DATE DUE

DEMCO 38-297

URANIAN

WORLDS

a guide to

alternative sexuality

in science fiction,

fantasy, and horror

SECOND EDITION

URANIAN

WORLDS

a guide to

alternative sexuality

in science fiction,

fantasy, and horror

SECOND EDITION

Eric Garber

and

Lyn Paleo

G.K. Hall & Co.

Boston, Massachusetts

First published 1990
by G.K. Hall & Co.
70 Lincoln Street
Boston, Massachusetts 02111

10 9 8 7 6 5 4 3 2 1

Library of Congress Cataloging-in-Publication Data

Garber, Eric.
    Uranian worlds: a guide to alternative sexuality in science fiction,
fantasy, and horror / Eric Garber, Lyn Paleo. – 2nd ed.
      p. cm.
    Includes indexes.
    ISBN 8161-1832-9
    1. Homosexuality in literature – Bibliography. 2. Fantastic
literature – Bibliography. 3. Science fiction – Bibliography.
I. Paleo, Lyn. II. Title.
Z6514.C5S43   1990
[PN56.H57]
016.80883'87608353 – dc20   90-37434
                                     CIP

The paper used in this publication meets the minimum requirements of
American National Standard for Information Sciences – Permanence of
Paper for Printed Library Materials. ANSI Z39.48-1984   ∞™
MANUFACTURED IN THE UNITED STATES OF AMERICA

Contents

The Authors

Eric Garber is the coeditor of *Worlds Apart: An Anthology of Lesbian and Gay Science Fiction and Fantasy* (with Camilla Decarnin and Lyn Paleo) (Alyson Press, 1986). He has written for the *Advocate, Out/Look*, and *The Dictionary of Literary Biography*. He has also written extensively on the Harlem Renaissance. He is currently compiling an anthology of gay-themed horror fiction.

Lyn Paleo is the coeditor of *Worlds Apart: An Anthology of Lesbian and Gay Science Fiction and Fantasy* (with Camilla Decarnin and Eric Garber) (Alyson Press, 1986) and several articles on AIDS in medical and nursing texts. She also has written for *Plexus, WomenNews*, and Science Fiction Amateur Press Association publications. She has been employed in the fields of AIDS education and American Sign Language translation for the deaf.

Preface

Purpose

Uranian Worlds is an annotated bibliography of variant sexuality in science-fiction, fantasy, and horror literature and film from A.D. 200 through 1989. It is a guide for use by both general and academic readers. Readers can skim the many annotations in *Uranian Worlds* to find entertaining and thought-provoking fiction (a simple coding system aids in quick identification of lesbian and gay male content in the works cited). The bibliography also can be used as a research tool and a teaching aid in the fields of science fiction, feminist studies, gay studies, social history, or human sexuality.

Uranian Worlds is a window to the changing popular attitudes toward sexual variance over several centuries. Fantastic literature is an ideal genre from which to examine these attitudes because of its ability to envision possibilities. Fantastic literature has always contained depictions of homosexuality, both female and male. It also has contained portrayals of androgynes, transsexuals, gender-switching people, and alien sexuality that is clearly not heterosexual. In the centuries before writers could deal explicitly with homosexuality, they used fantastic literature's various forms to disguise homoerotic passions. Some authors described fantastic voyages to single-sexed islands; others wrote of vampiric passion. Today, when the very subject of homosexuality is no longer shocking in print, writers use science fiction and fantasy to create utopias and dystopias and to invent social systems that deal with sexuality in a variety of ways. In doing so, these authors say a great deal about our own commonplace cultural views of variant sexuality.

The title of this bibliography is derived from the nineteenth-century word for homosexual, *Uranian*. The term was coined by the early German homosexual emancipationist Karl Ulrichs and was popularly used through the First World War. It refers to Aphrodite Urania, whom Plato had identified as the patron goddess of homosexuality in his *Symposium*. A slight variation, *Uraniad*, was used to describe lesbians.

Historical Overview

Early images of male homosexuality are more numerous than early images of lesbianism. In Lucian's *True History* (ca. A.D. 200), the bawdy Greek satirist used one of the earliest forms of fiction, the imaginary travelogue, to describe a trip to the moon and an encounter with homosexual moon-men who give birth through their calves. Among the many fantastic voyages of the classical period, the Middle Ages, and the Renaissance are several that describe uncharted lands inhabited by tribes of warrior women. An early fantasist, John Mandeville, in his epic twelfth-century poem of voyage and discovery, used hermaphroditism to explore variant sexuality by inventing an island inhabited by a strange third sex.

The emergence of Gothic fiction in the eighteenth century brought new fantastic venues for the depiction of homosexuality and lesbianism. Both William Beckford's influential "Oriental fantasy" *Vathek* (1787) and John Polidori's *The Vampyre* (1819) contain veiled autobiographical details of their authors' homosexual involvements. Subtle inferences of male homosexuality are unmistakable in works such as Oscar Wilde's *The Picture of Dorian Gray* (1890) and Henry James's "The Turn of the Screw" (1907). Oliver Wendell Holmes suggested lesbian emotions in his 1859 occult novel *Elsie Venner*, and H. Rider Haggard was much more explicit in his fantasy adventure *Allan's Wife* (1887), which contains a remarkable defense of same-sex love. Vampires who are unquestionably lesbian are the subjects of Joseph Sheridan Le Fanu's often reprinted "Carmilla" (1872) and Cora Lynn Daniels's more obscure *Sardia: A Story of Love* (1891).

Early feminists Mary Bradley Lane in her *Mizora: A Prophecy* (1880-1881) and Charlotte Perkins Gilman in *Herland* (1915) found utopian fantasy an ideal medium through which to express their nonsexual, woman-identified visions. To ridicule women like Lane and Gilman, some of their male contemporaries satirically wrote of worlds without men or cultures with reversed sex roles that make derogatory comments about the female characters' assuming of "masculine" behaviors.

During the first half of the twentieth century, gay men and lesbians appeared as secondary characters in fantasy fiction, as in Sinclair Lewis's *It Can't Happen Here* (1935) and Fletcher Pratt's *The Well of the Unicorn* (1948). Occasionally, authors created relatively overt gay characters; popular examples include the protagonists of E. F. Benson's *The Inheritor* (1930) and Radclyffe Hall's "Miss Ogilvy Finds Herself" (1934). More often, authors camouflaged their personal passions by writing fantasy stories of disguised intimate same-sex bonding. Works by Natalie Barney, Virginia Woolf, Forrest Reid, E. M. Forster, Hugh Walpole, and Gerald Heard are notable examples of this style.

During this period, the discussion of homosexuality brought up inevitable questions about the difference between physical sex and gender identification. Stories about switching sexes were published years before transsexuality was a medical possibility. Novels such as Barry Pain's *An Exchange of Souls* (1911), Isador Schneider's *Doctor Transit* (1925), Virginia Woolf's *Orlando* (1928), Thorne Smith's *Turnabout* (1931), and Seabury Quinn's posthumously published *Alien Flesh* (written ca. the 1940s) examine the identity crisis and social repercussions inherent in changing sex—a subject, at the time, particularly suitable to fantasy.

What is now referred to collectively as "science fiction and fantasy" was codified into a unique literary genre in early pulp magazines. Beginning near the turn of the century with magazines like *Argosy All-Story Weekly* and continuing in the 1920s and 1930s with the popular *Amazing Wonder Stories* and *Weird Tales*, these inexpensive pulp periodicals molded a genre out of Gothic horror stories, "scientific fictions," and adventure romances. They were extremely popular with the American middle class and sold by the thousands in drugstores and newsstands across America.

The intended audience for this early pulp fiction was teenage boys, and most of the stories rarely dealt with even the most superficial aspects of sex. But sexual material was not entirely absent, and occasionally even homosexuality was mentioned. David H. Keller's "The Revolt of the Pedestrians" appeared in *Amazing Stories* in 1928, and it features a "pathologically soul-sick" lesbian as a minor character. A more erotic and dangerous vision of lesbianism appeared in Robert E. Howard's "Red Nails," a "Conan the Barbarian" tale from 1936, in which the beautiful lesbian villain, Tascela, kidnaps and lovingly tortures another woman. Fourteen years later, John D. McDonald used an exaggerated "sissy" stereotype to imply a character's homosexuality in "The Big Contest" in the December 1950 issue of *Worlds Beyond*. But the possibilities for gay characterizations were limited and strictly circumscribed.

Male science-fiction authors carried over from the literature of the previous century the theme of single-gendered societies. The earliest is Wallace West's "The Last Man" (1929). During the next several decades a great many shallow and stylized variations on this theme appeared. Virtually all writers failed to develop this topic seriously, though a fascinating—albeit extremely negative—exception is David H. Keller's "The Feminine Metamorphosis" (1929).

Other pulp authors used the traditional vampire story to circumvent prohibitions and to disguise same-sex passion. C. L. Moore's classic tale "Black Thirst" first appeared in *Weird Tales* in April 1934. Her daring protagonist, Northwest Smith, becomes prey to a vampiric Venusian aristocrat's taste for the "beauty of men." Seabury Quinn used a similar disguise in "Claire de Lune" in *Weird Tales* (November 1947). Quinn's misogynistic psychic detective, Jules de Grandin, battles a beautiful ageless vampire over the soul of a young woman. In both these cases, same-sex attraction and sexuality were disguised as vampiric blood lust. But whether a "soul-sick lesbian," an effeminate caricature, a man-hating amazon, or a bloodthirsty vampire, the image of the homosexual was overwhelmingly stereotypic and one-dimensional.

Theodore Sturgeon is considered to have single-handedly opened the science-fiction field to explicit gay images with the publication of "The World Well Lost" in *Amazing* in 1952. The story concerns a pair of alien "lovebirds" who charm the Earth until it is learned that they are homosexual. Once their secret is out, the lovebirds face homophobic oppression and are extradited to their home planet. Sturgeon continued his trailbreaking exploration of gay subject matter in his 1957 "The Affair of the Green Monkey," in which an effeminate alien is taught the homosexual survival technique of "passing."

During the following decades, several science-fiction writers followed Sturgeon's lead. Alfred Bester's successful science-fiction thriller *The Demolished Man* (1953) featured a pair of effete, male secretaries, humorous characters who flit through the plot. Frederik Pohl and C. M. Kornbluth's *The Space Merchants* (1953), a blistering attack on the advertising industry, made perceptive comments on the "homosexual market." In Richard Matheson's *The Shrinking Man* (1956) a predatory pederast mistakes the shrinking hero for a young boy. Judith Merril's *The Tomorrow People* (1960) raised the question of homosexuality on single-sexed space flights. Frank Herbert's *Dune* (1965) offered the loathsome Baron Harkonnen, a sadistic pederast. Most of these images were fleeting and derogatory, but they signaled a willingness to explore previously restricted subject matter.

A number of lesbians and gay men who became pioneers of the early 1950s homophile movement originally met through science fiction fandom, a growing network of avid genre readers. Several of their amateur publications, called *fanzines* – such as Lisa Ben's *Vice Versa* and Jim Kepner's *Toward Tomorrow* – were among the first gay-community publications in this country. The format and the private distribution network of these fanzines made them ideal vehicles for communication and contacts among gay people.

The 1950s reemergence of homosexuality as a theme in fantastic literature and the open involvement of gay people within science-fiction fandom can be attributed to the increased visibility of lesbians and gay men in postwar American society. Several causes contributed to this visibility: the massive population shifts and gender segregation caused by the national war effort, the publication of the reports of sexologist Alfred Kinsey, and the courageous organizing efforts of homophile groups such as the Mattachine Society, the Daughters of Bilitis, and ONE, Inc.

Marion Zimmer Bradley stands out among the science-fiction authors of this period. Early in her career, Bradley incorporated homosexual themes into her fiction, as in her 1958 story *The Planet Savers*, set on the imaginary world of Darkover. In June 1963, *Fantasy and Science Fiction* published Bradley's "Another Rib," cowritten with her friend Juanita Coulson. "Another Rib" concerned an all-male crew's homosexual adaptation to an alien environment. Bradley's sensitivities were not surprising; she had been an early contributor to both the *Ladder* and the *Mattachine Review*.

The mid-1960s brought political activism and alternative life-styles to American life, and this social situation was reflected in a new kind of science fiction. J. G. Ballard, Samuel R. Delany, Thomas M. Disch, Michael Moorcock, Joanna Russ, and Robert Silverberg emerged as New Wave science-fiction writers, willing to experiment radically with style and content. Some of this experimentation involved sexuality. Moorcock's Jerry Cornelius series, begun in 1968 with *The Final Programme*, introduced a hip, bisexual, James Bond-type character who romps across the globe looking for adventure. Delany's award-winning "Time Considered as a Helix of Semi-Precious Stones" (1968) features a futuristic bisexual thief as a primary character. Disch's brilliant antiwar novel, *Camp Concentration* (1968), casually includes prison homosexuality. Russ's "Mr. Wilde's Second Chance" (1966) asserts that Oscar Wilde would have preferred his homosexual life to a "proper" one. The gay characterizations of these New Wave writers tended toward a new realism and overall veracity.

Social change continued to be reflected in science fiction throughout the 1970s. As lesbians and gay men came out of the closets by the tens of thousands to march in annual Gay Pride marches across the country, they also emerged as protagonists in science fiction and fantasy. Bradley, Delany, and Russ opened the floodgates to lesbian and gay male images in science fiction. Bradley's *The Heritage of Hastur* (1975), set among Darkover's psychic aristocracy, is, in large part, a classic gay male coming-out story. *The Shattered Chain* (1976) was her first examination of Darkover's Free Amazons. Her 1978 novel *The Ruins of Isis* presents a critique of lesbian separatism.

Samuel R. Delany produced his massive novel *Dhalgren* in 1975 after a long absence from publishing. The brilliant, kaleidoscopic blockbuster, revolving around a nameless, bisexual drifter in a near-deserted American city, shocked many with its passionate sexual descriptions. His novel *Triton* (1976), set in a social utopia where homosexuality is neither condemned nor proscribed, dissects the anachronistic sexist protagonist who does not fit into the feminist society. The hero of Delany's 1979 fantasy collection *Tales of Nevèrÿon* is a kinky gay ex-slave who leads a revolution for freedom.

As remarkable as Sturgeon's introduction of gay sexuality was Joanna Russ's introduction of lesbian feminism into science fiction. Her powerful short story "When It Changed" (1972) effectively turns the tables on prurient, male-authored visions – those which show a women's world collapsing at the first sight of men – by portraying an all-female society in a positive and down-to-earth fashion. Her novel *The Female Man* (1975), with its juxtaposition of four very different female realities, is recognized as both a science-fiction and a feminist classic.

Certain authors transformed old science-fiction conventions into something new – and often something openly gay. Joanna Russ's planet of

Whileaway, for example, was an all-female planet that didn't *want* to become heterosexual. James Tiptree, Jr., with "Houston, Houston, Do You Read?" (1976) and Suzy McKee Charnas with *Motherlines* (1978) also created feminist worlds. The vampires in Anne Rice's *Interview with a Vampire* (1976) feast on blood like their forebears, but they also fall passionately in love with each other. Unlike the sex, hangers in Thorne Smith's *Turnabout*, the androgynous inhabitants of Winter in Ursula Le Guin's brilliant *The Left Hand of Darkness* (1969) are portrayed with great seriousness and compassion.

Even science fiction's more traditional best-selling authors engaged in this discussion. One of the first attempts to incorporate the sexual revolution into the genre was a confused effort by science-fiction master Robert A. Heinlein to explore transsexuality, *I Will Fear No Evil* (1970). More effective was Robert Silverberg's 1972 novel *Book of Skulls*, which presents two very different gay men as protagonists. Arthur C. Clarke's 1975 novel *Imperial Earth* and Ray Bradbury's 1976 short story "A Better Part of Wisdom" contain strong gay male themes. Frederik Pohl's *Gateway* (1977) features a neurotic, repressed homosexual.

New writers with new ways of dealing with homosexuality also appeared. David Gerrold's intriguing examination of time travel, *The Man Who Folded Himself*, was published in 1973. Thomas Burnett Swann's retelling of the classic Jonathan and David story, *How Are the Mighty Fallen*, was published in 1974, as was *334*, Thomas M. Disch's description of a future urban housing project and its various gay and lesbian residents. Marge Piercy's 1976 feminist speculation, *Woman on the Edge of Time*, sends a young Puerto Rican woman into an androgynous, nonsexist future. In 1978, Elizabeth A. Lynn's *A Different Light* recounts the quest of a spacecraft pilot to find a male lover, George Nader's *Chrome* details the difficulties in falling in love with a gay robot, and Sally M. Gearhart portrays the amazonian Hill Women in *The Wanderground*. 1979 proved an even bigger year for gay science fiction as Thomas M. Disch's *On Wings of Song* explored a gay man's fight against moral fascism, Diane Duane's *The Door into Fire* pitted two homosexual lovers against the powers of darkness and evil, Zoë Fairbairns's *Benefits* described a future feminist revolution, and John Varley's *Titan* introduced lesbian space captain Cirocco Jones's exciting adventures. Publications as diverse as *In Touch for Men* and *Sinister Wisdom* began to publish science fiction specifically designed for the lesbian and gay male audience.

Since the first edition of *Uranian Worlds* in 1979, much has changed. The mainstream explosion of gay-themed science fiction peaked in the early 1980s. But even if lesbians and gay men are no longer as frequently the protagonists, such characters still abound within the genre and, in many cases, are no longer confined by stereotypes. The 1980s explosion in horror fiction has produced enjoyable gay stories from Clive Barker, Jewelle Gomez, Michael McDowell, and Jeffrey McMahan. Kathy Acker, Jonathan Littell, and W. T. Quick have produced gay-flavored cyberpunk, science fiction characterized by rock-and-roll imagery and best represented by the stylistic works of William Gibson and Bruce Sterling.

Inevitably, AIDS has entered the scope of science fiction. Within the last few years, several science-fiction and fantasy novels have appeared that use this current health crisis as a subject. One of the first science-fiction stories to use AIDS as a subject was Samuel R. Delany's "The Tale of Plagues and Carnivals," in which the story of an ancient plague in the barbarian world of Nevèrÿon is intercut with the author's candid observations and concerns about AIDS. Michael Bishop, in his *Unicorn Mountain* (1988), is equally profound in his quiet portrait of a young gay man with AIDS whose encounters with Native American culture and a small herd of unicorns result in a magical transformation. Several gay authors have produced dystopian warnings in their stories about concentration camps for people with AIDS, notably Tim Barrus's *Genocide* (1989), Jed Bryan's *A Cry in the Desert* (1987), and Geoff Mains's *Gentle Warriors* (1989).

Feminist- and lesbian-oriented science fiction and fantasy has remained a prominent component of the field. Strong, independent female protagonists are now more common. Jo Clayton's Duel of Sorcery trilogy (1982-85), Jessica Amanda Salmonson's Tomoe Gozen series (1981), Joan Slonczewski's *A Door into the Ocean* (1986), and Pamela Sargent's *The Shore of Women* (1986) are amazon stories with lesbian protagonists. J. F. Rivkin's Silverglass series (1986) features a swashbuckling bisexual barbarian. Caroline Forbes's *The Needle on Full* (1985), Katherine Forrest's *Daughters of the Coral Dawn* (1984), Sandi Hall's *The Godmothers* (1982), and Anna Livia's *Bulldozer Rising* (1987) are powerful lesbian feminist future visions.

Bibliographic Criteria

While compiling the bibliographic citations in *Uranian Worlds*, we noted the contrived and stereotypic images that predominate in science fiction and fantasy, and therefore we have given special attention to finding and annotating works that treat homosexuality with intelligence, validation, and verisimilitude. Our critical eye also noted the existence of other social dynamics based on factors such as race, gender, age, and physical condition.

We have used a broad definition of science fiction and fantasy in order to include visions of lesbians and gay men that may not typically be identified with the genre. Therefore, the bibliography lists horror and vampire stories such as Chelsea Quinn Yarbro's *Hotel Transylvania*, ghost stories such as Philip Loraine's *Voices in an Empty Room*, a few disaster novels such as Thomas Scortia and Frank M. Robinson's *The Nightmare Factor*, gay "camp" fantasies like Gore Vidal's *Myra Breckinridge*, feminist fantasies such as Sally M. Gearhart's *The Wanderground*, utopian speculation such as Ernest Callenbach's *Ecotopia*, pornographic science fiction such as Larry Townsend's *The Scorpius Equation*, and several non-science-fiction short stories that were published in science-fiction or fantasy anthologies or author collections, such as Ray Bradbury's "The Better Part of Wisdom."

While being flexible in our definitions of science fiction and fantasy, we have been more strict in our definition of homosexuality. We have avoided interpreting a character's sexuality. Instead, we have relied upon the author to label a character or situation as homosexual or to portray some form of physical expression of same-sex attraction. Only in a few cases, with works written before 1960, have we included items based solely on the stereotypic homosexual actions or mannerisms of a character. One fan at a science fiction convention made the novel suggestion that we assume all characters are gay, unless the author specifies differently – this certainly adds new flavor to old books!

Each item in this bibliography is listed alphabetically by the author's name as it appears in the work's first edition, then by the title of the work. If the item was published under a pseudonym, the actual name of the author, if it is known, is cross-referenced. Joint authors are also cross-referenced. Articles, interviews, and critical pieces about a specific author are listed with that writer's work. Articles about sexuality or sexual politics in science fiction and fantasy are listed under the author's name.

If a work was originally published in this country, we only list that edition. If it was originally published in the English language in another country, the original publishing citation is followed by the first American reprinting, if any. If a work was first published in a foreign language and then translated, the first English language edition and the first American edition are cited with the original foreign printing. Only those poems that appeared in science-fiction anthologies or collections are included in this bibliography. No items published after 1989 are annotated.

Following the bibliographic data is a letter code. This code indicates the kind and importance of sexuality within a work:

F – Lesbianism or female bisexuality is a major component within a work.

f – Lesbianism or female bisexuality is mentioned in the work but is not a major element.

M – Male homosexuality or bisexuality is a major component within a work.

m – Male homosexuality or bisexuality is mentioned in the work but is not a major element.

X – Some form of sexuality that is neither heterosexual nor homosexual appears. Transsexuality, hermaphroditism, three-sexed aliens, androgyny, and vampirism are examples.

? – A question mark following the letter code indicates that certain elements of the work are open to interpretation (i.e., latent homosexuality, same-sex societies, and overtly suggestive friendships).

Biographical notes for several authors are included. They contain references to non-science-fiction works with major lesbian and / or gay male content, some biographical information, and references to further information. The biographical notes are not intended to be complete.

Following the body of the work are three appendixes that supply further information and three indexes that allow quick access to the bibliography. Appendix 1 contains selected anthologies, Appendix 2 lists movies with content relevant to this bibliography, and Appendix 3 provides information about several science-fiction fan organizations. The first index lists the cited works in chronological order. The second index lists them in alphabetical order by title. Both give the authors' surnames and entry numbers. The third is an index to the biographical notes, keyed to page numbers.

Acknowledgments

Without some people whose input was crucial to us, *Uranian Worlds* could not have been written: Camilla Decarnin, Allan Galanter, Susan Edelberg, Elizabeth A. Lynn, and Debbie Notkin . . . thank you all.

Many individuals provided us with help and guidance during the completion of the first edition of *Uranian Worlds*. Some responded to our inquiries, shared their knowledge and memories with us, and opened extensive personal libraries to our scrutiny. Others read over our many rough drafts and gave us much-appreciated criticism and suggestions. Still others opened up their homes and lives to us, providing us with a network of support and friendship. These people include: Forrest J. Ackerman, Randy Alfred, Chester Anderson, Roger Austen, Melinda Basker, Allan Bérubé, Marion Zimmer Bradley, Walter Breen, Elaine Brown, Charlie Cockey, Rose Ann Cyrus, N. A. Diaman, Samuel R. Delany, Wayne Dynes, Charles Garber, Dorothy Garber, Sally M. Gearhart, David Gerrold, Charles Gilman, Penny Gray, Barbara Grier, Bert Hansen, Susan Hobbs, Mark Horn, Denys Howard, Mikhail Itkin, Jerry Jacks, Jonathan Ned Katz, Jim Kepner, Jason Klein, Martin Last, Elizabeth Lay, W. Dorr Legg, Craig Louis, Richard Lupoff, Lyndall MacCowan, Dave Nee, David Pasko, Marta Randall, Frank M. Robinson, Jane Robinson, Robin Rowland, Joanna Russ, Mary Kay Ryan, Jessica Amanda Salmonson, Joe Sandford, Susan Schneider, George Scithers, Carol Seajay, Baird Searles, Robert Silverberg, Don Slater, Stuart A. Teitler, Larry Townsend, Paula Wallace, Jeanne Winer, Tom Whitmore, Marta Wohl, Chelsea Quinn Yarbro, and Ian Young.

Ten years later, the following people suggested entries, verified citations, and offered critical support, all of which helped us update and improve our second edition: Clive Barker, Michael Bishop, F. M. Busby, Lisa Ben, Arthur C. Clarke, John Dumas, Laurie Edison, Kevin Esser, Doug Faunt, Jewelle Gomez, Stephen King, Elizabeth Holthaus, Franklin Hummell, Ellen Kushner, Richard Labonté, Mercedes Lackey, Adelia Lines,

Rachel MacLachlan, Steve McLaughlin, Jeffrey N. McMahan, Annie Ng, Felice Picano, W. T. Quick, J. F. Rivkin, Vito Russo, Melissa Scott, J. S. Stephens, Susanna Sturgis, Jeffrey Sunshine, Philip Tobin, Tim Williams, and Scott Winnett. We are grateful to fandom and particularly to the Gaylactic Network, a fan network of lesbians, gay men, and their friends.

Many institutions, libraries, and organizations were helpful to us. We would like to thank in particular: A Different Light Bookstore (San Francisco), Fantasy Etc. Bookstore (San Francisco), the Homosexual Information Center (Los Angeles), the Interlibrary Loan Department at the San Francisco Public Library, the Kennedy School of Government's Department of Computer Services (Harvard), Old Wives' Tales Bookstore (San Francisco), ONE Institute (Los Angeles), the Other Change of Hobbit Bookstore (Berkeley), the Lesbian Herstory Archives (New York), the J. Francis McComas Collection at the San Francisco Public Library, the National Sex Forum (San Francisco), the San Francisco Lesbian and Gay History Project, the South San Francisco Public Library Reference Department, and the Walt Whitman Bookshop (San Francisco).

Introduction

Samuel R. Delany

The situation of the lesbian in America is vastly different from the situation of the gay male. A clear acknowledgment of this fact, especially by male homosexuals, is almost the first requirement for any sophisticated discussion of homosexual politics in this country.

In the United States, lesbianism is characterized, traditionally, by very little information and consequently somewhat limited social options to lesbians for social and sexual expression. By comparison, there is a great deal of information abroad about gay males – the majority of it misinformation. But there are notably more social options for social expression of male homosexuality; and there are vastly more options for gay male sexual expression, however socially marginal those options are. What this means, however, is that the experience of growing up, living, and loving as a gay woman is going to be very different from the experience of growing up, living, and loving as a gay male.

The heterosexual world is of course made highly uncomfortable by the existence of both genders of homosexual. Against this discomfort, gay men and gay women may well express solidarity with each other. But in the day to day working out of the reality of liberation, the biggest help we can give each other is a clear and active recognition of the extent and nature of the different contexts and a rich and working sympathy for the different priorities these contexts (for want of a better term) engender.

Peruse this bibliography with a counter clicking at your side, and you will no doubt find the statistical emblems of that difference – in the comparative number of references to lesbians and gay males, in the variety and nature of the references in all categories. If you simply read along, however, and let the counter go, you will probably be far more struck by the variety and diversity.

I recently returned from the thirty-eighth annual World Science Fiction Convention, Noreastcon 2, held in Boston, with about 8,000 attendees. There was a panel sponsored by the convention in the Independence Ballroom of the Boston Sheraton Hotel, entitled "The Closed Open Mind – Homophobia in Science Fiction and Fantasy Stories," on which I sat with four other writers. Though there have been programs with gay themes at regional science-fiction conventions before – and feminist panels have practically become a standard feature of world and regional science-fiction conventions over the past handful of years – this was the first such panel at a World SF Convention. The ballroom, which held perhaps 200 people, was packed. Though the panel's title may well have been an attempt to limit the hour's program to a discussion of texts, almost immediately things launched off with an historical recounting.

We talked of the sf editor in the early fifties who, upon receiving Theodore Sturgeon's sympathetic portrayal of male homosexuality in his story "The World Well Lost," not only rejected the story, but called up every other magazine editor in the field to tell them not to accept the story either. The story was purchased, despite this campaign, by the feisty editor-publisher Ray Palmer. Raymond Palmer (1910-1977) stood four feet tall and had a deformed spine. The story appeared in the June 1953 issue of *Universe*, and helped establish that magazine's reputation as one of the era's more sophisticated sf periodicals. There were tales of tragic ostracisms in the fifties and sixties among that hypersocial group of sf fans whose younger friends and associates were putting on the very convention which was sponsoring our panel. Only then, having reminded ourselves of the real pain that oppressive attitudes toward homosexuality had caused, and the bravery they had elicited, could we turn to the topic of the reflection of these attitudes within sf stories themselves.

The question quickly articulated itself: aesthetic freedom versus political responsibility. How, if one believes passionately, and absolutely, in both (and four of our five panel members did), can the writer reconcile them.

Implicit in a book such as this is the basis for the resolution – at least as far as images of homosexuality are concerned. Though they do not particularly analyze them, the compilers are very ready to call a stereotype a stereotype. Frankly, they do not need to analyze them. We all know what they are. The truth is, as with all clichés, there is just not a shred of artistic life, aesthetic energy, or inventiveness left in them. In a way, by sparing us the details, the compilers have reminded us, through their reticence, just how similar, repetitive, and predictable such stereotypes are.

What this bibliography does is render dramatic Wittgenstein's 1916 assertion: "Aesthetics *is* ethics," as well as Lukac's assertion, made in the same year, that fiction "is the only art form where the artist's ethical position *is* the aesthetic problem," a problem a writer will solve or not solve through a single set of gestures.

Fictive texts – including science fiction – are complex statements made in, by, through, and out of a sense of play. But such play may be as serious as the writer can conceive; the stakes envisioned are limited only by the writer's ambition. Still, because they are play, they are free from a certain order of direct moral ascription of good and evil. And I would maintain anyone's freedom to write any clearly labeled fictive text, however offensive, repellent, or clichéd; but the very same gesture that upholds the writer's freedom to write upholds equally my own, or any critic's, freedom to declare such texts to *be* offensive, repellent or clichéd, and not to have the value of the paper it takes to print them – if that is how a text strikes a particular reader.

The argument is not over the freedom to write – which I would vouchsafe to anyone. The argument is over how (*not* what!) we should read: that is, do we read with an awareness of the breadth and range of what has been written, as we focus on a particular text; or do we read with our eyes half closed?

For many who have not thought about such problems as they entail images of lesbians and gay males in the demotic genres, this will be an eye-opening book. It has been compiled with energy and purpose. Though it is a bibliography, the compilers are not above judgment. Though I don't always agree with their judgments, I am glad the compilers make them – because the writer *is* free.

Science fiction is a demotic field of reading. By and large, opinions expressed throughout it reflect the most prevalent opinions to be found in the general cultural centers. (This is probably equally true for the vast bulk of contemporary literature, demotic or elite.) Without the energy and purpose of its compilers, this book might simply have been a dreary listing of stereotypes, drearily notated, noted? a depressing chronicle of aesthetic clichés at one with the ethical abominations by which they manifest themselves. But the compilers of this bibliography are interested in accurately cataloging what there is with a clear view to changing it. To that end they have put most of their energy into detailing the positive and/or astereotypical portrayals of gay men and women throughout the range of science fiction and fantasy; and they have made creative use of those works in which the general richness of fictive portraiture has tended to undercut a controlling stereotype – sometimes in spite of the author. Reading over any large body of science fiction referring to gay men and women, one can't avoid seeing it as a system of stereotypes with a few more or less effective tries at a kind of fashionable liberalism. And our compilers present that system to us – but with a clear eye toward dismantling it. They would seem to have a sense that we cannot change the way we write without concurrently changing the way we read. And what should be clear from even the most superficial perusal of the book: it represents a monumental, exhaustive, and triumphant act of *reading*.

Also, I would hazard that anyone who reads it, or reads through any significant part of it, will find it hard to read across passing references to female or male homosexual characters, not only in sf novels but in any other kind of fiction from now on, without a much clearer view of the larger system, positive or negative, that organizes such representations.

Introduction

Joanna Russ

How does one introduce a bibliography? A good bibliography is surely a good thing, but its virtues usually lie outside the realm of aesthetics. Thus one may say, "This bibliography is comprehensive," or "This bibliography is well organized," or "This bibliography is useful," but hardly "This bibliography is elegant, witty and full of dramatic contrast," or "This bibliography is adventurous and so suspenseful that you will stay up all night reading it."

And yet I can add one thing about this particular bibliography: When I was sixteen I would have given a very great deal for it.

That's because when I was sixteen (in 1953) not only was a bibliography like this unthinkable, so were most of the books in it. My literary-cultural education on the subject of lesbianism – and I had done a lot of very frustrating research – was, and continued for years after, to be limited to one film, "Maedchen in Uniform," one novel, Theophile Gautier's *Mademoiselle Maupin* (which had somehow found its way into the family bookcase), and one short story, a little parody of Mark Twain's which I read at the age of twelve and could never find again. The only other book I even knew about was *The Well of Loneliness* and to get that you had to go to the locked room in the college library and explain why you wanted it – a requirement that effectively prevented me from getting within a mile of it.

Samuel Delany – it wasn't his fault; he was eleven at the time and writing his first novel, but otherwise blameless – would have had a much better time of it, literarily speaking, since Wilde, Gide, and Verlaine were right there on the open library shelves, not to mention Truman Capote's *Other Voices, Other Rooms*, and works by Christopher Isherwood, and Hart Crane was actually known to have been – well, you know.

But Gertrude Stein wasn't.
Willa Cather wasn't.
Emily Dickinson wasn't.
H.D. wasn't.
Amy Lowell wasn't.
(And lesbian writers of color, like Angelina Weld Grimké, didn't even exist.)

Although our heterosexist/homophobic society still does its best to bury all signs of homosexuality, both in literature and in life, the jackboot – predictably – comes down much harder on women's love for women than it does on men's love for men. Here is my friend, Marilyn Hacker, the poet, on the subject:

> If a man sleeps with men and women he's *queer: vide* Wilde, Gide, Verlaine. A woman who does can be 'passionately heterosexual' (said Norman Pearson of H.D.) Anyone's love with women doesn't count....[1]

That is, since women's services, economic, emotional, and sexual, must be secured for men (some directly to all men, much indirectly to privileged men) women's sexual self-assertion must go the way of women's economic and political self-assertion: Not to Be Used Except in Response to Male Needs. Those gay men who envy lesbians' apparent freedom from direct persecution are forgetting that lesbians are already being persecuted – as women. And women's oppression includes the distortion and alienation from our sexuality, whatever it is. Years before Stonewall, I sat uncomprehending while Allen Ginsberg publicly read his poem, "Walt Whitman at the Supermarket," wondering mildly what certain men in the audience found so amusing. Only five years ago – to an extremely specialized, all-female audience – did a women's studies researcher suggest that Gertrude Stein's "Lifting belly is my ice cream" actually *meant* anything. Now that Jane Addams and Eleanor Roosevelt have joined our august ranks it's difficult to convey to the young the utter invisibility of lesbian writers or characters up to the last few years; instead of lesbians we had spinsters, neurotics, and psychotic bitches, both in literature and in life, that is, large, lesbian-shaped vacancies where people should have been.

As many feminists have said, lesbianism has simply been legislated out of existence for millions of women. So has (I would add) heterosexuality as a genuine choice for millions more.

And then there was science fiction.

Passionately speculative, daringly original, with the wildness and vaulting imagination that have been its trademark from the beginning, science fiction resolutely ignored the whole subject.

Hell, they didn't even have *girls* then, although some female characters, "handled in moderation," were admissible, as the chaste young Asimov remarked in an early fan letter he will probably never live down.[2] All those initials and male pseudonyms – known to other writers, of course, but not to the kids who read the books – and then as late as 1975 Poul Anderson was protesting that sf writers didn't *mean* to omit women from their stories; it's just that "love interest" was so rare in sf.[3] And here is André Norton, a year earlier, stating that she had to avoid showing friendship between "two women of this type" (strong and independent) because the friendship would be misunderstood by librarians and readers.[4]

Alas, when I was young I didn't misunderstand. I understood all too well. Sexuality – including homosexuality – was a male prerogative. We got to wear the chromium bathing suits and be rescued. When we were allowed a share in the plot (a good reason many female readers still enjoy Heinlein's female characters) we were usually an improbable combination of brainy scientist and purring calendar cutie (a bad reason many female readers, etc.). When women exist *for men*, women barely exist at all, and as for lesbian characters, the only lesbian I remember in sf, before the late sixties, occurred in C. S. Lewis's *That Hideous Strength*, where she expressed her love for women by stubbing out lit cigarettes on the heroine's shoulders. (Women who love women really hate women. What? Never mind.) Even in modern fiction one must beware. For example, *I Will Fear No Evil* is probably buried in here someplace, but that brand of lesbianism (like Fritz Leiber's "girls" in *Our Lady of Darkness*[5]) is designed for the titillation of straight men; read it and see. Better still, don't read it. Read other things. That is the fine thing about a bibliography; it tells you where the books are. You will find *The Left Hand of Darkness* here, an exciting "first" for many women, although its subject is not quite homosexuality but rather androgyny and identity. (Let's see, a woman writing about/observing a man who is really part woman in a world where women's work is absent, so that everyone seems to be a man, but. . . .) You will also find Marion Zimmer Bradley's *The Shattered Chain*. James Tiptree's "Houston, Houston, Do You Read?" (what a vanishing act!), Samuel Delany's *Triton*, Monique Wittig's *Les Guérillères*, Marge Piercy's *Woman on the Edge of Time*, my *The Female Man*, Elizabeth Lynn's "The Woman Who Loved the Moon," and many more.

Tracing the sudden visibility of lesbian and gay male characters in sf is a historical detective story. Some questions:

Are women writers underrepresented in terms of our presence (53%) in the population? (Bet you yes.)

Are we overrepresented in terms of our presence (about 18%) in The Science Fiction Writers of America? (Bet you yes.)

If the above is true, is it because women writing sf are more apt than men to be (a) feminist (b) lesbian (c) liberal in sexual matters or (d) interested in human relations? Or some combination of the above?

Are writers of color underrepresented here? (Bet you yes.)

Some caveats: women who write of all-female worlds are almost always feminists; men who do so usually aren't; men who write about gay men needn't be; men who create lusciously titillating lesbians seldom are; men who create humanly believable lesbians usually are.

To return to my first paragraph: this bibliography *is* different. It marks a chapter of considerable importance not only in sf but in the political and cultural history of the world – if you think literature matters. I do. I also believe that, outside of poetry, science fiction is still the literature that has the greatest potential to astonish readers and illuminate life. *Uranian Worlds* is packed with high drama; it is ironically witty, tragic, chucklesome, suspenseful, and likewise thrilling.

You may even stay up all night reading it.

NOTES

1. In a sonnet sequence, "Taking Notice," which is unpublished as of this writing but is scheduled for her next book of poems.

2. Dr. Asimov tells the story against himself in his autobiography, *In Memory Yet Green*, (Garden City: Doubleday, 1979).

3. Letter, *The Witch and the Chameleon* (September 1975).

4. Letter, *The Witch and the Chameleon* (November 1974).

5. In correspondence the author has self-critically called such characters "dream Lesbians."

Uranian Worlds

1 AARON, RICK. "Masters of Gravity." *Advocate Men* (Los Angeles), April 1986. [M]
In this amusing piece of gay male erotica, four male astronauts find love and sexual diversion while sealed in a spaceship a quarter of a million miles from Earth.

2 ACKER, KATHY. *Empire of the Senseless*. New York: Grove Press, 1988. [M]
Acker's novel is a challenge in both content and style. Abhor, a construct (part robot and part human), and her lover, a bisexual pirate named Thivat, inhabit the chaotic decay of the near future. The violence and misery of daily life comes through clearly in Acker's painful prose. A "punk" sensibility is noticeable throughout. This bleak future vision has developed a considerable following among intellectual circles, but, like that of Ballard and Burroughs, Acker's work will not appeal to everyone.

ACKERMAN, FORREST J. *See* ERMAYNE, LAURAJEAN (pseudonym)

3 ADAMS, DEREK. "The Alien." *Mandate* (New York), August 1989. [M]
Gay male erotica in which a man meets an extraterrestrial sexual companion.

4 ALDISS, BRIAN. *The Dark Light Years*. London: Faber, 1964. Reprint. New York: Signet, 1964. [m, X]
Utods, highly intelligent beings who periodically shift gender, have been discovered by interstellar explorers on the planet Dandrof. Utod

1

representatives are sent to Earth to establish communication, but unfortunately the personal appearance and characteristics of the alien species cause Earth-wide repulsion. A subplot concerns two human male lovers who seek freedom in the "Gay Ghetto," a haven for nonconformists of all kinds. Pessimistic view of humanity's potential for tolerance.

5 ALDISS, BRIAN. *The Primal Urge*. New York: Ballantine, 1961. [m]

By government decree, all British citizens between the ages of fourteen and sixty are forced to wear metal discs upon their foreheads which turn pink when the wearer becomes sexually aroused. Needless to say, this little device forces all out of their particular closets. The effects on the nation are monumental. While ingeniously handling these consequences, Aldiss cursorily glances at several gay male minor characters.

Biographical Note

Brian Aldiss (b. 1925) is also the author of many other science-fiction novels, including the Hugo-winning *Hothouse* (London: Faber and Faber, 1962), *Greybeard* (New York: Harcourt, 1964) and *The Malacia Tapestry* (London: Jonathan Cape, 1976). His non-science-fiction novel, *The Hand-Reared Boy* (London: Weidenfeld and Nicolson, 1970), has significant gay male content.

---

6 ALLEGRA, DONNA. "A Toast of Babatine." *Sinister Wisdom* (Berkeley, Calif.), no. 34 (1988). [F]

A young amazon from an egalitarian, woman-only tribal society discovers love and passion with a beautiful, dark-skinned woman "from across the waters."

7 AMIS, KINGSLEY. *The Alteration*. London: Jonathan Cape, 1976. Reprint. New York: Viking, 1977. [M?]

The Alteration is an enjoyable fantasy set in an alternate world similar to, yet different from, our own: the Reformation never happened and Europe is still a unified Catholic state. Two castrati, Viaventosa and Mirabilis, who have had an emotionally satisfying "marriage" for years, aid in an attempt to preserve a ten-year-old boy singer's voice by means of castration. The book has a serious message and moments of great humor.

8 AMIS, KINGSLEY. *The Green Man*. London: Jonathan Cape, 1969. Reprint. New York: Harcourt Brace & World, 1970. [f]

Amis uses a Gothic mode to create an intelligent and contemporary ghost story. Maurice Allington, proprietor of "The Green Man," a small pub forty miles outside of London, finds his life complicated by a pesky ghost. Although Allington's character is at times unpleasant, the book itself is likely to amuse. Lesbians in particular may enjoy the author's irony: Allington's wife and his mistress run off together – finding each other far more interesting than Maurice.

9 ANDERSON, CHESTER. *The Butterfly Kid*. New York: Pyramid, 1967. [m]

The hippie community of Greenwich Village is suddenly inundated with a strange new way to get high, the "Reality Pill." These pills cause a person's fantasies to become reality. The protagonist and a group of his friends turn sleuth to find the source of the unusual drug. As well as briefly mentioning several overtly gay men, Anderson portrays both the hero and his roommate as capable of homoerotic responses by including a flirtatious park bench scene in the first chapter. Although he has written an enjoyable book, the author uses 1960s sexist vernacular (i.e., women are called "chicks").

Biographical Note

Chester Anderson (b. 1932) is also the author of *Puppies* (Glen Ellen, Calif.: Entwhistle Books, 1979), a frolicking account of boy love written under the pseudonym of John Valentine, and *Fox and Hare* (Glen Ellen, Calif.: Entwhistle Books, 1980), a non-science-fiction novel in which a bisexual man is a major character.

---

10 ANDERSON, POUL. "Eutopia." In *Dangerous Visions*, edited by Harlan Ellison. Garden City, N.Y.: Doubleday, 1967. [M]

A homosexual man whose culture is based on logic, tolerance, and humanistic values is sent to a patriarchal world in a parallel universe where he unwittingly breaks the taboo against homosexual behavior. He flees and returns home to his male lover. The author maintains a heterosexual bias while giving approbation to a culture that accepts homosexuality.

11 ANDERSON, POUL. "The Fatal Fulfillment." *Fantasy and Science Fiction*, March 1970. Reprinted in *Five Fates*, edited by Keith Laumer. Garden City, N.Y.: Doubleday, 1970. [m]

A young scientist, Douglas Bailey devises a machine that stimulates various realities in an attempt to halt a growing mental illness epidemic. Among the many possible realities he visits by using this experimental device is one in which homosexuals have achieved a degree of privilege within society. Both the homosexuals and the world in which they live are depreciated.

12 ANDERSON, POUL. "The Peat Bog." In *Homeward and Beyond*. Garden City, N.Y.: Doubleday, 1975. [M]

This gay male story is more historical fantasy than science fiction, although it was published in a science-fiction anthology. Homosexuality is freely discussed as two Roman soldiers travel on horseback observing their recently conquered Germanic territories. The narrator falls in love with a heterosexual king who is unable to reciprocate the soldier's love. The few female characters are without substance.

13 ANDERSON, POUL. *Virgin Planet*. New York: Avalon, 1959. [F]

Cocky Davis Bertram takes off in his spaceship and discovers a planet populated entirely by women who have been anxiously awaiting the return of men for 300 years. At first sight the warrior women mistake Davis for an alien monster, but overnight he manages to convince them that he is attractive. Like most heterosexist world-without-men stories, the amazon culture collapses with the appearance of the first man. Lesbianism as an option ceases to exist and heterosexuality becomes the only form of sexual expression. In this novel, the women decide that Davis should leave the planet and return with a vanguard of male immigrants. The formerly strong, decisive women end up squabbling over who will be among the lucky few to accompany Davis on the trip.

14 ANDERSSON, DEAN. *Raw Pain Max*. New York: Popular Library, 1988. [F]

Andersson's nasty supernatural thriller revolves around a standard character in contemporary horror fiction and film: the Countess Elizabeth Bathory, an actual figure in criminal history whose eighteenth-century murders are legendary. In *Raw Pain Max* she is reincarnated as a beautiful employee in a sadomasochistic sex show. Because Bathory is bisexual and dominates both men and women, there is considerable lesbian sexuality portrayed. Some readers may find the novel titillating, but many may be repelled by the lengthy descriptions of sexual brutality.

ANDREWS, LEWIS M. *See* KARLINS, MARVIN (joint author)

ANONYMOUS. The Amplified Journal of D. G. Series. [M, X]:

15 ■ "And Always the Blood." *Mandate* (New York) 12, no. 4 (July 1986).

16 ■ "The Vampire Dance." *Mandate* (New York) 12, no. 7 (October 1986).

17 ■ "Beneath the Dead Stars." *Mandate* (New York) 12, no. 8 (November 1986).

18 ■ "The Whisperer." *Mandate* (New York) 13, no. 1 (December 1986).

19 ■ "Shallow Grave Revisited." *Mandate* (New York) 13, no. 2 (February 1987).

20 ■ "Blood on the Altar." *Mandate* (New York) 13, no. 3 (March 1987).
    The six published installments of the Amplified Journal of D. G. comprise the melancholy musings of a philosophic gay vampire who calls himself Dorian Gray, or "D. G.," because he was the inspiration for Wilde's masterpiece. D. G. roams Manhattan's gay discos and bathhouses in search of his nourishment.

21 ANONYMOUS. "Kiki." *Vice Versa* (Los Angeles), December 1947. [F]
    "Kiki" makes an amusing historical comment on lesbian subculture. In 1940s lesbian slang, "kiki" meant a lesbian who was neither butch nor femme. This story concerns just such a woman. Kiki begins loving women when she is thirteen, and she goes through both a "masterful" butch and a "flowerlike" femme before finding true love in the arms of another kiki lesbian. The story pivots on a supernatural entity known as the Cosmic Registrar who watches and records it all. The story is historically interesting in that it is representative of the connection between science fiction and the emerging gay consciousness of the time.

See also BEN, LISA

22 ANTHONY, JAMES. "Roger." *In Touch for Men* (Hollywood, Calif.), no. 42 (July-August 1979). [M]
    A ghostly encounter leads to sexual gratification in this short gay male erotic piece.

23 ARCHER, ROD. "Wrestling with Hallowe'en." *In Touch for Men* (Hollywood, Calif.), no. 119 (October 1986). [M]
    A young gay man finds his sensuality heightened under the influence of an enchanted Grecian cup.

24 ASIMOV, ISAAC. *Currents of Space*. Garden City, N.Y.: Doubleday, 1952. [m]
    The absorbing political intrigue in this novel revolves around Ric, an Interstellar Spatio-Analyst. Ric has been psychically probed into amnesia by persons unknown and used as a political pawn. The

homosexual element in the book is the characterization of one of the villains, the Squire of Steen, as a bisexual coward.

25 ASIMOV, ISAAC. "The Encyclopedists." In *Foundation*. New York: Gnome, 1951. [M?]

"The Encyclopedists" is the first story in Asimov's celebrated Foundation series. It is the autumn of a dying age. The Empire has flourished as an intergalactic power for 12,000 years, but its omnipotence is crumbling and its domains are slowly falling into chaos. For fifty years a small scientific community on the fringe world of Terminus has struggled with growing isolation as an Imperial outpost and internal domestic problems. A crisis finally has been reached and is accentuated by the arrival of Lord Dorwin, a representative of the Empire. Dorwin is effete and foppish, and the story's primary character develops an "instant detestation" of him. Although never clearly defined as homosexual, Dorwin's affected character obviously represents the loss of the Empire's remaining virility.

26 ASIMOV, ISAAC. *Foundation and Earth*. New York: Doubleday, 1986. [X]

The fifth installment of Asimov's famous Foundation series. A quest for the origins of human beings leads Golan Trevize, former Councilman of the First Foundation, planet-hopping across the galaxy. Trevize and his band visit six planets before finding their goal. Among these planets is Solaria, where a small population of hermaphroditic humans are cared for by an army of robots. A hermaphroditic child joins the expedition and proves important to the novel's conclusion.

27 ASIMOV, ISAAC. *The Gods Themselves*. Garden City, N.Y.: Doubleday, 1972. [X]

A new, endless source of energy is discovered and Earth's problems seem solved. But it soon becomes apparent that not only will continued use of this free energy blow up our solar system, but it will also destroy another universe. The inventive characterization of the inhabitants of this other universe makes the story relevant to this bibliography. They have three different sexes, each an aspect of a whole personality, which permanently merge into a single being through their lovemaking. The energy that the Earth is using so abundantly is necessary for these trisexual aliens' survival, but contact between the two universes, let alone communication, seems impossible.

28 ATWOOD, MARGARET. *The Handmaid's Tale*. Toronto: McClelland and Stewart, 1985. Reprint. New York: Houghton Mifflin, 1986. [f]

Canadian poet and novelist Margaret Atwood delivers a bleak vision of the future. Conservative religious and political forces have forced a fundamentalist dictatorship onto the people of the United States. The country now calls itself the Republic of Gilead; a racist and misogynistic administration is in power. Because the wives of the ruling class are rarely fertile, a group of women are drafted to be "handmaids," surrogate mothers for the elite. Offred (literally "owned by Fred") is such a handmaid, who finds herself controlled and exploited at every turn. One of her few friends, fellow handmaid Moira, was once involved in lesbian feminist politics. A strong and unforgettable feminist vision.

29 BAKER, SHARON. *Quarreling, They Met the Dragon*. New York: Avon, 1984. [M]

Baker's fascinating and kinky first novel manages to cover hustling, sadomasochism, and boy love in one big leap. Senruh is a young slave and male prostitute on the cruel world of Naphar. When Senruh meets an aristocratic Lady he imagines a rescue from bondage, but his hopes are dashed when he discovers the Lady's sadomasochistic desires. Senruh escapes her manipulations, helped in large part by his love for Pell, a younger friend. Baker has returned to Naphar twice, in *Journey to Memblair* (New York: Avon, 1987) and its sequel *Burning Tears of Sassurum* (New York: Avon, 1988), but neither utilizes as strong a homosexual theme.

30 BALL, BRIAN N. *Planet Probability*. London: Dennis Dobson, 1968. Reprint. New York: DAW, 1973. [m]

A sequel to the author's *The Probability Man*, this novel continues the author's examination of a future in which humanity, with nothing left to accomplish, spends most of its time within "total-experience simulators." A cliché-ridden bisexual is introduced within the novel's first few pages, but he soon flits out of the story.

31 BALLARD, J[AMES] G. *The Atrocity Exhibition*. London: Jonathan Cape, 1970. Reprinted as *Love and Napalm: Export USA*. New York: Grove, 1972. [m]

A surrealistic voyage across the convoluted landscape of a severely disturbed man obsessed with the relationship between the violence of contemporary life and his own internal chaos. His mind continually generates a series of fantasies, some homoerotic and all utilizing his personal iconography. To convey his protagonist's emotional turmoil, the author adopts a style as experimental as his subject matter by using fragmentary, puzzlelike images that pose some very disturbing questions about the ways in which mass violence and unconscious sexuality relate.

32 BALLARD, J[AMES] G. *Crash*. London: Jonathan Cape, 1973. Reprint. New York: Farrar Straus, 1973. [M]

In *Crash*, Ballard again explores the connections between human sexuality and violence. The narrator recounts his friendship with a young man who eroticizes the wreckage of both vehicles and human beings. As the narrator's friendship with the young man, Vaughan (a minor character in *The Atrocity Exhibition*), deepens, he finds himself beginning to share Vaughan's morbid obsessions. By the end of the novel, the two men have made love with each other. The book is filled with graphic depictions of violence, mutilation, and sex (largely heterosexual), but the book has significance beyond this carnage.

33 BALLIET, BEV. "The Many Women in the Woman I Love." In *A Woman's Touch*, edited by Cedar and Nelly. Eugene, Oreg.: Womanshare Books, 1979. [F]
Sexually explicit lesbian erotica with sadomasochistic role-playing fantasy elements. Written and published by lesbian feminists.

34 BAMBER, GEORGE. *The Sea Is Boiling Hot*. New York: Ace, 1971. [f?, m]
Pollution has finally destroyed the delicate environmental systems that make life on our planet possible. The air is unbreathable; the ocean boils. Humanity has retreated to enormous cities shielded inside gigantic plastic domes. Society has degenerated into a hedonistic herd of cattle awaiting extinction. To depict the decadence of future life, all aspects of sexuality are derogatorily portrayed, but the author is particularly contemptuous of homosexuality. Sexuality between women is shown as infantile regression and male homosexuality is personified by a predatory, senile degenerate.

BARBOUR, DOUGLAS. *See* DELANY, SAMUEL R.

35 BARKER, CLIVE. "The Age of Desire." In *Clive Barker's Books of Blood, Volume Four*. London: Sphere, 1985. Reprinted as *The Inhuman Condition*. New York: Poseidon, 1986. [m]
In an ethically questionable medical experiment, a hallucinogenic aphrodisiac is injected into a human volunteer. His erotic cravings soon become uncontrollable and he begins to sexually assault anyone, female or male, who gets near him. Ultimately the experiment proves fatal and the young man literally burns up with sexual desire.

36 BARKER, CLIVE. "Coming to Grief." In *Prime Evil*, edited by Douglas E. Winter. New York: New American Library, 1988. [f]
After her mother's death, Miriam Blessed must return to her family home and take care of the funeral details. In doing so, she must also confront and overcome her childhood fears. She is helped by an old

friend, now a lesbian. A very sensitive and haunting story, surprisingly free of Barker's trademark violence and gore.

37 BARKER, CLIVE. "Human Remains." In *Clive Barker's Books of Blood, Volume Three*. London: Sphere, 1984. Reprint. New York: Berkley, 1986. [M]

Another chilling horror story from Barker, this time with a bisexual protagonist. Gavin is a jaded, narcissistic male prostitute living on the streets of London. One evening, after following an older man home to an eerie, antique-filled flat, Gavin meets a client who wants not only his body but also his soul. Well-drawn, graphic, and very scary.

38 BARKER, CLIVE. "In the Hills, the Cities." In *Clive Barker's Books of Blood, Volume One*. London: Sphere, 1984. Reprint. New York: Berkley, 1984. [M]

Barker's "In the Hills, the Cities" has received justifiable critical acclaim for its portrayal of mass psychosis and its transcendental conclusion, but few critics mention the story's gay male content. In fact, this is one of the finest examples of gay male characterizations in the horror genre. Mick and Judd, a bickering gay male couple vacationing in Eastern Europe, find their destinies changed forever when they accidentally stumble upon a weird bloody ritual.

39 BARKER, CLIVE. "Sex, Death, and Starshine." In *Clive Barker's Books of Blood, Volume One*. London: Sphere, 1984. Reprint. New York: Berkley, 1984. [m]

The Elysium Theater is about to be closed. Director Terence Calloway has been holding the company together with luck and ingenuity (and an affair with a leading soap opera actress), but shoddy performances and falling box office sales have brought about the inevitable. The final performance is scheduled until an offer from a mysterious stranger gives the theater new hope. A secondary character is the gay Edward Cunningham, a flouncy, but not unsympathetic, member of the troupe.

40 BARKER, CLIVE. "The Yattering and Jack." In *Clive Barker's Books of Blood, Volume One*. London: Sphere, 1984. Reprint. New York: Berkley, 1984. [f]

Barker renders a surprisingly humorous account of an inconsequential gherkin importer named Jack Polo who must battle a minor demon assigned by Satan to deliver Jack's soul to hell. One of Jack's daughters is lesbian.

Biographical Note

Clive Barker (b. 1952) has developed an impressive reputation as a writer of horror fiction. His clean writing, graphic violence, and wry humor have given him a wide following. He is the author of the six-volume Books of Blood series (London: Sphere, 1984-86). When reprinted in the United States, volumes 4 and 5 of this series were retitled *The Inhuman Condition* (New York: Poseidon, 1986), and *In the Flesh* (New York: Poseidon, 1986). *Cabal* (New York: Poseidon Press, 1988) includes all the stories from volume 6, in addition to the title novella. He has also written *The Damnation Game* (New York: G. P. Putnam's Sons, 1987), *Weaveworld* (New York: Poseidon Press, 1987), and *The Great and Secret Show* (London: Collins, 1989; New York: Harper and Row, 1990). He wrote and directed the horror films *Hellraiser*, *Hellbound: Hellraiser II*, and *Nightbreed*.

One of Barker's trademarks is his sophisticated approach to sexuality; unlike many horror writers, he displays no moral contempt for variant sexual behavior. All his work should be examined carefully for homosexual images. Both "Human Remains" and "In the Hills, the Cities" are included in *Tapping the Vein, Book One* (Forestville, Calif.: Eclipse, 1989) and *Tapping the Vein, Book Two* (Forestville, Calif.: Eclipse, 1989).

Biographical material on Barker can be found in Douglas E. Winter's *Faces of Fear* (New York: Berkley, 1985). See also "Meet the New (Stephen) King of Horror, Briton Clive Barker" in *People*, 15 June 1987.

BARNES, STEVEN. Aubry Knight Series:

41 ■ *Streetlethal*. New York: Avon, 1983. [m]

42 ■ *Gorgon Child*. New York: Tor, 1989. [f, m]

Aubry Knight is a trained martial-arts killer in twenty-first century Los Angeles. He is sent to prison for a murder he did not commit. Knight escapes, teams up with an exotic dancer named Promise, and fights against crime and tyranny in two action-packed novels. Barnes's future society is rife with disease, social corruption, and intolerance, but there are elements of resistance and hope. For example, within the underground, racial barriers have eroded. The author is an African-American and so are many of his characters, including the protagonist. Barnes writes with a tolerance towards homosexuals. An important element of both *Gorgon Child* and *Streetlethal* are the "NewMen," supermen genetically engineered from XXY ova in male separatist camps. A feminist (predominantly lesbian) commune in Oregon also figures in the plot. An odd view of homosexuality perhaps, but not condemnatory.

BARNETT, LISA. *See* SCOTT, MELISSA (joint author)

43 BARNEY, NATALIE CLIFFORD. *The One Who Is Legion: or, A. D.'s Afterlife*. Illustrated by Romaine Brooks. London: Eric Partridge, 1930. [F, X]

Privately printed for the author, *The One Who Is Legion* concerns a strange, multiconscious, hermaphroditic spirit who assumes the body and identity of A. D., a recent suicide. Although the author cleverly obscures the sex of A. D., careful reading reveals her to be a lesbian (probably autobiographically drawn) who is despondent over the death of a former lover. The spirit spends much of the story figuring out who A. D. was and what the spirit is now. Unfortunately, the author's ability to characterize her sexless creation is uneven, and the book occasionally becomes impenetrable. The overall atmosphere is morose, probably due to the influence of Barney's friend and lover, Romaine Brooks, who contributed two illustrations to the text. The book was printed in an edition of 560 copies. An excerpt from the novel was originally published in the *Dial*, June 1927.

Biographical Note

Natalie Clifford Barney (1876-1972) was one of the most influential lesbians of her day. Information on Barney can be found in Jean Chalon's *Portrait of a Seductress: The World of Natalie Barney* (New York: Crown, 1979), Karla Jay's *The Amazon and the Page: Natalie Clifford Barney and Renee Vivien* (Bloomington: Indiana University Press, 1988) and George Wiches's *The Amazon of Letters* (New York: Putnam, 1976).

---

44 BARR, DONALD. *Space Relations: A Slightly Gothic Interplanetary Tale*. New York: Chatterhouse, 1973. [m]

John Craig, a robust heterosexual Terran diplomat, is kidnapped and sold into slavery on the feudal planet Kossar. He is bought by the aristocratic slave owner, Lady Morgan Sidney, and soon rises from the degradation of working in her dangerous mines to the pleasures of his labor at her bedside. He escapes from Kossar, but he later returns to abolish slavery and to reclaim his beloved former owner, Lady Sidney. The author rarely strays from his heterosexual love story, but he manages to introduce a gay character. The villainous minor character, like a space-age Dr. Moreau, genetically alters his young male slaves into simpering hermaphroditic creatures.

45 BARRETT, NEAL, Jr. *Highwood*. New York: Ace, 1972. [F, M]

On a heavily forested planet, Sequoia, a native population of monkeylike Lemmits have a social system that, outside of yearly ritual matings, is entirely homosexual. The homosexuality of the Lemmits is treated as unnatural by the author and is eventually explained as the result of some long-forgotten civil strife. The human female protagonist, although starting out independent, ends up as a submissive female clinging to her hero.

46 BARRUS, TIM. *Genocide: The Anthology*. Stanford, Conn.: Knights Press, 1989. [M]
     This nightmarish gay male novel, which reads like the contemporary experience of the AIDS epidemic, is set in a distant future in which a horrible virus has destroyed civilization. Internment/concentration camps have been set up around the world to incarcerate the infected. The images Barrus evokes are bitter, violent, and ugly. Yet despite his nihilist outlook (and stated intentions) there is an element of hope in *Genocide*, largely in the love, support, and passion (often sadomasochistic) that gay men give to each other. In both form and content, Barrus resembles William Burroughs, and like that of the older writer, Barrus's vision will be appreciated only by some.

Biographical Note
Tim Barrus is also the author of the gay-themed, non-science-fiction novels, *My Brother, My Lover* (San Francisco, Calif.: Gay Sunshine Press, 1985) and *Anywhere, Anywhere* (Pound Ridge, N.Y.: Knights, 1987).

---

47 BARTH, ROGER. "The Homosexual Aid Society in the Middle of the 21st Century." *ONE Magazine* (Los Angeles), May 1962. [F, M]
     A short future vision of the world of 2060 in which homosexuals have been emancipated in cities of over 10,000 in population. Within these cities, lesbians and gay men have developed their own culture and institutions, which include a cultural museum, a gay history school, gay bars, and computer dating services.

48 BARTTER, M. A. "Be Ye Perfect." *Galaxy*, January 1975. [F]
     "Be Ye Perfect" concerns a society almost entirely homosexual in which women and men are kept totally isolated except for brief periods of required heterosexuality for the purposes of propagation. These periods are looked upon with fear and disgust. The plot revolves around a lesbian who is forced into motherhood.

49 BAYER, SANDY. *The Crystal Curtain*. Boston: Alyson, 1988. [F]
     A lesbian psychic, Stephanie Nowland, helps the police locate a psychotic rapist and murderer in a rural Georgia town. The murderer is incarcerated, but he escapes and stalks Stephanie and her lover. Bayer effectively builds suspense throughout her gripping page-turner, but her depiction of violence may unsettle some.

50 BEAR, GREG. "Tangents." *Omni* (New York) 8, no. 4 (January 1986). Reprint. *Tangents*. New York: Warner, 1989. [M]

Bear pens an uplifting story about the friendship between a brilliant, middle-aged gay mathematician (living in obscurity because of his sexuality) and a lonely Korean-American boy. Their deepening nonsexual friendship proves crucial to them both and leads to a remarkable scientific breakthrough. Bear's mathematician is obviously patterned on the British mathematician Alan Turning, a national hero until his open homosexuality destroyed his career.

51 BEAUMONT, CHARLES [pseudonym of Charles Nutt]. "The Crooked Man." *Playboy*, August 1955. Reprinted in *Hunger, and Other Stories*. New York: Putnam, 1958. [F, M]

Overpopulation pressures have caused homosexuality to become the Earth's social norm. "Heteros" are now forced to hide their sexuality and to disguise themselves as gays. The two protagonists of "The Crooked Man," heterosexual lovers, are arrested by the vice squad. An interesting examination of social oppression that is ultimately homophobic: gays are portrayed as universally cruel and their relationships are totally depersonalized.

52 BEAUMONT, CHARLES [pseudonym of Charles Nutt]. "Miss Gentilbelle." In *Hunger, and Other Stories*. New York: Putnam, 1958. [F?, X]

In this haunting story an abusive mother, Miss Gentilbelle, has raised her son strictly as if he were a girl because she hates men. When her son asks questions about his true gender, Miss Gentilbelle punishes her "daughter" by butchering a pet frog. The boy breaks under the constant abuse and creates a scene of supreme horror. A carefully crafted, weird story.

53 BECKFORD, WILLIAM. *The History of the Caliph Vathek*. London: J. Johnson, 1786. [M?]

This fantastic Arabic tale is both captivating and horrifying. Beckford recounts the epic tale of the Caliph Vathek and his unceasing quest for power and riches. This search leads Vathek to commit villainous crimes, to deal with sorcery and demons, and eventually to face damnation in the depths of hell. Homosexual elements are subtle but unmistakable. Beckford's homosexuality was the subject of much public comment during his life, and it is quite clear that the character of Vathek is autobiographically drawn. The young Prince Gulchenrouz, described as "the most delicate and lovely creature in the world," can be none other than Beckford's lover, William Courtenay. Rich and vivid, this Oriental extravaganza was immensely popular in its day, and it is still considered a classic Gothic romance.

54 BEECHING, JACK. *The Dakota Project*. London: Jonathan Cape, 1968. Reprint. New York: Delacorte, 1969. [F, m]

A British technical copywriter, Richard Conroy, is recruited for a top-secret research project located somewhere in the Black Hills of the United States. When he arrives at the mysterious Dakota Project, the intense security precautions make him question his decision. His apprehension grows when he realizes that he has become a virtual prisoner. When Conroy discovers the nature of the Dakota Project's research he decides to take matters into his own hands. His primary allies throughout the novel are two loving lesbians, whose positive depiction is a sharp contrast to that of the unpleasant gay men scattered throughout the book.

55 BELL, NEIL. *Gone to Be Snakes Now*. New York: Popular Library, 1974. [F?, M?]

Surreal and semiallegorical, this novel emerges through the perceptions of Walter Wence, a young boy from Exxon, one of the towns centered around giant gas pumps, prepared by aliens for the survivors of Earth's nuclear holocaust. Most of the female characters are treated with sensitive humor, amid much sardonically light-hearted violence. Throughout, there are hints that Walter is worried about his sexual orientation; he decides that anyone he does not like is a "homo," though his young friends, Jane and Elena, impatiently try to broaden his views. The Freudian overtones to Walter's fear of snakes, an ambiguous declaration of love from Francis Cragley (also called the Great Bird), and a homoerotic dream add up to an ambivalent homosexual statement. The book winds up focusing more on death than sex, even though the writing is witty and alert. Just before the end of the novel, however, Jane states that "in a way" she is in love with Elena.

56 BEN, LISA [pseudonym]. "New Year's Revolution." *Vice Versa* (Los Angeles), January 1948. [F, m]

Apparently written in a fit of anger over the injustices gay people face daily, "New Year's Revolution" concerns a drunk straight man who stumbles accidentally into a gay bar on New Year's Eve and promptly falls into an alcoholic stupor. While unconscious, he dreams of visiting "Fruitvale Heights," the author's vision of lesbian / gay utopia. Openly gay people are everywhere, lesbian and gay male love is encouraged, and heterosexuality is considered a deviation. The protagonist experiences his hallucination as a nightmare, but sympathetic readers will enjoy every sentence.

Biographical Note

Lisa Ben (an anagram of lesbian) is a pseudonym of a lesbian who actively participated in science-fiction fandom during the 1940s. Her involvement with the Los Angeles Science Fiction Association led her to help organize the first major West Coast science-fiction convention, the Pacificon, in 1946. Later, under another pseudonym, Lisa Ben had several science-fiction stories professionally published.

In 1947, as a result of her rising lesbian consciousness, Lisa Ben began publishing a small magazine specifically directed toward lesbians. Called *Vice Versa*, the magazine was the first American publication of its kind, and its fan origins are clear. Published in the same amateur format that fanzines have used for decades, *Vice Versa* carried at least two fantasy stories during its nine-issue run: "New Year's Revolution" and "Kiki." It also featured a lesbian critique of Vardis Fisher's prehistoric fantasy, *The Darkness and the Deep*. Lisa Ben later wrote for the *Ladder*, and in the early 1960s she recorded an early example of lesbian music: a lesbian version of "Frankie and Johnnie."

Additional biographical information can be found in "An Interview with Lisa Ben" by Leland Moss in *Gaysweek* (New York), no. 49 (23 January 1978).

---

57 BENFORD, GREGORY. *In the Ocean of Night*. New York: Dial Press, James Wade, 1972. [f]

Astronaut Nigel Walmsly's life comprises his work with NASA and his comfortable home life with his wife and their mutual female lover, Shirley. After he disobeys a NASA directive during the first close encounter with an alien spaceship, NASA tries to ruin his life. His mental health worsens when Alexandria, his wife, becomes a resurrected Christ figure for a politically inclined religious sect. Without Alexandria, Shirley finds no satisfaction in a relationship with Nigel, and she leaves to follow Alexandria's mass preaching tours. The author spends few words on the two women's support and love for each other, and he soon shifts the attention back to Nigel.

See also EKLUND, GORDON (joint author)

58 BENSON, E[DWARD] F[REDRIC]. *The Inheritor*. London: Hutchinson, 1930. Reprint. Garden City, N.Y.: Doubleday, 1930. [M]

Benson's important but overlooked fantasy is both an effective horror story and a classic coming-out novel. Maurice Crofts, scholar of Ancient Greek culture and a repressed homosexual, has settled down to a refined and celibate existence as a don at a distinguished British university. Although he adores the cloistered all-male society that the academic environment provides, Maurice longs for "perfect comradeship," and is jealous of the "engrossing intimacy" between undergraduate Steven Gervase and his friend, Merriman. Maurice is overjoyed when Gervase turns to him after breaking off the affair. Their new friendship heralds Maurice's homoerotic awakening. The plot thickens when a supernatural curse upon Gervase's family is revealed and brings *The Inheritor* to its startling conclusion. Homosexuality, though disguised as nonsexual, homoemotional friendship, remains a prominent theme throughout, and it is intriguing that this went unnoticed in the book's initial reviews. The author's misogyny is unmistakable.

59 BENSON, E[DWARD] F[REDRIC]. *Ravens' Brood*. London: Arthur Barker, 1934. Reprint. Garden City, N.Y.: Doubleday, 1934. [M]

Ravens' Brood is a slow-moving Gothic novel. It tells the tale of the Pentreaths, an eccentric Cornish family. Although by no means the primary focus of *Ravens' Brood*, mystical powers, evil omens, and heathen rituals appear within the novel. The homosexual content is quite explicit. An effeminate boarder the Pentreaths take on for the summer is known simply as the "girlie." In sharp contrast, the hero, Dennis Pentreath, has a close Jonathan and David-type relationship with his best friend.

Biographical Note

E. F. Benson (1867-1940) was a well-respected and highly prolific British author who wrote several notable classics of fantasy literature. While many of his novels touch upon the supernatural, Benson is remembered for his brilliant fantasy short stories and his nonfantasy, campy comedies of manners. Other fantasy novels not listed in the above citations include: *The Angel of Pain* (London: William Heinemann, 1906); *Colin: A Novel* (London: Hutchinson, 1923); and *Colin II* (London: Hutchinson, 1925). His fantasy short stories can be found in the following collections: *The Room in the Tower, and Other Stories* (London: Mills & Boon, 1912); *Visible and Invisible* (London: Hutchinson, 1923); *Spook Stories* (London: Hutchinson, 1928); and *More Spook Stories* (London: Hutchinson, 1934).

Benson was homosexual, and homosexual themes occur regularly in both his fantasy and nonfantasy work. Significant examples of this can be seen in *Rex* (London: Hodder & Stoughton, 1926) and in *David Blaise* (London: Hodder & Stoughton, 1930). His entire Lucia series, beginning with *Queen Lucia* (London: Hutchinson, 1920), is of some relevance to both gay men and lesbians.

Autobiographical information is available in Benson's *Our Family Affairs* (1920) and his *Final Edition* (1940). Biographical / critical information on Benson is available in *Twentieth Century Authors*, ed. Stanley J. Kunitz and Howard Haycraft (New York: Wilson, 1942); in "Luciaphiles and Anglophiles: The Benson Mania," by Karl Maves in the *Advocate* (San Mateo, Calif.), no.

236 (8 March 1978); in Davis Williams's *Genesis and Exodus: A Portrait of the Benson Family* (London: Hamish Hamilton, 1979); and in Cynthia and Tony Reavell's *E. F. Benson: Mr. Benson Remembered in Rye, and the World of Tilling* (n.p.: Martello Bookshop, 1984).

---

60 BERENSFORD, JOHN D[AVYS]. *Goslings*. London: Heinemann, 1913. Reprinted as *A World of Women*. New York: Macaulay, 1913. [F?]

Berensford's novel focuses on the efforts of a British family to survive the devastating effects of a worldwide plague. The plague has filtered out of China and is fatal only to men, leaving a world of women and only a handful of men. Society collapses, traditional social values disappear, and starvation becomes widespread. Blanche Gosling, her mother, and her sister flee a deserted London and travel to the isolated community of Marlow. In Marlow, a new communal woman-run government has been established. Despite the author's expressed dedication to equality between the sexes, the book's basic premise is one of male superiority. The Marlow community, though temporarily stable and self-supporting, is nonetheless destined for collapse until a boatload of American men arrive. The novel contains several strong female characters who wear men's clothes and have no need for the male sex. There is also an oblique reference to "sexual perversions" resulting from the severe shortage of men.

BERRY, D. BRUCE. *See* OFFUTT, ANDREW J. (joint author)

61 BESTER, ALFRED. *The Demolished Man. Galaxy*, January-March 1952. Revised and reprinted. Chicago: Shasta, 1953. [m]

A suspenseful science-fiction mystery thriller. An interplanetary businessman has been found murdered, and psychic detective Lincoln Powell is assigned to the case. Both Powell and the reader know the culprit; Powell's problem is to find out how and why the murder was committed. The crime is set in a future in which telepaths make up a growing percentage of the population. Bester successfully conveys the telepathic communications of this mind-reading society by utilizing a dissimilar typeface. Male homosexuals are depicted as effete, gushy social secretaries; their appearances are brief and have little effect upon the story. The book was very successful when released (winning the first Hugo Award in 1953) and has remained popular since.

62 BESTER, ALFRED. *The Indian Giver. Analog*, November 1974-January 1975. Reprinted as *The Computer Connection*. New York: Berkley, 1975. [m, X]

A band of eccentric immortals find that their newest member, a brilliant Cherokee scientist, Dr. Sequoya Guess, is being manipulated by the Earth's largest and most powerful computer, Extro. Guess's noble experiment, the creation of an advanced race of human hermaphrodites, is threatened, and the wacky immortals must work together to fight Extro. The plot is played for laughs, but the humor is often insensitive. For example, Bester uses stereotypic mannerisms and the epithets "faggot" and "queenie" to denote male homosexuality. The author's treatment of homosexuality remains unchanged in the twenty years since the publication of *The Demolished Man*.

Biographical Note
Alfred Bester (b. 1913) is also the author of the classic science-fiction novel *My Stars My Destination* (New York: New American Library, 1956). He discusses his attitudes toward homosexuality and the gay rights movement in Jeremy Hughes's article "Sex in the Year 2500," *In Touch for Men*, July 1982.

---

63 BEY, HAKIM. "The Antarctic Autonomous Zone: A Science-Fiction Story." In *Semiotext(e): SF*, edited by Rudy Rucker, Peter Lamborn Wilson, and Robert Anton Wilson. Brooklyn, N.Y.: Autonomedia, 1989. [M]
   An erotic image poem replete with ice-covered flying saucers, alien planets, and horny boy astronauts.

64 [BEY], HAKIM. *Crowstone*. Amsterdam: Acolyte Press, 1983. [M]
   This unabashed Sword and Sorcery boy-love tale has been the object of official harassment in Britain because of its explicit depiction of intergenerational gay sex. Subtitled "The Chronicles of Qamar," the novel takes place on the fairest of the 108 moons orbiting the planet of Algol. On Qamar, the citizens worship Varon, the boy-love god. The atmosphere is a mixture of medieval and Arabic. A traveling scholar and a barbarian mercenary meet in a boy brothel and set out to locate the magical Crowstone, battling dragons, ghosts, and sorcery along the way. Controversial and pornographic, but fast-paced and rich with imagination nonetheless.

65 BIGELOW, JANE M. H. "Tactics." In *Free Amazons of Darkover*, edited by Marion Zimmer Bradley. New York: DAW, 1985. [F]
   A feminist short story based on Marion Zimmer Bradley's popular Darkover series. A young fifteen-year-old dreams of escaping her boring life and joining the Free Amazons. There are lesbian implications in the story, but to tell them would give away the plot.

66 BINGLEY, MARGARET. *Seeds of Evil*. London: Piatkus, 1988. Reprint. New York: Carroll & Graf, 1989. [m]

Bingley pens a fairly typical *Rosemary's Baby*-type horror novel. A young British mother becomes more and more frightened as her strange twins, the results of artificial insemination, begin to exhibit destructive psychic powers and a morbid fascination with violence and blood. The twins soon murder her homosexual husband and arrange for her to meet an oddly sinister man.

67 BIRDSTONE, ALABAMA. *Queer Free.* New York: Calamus Books, 1981. [f, M]

Birdstone issues a dire warning about intolerance, homophobia, and political awareness by depicting a dystopia in which a fascist religious movement takes over the United States and establishes death camps for lesbians and gay men. San Francisco's Castro Street district becomes a center of organized resistance. *Queer Free* focuses upon a group of gay men who find themselves caught in the worsening situation. Birdstone's vision is a strong one, vividly depicted, but unfortunately he is less successful with his characterizations and plot development. His handsome and horny actors, artists, and magazine publishers are shallow and predictable. Birdstone's gay dystopia can be compared with similar treatments by Barrus, Bryan, Mains, and Welles.

68 BISHOP, MICHAEL. "Icicle Music." *Fantasy and Science Fiction*, November 1989. Reprinted in *Spirits of Christmas*, edited by David G. Hartwell and Shirley Cramer. New York: Wynwood, 1989. [M]

A gay man hospitalized with a fatal illness remembers a surreal Christmas of his youth and the subsequent supernatural visits of his father.

69 BISHOP, MICHAEL. *Unicorn Mountain.* New York: Arbor House, 1988. [M]

Bishop's touching and heartfelt fantasy novel combines condoms, AIDS, Native Americans, and unicorns in a magical story. Libby Quarrel, a divorced rancher trying to eke out a living in the isolated Colorado Rockies, grudgingly shares her place with ranch hand and friend Sam Coldpony, a Ute Indian. She takes in Bo Gavin, a young gay relative with AIDS, after he has been rejected by his lover and his family. These three people find their lives transformed when a small herd of unicorns is discovered on the ranch. Bishop creates complex characters and relationships and his novel is one of the best.

Biographical Note
Michael Bishop (b. 1945) is also the author of the Nebula Award-winning novel *No Enemy but Time* (New York: Timescape, 1982). His non-science-

fiction story, "Unlikely Friends," in *Ellery Queen's Mystery Magazine*, November 1982, is also of gay male interest.

---

70 BIXBY, JEROME. "The Strange Habits of Robert Prey." In *Devil's Scrapbook*. North Hollywood, Calif.: Brandon House, 1964. [M]

A brief horror story concerning an attempt to blackmail a suspected homosexual.

71 BIXBY, JEROME, and DEAN, JOE. "Share Alike." *Beyond*, July 1953. Reprinted in *Galaxy of Ghouls*, edited by Judith Merril. New York: Lion, 1955. [M]

Two survivors of a shipwreck await rescue in a lifeboat. One is a male human; the other is a male vampire. The relationship that develops between them is erotic. The story is gripping.

BLIXEN, KAREN. *See* DINESEN, ISAK (pseudonym)

72 BLOCH, ROBERT. "A Toy for Juliette." In *Dangerous Visions*, edited by Harlan Ellison. Garden City, N.Y.: Doubleday, 1967. [f]

A gruesome story in which a time-traveling grandfather collects "toys" for his granddaughter, Juliette. These toys, actually women and men from the past, are the playing pieces in Juliette's games of sexual activity and human dismemberment. The tables are turned when her grandpappy transports Jack the Ripper to her playroom.

73 BLUEJAY, JANA [pseudonym of Terry Woodrow]. *It's Time*. Little River, Calif.: Tough Dove, 1985. [F]

A simple, good-hearted glimpse of a lesbian feminist dystopia. The women of the Enchanted Forest must overcome their class and ethnic differences and challenge the "tree eaters" who live in the "Power Tower." The narrative follows a vegetarian pacifist woodswoman and her adventuresome lover, Meriwyn ("of the far reaches, frosted layers, and greater worlds"). Add to the adventure three urban escapees, Darlene, Carolyn, and Sandra, who join the forest women's fight. Bluejay's vision will appeal to audiences who enjoy Sally Gearhart's *Wanderground*.

74 BOAL, NINA. "Flight." In *Red Sun over Darkover*, edited by Marion Zimmer Bradley. New York: DAW, 1987. [M]

Boal's short story is based on Marion Zimmer Bradley's popular Darkover series. Lewis-Gabriel Ridenow, one of Darkover's Comyn aristocracy, has been kidnapped, castrated, and sold to a Dryland lord as a servant and a sex partner. "Flight" concerns his escape to freedom.

BONA DEA, MARIDES. *See* ESTACADA, ALIX (joint author)

75 BORGMAN, C. F. "A Queer Red Spirit." In *Men on Men*, edited by George Stambolian. New York: New American Library, 1986. [M]
The spirit of an older gay man communicates with a young 1980s one.

76 BORGMAN, C. F. *River Road*. New York: New American Library, 1988. [f, M]
River Road is a critically acclaimed mainstream gay novel with a science-fiction twist centering on poet and performance artist Eugene Goessler. Comprised of brief vignettes from various periods of Goessler's life, the novel begins with his Midwest youth in the 1950s and extends through his homosexual awakening, his struggles as an artist, and his eventual international fame in the twenty-first century. The novel's time frame extends well into the future, but the science-fiction elements are limited to cursory extrapolations of contemporary trends.

77 BOSTON, BRUCE. "Break." *New Worlds Quarterly*, June 1974. Reprinted in *New Worlds Seven*, edited by Charles Platt and Hilary Bailey. London: Sphere, 1974. Reprinted as *New Worlds Six*. New York: Avon, 1975. [M]
An eerie story about a carefully planned prison escape. At first, it seems that there are two men involved, but the ending leaves the reader wondering if actually only one very schizophrenic convict plotted the jail break. Nonconsensual homosexuality is an integral element of this bizarre and fascinating story.

78 BOYD, JOHN [pseudonym of Boyd Bradfield Upchurch]. *Sex and the High Command*. New York: Weybright & Talley, 1970. [F?, m, X]
A science-fiction satire based on the premise that women have developed a cream that gives them both sexual satisfaction and the ability to reproduce independently, thus eliminating their need for men. Of course, the United States military (who else?) shifts into high gear to defend patriarchy. A minor character, Dr. Houston Drexel, changes his sex toward the end of the novel. Homosexuality (both male and female) is mentioned in passing; male homosexuality is linked with polarized role-playing.

79 BOYETT, STEVEN R. "The Answer Tree." In *Silver Scream*, edited by David J. Schow. Arlington Heights, Ill.: Dark Harvest, 1988. [m]
Boyett writes an unusual horror story in which a professor of film criticism finds himself becoming seriously obsessed with the work of a sadistic bisexual Spanish film director.

80 BRADBURY, RAY. "The Better Part of Wisdom." In *Long after Midnight*. New York: Knopf, 1976. [M]

A warm, touching story about an Irish grandfather's acceptance of his grandson's loving relationship with another man. (This story contains no science-fiction or fantasy elements but was published in a science-fiction collection.) Recommended.

81 BRADBURY, RAY. "The Cold Wind and the Warm." *Harper's*, July 1964. Reprinted in *I Sing the Body Electric!* New York: Knopf, 1969. [M]

A lovely story in which six gay men descend upon a small town in Ireland, evoking a strong response from the men of the village. The stereotypic presentation of the homosexuals is qualified by a validating ending. (This story contains no science-fiction or fantasy elements but was published in a science-fiction collection.)

82 BRADBURY, RAY. "Long after Midnight." In *Long after Midnight*. New York: Knopf, 1976. [M?]

Two seasoned ambulance attendants help a third, less experienced colleague deal with his reactions to the suicide of a male sexual variant. The story focuses on the new attendant's sexual prejudices and possible homophobia. The melodramatic suicide is reminiscent of a more sexually repressive era. (This story contains no science-fiction or fantasy elements but was published in a science-fiction collection.)

83 BRADBURY, RAY. "The Parrot Who Met Papa." In *Long after Midnight*. New York: Knopf, 1976. [m]

Panic strikes Havana when an old pet parrot, once an intimate of Ernest Hemingway, is kidnapped. The guilty party turns out to be the malicious rival author Shelley Capon, a Truman Capote-like character described as a giggling "Kewpie doll" wearing a velveteen jacket, a loud bow tie, and little green booties. (This story contains no science-fiction or fantasy elements but was published in a science-fiction collection.)

84 BRADLEY, MARION ZIMMER. "Centaurus Changeling." *Fantasy and Science Fiction*, April 1954. [F?]

"Centaurus Changeling" concerns the conflicts resulting from a Terran woman's pregnancy on an alien world. The Terran develops strong emotional relationships with several alien women while she is pregnant. Although it is questionable whether these relationships can be termed lesbian, they have been noted as such.

85 BRADLEY, MARION ZIMMER. *City of Sorcery*. New York: DAW, 1984. [F]

This novel, like much of Bradley's science fiction, is set in her Darkover universe. Darkover is an Earth-settled planet, but the colonizers have been out of communication with their mother world for centuries and have interbred with an indigenous, telepathic people. This has caused Darkover to develop its own unique culture: aristocratic and feudal, yet psychically advanced. *City of Sorcery* is set decades after Earth has rediscovered Darkover and Terran-Darkover relations have been normalized. Free Amazons, women who live outside the cultural values that keep the rest of Darkover's female population subservient – sometimes enchained – have become an important link between the two cultures. Each Free Amazon swears an oath to forsake male domination, to define her own sexuality, and to protect each other no matter what the cost. Camilla, an *emmasca* (a voluntarily neutered woman) and Magda Lorne, a Terran, are Free Amazonian lesbian lovers who search for a mysterious city of telepathic Amazons. Chronologically follows *The Shattered Chain* and *Thendara House*.

86 BRADLEY, MARION ZIMMER. *The Forbidden Tower*. New York: DAW, 1977. [F?, M]
On Darkover, psychic power is generated through "towers" – small groups of powerful psychics who channel their psi power, or *laran*, together. *The Forbidden Tower* concerns four rebellious telepaths, two women and two men, including one Terran, who band together to create a nontraditional tower. There is explicit sexuality between the two men, and the book implies pansexual group expression among them.

87 BRADLEY, MARION ZIMMER. "Hawk-Master's Son." In *The Keeper's Price*, edited by Marion Zimmer Bradley. New York: DAW, 1980. [M]
Darkover short story that examines the early life of the homosexual nobleman Dyan Ardis, prior to the events of *Heritage of Hastur*, and his youthful love affair with Kennard Alton.

88 BRADLEY, MARION ZIMMER. *Hawkmistress!* New York: DAW, 1982. [F?, m]
Bradley explores the options for Darkover women who choose not to become Free Amazons with the story of Romilly, a young Darkover woman with *laran*. Romilly can mentally communicate with hawks and horses, and she would like nothing more than to be a keeper and trainer of hawks all her life. But her tyrannical father thinks the vocation unfeminine and has arranged a marriage for her instead. Romilly decides that she would rather choose her own destiny and runs away, traveling disguised as a boy for a time with a group of men. She is thought by some to be the leader's catamite. In Romilly's case, transvestism does not infer lesbianism.

89 BRADLEY, MARION ZIMMER. *The Heritage of Hastur*. New York: DAW, 1975. [f, M]

This landmark in gay male science fiction concerns Regis Hastur, a young member of the Comyn, Darkover's telepathic aristocracy, and the slow, stormy awakening of both his homosexuality and his psychic abilities. The author's comparison of sexuality with psychic abilities is particularly well done. When Hastur, Darkover aristocrat and heir to the throne, represses his youthful homosexual affair with Lew Alton, he represses his psychic abilities as well. The primary adult homosexual character is a frustrated nobleman, Dyan Ardis, who uses his telepathy to torment young men unwilling to sleep with him. Thus, it is implied, perhaps unintentionally, that homosexuality is tolerable only during adolescence; it is either outgrown or misused by adults. (Bradley tempers Ardis's character in later works.)

90 BRADLEY, MARION ZIMMER. "The Incompetent Magician." In *Greyhaven*. New York: DAW, 1983. [F]

A story from outside Bradley's Darkover universe. The author sets her tale in Sanctuary, the archetypal Sword and Sorcery town invented by a group of science-fiction authors at a particularly imaginative science-fiction convention. Bradley tells of Lythande, a tall, blond, mysterious magician with a blue star tattooed upon "his" forehead. Each magician must have a secret that will bind his magical powers to him, and the magician must never divulge this secret to anyone. In "The Incompetent Magician" Lythande reveals her lesbian past.

91 BRADLEY, MARION ZIMMER. "The Legend of Lady Bruna." In *Free Amazons of Darkover*, edited by Marion Zimmer Bradley. New York: DAW, 1985. [F]

The Darkover legend of Bruna Leynier, a woman who picked up the sword after the death of her brother, was first mentioned in *The Forbidden Tower*. Here Bradley expands the story to explain this occurrence and why Lady Bruna married her brother's sister.

92 BRADLEY, MARION ZIMMER. "Man of Impulse." In *Four Moons of Darkover*, edited by Marion Zimmer Bradley. New York: DAW, 1988. [M]

Dyan Ardis is a villainous character in *The Heritage of Hastur*, but in "Man of Impulse," Bradley shows another side of the homosexual nobleman and explains how he once fathered a child.

93 BRADLEY, MARION ZIMMER. "Of Men, Halflings, and Hero Worship." Rochester, Tex.: privately printed, 1961. Reprint. Baltimore: T-K Graphics, 1973. Drastically expurgated and reprinted in *Tolkien*

and the Critics, edited by Neil Isaacs and Rose A. Zimbardo. Notre Dame, Ind., and London: Notre Dame Press, 1968. [Nonfiction]

This essay speculates on the possible homosexual nature of the friendship between Sam and Frodo in J. R. R. Tolkien's fantasy classic *The Lord of the Rings*.

94 BRADLEY, MARION ZIMMER. *The Planet Savers*. *Amazing*, November 1958. Reprint. New York: Ace, 1962. [M?]

An early Darkover novel that revolves around two personalities inhabiting one body. One of the personalities is a misogynist and a repressed homosexual. Regis Hastur is also a character, but there is no mention here of his sexual orientation.

95 BRADLEY, MARION ZIMMER. *The Ruins of Isis*. Norfolk, Va.: Donning Press, 1978. [F]

The Ruins of Isis clearly states the author's ongoing criticism of lesbian separatism, and it places the duty of motherhood above all else. The novel, not part of the author's popular Darkover series, depicts a world in which a matriarchal society is firmly established. The enchained men bow to women's superiority and gracefully serve the Supreme Mother in all women. The culture is in transition as contact with patriarchal worlds increases. None of the women questions their right to rule, but half of them want to trade with male-dominated worlds and the others want to keep their planet closed to outside intrusion. When an off-world heterosexual couple land on the planet, they quickly adopt the roles ascribed to them by the matriarchal culture. While the wife forms emotional and sexual relationships with the separatist women, her husband is inciting the oppressed men to revolt.

96 BRADLEY, MARION ZIMMER. "The Secret of the Blue Star." In *Thieves World*, edited by Robert Asprin. New York: Ace, 1979. [F]

This is Bradley's original Lythande story, set in the mythical "Thieves World." The cross-dressing magician's deepest secret is momentarily threatened when a young maiden, bewitched by a sorcerer's spell, falls in love with her.

97 BRADLEY, MARION ZIMMER. "The Shadow." In *Red Sun of Darkover*, edited by Marion Zimmer Bradley. New York: DAW, 1987. [M]

Danilo has been adopted by Dyan Ardis, his cruel tormentor in *The Heritage of Hastur*, and must come to terms with his foster father as well as his love for Regis Hastur. Chronologically lies between *The Heritage of Hastur* and *Sharra's Exile*.

98 BRADLEY, MARION ZIMMER. *Sharra's Exile*. New York: DAW, 1981. [M]

A sequel to *Heritage of Hastur* in which Lew Alton returns the Sharra matrix to Darkover. Alton's heterosexual love affair is the central theme of the novel, but significant gay male subplots abound. Regis Hastur reaffirms his love for Danilo, decadent bisexual Lerrys Ridenow secretly plots treason, and the manipulative Lord Dyan ultimately redeems himself. Under the leadership of Regis Hastur, Darkover develops ongoing relations with the Terrans.

99 BRADLEY, MARION ZIMMER. *The Shattered Chain*. New York: DAW, 1976. [F?, m]

The Shattered Chain is one of the most popular lesbian science-fiction novels. A group of Free Amazon mercenaries rescue a girl and her telepathic, pregnant mother from chains. The daughter, Jaelle, travels with the Free Amazons and grows up to become one of their leaders. While scouting, Jaelle discovers a Terran agent, Magda Lorne, who is impersonating an Amazon. A strong friendship develops between the two women. Magda's growing woman-identification is contrasted with Jaelle's dilemma: how to be a strong and self-determining woman while loving a man in a sexist society. The author shies away from the inclusion of a strong lesbian theme within the context of the all-women society, but mention is made of the *emmasca*, women who voluntarily neuter themselves, and of woman-woman sexuality. There is a brief, uncharitable mention of male homosexuality. Jaelle and Magda's story continues in *Thendara House* and *City of Sorcery*.

100 BRADLEY, MARION ZIMMER. *Star of Danger*. New York: Ace, 1965. [X]

An early Darkover novel revolving around the friendship between two sixteen-year-old boys, one Terran and one from Darkover. There is a brief appearance of a *chieri*, one of a hermaphroditic race indigenous to Darkover.

101 BRADLEY, MARION ZIMMER. *Survey Ship*. New York: Ace, 1980. [M]

A cosexual and multiethnic group of six young Terrans, trained since childhood in their individual talents and specialties, are sent into space by the United Nations to discover new planets to develop. Before the survey ship crew can effectively function as a team, each of the six crew members must learn to trust and support the others. On this ship, the process often entails sexual issues. For example, David Akami, a black, gay South African doctor, must forget about the gay lover he has left behind before he can successfully work with the crew. A story outside of the Darkover series.

102 BRADLEY, MARION ZIMMER. *Thendara House*. New York: DAW, 1983. [F, m]

The protagonists of *The Shattered Chain*, Terran agent Magda Lorne and Free Amazon Jaelle, switch places. Jaelle moves to the Terran complex with her heterosexual "freemate," starts a Terran job, and tries to reconcile her Amazon oath with her new life. When she becomes pregnant, her conflicting loyalties to her husband, to her Amazon sisters, and to her Comyn heritage are questioned. Meanwhile, Magda enters an Amazon Guild house and eventually discovers her love of women, taking Camilla, the *emmasca*, as her partner. Events cause Magda and Jaelle to learn that their love for each other is of primary importance to them both. There is a nonjudgmental mention of male homosexuality. The story continues with *City of Sorcery*.

103 BRADLEY, MARION ZIMMER. "To Keep the Oath." In *The Bloody Sun*. New York: Ace, 1979. [F?]

One of Darkover's Free Amazons questions her commitment to the laws of compromise between her Amazon Guild and the patriarchal Darkover society when she assists two women who desperately need her help. One of these is Camilla, the *emmasca* who eventually becomes Magda Lorne's lover, but no mention is made here of her sexuality. There is, however, overt mention of lesbianism among the Free Amazons. A "prequel" to *The Shattered Chain*.

104 BRADLEY, MARION ZIMMER. "The Wandering Lute." *Fantasy and Science Fiction*, February 1986. Reprinted in *Lythande*. New York: DAW, 1986. [F]

Another of Bradley's Lythande stories in which the cross-dressing magician obtains an enchanted lute that causes women to pursue her.

105 BRADLEY, MARION ZIMMER. *Warrior Woman*. New York: DAW, 1985. [F]

Bradley's swashbuckling novel concerns Zadieyed of Gyre, a fierce lesbian in a far-off world, who suddenly awakens to find herself a chained slave unable to remember anything about her past. After rape and abuse, she is sold to the gladiator's arena, where she proves herself an innately skilled fighter. She is then bought by an amorous noblewoman hoping to establish an all-women's group of gladiators. But all the while, Zadieyed is beginning to regain her memory. Lesbian relationships, positively portrayed, are primary to the plot. This is not part of the author's Darkover series.

106 BRADLEY, MARION ZIMMER. *The World Wreckers*. New York: Ace, 1971. [F?, m, X]

Members of Darkover's telepathic ruling class are being murdered one by one in an attempt to ruin the planet's economy and to open it up for exploitation by off-worlders. Regis Hastur asks telepaths from all corners of the galaxy to form a psychic net to snare the destroyer. Keral, a *chieri*, emerges from the dying forest to join the telepathic net. This hermaphrodite, temporarily of masculine gender, and David Hamilton, a Terran telepath, begin a sexual relationship that is described in detail. Hamilton relinquishes his prejudice toward homosexuality and refers to his hermaphroditic lover as "he" throughout their involvement, even when Keral is pregnant. In addition, Regis Hastur and several other Darkover telepaths discuss their experiences with same-sex love, generally with an attitude of acceptance. While maintaining that a woman's higher duty and fulfillment are found in motherhood, Bradley makes several of the female characters, particularly two amazons, decisive and vital to the plot. One of the best Darkover novels.

107 BRADLEY, MARION ZIMMER, and WELLS, JOHN J. [pseudonym of Juanita Coulson]. "Another Rib." *Fantasy and Science Fiction*, June 1963. [M]
Sun flares have destroyed the solar system. The spaceship containing the sole human survivors is stranded on an alien planet with only one other inhabitant: an intelligent life-form named Fanu. The story revolves around the all-male crew of the spaceship, their adaptation to their new environment, and their eventual procreation. Odd and complimentary for its time.

Biographical Note

Marion Zimmer Bradley (b. 1930) is a prolific author who has made significant contributions to both science fiction and gay / lesbian literature. She is the author of the best-selling novels *The Mists of Avalon* (New York: Knopf, 1982) and *The Firebrand* (New York: Simon and Schuster, 1987). Her Lythande stories are collected in *Lythande* (New York: DAW, 1986).

Since the start of her writing career in 1954, Bradley has consistently included substantial homosexual elements in her work, and all her writings deserve close examination. Her strong belief in freedom and tolerance is evidenced throughout her work. Bradley was an early contributor to the *Ladder*, and under various pseudonyms she wrote several lesbian paperback novels during the 1960s. In 1958 she expanded her fanzine *Astra's Tower* to create a supplement to Dr. Jeanette Foster's *Sex Variant Women in Literature* (New York: Vantage, 1957), and with Barbara Grier she continued to issue periodic updates for several years. This supplement and its updates have been reprinted in *A Gay Bibliography* (New York: Arno, 1975). Bradley has also contributed to the *Mattachine Review*, the *International Journal of Greek Love*, *WomanSpirit*, *Ms.*, and *Sinister Wisdom*.

Her non-science-fiction novel *The Catch Trap* (New York: Random House, 1979) is of major gay male interest.

Biographical information can be found in *Contemporary Authors*, vols. 57-60, ed. Cynthia Fadool (Detroit: Gale Research, 1976). Autobiographical information is provided in "Behind the Borderline" by Miriam Gardner (pseudonym of Marion Zimmer Bradley) in the *Ladder*, October 1960. Supplemental information can be found in the exchange of letters between Bradley and Joanna Russ in *The Witch and the Chameleon*, ed. A. Bankier, nos. 3-6, 1975. See also Marion Zimmer Bradley, "Responsibilities and Temptations of Women Science Fiction Writers," in *Women Worldwalkers: New Dimensions of Science Fiction and Fantasy*, ed. Jane B. Weedman (Lubbock, Tex.: Texas Tech Press, 1985), and "One Woman's Experience in Science Fiction," in *Women of Vision: Essays by Women Writing Science Fiction*, ed. Denise DuPont (New York: St. Martin's, 1988).

There are several feminist-oriented critiques of Bradley's work: "Marion Zimmer Bradley and Darkover" by Linda Leith, *Science Fiction Studies*, no. 20 (March 1980); Susan M. Shwartz's "Marion Zimmer Bradley's Ethic of Freedom," *The Feminine Eye: Science Fiction and the Women Who Write It*, ed. Tom Staicar (New York: Ungar, 1982); Barbara Hornum's "Wife / Mother, Sorceress / Keeper, Amazon / Renunciate: Status Ambivalence and Conflicting Roles on the Planet Darkover"; and Diane S. Wood's "Gender Roles in the Darkover Novels of Marion Zimmer Bradley" (the last two are both in *Women Worldwalkers: New Dimensions of Science Fiction and Fantasy*). Another useful resource is Rosemarie Arbur's *Marion Zimmer Bradley* (Mercer Island, Wash.: Starmont House, 1985).

Bradley's Darkover series has generated a great deal of popular interest. The most comprehensive reference on Darkover is Walter Breen's *The Darkover Concordance* (Berkeley, Calif.: Pennyfarthing Press, 1979). Several fanzines and anthologies have been published with Darkover as their central theme. There is explicit homosexual and lesbian content in many of these. Of particular interest is *Free Amazons of Darkover*, ed. Marion Zimmer Bradley (New York: DAW, 1985).

See also BIGELOW, JANE M. H.; BOAL, NINA; LACKEY, MERCEDES; McINTYRE, VONDA; MATHEWS, PATRICIA; PAXTON, DIANA L.; SHWARTZ, SUSAN M.

108 BRALY, MALCOLM. "An Outline of History." In *Bad Moon Rising*, edited by Thomas M. Disch. New York: Harper & Row, 1973. [m]

Braly's story is an ironic prison drama set in the not-too-distant future. Consensual gay male sexual activity is mentioned briefly and without judgment.

109 BRINTON, HENRY. *Purple Six*. London: Hutchinson, 1962. Reprint. New York: Walker, 1962. [M]

In the very near future's cold war, someone has slipped a top-secret nuclear device to the Soviets. Who could it be? Among the suspects is a slightly effeminate homosexual identified only as "C. H."

110 BROOKE, [BERNARD] JOCELYN. *The Scapegoat*. London: Bodley Head, 1949. Reprint. New York: Harper, 1950. [M?]

A rainswept evening, a desolate and foreboding family estate, a sinister and mysterious male relative, and strange supernatural goings-on ... the author of *The Scapegoat* uses all the classic elements of the Gothic novel except one: nowhere in the story does the "helpless maiden in distress" appear. Instead, the author introduces Duncan Cameron, a sensitive, recently orphaned, thirteen-year-old boy. Duncan is sent to live with his Uncle Gerald in the old family manor, March House. An attraction, ripe with erotic tension, immediately springs up between the boy and his uncle. It is not until young Duncan has been thoroughly corrupted by the ancient and occult forces of March House that their relationship reaches its macabre consummation. The fantasy elements are subtly expressed but essential to the plot.

111 BROPHY, BRIGID. *Palace without Chairs*. London: Hamilton, 1978. Reprint. New York: Atheneum, 1978. [F, m]

This farcical satire by a popular British author, noted for her mainstream fiction, is set in a tiny, modern, mythical country that is home to a nutty royal family, a Communist party, and seemingly scores of lesbians and gay men. With macabre humor, the members of the royal family are assassinated, commit suicide, die of old age, or abdicate the throne, leaving the door wide open for a revolutionary party to take power. The author brings one character after another out of the closet; of particular interest is Princess Heather who has a penchant for amorous affairs with her governesses.

BROSNAN, JOHN. *See* KNIGHT, HARRY ADAM (pseudonym)

112 BROSTER, D. K. "Couching at the Door." In *Couching at the Door*. London: William Heinemann, 1942. [M?]

After dabbling in satanism while in Europe, a decadent British poet, patently based on Oscar Wilde, finds himself haunted by a brown, furry demon. For a time he is able to rid himself of his pesky curse by giving it to a younger illustrator, a character based on Aubrey Beardsley, but it eventually returns to him in a more horrifying incarnation. There is no overt homosexuality in the story, but the implications are obvious.

113 BROWN, ALICE. "There and Here." *Harper's Monthly*, November 1897. Reprinted in *High Noon*. Boston and New York: Houghton Mifflin, 1904. [F?]

In Brown's thoughtful exploration of life after death, Ruth Hollis, a New England spinster, finds her loneliness abated with the surprise visit of a beloved woman friend. Brown includes passionate declarations of friendship and a suspicious bedroom scene, but nothing overtly lesbian.

114 BROWN, FREDRIC. "Nightmare in Green." In *Nightmares and Geezenstacks*. New York: Bantam, 1961. [F]

A very short story about the nightmare of an insecure man who feels his wife is superior to and stronger than him in every way. The lesbian content is major and can be enjoyable despite the author's oblique intentions.

115 BROWN, FREDRIC. *Rogue in Space*. New York: Dutton, 1957. [m]

A homophobic, misogynistic space criminal gets involved in a corrupt judge's scheme to rule the solar system. The scheme fails and almost proves fatal for Brown's bigoted hero, but he is saved in the nick of time by a unique, nonhuman entity. Several effeminate stereotypes appear within the novel; the protagonist's often violent reactions to them are consistent with his character.

BROWN, ROSEL GEORGE. *See* LAUMER, KEITH (joint author)

116 BRUNNER, JOHN. *Children of the Thunder*. New York: Ballantine, 1989. [m]

A British reporter and an American scientist explore with growing concern the possibility that antisocial behavior is genetically determined. They discover a group of criminally inclined adolescents with terrifying inborn psychic powers. One of these amoral youths is a bisexual thirteen-year-old who once ran a brothel out of his all-male boarding school.

117 BRUNNER, JOHN. "An Elixir for the Emperor." *Fantastic*, November 1964. Reprinted in *From This Day Forward*. Garden City, N.Y.: Doubleday, 1972. [M?]

This short fantasy story deals with political intrigue in ancient Rome. Although Marcus Placidus, the villain, is not explicitly homosexual, his lisping manner and the well-known sexual practices of the historical setting lend that interpretation to his character.

118 BRUNNER, JOHN. *The Productions of Time*. *Fantasy and Science Fiction*, August 1966. Reprint. New York: Signet, 1967. [f, m]

Murray Douglas was a stage star until alcoholism ended his career. On the wagon, Douglas attempts to make his comeback in a play by the strange Argentine director, Manuel Delgado. As the play develops, each actor finds her or his addictions fed by the director. The heroin addict locates an endless supply of narcotics, Douglas finds bottles of liquor wherever he goes, and a young woman, Heather Carson, is provided for the lesbian actress Ida Marr, whose sexual preference is equated with instability. An important point is made when Carson states that "there's a bit of it [homosexuality] in all of us." A minor gay male character is also included in the action.

119 BRUNNER, JOHN. *The Sheep Look Up.* New York: Harper & Row, 1972. [f, m]

This dense novel chronicles humanity's final year, month by painful month. Governmental bureaucracy and the insensitivity and greed of capitalism have allowed toxins to spread unchecked in the environment. Epidemics inevitably run rampant, health foods are found to be poisonous, and water-purifying systems clog with excessive bacteria. Environmentalists arm themselves for revolution and await their leader, Austin Train, a garbage collector. Many minor references to homosexuality appear throughout the book. Among the numerous characters are two male lovers, Hugh Pentingill and Carl Travers, and a lesbian, Petronella Page.

120 BRUNNER, JOHN. *Stand on Zanzibar.* Garden City, N.Y.: Doubleday, 1968. [f, m]

This massive dystopian novel depicts an overpopulated Earth at the dawn of a new century. Eugenics legislation is in full swing. Rape, drug dependence, robbery, and murder are ever on the increase. Improvement in the situation of African-Americans is barely perceptible; women, with few exceptions, are either mothers or prostitutes. Minor references to homosexual behavior throughout show it to have become accepted by society. Three individuals are revealed in depth, although there are numerous minor characters that give the novel its social context. This novel has won the Hugo Award, the 1970 British Science Fiction Award, and the Prix Apollo in 1973 for its French translation.

121 BRUNNER, JOHN. *The Stone That Never Came Down. Amazing*, November-December 1973. Expanded and reprinted. Garden City, N.Y.: Doubleday, 1973. [m]

A miracle drug is discovered that will solve the problems of prejudice, war, poverty, hate, and tyranny by heightening its users' empathy and their ability to synthesize information. When the fascist Christian government gears up for World War III, a small, courageous group attempts to dose the military authorities with the new drug. The group's methods are both ingenious and funny. Two homosexual secondary characters represent the extremes of this polarized future society. One is a closeted servant of the head of the right-wing religious and political system; the other is openly gay and supportive of the underground proponents of the miracle drug.

122 BRUNNER, JOHN. *Timescoop*. New York: Dell, 1969. [m]
     A rich capitalist in the far future develops a new technological method of traveling through time and immediately begins plundering the past. To celebrate his good fortune, he decides to hold an intergalactic family reunion and "timescoops" nine of his illustrious ancestors for the fete. To his disappointment, all nine turn out to have skeletons in the closet. For example, one eighteenth-century composer is found to be a pederast.

123 BRUNT, Captain SAMUEL [pseudonym]. *A Voyage to Cacklogallinia with a Description of the Religion, Policy, Customs, and Manners of That Country*. London: J. Watson, 1727. Reprint. New York: Columbia University Press, 1940. [M?]
     This sixteenth-century satire relates the adventures and misadventures of Samuel Brunt, including his trip to the moon. He finds the moon inhabited by "Selenites," an exclusively male species. They live a peaceful life without passion and greed, thinking only of philosophy and religion. There is no overt homosexuality in this male-only world.

124 BRYAN, JED A. *A Cry in the Desert*. Austin, Texas: Banned Books, 1987. [f, M]
     Bryan pens a mix of science fiction and adventure thriller in which archetypal mad scientist Alfred Botts uses the public hysteria surrounding the AIDS epidemic to unleash a villainous, homophobic plot. Under the guise of public health, gays are rounded up and sent to death camps in the mountains of Nevada. The gay community reacts strongly to this homophobic campaign–Reverend Terry Bridges preaches gay militancy from his Metropolitan Community Church pulpit, and lesbian poet Miriam Speth gives a benefit reading–but few escape the dragnet. The evil Dr. Botts, a repressed homosexual, was abused as a child by his fundamentalist father, and he seeks to ease his pain by inflicting it on others. Dr. Carl Woodford and his lover Larry Armstrong try to stop the genocidal closet case. Similar visions of homophobic pogroms appear in works by Barrus, Birdstone, Mains, and Welles.

125 BRYANT, DOROTHY. *The Comforter*. Berkeley, Calif.: Moon Books, 1971. Reprinted as *The Kin of Ata Are Waiting for You*. New York: Moon Books, 1976. [F?, m?]

In this avidly feminist, utopian novel, a sexist male author has a car accident and suddenly awakens on an island paradise called Ata. The beauty and simplicity of the island culture and its effect upon the writer are Bryant's subject. Homosexuality is totally accepted within Ata's culture, though none of the characters are specifically identified as homosexual.

126 BRYANT, EDWARD. "Dancing Chickens." In *Light Years and Dark*, edited by Michael Bishop. New York: Berkley, 1984. [M]

A sad, yet touching, tale about an unhappy teenage runaway, his older mentor / lover, their gay friends, and a mysterious invasion of aliens.

127 BUCK, CHARLES H. *The Master Cure*. New York: Jove, 1989. [m]

In this fast-paced political thriller set in the near future, a secret network of Christian fundamentalists, American racists, and South African whites develop an AIDS-like virus and begin selectively releasing it across the country. The targets are African-Americans, Jews, and homosexuals. It is up to black reporter Gloria Day to track down the killers of her gay friend Kim Carsons and to stop the conspirators. Sound good? Unfortunately, reporter Day is neither convincing nor likable; she "passes" for white, is prone to nymphomania, and eventually falls in love with a recovering addict who has killed hundreds of black South Africans for the Nazis.

128 BUJOLD, LOIS McMASTER. *Ethan of Athos*. New York: Baen, 1986. [M]

Bujold sets her novel on Athos, a planet founded by misogynistic religious fanatics and now entirely homosexual. Athonians reproduce by manipulating ovarian cultures in mechanical wombs. When some imported cultures prove infertile, Dr. Ethan Urquhart is sent off-planet to procure more. There, he finds intrigue and adventure and discovers that women are not the monsters he had been taught they were. But his response is atypical in the genre: he surprisingly does *not* succumb to the temptations of heterosexuality and instead returns to Athos with a potential new male lover.

BURDEKIN, KATHARINE. *See* CONSTANTINE, MURRAY

129 BURFORD, LOLAH. *The Vision of Stephen: An Elegy*. New York: Macmillan, 1972. [M?]

Stephen, a young prince of Deira in eighteenth-century Britain, is captured by the equally young prince of an enemy kingdom. During the brief time they spend together, they form a very intimate friendship. The loyalty Stephen feels for his friend ultimately leads to Stephen's capture and torture. At this point the book shifts from historical fiction to fantasy fiction. Stephen is transported in time to the year 1882. Through the love and concern of two nineteenth-century youngsters, Stephen is finally rescued from his misery. This book, designed for juveniles, throbs with homoemotional feelings and is overtly sadomasochistic. The author shows little awareness of sexism.

130 BURGESS, ANTHONY [pseudonym of John Anthony Burgess Wilson]. *The Eve of Saint Venus*. Illustrated by Edward Pagram. London: Sidgwick & Jackson, 1964. Reprint. New York: W. W. Norton, 1970. [F]
      On the eve of his wedding, a young man happens to place his ring on the finger of a magical statue of Venus and suddenly finds the goddess herself preempting his marriage bed. Meanwhile, a lesbian talks the bride-to-be out of matrimony and they run off together. Most of Burgess's characterizations are exaggerated and farcical, but the lesbian's is more realistic. In the end the goddess releases her grip on the young man, the bride rejects lesbianism, the marriage takes place, and all of the characters, except (of course) the lesbian, live happily ever after.

131 BURGESS, ANTHONY [pseudonym of John Anthony Burgess Wilson]. *The Wanting Seed*. London: Heinemann, 1962. Reprint. New York: W. W. Norton, 1963. [F, M]
      Burgess's bitter satire depicts a desperately overcrowded future Britain in which the government takes extreme measures to stop population growth. Mothers who practice infanticide are given "condolence stipends" by the government. Homosexuality becomes not only the sexual norm but also a requirement for employment. Nature, following society's example, reflects this vogue for infertility; crops wither and animals cease to reproduce. Food shortages result, and people revert to cannibalism. Almost-forgotten religions are resurrected and fertility rituals are performed in the barren fields. Finally, an artificial war between the sexes is created by entrepreneurs, who sell the casualties to civilians as packaged luncheon meat. In this bleak, inhumane future, Beatrice Foxe vacillates between two lovers: her mousy husband and her ambitious, heterosexual brother-in-law, who passes as an effeminate homosexual.

132 BURROUGHS, WILLIAM S. *Blade Runner: A Movie*. Berkeley, Calif.: Blue Wind, 1979. [M]

In this intriguing story, written in cinematic montage style, Burroughs envisions a future in which the medical establishment, the major drug companies, and the federal government have conspired to make health care available only to the privileged few. Consequently, an underground medical system has arisen. Operating out of basements and deserted subway tunnels, the system relies largely on holistic medicine and is the object of intense harassment by the authorities. Burroughs's short book focuses on Billy, a blade runner, who transports drugs and surgical instruments to the underground clinics. Both Billy and his male lover are positively portrayed. Based on a novel by Alan E. Nourse.

BURROUGHS, WILLIAM S. Cities of the Red Night Series. [M]:

133 ▪ *Cities of the Red Night*. New York: Holt, Rinehart, & Winston, 1981.

134 ▪ *The Place of Dead Roads*. New York: Holt, Rinehart, & Winston, 1983.

135 ▪ *The Western Lands*. New York: Viking Penguin, 1987.
Although little continuity exists between these novels, the author wrote them as a trilogy. They are tied together by theme and style rather than by narrative. In his first volume, Burroughs introduces three different plots: scenes of eighteenth-century pirates fighting for equality; tales of the mythical desert Cities of the Red Night; and a detective story featuring private eye Clem Snide, a character from the earlier *Naked Lunch*. By the trilogy's end, the author has shifted to a hallucinatory trip through ancient Egyptian mythology. In fact, the only consistent thread throughout the conglomeration is Burroughs's superior race of homosexual "wild boys" who make love and fight for freedom throughout much of Burroughs's later fiction. But even if lacking in plot, the trilogy does offer some eclectic and often hilarious insights into contemporary society, nuclear warfare, and the human condition.

136 BURROUGHS, WILLIAM S. *Exterminator!* New York: Viking, 1973. [f, M]
Exterminator!, comprising short stories and bits of previously unpublished material, is occasionally sketchy but consistently vivid and intense. Fantasy and homoerotic elements appear in many of the book's sequences. In "Short Trip Home," for example, two boys make love while turning into wolves, and in "My Face," Burroughs deals with personality transference while subtly implying bizarre sexual practices. As with most of Burroughs's work, parts of this book are explicitly misogynistic.

137 BURROUGHS, WILLIAM S. *The Naked Lunch*. Paris: Olympia, 1959. Reprinted as *Naked Lunch*. New York: Grove, 1962. [f, M]

With trenchant wit and rancor, Burroughs, a homosexual and longtime heroin addict, records his hysterical perceptions of contemporary society. The author portrays a world dominated by "control addicts," loathsome people who sexually, socially, and politically control others. A series of fantasy vignettes, often surreal and hallucinatory, simulate the consciousness-altering effects of drugs. Male homosexual characters fill the book, usually in the form of detestable control addicts, but the author balances these negative gay male images with lyric and intensely erotic gay male fantasies. Misogyny permeates the work, affecting Burroughs's fleeting lesbian characterizations in particular and contradicting the author's expressed opposition to oppression. The book was controversial when first published in the United States and was the object of several obscenity trials during the early 1960s.

138 BURROUGHS, WILLIAM S. *Nova Express*. New York: Grove, 1964. [M]

In *Nova Express*, Burroughs's dystopian nightmare has become more developed and detailed. Burroughs depicts a corrupt, degenerate future America, terrorized by a malevolent Nova Mob and protected by the Nova Police. Drug addiction and explicit gay male sexuality figure prominently in the author's acid-etched visions. Burroughs also makes extensive use of an experimental literary technique, known as "cut-ups," in which a manuscript is cut, jumbled up, and then reassembled in an apparently random order. "Cut-ups" were first used in some of the author's earlier works, but they reach their zenith in *Nova Express*. Their effect is poetic–short, rhythmic burst of words, sentence fragments, and images–but the technique renders an already hallucinatory novel even more inaccessible to the general reader.

139 BURROUGHS, WILLIAM S. *Port of Saints*. London: Covent Garden, 1975. Revised edition. Berkeley, Calif.: Blue Wind, 1980. [M]

Port of Saints offers an important key to Burroughs's "wild boy" mythos. Aubrey Carsons, a repeating character throughout the author's later fiction, becomes one of the "wild boys" and joins their revolution. Aubrey and the boys jump through time to "rewrite all the wrongs of history." For example, they battle European colonialism in the nineteenth-century West Indies. But after discovering linear storytelling in *The Wild Boys*, Burroughs again experiments with style, creating an episodic collage of story pieces, none of which is a complete narrative. As usual, *Port of Saints* is filled with the author's ongoing sexual and political fixations.

140 BURROUGHS, WILLIAM S. *The Soft Machine*. Paris: Olympia, 1961.
Reprint. New York: Grove, 1966. [M]

The Soft Machine is virtually indistinguishable from *Naked Lunch*,
the book preceding it, except for the Central American locale. Kinky
scenes of a nightmarish future and sometimes unnervingly paranoid,
drug-related images are ever-present, as are Burroughs's erotic and
explicit homosexual fantasies, predominantly involving handsome
Mexican youths. Burroughs's biting humor is still present in the plotless
succession of episodes that are as difficult to understand as his earlier
work due to the use of the "cut-up" technique. Female characters are
not present in *The Soft Machine*; its dreamlike world is apparently
populated entirely by sexually available boys, junkies, and villainous
control addicts.

141 BURROUGHS, WILLIAM S. *The Ticket That Exploded*. Paris:
Olympia, 1962. Reprint. New York: Grove, 1967. [M]

Another of Burroughs's for-the-most-part-interchangeable,
dystopian fantasies. As in his other work, the reader must enter the
consciousness of the paranoid and hallucinating narrator to appreciate
the book. The theme of the novel is again the nefarious Nova Mob's
vicious attempts to control the universe. Homosexual and pederastic
episodes often have violent overtones. Despite the confusion resultant
from the "cut-up" technique, the author is able to create beautifully
poetic imagery and some very outrageous moments.

142 BURROUGHS, WILLIAM S. *The Wild Boys: A Book of the Dead*.
New York: Grove, 1971. [f, M]

Much of *The Wild Boys* mirrors the author's earlier fiction. What
distinguishes it is the abandonment of the "cut-up" technique and the
adoption of a cohesive plot, features absent in much of the author's
previous work. Society in the future is controlled by a military / CIA /
governmental group very similar to the Nova Mob of earlier vintage.
There develops an evolutionarily superior race of pansexual "wild boys"
to counter this repression. The boys overrun and lay waste the Earth,
but not before indulging in numerous, explicitly depicted orgies. Some
passages are misogynistic, and the one lesbian character is authoritarian
and repressive. The "wild boys" subsequently become a consistent thread
in Burroughs's later fiction. Comparable to Esser's *Dance of the
Warriors*.

Biographical Note

William S. Burroughs (b. 1914) is an influential and highly controversial
American author who writes with a style both fascinating and frustrating.
Although most of his work is marginally science fiction, Burroughs is best

known as a mainstream writer, perhaps because of his personal associations with Beat writers such as Allen Ginsberg and Jack Kerouac.

Burroughs has always been outspoken about his homosexuality and has contributed to journals such as *Fagrag*, *Blueboy*, *Gay Sunshine*, *Christopher Street*, and the *Advocate*. His nonfantasy novel *Queer* (New York: Viking Penguin, 1985) is of major gay male significance. He discusses his sexual politics in the essay entitled "The Whole Tamale," in *Roosevelt after Inauguration* (San Francisco: City Lights, 1979), and in *Gay Sunshine Interviews,* vol. 1, ed. Winston Leyland (San Francisco: Gay Sunshine Press, 1979).

Biographical information on Burroughs is found in *Current Biography 1971*, ed. Charles Moritz (New York: Wilson, 1971), and in Ted Morgan's *Literary Outlaw: The Life and Times of William S. Burroughs* (New York: Holt, 1988). See also Jennie Skerl's *William S. Burroughs* (Boston: Twayne, 1985). Two particularly relevant critical essays are Gerard Cordess's "The Science Fiction of William Burroughs," *Caliban* 12 (1975), and "William Burroughs's Quartet of Science Fiction Novels as Dystopian Social Satire," by Donald Palumbo, in *Extrapolation* (Winter 1979).

---

143 BUSBY, F. M. *The Alien Debt*. New York: Bantam, 1984. [X]

Set in the U.E.T. universe originally formulated in the Rissa Kerguelen saga (see citation below), this novel features a three-sexed alien race, the Tsa. Bran and Rissa now have two children. They have conquered the U.E.T. and allied themselves with an alien race, the Shraken. The Tsa are destroying the Shraken, so the dauntless Bran and Rissa step up to save their friends. But it turns out to be their teenage daughter who does most of the saving.

144 BUSBY, F. M. *The Breeds of Man*. New York: Bantam, 1988. [X]

Busby sets his intriguing, fast-paced science-fiction thriller in the near future, in which American scientists have tampered with the human genetic structure in their search for a cure for AIDS. Their evolutionary experiment is successful, but the resulting mutants are not only immune to the deadly virus – they are also cyclic hermaphrodites, alternating between male and female phases. Although these new humans, called Mark Twos, are potentially the answer to many of the world's problems, they must be hidden and protected from the growing wave of religious and political fundamentalism that would destroy them.

145 BUSBY, F. M. "For a Daughter." In *Amazons II*, edited by Jessica Amanda Salmonson. New York: DAW, 1982. [f]

A young amazon joins her all-female culture's annual heterosexual mating ritual with both excitement and trepidation: she has had women lovers before but has never slept with a man.

BUSBY, F. M. The Rebel Dynasty Series. [f, m]:

146 ▪ *The Rebel Dynasty, Volume I*. New York: Bantam, 1987.

147 ▪ *The Rebel Dynasty, Volume II*. New York: Bantam, 1988.

The Rebel Dynasty books are compendium volumes to the Rissa Kerguelen saga (see citation below). The story follows Bran Tregare's life from childhood. Abandoned by his family in the U.E.T. space academy (the Slauterhouse), Tregare experiences the horrors inflicted upon adolescents at the academy. He escapes U.E.T.'s control and takes his armed ship to the rebels' Hidden Worlds. Two homosexual crew members play a significant role.

BUSBY, F. M. The Rissa Kerguelen Saga. [f, m]:

148 ▪ *The Long View*. New York: Berkley, 1976.

149 ▪ *Rissa Kerguelen*. New York: Berkley, 1976.

The megalithic United Energy and Transport Corporation (U.E.T.) has absolute domination over the Earth's population. For many, life comprises the excessively dreary and at times brutal conditions of the U.E.T.'s total welfare institutions. The corporation's power has remained unchallenged for decades. And then comes Rissa Kerguelen – straight out of an U.E.T. orphanage and into the capable hands of a rebel group in Argentina headed by a bisexual, parthenogenetically reproducing woman. After being trained by the Argentineans, Kerguelen heads for space where she teams up with the infamous Bran Tregare, who matches Kerguelen's vehement determination to topple the U.E.T. And the adventure begins. . . . Kerguelen is marginally bisexual, and two of Tregare's male crew form a comfortable homosexual marriage. The saga has been published in one, two, and three volumes. It serves as the centerpiece for the series of books set in the U.E.T. universe.

150 BUSBY, F. M. *Zelda M'Tana*. New York: Dell, 1980. [f, m]

Zelda M'Tana is set in the same U.E.T. universe as the Rissa Kerguelen saga (see citation above) and chronologically precedes Kerguelen's story. It follows the rough childhood of Zelda M'Tana in the gangs of Wild Children scraping by just beyond edges of U.E.T.'s authority. Like Rissa Kerguelen, M'Tana escapes the corporation's clutches and finds action on a rebel starship. M'Tana is bisexual and has two affairs with women during the novel's action, though she spends a good portion of the story romantically involved with the starship captain. M'Tana is also black, a rare treat in the genre. There are other bisexual characters throughout the book. A feel-good, fast-paced adventure series in which women are as much involved as men in the heat of the action.

151 BUTLER, OCTAVIA. *Patternmaster*. New York: Doubleday, 1976. [f]
Butler's fascinating Patternist series concerns a race of telepathic mutants, feared and scorned by humans in the 1600s, who eventually overpower civilization. Butler uses the telepaths, often black, to draw parallels with contemporary social inequities and to explore important issues of racism and patriarchy. In *Patternmaster*, two powerful brothers vie for control of the psychic Pattern that holds a far-future, disease-ravaged southern California together. Teray, one of the two, falls in love with a feisty, independent, bisexual black woman named Amber (who sleeps with both women and men, but prefers women). Butler's Patternist novels also include *Mind of My Mind* (New York: Doubleday, 1977), *Survivor* (New York: Doubleday, 1978), *Wild Seed* (New York: Doubleday, 1980), and *Clay's Ark* (New York: St. Martin's, 1984).

BUTLER, OCTAVIA. Xenogenesis Trilogy. [X]:

152 ■ *Dawn*. New York: Warner, 1987.

153 ■ *Adulthood Rites*. New York: Warner, 1988.

154 ■ *Imago*. New York: Warner, 1989.
The future Earth has been rescued from nuclear suicide by a three-sexed species of alien, the Oankali. The Oankali want to mate with humans to engineer a cross-species form of life. Humans resist this idea, but they are given the choice between sterilization and reproduction with the Oankali, the choice between the death of humanity and its complete merger. With each successive generation, the humans respond with less xenophobia, though many do not accept the genetic and cultural merger. Lillth, the central character of the trilogy, joins with four others in marriage: a human man, an Oankali woman and man, and a member of that species' third sex. Her children, protagonists in the successive volumes, manifest both human and Oankali sexual aspects. Throughout the series, but especially in *Imago*, the sexuality depicted between the Oankali and humans is quite sensual. Since only in the southern hemisphere were there survivors of the nuclear holocaust, the majority of characters in the trilogy are people of color.

155 CABELL, JAMES BRANCH. *The High Place: A Comedy of Disenchantment*. New York: McBride, 1923. [M?]
During the first years of this century, Cabell wrote a long series of popular, satiric, witty, and sometimes risqué fantasies collectively titled

Biography of the Life of Manuel. All are set in the imaginary medieval country of Poicesme. In the first chapter of *The High Place*, young noble Florian de Puysange falls asleep in Poicesme's forest while reading a book of fairy tales and dreams of the beautiful princess Sleeping Beauty. Throughout his adult life–which is punctuated by crime, murder, and debauchery–he remembers his magical childhood dream and eventually finds his own enchanted princess. Florian has several wives and a young boy lover (all of whom he murders without remorse when his affections ebb). Although the homosexual passages are exceedingly tame by today's standards, they were considered shocking in 1923. (The *New York Times* noted, "This book is definitely distasteful in its explicit ... suggestion of sexual aberration and sexual perversion.")

156 CADIGAN, PAT. "Pretty Boy Crossover." *Isaac Asimov's Science Fiction Magazine*, January 1986. Reprinted in *The 1987 Annual World's Best SF*, edited by Donald Wollheim. New York: DAW, 1987. [M]

Cadigan offers an effective mix of hard-edged cyberpunk style and a refreshing gay sensibility. A sixteen-year-old Pretty Boy haunts the ultrachic downtown video clubs where "only the Prettiest Pretty Boys can get in any more." But he's getting older and will soon be unable to get past the doorman. Should he follow his friend Bobby and "crossover"?

157 CALIFIA, PAT. "The Vampire." In *Macho Sluts*. Boston: Alyson, 1988. [F]

Lesbian sadomasochistic pornographic vampire fantasy; whew!

Biographical Note

Pat Califia is also the author of the futuristic erotic fantasy "The Hustler," in *Macho Sluts* (Boston: Alyson, 1988). Her novel *Doc and Fluff* (Boston: Alyson, 1990) was published too late for inclusion in this bibliography.

---

158 CALLENBACH, ERNEST. *Ecotopia: The Notebooks and Reports of William Weston and Ernest Callenbach*. Berkeley, Calif.: Banyan Tree Books, 1975. [f, m]

The year is 1999. Oregon, Washington, and northern California have seceded from the United States to form Ecotopia, a country founded upon strong ecological principles. Reporter Will Weston visits Ecotopia on assignment from a major newspaper. The book consists of his reports and excerpts from his journal. Homosexuality is mentioned twice: in Weston's column concerning Ecotopia's family units and when Weston has a sexual encounter with two bisexual women. The author is well-versed in ecological politics, but he is less sensitive to issues surrounding class and race.

159 CAMPBELL, RAMSEY. *Ancient Images*. New York: Scribner's Sons, 1989. [m]

The protagonist of this well-written horror novel is a female film editor who investigates the murder of her friend, an older gay-film collector. He had discovered a "lost" Boris Karloff film, since stolen, and the editor suspects it holds the key to the murder. Her search for clues leads to a mysterious community in rural England and to an old secret. The film collector is gay, and he and his lover are both well portrayed.

Biographical Note

Ramsey Campbell is also the author of *The Face That Must Die* (Santa Cruz, Calif.: Scream / Press, 1983), a nonfantasy crime thriller with significant gay male content.

---

160 CARD, ORSON SCOTT. *A Planet Called Treason*. New York: St. Martin's, 1979. [f, m, X]

Each of the tribes on the prison planet of Treason has developed a different talent or metaphysical power. It is up to one man, Lanik, to unite Treason's myriad cultures by traveling through them and taking on each of their special powers. He first grows breasts and ovaries and becomes a hermaphrodite, allowing him to pass as what the author perceives to be a feminist from Treason's single matriarchal nation. Although Lanik is treated as a woman, and even seduced by a black lesbian, the hermaphrodite remains male-identified. Upon reaching the desert and having grown several more arms and legs, Lanik falls in love with an ageless boy–perhaps because the boy rids Lanik of the "disgusting" feminine physical characteristics and excess limbs. Intriguing metaphysical ideas are mixed with a sexist portrayal of women, a heroic depiction of mass murder, and racist passages. *A Planet Called Treason* was extensively rewritten and republished as *Treason* (New York: St. Martin's, 1988).

161 CARD, ORSON SCOTT. *Songmaster*. New York: Dial, 1980. [M]

On the distant planet of Tew, talented singing youngsters, called "Songbirds," are trained in voice and then sent to deserving hosts for extended visits. Mikal the Terrible, conqueror of the galaxy, wants a Songbird for his own, but must wait years before the beautiful young boy, Ansset, is sent to him. Mikal and his Songbird develop a deep and intense love for each other. Although not sexual, this relationship is an extraordinarily sympathetic depiction of man-boy love. Ansset is kidnapped by Mikal's enemies and unwillingly takes part in an assassination attempt. Later, Ansset becomes the planetary "manager" of Earth, and he develops a close friendship with a gay man, Josif.

Ansset's abduction has rendered him sexually impotent, but his emotional orientation is clearly toward men.

162 CARLISLE, ANNE. *Liquid Sky: The Novel*. New York: Doubleday, Dolphin, 1987. [F]

Based on the cult science-fiction film *Liquid Sky*, Carlisle's adaptation revolves around outer-space aliens who invade the trendy Manhattan underworld of drugs, sex, and rock and roll (as well as performance art and other forms of nightlife). The primary character, a lesbian named Margaret, finds herself possessed by a strange power: all her lovers dissolve after orgasm.

163 CARLSON, WILLIAM. "Dinner at Helen's." In *Strange Bedfellows*, edited by Thomas Scortia. New York: Random House, 1972. [X]

A radio repairman meets a woman he finds voluptuous and exciting. His interest turns to shock, however, when "Helen" turns out to be neither female nor male. An unconventional story.

164 CARR, ROBERT SPENCER. *The Room Beyond*. New York: Appleton-Century-Crofts, 1948. [f]

This carefully revealed mix of metaphysics and melodrama involves a man's search for the one person who has put meaning into his life. Dan Bryce, while a youth, meets a beautiful young nurse named Cristina who performs relief work among the poor. She delights and inspires him, then breaks his heart with her sudden departure. He finds her again while in college, and again when he is middle-aged, but each time the still-youthful Cristina eludes him. While in medical school Bryce has an affair with a pretty coed who becomes "doomed" to a life of lesbianism because of Bryce's inability to love anyone but Cristina. This interlude is incidental to the plot.

165 CARRINGTON, LEONORA. *The Hearing Trumpet*. Illustrated by Pablo Weiez-Carrington. New York: St. Martin's, 1976. Originally published as *Le Cornet Acoustique*. Paris: Éditions Flammarion, 1974. [m]

A hearing-impaired, ninety-two-year-old feminist, Marion Leatherby, is incarcerated in an unconventional home for supposedly senile ladies. At the institution, housed in a Spanish castle, Marion gradually befriends the other inmates, all of them eccentric. One is Maud, an old transvestite discovered to be a man only after his death. Another is a black woman, Christabel, possessor of magical knowledge and ancient Spanish texts (one of which deals with a homosexual boys' choir conductor). The plot is hilarious and surreal; the characters are the antithesis of pasteboard cutouts propped in rocking chairs. Carrington, a noted painter as well as an author, challenges social attitudes toward old people with wit and charm – and she provides great fun.

166 CARTER, ANGELA. *The Infernal Desire Machines of Doctor Hoffman*. London: Hart-David, 1972. Reprinted as *The War of Dreams*. New York: Harcourt Brace Jovanovich, 1974. [f, M]

Society has been driven past the edge of sanity by the mad Dr. Hoffman who has created a machine that changes physical reality every few seconds. A young man, Desidero, is sent on a mission to restore world order by killing Dr. Hoffman. Desidero falls in with a traveling circus where he meets an outrageous gun-slinging lesbian and is raped by a group of male Moroccan acrobats. Sexual violence is graphically depicted. The story's pervasive weirdness, similar to an adventurous LSD trip, may make the novel compelling.

167 CARTER, ANGELA. "Overture and Incidental Music for *A Midsummer Night's Dream*." In *Shakespeare Stories*, edited by Giles Gordon. London: Hamish Hamilton, 1982. [X]

An imaginative addition to Shakespeare's famous dramatic fantasy in which the main character is a hermaphrodite.

168 CARTER, ANGELA. *The Passion of New Eve*. London: Gollancz, 1977. Reprint. New York: Harcourt Brace Jovanovich, 1977. [f, m, X]

In the convoluted narrative of *The Passion of New Eve*, Carter makes an explicit feminist statement. She argues that gender is not biologically defined but is rather a socially defined construction. She also delivers a hilarious and scathing satire of the lesbian separatist movement. Evelyn, a randy and opinionated Englishman, travels to a near-future New York for a university teaching position. The United States is a war-torn landscape where African-Americans and feminists battle conservative Christian forces. Evelyn is captured by separatists, raped, castrated, surgically changed into a woman, and impregnated. Evelyn becomes the "New Eve" of the title. Eve escapes and flees across the country, battling wife-beating patriarchs, born-again zealots, and aging transvestites.

Biographical Note

Angela Carter (b. 1940) is a noted British writer and feminist. Her novel *Heroes and Villains* (London: Heinemann, 1969) is set in a postholocaust England.

169 CASPERS, NONA M. "Harmonic Conception." In *Memories and Visions: Women's Fantasy and Science Fiction*, edited by Susanna J. Sturgis. Freedom, Calif.: Crossing Press, 1989. [F]

A lesbian finds herself miraculously pregnant after a visitation by a supernatural entity in Caspers's humorous short story.

170 CASTELL, DAPHNE. "Come Up and See Me." In *Alchemy and Academe*, edited by Anne McCaffrey. Garden City, N.Y.: Doubleday, 1970. [m]

Bizarre transmutations originating in a mysterious country garden affect a placid English village. The village inhabitants, including an inoffensively drawn gay male couple, are irresistibly drawn into the garden from which escape appears impossible. Neither the strange metamorphoses nor the garden itself is fully explained, and this adds to the poetic surrealism of Castell's enigmatic tale.

171 CHALKER, JACK L. *Cerberus: A Wolf in the Fold*. New York: Del Rey, 1981. [X]

The hero of Chalker's Four Lords of the Diamond series is a Federation operative who, with the assistance of his computer, swaps minds with various individuals in order to investigate in four sequential books the four prison planets of the Diamond Cluster: Charon, Lilith, Cerberus, and Medusa. On *Cerberus* body shifting is common, and the agent changes sex on several occasions. Chalker expends little energy on the psychological or social aspects of these profound changes.

172 CHAMBERS, JANE. *Burning*. New York: Jove, 1978. [F]

Cynthia plans a quiet vacation in a rustic New England village to get out of humid New York City and to focus on her oil painting. A young neighbor, Angela, goes along to watch Cynthia's children. While in the small village, the two women are possessed by the spirits of two eighteenth-century lesbians, Abigail and Martha. The lesbians had rebelled against the roles ascribed to women in Puritan America and had become lovers. Subsequently, they were condemned as witches and killed by the village's men. Cynthia and Angela care for each other as they are possessed and released by the two lesbians whose desire, strength, and suffering have endured death. An effective blend of lesbian romance and horror presented from a feminist viewpoint.

173 CHAMBERS, JANE. *Chasin' Jason*. New York: JH Press, 1983. [f, m]

Chambers relates a wry account of the second coming of Christ in the near future as told by Josephine Mary Caldwell, his mother. Caldwell is a television reporter who adopts a young Korean baby named Jason, not realizing that her new son will eventually work miracles. Among the novel's secondary characters are several lesbians and gay men.

Biographical Note
Jane Chambers (1937-83) was a noted playwright and a novelist. Her lesbian drama, "A Late Snow," has been reprinted in *Gay Plays: The First Collection*, ed. William Hoffman (New York: Avon, 1979). Her play *My Blue Heaven* (New York: JH Press, 1982) is also of lesbian interest. A collection of her poetry, *Warrior at Rest* (New York: JH Press, 1984), is also available. Further information on Chambers can be found in "Playwright Jane Chambers: The Long Road to 'Last Summer at Bluefish Cove,'" by Emily Sisley in the *Advocate* (San Mateo, Calif.), no. 305 (13 November 1980).

174 CHAMPAGNE, ROSARIA. "Womankind." In *Memories and Visions: Women's Fantasy and Science Fiction*, edited by Susanna J. Sturgis. Freedom, Calif.: Crossing Press, 1989. [F]
   Strange, surreal story about a woman who travels to a women-only world after stealing a man's penis.

175 CHANDLER, A[RTHUR] BERTRAM. *False Fatherland*. London, Melbourne, Sydney: Horwitz, 1968. Reprinted as *Spartan Planet*. New York: Dell, 1969. [M]
   On New Sparta, the all-male world depicted in this novel, homosexuality is the social norm. The sexual roles in this culture are rigidly defined and copy our society's: the effeminate males hold less power and always pair off with a more masculine partner. The plot is the standard formula used in most stories about single-sexed worlds: a strange ship carrying a sexually mixed crew lands on the planet and homosexuality, once the norm, is immediately dropped from the culture. In this instance, not only is heterosexuality adopted, but actions ranging from rape to men opening doors for women are spontaneously incorporated into the culture as if such conditioning were innate in men's genetic makeup. Heterosexuals John Grimes and Maggie Lazenby attempt to turn the planet around. Maggie is an anomaly in that she is intelligent, bold, and capable. Her function is as a catalyst for the Spartan planet's social transformation.

176 CHANDLER, A[RTHUR] BERTRAM. *The Last Amazon*. New York: DAW, 1984. [F?, m]
   The Last Amazon, sequel to *False Fatherland*, is also set on New Sparta. A group of neo-amazon separatists plot to take over the planet, and once again Grimes and Lazenby must literally straighten things out. There is minor mention of both lesbians and gay men.

177 CHARNAS, SUZY McKEE. *Motherlines*. New York: Berkley, 1978. [F]
   Charnas's sequel to *Walk to the End of the World* (cited below) is set on the barren desert outside the men's territory. The author

contrasts two very different women-only cultures. One group has lived without men since Earth's holocaust centuries before. Their desert society relies on horses for food, trade, transportation, and a form of reproduction that most readers find controversial. The other group, called "fems," is made up of escaped female slaves learning to survive without male masters. Patriarchy has left its mark on the fems' personalities; their culture is organized hierarchically and many of their attitudes and behaviors remain male-identified. Both groups are lesbian. The fem protagonist questions the politics and values of both groups and endeavors to synthesize the best parts of the cultures. There are no male characters in the novel, an aspect unusual even within the science-fiction genre. The narrative's tension is built solely on the individual and cultural dynamics among the women.

178 CHARNAS, SUZY McKEE. *Vampire Tapestry*. New York: Simon & Schuster, 1980. [f, m]

Dr. Edward Weyland is brilliant, erudite, graying anthropologist – and an ageless vampire. From contemporary college campuses to cruising areas in Central Park to the deserts of New Mexico, Weyland stalks his human prey. Charnas skillfully depicts Weyland's growing sympathy for his "food" in a series of interconnected episodes and reveals his ensuing psychological struggle. Both lesbian and gay male characters are introduced – in fact, a lesbian couple proves pivotal to the plot – and all are treated with care and respect.

179 CHARNAS, SUZY McKEE. *Walk to the End of the World*. New York: Ballantine, 1974. [f, M]

This book departs from standard treatments of homosexuality in science fiction by viewing it as a logical result of the contemporary polarization of the sexes. The setting is a postholocaust Earth where sexual apartheid is the rule, male homosexuality is the norm, and women are kept as slaves and breeders. The story centers on two male lovers who plan the downfall of society for their own gain, and, to a lesser degree, on their woman slave who carries a message of female rebellion to the escaped women living in the desert. The grim theme is relevant to both women and men. Charnas's writing is lucid and original.

Biographical Note

Suzy McKee Charnas (b. 1939) is a well-known science-fiction author who regularly incorporates a feminist perspective into her work. She is also the author of *The Bronze King* (New York: Houghton Mifflin, 1985), *Dorthea Dreams* (New York: Arbor House, 1986), and *The Silver Glove* (New York: Bantam, 1988).

Charnas discusses her feminism in "A Woman Appeared," in *Future Females: A Critical Anthology*, ed. Marleen S. Barr (Bowling Green, Ohio: Bowling Green State University Popular Press, 1981). See also her "No-Road" in *Women of Vision: Essays by Women Writing Science Fiction*, ed. Denise DuPont (New York: St. Martin's, 1988). Margaret Miller compares *Motherlines* and Gilman's *Herland* in "The Ideal Woman in Two Feminist Science-Fiction Utopias," in *Science Fiction Studies* (Montreal), no. 10 (July 1983), and Marleen Barr examines the author's sexual politics in "Utopia at the End of a Male Chauvinist Dystopian World: Suzy McKee Charnas's Feminist Science Fiction," in *Women and Utopia: Critical Interpretations*, ed. Marleen Barr and Nicholas D. Smith (Lanham, Md.: University Press of America, 1983). See also Barr's examination of *The Vampire Tapestry* in "Holding Fast to Feminism and Moving Beyond: Suzy McKee Charnas's *The Vampire Tapestry*," in *The Feminine Eye: Science Fiction and the Women Who Write It*, ed. Tom Staicar (New York: Ungar, 1982).

Biographical information on Charnas can be found in "Interview: Suzy McKee Charnas," by Neal Wilgus, *Algol / Starship*, Winter 1978-79, and in *Contemporary Authors, New Revision Series*, vol. 18, ed. Linda Mertzer and Deborah A. Straub (Detroit: Gale, 1986).

---

180 CHRISTOPHER, JOHN [pseudonym of Christopher Samuel Youd]. "A Few Kindred Spirits." *Fantasy and Science Fiction*, November 1965. Reprinted in *Best from Fantasy and Science Fiction: Sixteenth Series*, edited by Edward Ferman. Garden City, N.Y.: Doubleday, 1967. [M]

A heterosexual man comes upon a pack of dogs and recognizes in them the personalities of his former circle of homosexual acquaintances. In a flashback the lives of this shoddy literary bunch are detailed. Years later, the man again happens upon his former associates, this time manifested in a flock of parakeets.

181 CLARK, CARO. "The Rational Ship." In *Memories and Visions: Women's Fantasy and Science Fiction*, edited by Susanna J. Sturgis. Freedom, Calif.: Crossing Press, 1989. [F]

A lesbian starship captain pilots her craft using an intense, highly erotic interaction with one of her crew.

182 CLARK, KEITH, and KELLER, DENISE. "Future Sex: The Science Fiction Connection." *Gay News* (Pittsburgh, Pa.), 6 March 1976. [Nonfiction]

This article briefly reviews a wide variety of science-fiction novels and short stories that all deal in varying ways with sex. There is an emphasis on male homosexuality and lesbianism.

183 CLARKE, ARTHUR C[HARLES]. *Imperial Earth*. London: Gollancz, 1975. Expanded and reprinted. New York: Harcourt Brace Jovanovich, 1976. [M]

A strong homosexual foundation underlies this fascinating extrapolation. Duncan Makenzie, Clarke's bisexual protagonist, has been raised on Titan, one of Saturn's moons. He is a clone of Titan's founder, Malcolm Makenzie, and lives with Malcolm and their other clone, Colin, in a unique male family. The United States' 500th anniversary offers the Makenzies an opportunity to send Duncan back to Earth to clone another member for the family, so Duncan becomes Titan's official representative to the Quintennial. While exploring the technological wonders of Earth, Duncan runs into Karl Helmer, an old love from whom he has become estranged. While Clarke shies away from expressing open approval of exclusive homosexuality, he portrays male bisexuality with great acceptance. The novel is dedicated "for a lost friend."

184 CLARKE, ARTHUR C[HARLES]. *The Songs of Distant Earth*. New York: Ballantine, 1986. [m]

Thalassa is an earth colony founded centuries ago. Thalassans know neither hatred nor violence until visited by the enormous spaceship *Magellan* traveling from Earth. The sun has gone nova, the planet is destroyed, and the *Magellan* bears millions of refugees to colonize a new home world for the human race. The interaction between the spaceship crew and the Thalassans is fascinating and insightful. Several of the novel's secondary characters are gay or bisexual men. This entertaining novel first appeared as a short story in 1958.

185 CLARKE, ARTHUR C[HARLES]. *2061: Odyssey Three*. New York: Ballantine, 1987. [m]

Dr. Heywood Floyd prepares for another journey into space; a strange mountain develops on a moon of Jupiter, and Halley's comet returns to our solar system. The mysterious intelligence controlling the huge black monoliths, which Clarke introduced in *2001: A Space Odyssey* (New York: New American Library, 1968) and returned to in *2010: Odyssey Two* (New York: Ballantine, 1982), is the connection between these seemingly unrelated events. Once again, Dr. Floyd must confront star-child David Bowman, the computer HAL, and a strange alien race. A sympathetic pair of emotionally stable gay male lovers, Floyd's oldest and closest friends, are introduced early in the novel.

186 CLARKE, ARTHUR C[HARLES], and LEE, GENTRY. *Cradle: A Novel*. New York: Warner, 1988. [f, m]

Clarke's first collaborative novel, with engineer Gentry Lee, is another magnificent tale of human contact with an extraterrestrial intelligence. Resourceful feminist reporter Carol Dawson joins forces with a crusty Key West treasure hunter and his black crewman to investigate a mysterious golden underwater artifact. The authors include both gay men and lesbians among their varied cast. The homosexual director of Key West's repertory theater company is a positive character, unlike the kinky bisexual Aryan beauty Greta Erhard.

CLARKE, ARTHUR C[HARLES], and LEE, GENTRY. The Rama Trilogy. [f?, m]:

187 ▪ *Rama II*. New York: Bantam, 1989.

In the award-winning 1973 novel *Rendezvous with Rama*, Clarke describes the visit by an immense alien starship to our solar system. In *Rama II*, the first novel of a trilogy, the alien starship returns. A multicultural, cosexual crew of scientists, military, and civilians is assembled to rendezvous with the enigmatic craft. Among the crew members are Janos Tabori, a Hungarian engineer once active in Gay Liberation, and Irina Turgenyev, a possibly lesbian Soviet pilot. The second and third volumes of the trilogy, *The Garden of Rama* and *Rama Revealed*, are forthcoming.

Biographical Note

Arthur C. Clarke (b. 1917) is the author of many science-fiction and nongenre books, including the classic *Childhood's End* (New York: Ballantine, 1953), the screenplay (with Stanley Kubrick) for *2001: A Space Odyssey*, and *Rendezvous with Rama* (London: Gollancz, 1973), winner of the Hugo, the Nebula, the John W. Campbell, the British Science Fiction, and the Jupiter awards.

Other relevant works include "The Steam-Powered Word Processor," in *Astounding Days* (New York: Bantam, 1990), and the forthcoming novel *The Ghost from the Grand Banks*, which features a lesbian theme. Neither will be published soon enough for annotation in this bibliography.

Clarke discusses his opinions on sexuality and homosexuality in Jeremy Hughes's article "Sex in the Year 2500," in *In Touch for Men*, July 1982. Reinald Werrenrath's "Some Thoughts on the Sexual Nature of HAL" in *Northwest Gay Review*, February 1977, is a fascinating article exploring the personality, gender, and sexual orientation of HAL, the independently intelligent computer from Clarke's *2001: A Space Odyssey*.

CLAYTON, JO. The Duel of Sorcery Trilogy. [F?]:

188 ▪ *Moongather*. New York: DAW, 1982.

189 ▪ *Moonscatter.* New York: DAW, 1983.

190 ▪ *Changer's Moon.* New York: DAW, 1985.

Jo Clayton is a prolific fantasy and science-fiction author known for including assertive and adventuresome female protagonists in her works. In her Duel of Sorcery trilogy, Clayton makes her hero not just a female but also a lesbian ... well, at least sort of. Serroi, a warrior woman, finds herself a literal pawn in a dueling match between a fallen sorcerer and the Goddess. Serroi's beloved "shieldmate" Tayyan is apparently also her lover, which implies a lesbian sexuality. But Tayyan is murdered within the trilogy's first pages, and Serroi's lesbianism evaporates. By the trilogy's second novel, Serroi's heterosexuality is blossoming. Despite this minor irritation the Duel of Sorcery trilogy is worth reading.

191 CLAYTON, JO. *Irsud.* New York: DAW, 1978. [f]

Irsud is the third novel in Clayton's popular Diadem series. Aleytys is a strong, independent young woman who flees her repressive home planet and travels throughout the galaxy to find her heritage. She is electronically attached to the potent diadem of the series's title. In *Irsud,* Aleytys is sold into slavery. The inhabitants of Irsud are insectlike, intelligent, and highly organized; females dominate and males serve. One of the young females is said to get more pleasure from inflicting pain than from having more conventional sex and makes explicitly sexual overtures toward Aleytys. The Diadem series of novels, now over eight volumes, began with *Diadem from the Stars* (New York: DAW, 1977).

192 CLAYTON, JO. "Nightwork." In *Amazons II,* edited by Jessica Amanda Salmonson. New York: DAW, 1982. [F?]

Yassim, a moon-worshiping warrior, becomes involved in the affairs of a farming community while investigating the death of a temple keeper. Although she is accused of being "woman-loving," Yassim's sexuality can only be conjectured as she is celibate throughout the story.

193 CLENDENEN, BILL. *Stigma.* New York: Bantam, 1988. [m]

In a run-down Los Angeles hotel, a young woman miraculously begins to bleed from her palms and to have religious visions. A male hustler and a transsexual are secondary characters. A relatively sleazy and sordid viewpoint.

194 COMPTON, D. G. *Farewell, Earth's Bliss.* London: Hodder & Stoughton, 1966. Reprint. New York: Ace, 1971. [m]

Mark, a gay man, is sent to a Martian penal colony for attempting an assassination. He expects the hard work, scarce food, and even the strict discipline of the all-prisoner society, but he is not prepared for the staunchly religious inmates who believe in redemption through ignorance and their racist, sexist, and homophobic attitudes. The many unsympathetic characters include Ruth, who becomes a kept woman, a self-hating black artist, and a white, power-hungry bully. Mark, the only character with decency, is sent to his death for suspected homosexuality. Cynical.

195 CONEY, MICHAEL. *Friends Come in Boxes*. New York: DAW, 1973. [m]

These related short stories are set in a future when, in an attempt to save the resources and the knowledge of older citizens, every newborn's brain is surgically removed and thrown away to be replaced by an adult's brain. The citizens' infanticide thus insures their own immortality. The population is kept under tight control by denying immortality to citizens who have committed even a slight infraction of the law. Many people attempt to protect their children by hiding them from the state. A gay male minor character assists in this process in one story. Coney again uses a male homosexual image later in the book, that of a man who demands a woman's body. The stories are ironic, often with trick endings.

196 CONNER, MICHAEL. "Vamp." In *Orbit Nineteen*, edited by Damon Knight. New York: Harper & Row, 1977. [M]

Conner effectively maintains a heavy ambience of decay and corruption in "Vamp," and it is this ambience that gives the story its punch. The plot revolves around an upwardly mobile young artist working in a new medium, holo projection, which is a combination of photography and electronic surveillance. The artist, his employer, and perhaps the man under surveillance are homosexual.

197 CONSTANTINE, MURRAY [pseudonym of Katharine Burdekin]. *Swastika Night*. London: Gollancz, 1937. Reprinted under the author's name. New York: Feminist Press, 1985. [m]

First published during World War II, *Swastika Night* imagines a feudal, sexist Europe seven centuries into post-Hitlerian society. Hitler is worshiped as a god. Jews have been exterminated, and Christians are now being sent to death camps. Women are viewed as animals and kept in cages, while men are reared in comfortable, all-male environments. Male homosexuality is condoned. Yet despite her bleak setting, the author envisions the possibility for change. A young British technician, a secret revolutionary, discovers that the only way to overthrow fascism is through the emancipation of women. Constantine's novel offers a brilliant feminist examination of nazism years ahead of its time. This feminist dystopia is similar in many ways to Charnas's *Walk to the End of the World* published forty years later.

CONSTANTINE, STORM. The Books of Wraeththu Trilogy. [M, X]:

198 ▪ *The Enchantments of Flesh and Spirit*. London: Macdonald, 1987.

199 ▪ *The Bewitchments of Love and Hate*. London: Macdonald, 1988.

200 ▪ *The Fulfillments of Fate and Desire*. London: Macdonald, 1989.

Storm Constantine's inventive series about a exotic quasi-human species deserves a wide audience. At some unspecified time in the future, a mutated human species, the Wraeththu, has risen to dominance. The Wraeththu are telepathic, stunningly beautiful, and immersed in occult rituals. Their spiritual advancement is furthered by sexual contact. Like vampires, the Wraeththu can reproduce by sharing their blood with humans – but only with adolescent males. A young human falls in love with a handsome Wraeththu and deserts his family to travel with his lover. Unknown to both, they are destined for far greater glories. While technically the Wraeththu are hermaphroditic, their masculine appearance, their sexuality, and their assumption of masculine pronouns make a gay male interpretation of their culture unavoidable.

COOKE, CATHERINE. The Winged Assassin Trilogy. [M]:

201 ▪ *The Winged Assassin*. New York: Ace, 1987.

202 ▪ *Realm of the Gods*. New York: Ace, 1988.

203 ▪ *The Crimson Goddess*. New York: Ace, 1989.

In Cooke's richly woven Arabian Nights fantasy, Arris is just a young boy when his life is plunged into political and spiritual intrigue. Unknown to him, he is actually a chosen one of the Crimson Goddess. Her manipulations force Arris into a series of dangerous and exotic adventures, including being a slave and skilled lover of a cruel emperor. While living with the emperor, Arris is trained as an assassin and is sent on a mission to kill the powerful Prince Saresha. But instead of killing the Prince, Arris falls in love with him. The fast-paced action continues through the three volumes. Recommended.

204 COOKE, JOHN PEYTON. *The Lake*. New York: Avon, 1989. [M]

Cooke's novel is a predictable but entertaining horror fantasy with significant gay male content. Young teenager Jill Beaumont feels trapped in her hometown of Sherman, Wyoming. Her only companions are her boyfriend, Sam, and her best friend, Curtis. When the stagnant

Stink Lake is drained, a generations-old witch's curse is unleashed, and it is up to the trio to do something. Curtis is gay and in love with Sam; this relationship proves pivotal to the plot.

205 COONEY, ELLEN. *The Silver Rose*. San Francisco: Duir Press, 1979. [F, M, X]

This book-length poem tells the story of Morgan, an only child of the bisexual Goddess of the Moon and Sea. Morgan is a hermaphrodite until s/he is separated into two oppositely gendered beings by the Fire God. Both of Morgan's halves then enter the world as homosexuals, but both long to return to their former androgynous state. For years they search the globe seeking their other halves, and they are overjoyed when finally reunited. After a blissful period as heterosexual lovers they are miraculously merged again, becoming a single, epicene individual. The poet is consciously feminist and avoids any homophobic expressions.

206 COOPER, EDMUND. *Five to Twelve*. London: Hodder & Stoughton, 1968. Reprint. New York: Putnam, 1969. [F?]

There are five men for every twelve women in this female-dominated society of the future. Dion Quern, a misogynist, rebels against the women rulers while developing a love-hate relationship with one of them. Dion eventually comes to an unhappy end. This is a surprising variant from the standard treatment of the "evil dominating women subjugating helpless men" theme, but Dion's downfall does not mitigate the sexism in the novel. Lesbianism is overtly mentioned at an orgy for the women rulers, and the implication is that most women are lesbians.

207 COOPER, EDMUND. *Who Needs Men?* London: Hodder & Stoughton, 1972. Reprinted as *Gender Genocide*. New York: Ace, 1973. [F]

This is a true classic in the misogynists writing about misandry department: a pernicious and twisted view of lesbianism. Rura, raised to hate and kill the few remaining men in the British Isles, graduates from her special training as an executioner, and after an orgy with her women friends, sets out to hunt men. She falls in love with the first man she meets. He rapes her, and immediately she is won over to his way of thinking: that women need men. The speed with which she acclimates to an oppressed and self-effacing role would indicate that it is a more natural one than the self-asserting role her society practices.

208 COOPER, PARLEY J. *The Feminists*. New York: Pinnacle Books, 1971. [f, m]

A weak vision of a matriarchal society in New York City, 1992. The protagonist, Keith Montalvo, is an enlistee in the Revolutionary

Underground, a group of men attacking the Feminists. The Feminists are depicted as power-hungry and hierarchial. Homosexuality is introduced through a cowardly gay man who betrays the Underground and through a lesbian sadist. The treatment of the propatriarchal theme lacks originality.

COULSON, JUANITA. *See* BRADLEY, MARION ZIMMER (joint author), and WELLS, JOHN J. (pseudonym)

209 COURT, LEIGH. "Suck My Blood." *Mandate* 8, no. 8 (November 1982). [M, X]

Two handsome young men (whose romance began during a midnight screening of *Curse of Dracula's Castle*) find their erotic interaction becoming dangerously bloody and vampiritic.

210 COVINA, GINA. *The City of Hermits*. Berkeley, Calif.: Barn Owl, 1983. [F]

The City of Hermits is a near-future fantasy novel set amid the redwood groves of Guerneville, California. Covina, a former editor of *Amazon Quarterly*, focuses on several dynamic lesbian women in her novel, including the owner of Sister Spa, a feminist resort. During the course of the story there is a major earthquake in San Francisco, causing considerable damage.

211 COX, JOAN. *Mindsong*. New York: Avon, 1979. [M]

Cox's novel is a moody and ambiguous exploration of thwarted homosexual passion. Don Eel of Erl, sentenced to death in his own country, is rescued by a handsome traveling prince, Pollo of Delpha. Immediately becoming fast friends, the two embark upon an adventure that crosses time, space, and consciousness. Strange and ominous events have been occurring near Delpha's mines; innocent people have been kidnapped and murdered. The two young men are sent by Pollo's father to investigate. With the help of Don Eel's father, one of the winged race of nonhumans, the pair not only solve the mystery surrounding the mines but also solve an even greater mystery regarding humans' relationship to the cosmos. The emotional involvement between the two heroes is central to the plot. Pollo is overtly bisexual and wishes to make love with Don Eel. Don Eel's sexual feelings are ambivalent. He rejects Pollo's advances, yet he maintains his intense friendship with the prince and marries Pollo's look-alike sister. Women play only a small part in Cox's drama; the novel focuses almost entirely upon men.

212 COX, JOAN. *Star Web*. New York: Avon, 1980. [M?]

Star Web is another homosexual science-fiction novel from Cox. A bisexual starship captain faces alien adventure with his two lovers in tow, one male and one female. An enjoyable and exciting saga.

213 COYLE, JOHN. *Fury*. New York: Warner Books, 1989. [f, m]
Coyle explores the New Age phenomenon of channeling in this horror novel about a troubled young woman who resolves a conflict in a past life through spiritualism. Among the many previous existences that she discovers using channeling are those of a lesbian nun during the Renaissance and of a boy-loving poet in classical Greece.

214 COYLE, JOHN. *The Piercing*. New York: Putnam, 1978. [M?]
The hero of *The Piercing* is Father Stephen Kinsella, a priest investigating an authenticated case of stigmatic ecstasy. Kinsella is constantly being tempted with and tormented by a homosexual incident in his youth. Both the stigmata and the homosexual temptation are eventually revealed to be the villainous work of the Devil.

CULBRETH, MYRNA. *See* MARSHANK, SONDRA (joint author)

215 CURZON, DANIEL. "The Hideous Beast." In *The Revolt of the Perverts*. San Francisco: Leland Mellott Books, 1978. [M]
An attack by a hideous monster causes a young gay man to age rapidly and supernaturally. A curiously effective tale about death and dying.

216 CURZON, DANIEL. "Mr. Right." In *The Revolt of the Perverts*. San Francisco: Leland Mellott Books, 1978. [M]
This amusing rendition of a classical Greek myth concerns Zeus and his young male lover, Ganymede.

217 CYWIN, LARRY. "Blood Lust Valentine." *Torso* (New York), February 1987. [M]
Gay male vampire erotica.

218 DANAAN, TARA. "The Grave's a Fine and Private Place." *Sinister Wisdom* (Berkeley, Calif.), no. 34 (1988). [F, X]
A lesbian vampire meets a female lover in a graveyard.

219 DANIELS, CORA LYNN [MORRISON]. *Sardia: A Story of Love*. Boston: Lee & Shepard, 1891. [F]
A delightful, now-obscure American Gothic fantasy. Mysterious and beautiful Sybil Visconti has the vampiric ability to mesmerize people and to drain them of their vital energy. She has totally infatuated Ralfe Fielding in an attempt to ruin his marriage and secure his money.

Sybil uses her spellbinding powers on women as well as men, and her lesbian attachment to another woman is described in detail. It is easy to interpret the character of the exotic Russian princess, Madame Menshikoff, as lesbian. The scene at a nineteenth-century Bohemian hashish party is remarkable.

220 DANIELS, LES. *Citizen Vampire*. New York: Scribner's, 1981. [m]
Don Sebastian, the vampire protagonist of a sequence of Daniels's novels, experiences the French Revolution. The bisexual Marquis de Sade is a minor character.

221 DANN, JACK, and ZEBROWSKI, GEORGE. "Faces Forward." In *Dystopian Visions*, edited by Roger Elwood. Englewood Cliffs, N.J.: Prentice-Hall, 1975. [m]
A stream-of-consciousness style is used to write about the depersonalization of sex. A minor character is a homosexual "greaser."

222 DARK, JON. *Satan's Victor*. Chatsworth, Calif.: GX, 1972. [M]
Gay male pornographic horror novel.

223 D'ARRIGO, STEPHEN. "Man Made." *In Touch for Men* (Hollywood, Calif.), no. 47 (May-June 1980). [M]
In the twenty-second century, a robot finds himself erotically attracted to male humans.

224 DAVIS, CHERYL ELAINE. "Stone Hands." *Sinister Wisdom* (Berkeley, Calif.), no. 34 (1988). [F]
An intelligent and independent young woman living in a repressive postapocalypse world discovers rebellion following a rapturous sexual encounter with another woman.

225 DAVIS, CHRISTOPHER. "Histories." In *The Boys in the Bars*. Pound Ridge, N.Y.: Knights, 1989. [F]
Short story set in the near future about the gay survivors of the AIDS epidemic.

226 DAVIS, GRANIA. "New-Way-Groover's Stew." *Fantastic*, August 1976. [F, M]
An older butch lesbian and her close friend, a swishy gay male author, live in San Francisco's Haight-Ashbury district and watch the hippies' "Summer of Love." Their age and sexual preferences alienate them from the hippie movement, but, hoping to form same-sex affairs, they aid and shelter the naive flower children. A fiery member of the New-Way-Groovers (a group similar to the Diggers) and the gay man begin a sexual relationship likened to the roles of von Sacher-Masoch

and the Marquis de Sade. The gruesome narrative about emotional and physical devourment is surprisingly sensitive in its portrayal of the two gay characters.

DEAN, JOE. *See* BIXBY, JEROME (joint author)

227 De CAMP, L. SPRAGUE. *The Hostage of Zir*. New York: Berkley, 1977. [m]
Fergus Reith, a Terran, leads a group of bungling interplanetary tourists to the distant planet Krishna. The tourists proceed to involve themselves in a variety of comical situations from which Reith must rescue them. Among Reith's charges are two gay male lovers who break up and become heterosexual by the end of the novel. Part of the author's Krishna series.

228 De CAMP, L. SPRAGUE. *Rogue Queen*. Garden City, N.Y.: Doubleday, 1951. [f]
On the matriarchal planet of Ormazd, society is arranged like a beehive. Queens rule and reproduce hundreds of children; the male drones' sole function is to aid the queens in reproduction. And the tall amazonian women are the workers. When Iroedh, a worker, comes into contact with the first Earth men to land on the planet, she finds their customs preferable to her own. Her love for an Earth man leads her to the discovery that all women can bear children. Iroedh changes the customs of her world to more closely resemble those of Earth. Vardh, also a worker, is deeply in love with Iroedh, proclaims this love loudly, and refuses to "submit to the horrid embraces of some drooling drone." That Vardh proclaims her love after the society has begun its transition away from a matriarchy is a slight variation on a common science-fiction theme.

229 DELANY, SAMUEL R[AY]. "Aye, and Gomorrah." In *Dangerous Visions*, edited by Harlan Ellison. Garden City, N.Y.: Doubleday, 1967. [f, m, X]
In the future it has become necessary to develop "spacers," neutered human beings able to withstand the rigors of space travel. By creating this new breed of human, neither male nor female, society has also caused another type of person to develop–"frelks"–persons sexually attracted to spacers. Nebula Award-winning exploration of the concept of sexual deviation using minor lesbian and gay male characters.

230 DELANY, SAMUEL R[AY]. *Babel-17*. New York: Ace, 1966. [m]
Rydra Wong is a poet admired in five galaxies, an uncanny linguist, and a seemingly schizophrenic spaceship captain. While

working for the Alliance during their war against the Invaders, she is exposed to an insidious new weapon known as Babel-17. Using her rare ability to cut through cultural chauvinism, Delany's Asian protagonist assembles a racially mixed crew and takes off to seek the language's inventors. The novel couples fast-paced adventure with intriguing ideas about language. During the story Rydra is celibate, but she was formerly "tripled" (in a three-person sexual, emotional, and financial partnership) and talks about this to aid a crew member in solving problems within his own triple. Both triples involve male-male sexual relations.

231 DELANY, SAMUEL R[AY]. *Dhalgren*. New York: Bantam, 1975. [f, M]

A young amnesiac, whose grasp of reality is sporadic, wanders through the ruins of a devastated American city that apparently is becoming physically disjointed from the rest of the world. The young man, dubbed Kid (or Kidd, or The Kid), mingles within each of the city's social circles and so is able to take on several roles. He is a handyman for a white nuclear family that is vainly trying to continue a normal existence in the midst of increasing chaos, and he is a poet laureate for the city's sophisticates. The members of the fearsome and tough leather gang that rules the city draft him as their leader, and a black lesbian therapist convinces him to become her patient. Many of the novel's characters, including the Kid, are bisexual, and descriptions of sex are plentiful throughout the book; when occurring between men the encounters are described with more passion. The unreliability of the character's memory, the complex point of view, and the detailed descriptions of impossible events effectively create a hallucinatory effect that is intensified by the use of an experimental writing style and poetic diction in this monumental and controversial novel.

232 DELANY, SAMUEL R[AY]. *The Einstein Intersection*. New York: Ace, 1967. [X]

Long ago all humans left Earth. A trisexual race of aliens has been drawn to the planet to take on human form and cultural memories, using various myths of the planet as a basis for their interpretation of what is human. The aliens do not easily fit into a human mold, so that many variations, or mutations, are born. Lo Lobey, a young musician caught in the role of Orpheus, searches for La Friza, his lost Euridice. On his journey, Lo Lobey meets many unusual characters, each born with some kind of psychic power that sets them apart from their contemporaries. Among these characters are two hermaphrodites, Le Dorik and Le Dove, both of whom are erotically involved with the protagonist. Just as the aliens are different from humans (though what they are lacking or have added that makes them different is vague), the mythic plot lines that several of the characters live out have resolutions that are also different from those of the original myths.

233 DELANY, SAMUEL R[AY]. *Empire Star*. New York: Ace, 1966. [m]

A dirty red-haired youth, Comet Jo, rock climbing on his parochial home world, looks up in consternation as a small spaceship lands. A figure, looking very much like an older version of Comet Jo, stumbles out, orders the youth to deliver a message to the distant Empire Star, then dies. As Jo travels to Empire Star, he finds that not only must he deliver the message that proclaims the freedom of an enslaved race, but he must also set up the necessary conditions to make this message accurate. This humorous novel, a favorite among Delany fans, is like a delightful puzzle. Because space and time are strained and twisted around Empire Star, those who travel there are flung into either the past or the future. Thus, characters are able to meet themselves and to meet other characters who are younger with each reunion. Homosexuality is introduced by literary allusions to homosexual writers and lovers, which clarify the major but inexplicit homosexual relationship between two of the characters, Ni Ty Lee and Muels Aranlyde.

234 DELANY, SAMUEL R[AY]. *The Jewel-Hinged Jaw: Notes on the Language of Science Fiction*. Elizabethtown, N.Y.: Dragon Press, 1977. [Nonfiction]

A collection of Delany's essays and criticism includes some autobiographical material, a gay / feminist critique of Le Guin's *The Dispossessed*, and discussion on fellow authors Joanna Russ, Thomas Disch, and Roger Zelazny.

DELANY, SAMUEL R[AY]. Return to Nevèrÿon Series. [f, M]:

235 ▪ *Tales of Nevèrÿon*. New York: Bantam, 1979.

236 ▪ *Neveryóna, or the Tale of Signs and Cities*. New York: Bantam, 1983.

237 ▪ *Flight from Nevèrÿon*. New York: Bantam, 1985.

238 ▪ *The Bridge of Lost Desire*. New York: Arbor House, 1987.

The novel and short stories of Delany's four-volume Return to Nevèrÿon series are set in the untamed land of Nevèrÿon, some 9,000 years ago. The characters are some of those most loved by Delany fans: Gorgik, in turn a slave, a royal favorite, a trader, and a revolutionary soldier; Small Sarg, once a barbarian prince, now a slave and Gorgik's lover; Norema, an island fisherwoman; and Raven, the masked warrior woman. As Delany is so very capable of doing, he mixes Sword and

Sorcery adventure (which tingles with homoerotic passion) and brilliant (though sometimes long-winded) monologues about historical philosophy, the development of capitalism, sadomasochism, AIDS, and the meanings of freedom.

239 DELANY, SAMUEL R[AY]. "The Star Pit." *Worlds of Tomorrow* (London) 4, no. 3 (February 1967). Reprinted in *SF12*, edited by Judith Merril. New York: Delacorte, 1968. [m]

This well-crafted story works on different levels to describe the feeling of being trapped. Human society has expanded to the edge of the galaxy and wants to push further, but certain physical laws cause insanity and death to most who pass the galactic border. A few psychotic individuals, dubbed "golden," are able to travel to other galaxies and therefore have become an exploited, privileged, and despised class. The forty-two-year-old alcoholic black narrator, rejected in his bisexual group marriage, sets up a spaceship repair garage at Star Pit. His resentment of goldens dissolves when he hires a jaded youth who reveals that goldens also have physical limitations on how far they can travel. Male homosexuality is presented in two ways – stereotypically in a fat pederast smoking perfumed cigarettes and with depth in the context of a group marriage.

240 DELANY, SAMUEL R[AY]. *Stars in My Pockets, Like Grains of Sand.* New York: Bantam, 1984. [M]

Rat Korga is a slave on the planet Rhyonon until a planetary cataclysm completely alters his circumstances. He is discovered to be the ideal erotic partner of Marq Dyeth, a diplomat from the planet Velm. (Korga is into short, hairy men like Dyeth and the diplomat likes big men like Korga.) But fate and social prejudice soon separate the lovers. This is classic science-fiction space opera, but of a highly intellectual sort. Delany is a meticulous stylist and not always easy reading. But for the many who are enamored of Delany's work, *Stars in My Pockets, Like Grains of Sand* is delicious. Will Korga and Dyeth get back together? The answer must wait until Delany's sequel, *The Splendor and Misery of Bodies, of Cities*, is released.

241 DELANY, SAMUEL R[AY]. "Time Considered as a Helix of Semi-Precious Stones." *New Worlds* (London), November 1968. Reprinted in *World's Best Science Fiction: 1969*, edited by Donald Wollheim and Terry Carr. New York: Ace, 1969. [f?, M]

This dazzling short story concerns the narrow escapes of H. C. E., a quick-change artist and prosperous thief living in the far future. H. C. E. is relentlessly pursued by Maud, a special kind of cop and a remarkable woman. His friends include Hawk, whose songs inspire transcendental emotion in a population otherwise satiated by mass media, and Edna, also a famous singer and perhaps a lesbian. H. C. E. and Hawk were once lovers, and the subtle presentation of their relationship is sympathetic. Hawk's sexual masochism is described as a jumbled brain's interpretation of pleasure. Winner of both the Hugo and Nebula awards.

242 DELANY, SAMUEL R[AY]. *Triton*. New York: Bantam, 1976. [f, M]

Delany brilliantly constructs a believable nonsexist culture while exposing the confused internal workings of the macho kind of heroic character typically found in science fiction. People on the Outer Satellites can switch sexual preference or gender at whim; these qualities do not determine social roles or economic position. Because there is no stigma attached to the labels, many identify themselves as gay or lesbian, and the novel is replete with gay characters. In sharp contrast to his postsexist, collectively oriented society, the protagonist Bron is sexist and selfish. He falls in love with the famous theatrical director, the Spike, and begs her to give up her art and her career to reciprocate his love. Of course, being who she is and living in the society she does, she refuses. Their stormy relationship occurs against the background of a quick but devastating war between the worlds. When both the war and the relationship end, Bron changes gender and sexual orientation and tries to act like her definition of a "real" woman existing solely for the benefit of "real" men. But "real" men are hard to find on Triton.

Biographical Note

Samuel R. Delany (b. 1942), winner of four Nebula awards and one Hugo Award, is one of the most gifted science-fiction writers. He published his first novel in 1962 and was heralded as a wunderkind. In 1970 Delany and Marilyn Hacker jointly edited the influential *Quark: A Quarterly Journal of Speculative Fiction*. During its four-issue run *Quark* published some of the best American New Wave science fiction. He frequently writes about racial and sexual dynamics, political change, and social revolutions. His protagonists are usually not Caucasian; they are frequently female.

Homosexuality and bisexuality appear throughout Delany's work. *The Ballad of Beta-2* (New York: Ace, 1965), *Nova* (Garden City, N.Y.: Doubleday, 1968), and *Empire* (New York: Berkley, Windhover, 1978) all contain noticeable elements of sexual variation, but these are either too minor or too subjective to annotate here. Delany's non-science-fiction pornographic novel, *The Tides of Lust* (New York: Lancer, 1973), is of primary gay male significance and foreshadows the hallucinatory style of *Dhalgren*.

Delany discusses his sexuality and its influence on his science fiction in his memoir *The Motion of Light in Water* (New York: Arbor House, Morrow,

1988). See also "Samuel R. Delany: The Possibility of Possibilities," by Samuel R. Delany and Joseph Beam, in *In the Life: A Black Gay Anthology*, ed. Joseph Beam (Boston: Alyson, 1986); "Samuel Delany: Setting Future Limits" by Pat Califia, in the *Advocate*, no. 332 (9 December 1982); and "To Read *The Dispossessed*," in *The Jewel-Hinged Jaw: Notes on the Language of Science Fiction* (Elizabethtown, N.Y.: Dragon Press, 1977). He is also the author of *Starboard Wine, More Notes on the Language of Science Fiction* (Pleasantville, N.Y.: Dragon Press, 1984). Material from Delany's journals was extensively used to write an account of communal life in *Heavenly Breakfast* (New York: Bantam, 1979).

Relevant criticism of Delany can be found in Douglas Barbour's *Worlds out of Words: The SF Novels of Samuel R. Delany* (Somerset, England: Bran's Head Books, 1979) and in Seth McEvoy's *Samuel R. Delany* (New York: Ungar, 1984). The most comprehensive biographical information available on Delany is Michael W. Peplow and Robert S. Bravard's *Samuel R. Delany: A Primary and Secondary Bibliography, 1962-79* (Boston: G. K. Hall, 1980). Other sources of biographical information include *Contemporary Authors*, vols. 81-84, ed. Frances Carol Locher (Detroit: Gale, 1979), and Michael W. Peplow's "Meet Samuel R. Delany, Black Science Fiction Writer" in *Crisis*, April 1979.

---

243 DERLETH, AUGUST. "Bat's Belfry." *Weird Tales*, May 1926. Reprinted in *Not at Night!* edited by Herbert Asbury. New York: Vanguard, 1928. [M?]

Three collegiate men move into a mysterious English house with a very shady reputation. Known to locals as the Bat's Belfry, the estate is rumored to be haunted with vampires, and these rumors are subsequently confirmed. Homosexuality enters into the story with a midnight visit to one of the men by a handsome old man (the other men have been visited by beautiful women). The visited man is upset because the old man "kissed" him.

244 DIAMAN, N[IKOS] A. *Ed Dean Is Queer*. San Francisco: Persona Press, 1978. [F, M]

Diaman uses Anita Bryant's much-publicized 1977 "Save Our Children" campaign as a springboard for his utopian fantasy. The novel charts the reactions of two individuals to Bryant's homophobic crusade. Luis Rivera, a Latin reporter investigating the Miami vote, falls in love with another man. Joanna Jefferson, an Asian-African-American lesbian, becomes politically radicalized in response to the organized bigotry. The novel concludes when San Francisco secedes to form the Pacific Republic, a gay / feminist utopia, and Jefferson is elected premier of the new country. A simplistic but enjoyable roman à clef.

245 DIAMAN, N[IKOS] A. *The Fourth Wall*. San Francisco: Persona Press, 1980. [M]
Diaman uses an intentionally minimalist style to describe a future in which television has become the controlling social influence. The author follows three characters through a single day: a gay man, his mother, and the President of the United States.

Biographical Note

N[ikos] A. Diaman (b. 1938) edited *Paragraph: A Quarterly of Gay Fiction*. He is also the author of *Reunion* (San Francisco: Persona Press, 1983) and *Castro Street Memories* (San Francisco: Persona Press, 1988). Both of these novels have significant gay male content.

---

246 DICK, PHILIP K. *Flow My Tears, the Policeman Said*. Garden City, N.Y.: Doubleday, 1974. [F, m]
One day everyone knows Jason Taverner from his guest-host television show; however, the next day no one has ever heard of him. His fans, his girlfriend, and the police have no remembrance nor record of him. He is bewildered until he meets Alys, a drugged-out, sadistic, spoiled brat. She is responsible for Jason's loss of identity and has secretly been a lover of Jason's fiancée, Heather Hart. In the epilogue, Alys wills her estate to a lesbian organization, The Sons of Caribon. The gay male imagery, though brief, is memorable. A John Campbell Award winner.

247 DICK, PHILIP K. *The Man in the High Castle*. New York: Putnam's, 1962. [m]
A well-drawn fantasy of a parallel universe in which Franklin Roosevelt was assassinated during his second term and the Axis powers went on to win World War II. The United States has been divided among the victors, with the East Coast given to the German Nazis and the West Coast controlled by the more moderate Japanese. The death of Martin Bormann, Chancellor of the Reich, starts a chain of events around which *The Man in the High Castle* is built. The author is particularly successful in developing the novel's varied cast of characters and their respective cultures. Only one woman emerges as a primary character, a physically strong, emotionally male-dependent judo instructor. The author's fleeting inclusion of "simpering, blond, baby-like SS fairies" is historically misleading. The novel is a classic in the science-fiction genre and won the 1963 Hugo Award.

248 DICKINSON, PETER. *King and Joker*. London: Hodder & Stoughton, 1976. Reprint. New York: Pantheon, 1976. [F]

Dickinson, a popular British author, utilizes the science-fiction concept of parallel worlds to write this witty murder mystery. Someone is playing nasty tricks on Dickinson's imaginary modern royal family, and when harmless pranks lead to murder, Scotland Yard is called in. Buckingham Palace is turned upside down in the search for the murderer. The royal family's nursemaid, Miss Durdy, is a lesbian. Her characterization is both sympathetic and important to the plot. A delightful novel.

249 DICKSON, JAN. "Moonshine Quartet." *Women* (Baltimore) 5, no. 1 (1976). [F]

A lesbian narrates this humorous fantasy story about menstruation.

250 DIESBACH, GHISLAIN De. "The Chavalier d'Armel's Wedding." In *The Toys of Princes*, translated by Richard Howard. New York: Pantheon, 1962. Originally published as *Iphigénie en Thruinge; Nouvelles*. Paris: R. Julliard, 1960. [m, X]

Diesbach writes enchanting adult fairy tales similar in style to the fiction of Isak Dinesen. In this tale, a duchess undergoes a metamorphosis that changes her into a man, causing major complications for her fiancé. Minor male homosexuality is included.

251 DIESBACH, GHISLAIN De. "The Margravine's Page." In *The Toys of Princes*, translated by Richard Howard. New York: Pantheon, 1962. Originally published as *Iphigénie en Thruinge; Nouvelles*. Paris: R. Julliard, 1960. [M]

A handsome young page receives a premonition about the death of a beautiful prince. The prince later becomes the page's lover.

252 DINESEN, ISAK [pseudonym of Karen Blixen]. "The Monkey." In *Seven Gothic Tales*. New York: H. Smith & R. Hass, 1934. [F?, M]

A young Bavarian nobleman, enmeshed in an unpleasant homosexual scandal, seeks the counsel of his wise Aunt Cathinka, prioress of a wealthy cloister for unmarried ladies. Together they trick an eighteen-year-old neighbor (who is very likely a lesbian) into a marriage of convenience with the nephew. The title of the story refers to the prioress's supernatural pet, on which the story's conclusion pivots.

253 DINESEN, ISAK [pseudonym of Karen Blixen]. "The Sailor-Boy's Tale." In *Winter's Tales*. New York: Random House, 1943. [m]

A young sailor rescues a trapped falcon. He later kills a homosexual Russian sailor who, by making passes at the younger man, has been detaining the sailor from his girlfriend. The falcon turns out to be an old witch, who returns the favor and rescues the sailor from danger. A classically written Gothic tale.

254 DISCH, THOMAS M[ICHAEL]. "Apollo." In *Getting into Death and Other Stories*. London: Rupert Hart-Davis, 1973. Reprint. New York: Knopf, 1976. [M]

The bisexual god Apollo makes the contemporary Greenwich Village scene. Among his conquests is the Frisbee-throwing Hyacinthus, and their affair is described with warmth and humor.

255 DISCH, THOMAS M[ICHAEL]. *The Businessman*. New York: Harper & Row, 1984. [M]

Bob Glandier, a thoroughly despicable businessman, plots to murder his wife Giselle, but he finds himself haunted by her ghost after her death. Secondary characters include Giselle's gay uncle, famous nineteenth-century actress Adah Menken, and poet John Berrymore. A brutally funny yet genuinely scary horror novel in which a gay sensibility is notable throughout.

256 DISCH, THOMAS M[ICHAEL]. *Camp Concentration*. London: Rupert Hart-Davis, 1968. Reprint. Garden City, N.Y.: Doubleday, 1969. [m]

A powerful work that is rich in allegory and steeped in literary allusion. Louis Sacchetti and other Vietnam War resisters are put in a camp and subjected to horrifying medical experimentation. The United States government has inoculated them with a serum that drastically increases human intelligence yet ultimately brings death. Louis journalizes the interactions among the prisoners as their minds geometrically expand while their physical condition deteriorates. This absorbing book contains a single woman character – a perpetrator of the inhumane experiment – and two plaintive gay males.

257 DISCH, THOMAS M[ICHAEL]. "The Colors." *New Worlds*, December 1969. Reprinted in *Getting into Death and Other Stories*. London: Rupert Hart-Davis, 1973. Reprint. New York: Knopf, 1976. [m]

Using his gay friend's consciousness-altering device that utilizes color and light for its hallucinatory effect, a young man finds himself increasingly drawn into a dreamlike trance. The friend's homosexuality is handled in a subtle yet matter-of-fact manner.

258 DISCH, THOMAS M[ICHAEL]. "Displaying the Flag." In *Getting into Death and Other Stories*. London: Rupert Hart-Davis, 1973. Reprint. New York: Knopf, 1976. [M]

Leonard Dworkin, a young business executive guilt-ridden over his fetish for black leather, flies to a behavior clinic in Britain to eliminate his deviation through aversion shock treatments. He returns a changed man. He avoids leather bars but gravitates toward a small restaurant that serves "Libertyburgers" and glorifies the American flag. Dworkin's suppression of the original turn-on for leather causes displays of superpatriotism, which develop into fascism. The story gives no insight into the gay male leather scene itself and it equates sadomasochism with reactionary politics.

259 DISCH, THOMAS M[ICHAEL]. "Et in Arcadia Ego." In *Quark/2*, edited by Samuel R. Delany and Marilyn Hacker. New York: Paperback Library, 1971. [m]

In this disquieting memorial to a slain captain, the crew of a starship relate their discovery of an agrarian world and the subsequent murder of their mission's leader. The planet's inhabitants sacrifice the captain to their deity. In retaliation, the starship crew destroys the planet, obliterating an entire people. The deceased was loved, physically and emotionally, by both the men and women of the crew.

260 DISCH, THOMAS M[ICHAEL]. "The Joycelin Shrager Story." In *Getting into Death and Other Stories*. London: Rupert Hart-Davis, 1973. Reprint. New York: Knopf, 1976. [m]

When Donald Lang, a pioneer in New York's experimental film movement, meets promising young filmmaker Joycelin Shrager, he thinks himself invulnerable to love, but he soon finds this to be untrue. The story chronicles Lang's developing involvement with Shrager's hectic life and surreal artistic vision. Two of Shrager's best friends are gay men whose personalities are a bit sensationalized but believable.

261 DISCH, THOMAS M[ICHAEL]. "Let Us Quickly Hasten to the Gate of Ivory." In *Quark/1*, edited by Samuel R. Delany and Marilyn Hacker. New York: Paperback Library, 1970. [m]

A sister and brother get trapped in an eerie, supernatural cemetery while on their annual pilgrimage to their parents' grave. As the two meander among the tombstones they begin to reminisce, and it is slowly revealed that the sister was once married to a homosexual.

262 DISCH, THOMAS M[ICHAEL]. "Narcissus." In *Holding Your Eight Hands*, edited by Edward Lucie-Smith. Garden City, N.Y.: Doubleday, 1969. [M]

In this science-fiction poem, Disch imagines a future in which technology has developed perfect electronic facsimiles of human beings. These cyborgs are based on an antimatter theory, making it impossible for a cyborg's "original" ever to meet her or his facsimile. Disch depicts an exception to this rule: an unhappily married twenty-first-century

mathematician meets and falls in love with his own computerized image.
A splendid rendition of the Greek Narcissus myth.

263 DISCH, THOMAS M[ICHAEL]. *On Wings of Song*. *Fantasy and Science Fiction*, February-April 1979. Reprint. New York: St. Martin's Press, 1979. [M]

In twenty-first-century America, "flying," a new form of astral projection that allows people to leave their bodies by a combination of technology and singing, has become popular. The travelers, whose physical bodies are left earthbound, are called fairies. The right-wing Christian government morally disapproves of flying but its vituperative laws do not lessen the growing number of fairies. The lifelong quest of a Bible-belt farm boy, Daniel Weinreb, is to escape his body and to fly. His attempts lead him to New York City, where flying and other forbidden pleasures are openly available. In the hope that technical training will increase his singing (and thus flying) abilities, Daniel takes voice lessons from a renowned castrati opera singer. In exchange, he is required to wear a chastity belt and to dye his skin and hair in emulation of the city's black elite. Disch handles both his male and female characters well. Daniel's bisexuality is integrated into the plot. The novel is humorous and entertaining, and it works as narrative, as irony, as satire, and as metaphor.

264 DISCH, THOMAS M[ICHAEL]. "Thesis on Social Forms and Social Controls in the U.S.A." *Fantastic*, January 1964. Reprinted in *Fun with Your New Head*. Garden City, N.Y.: Doubleday, 1971. [f, m]

An examination of twenty-first-century American society identifying schizophrenia as the predominant societal characteristic is written by a future sociology student. It examines the economic, militaristic, and sexual behavior in the United States, offering some interesting insights into American culture. Sexual freedom, including same-sex sexuality, is totally accepted and is discussed in some depth.

265 DISCH, THOMAS M[ICHAEL]. *334*. New York: Avon, 1974. [F, m]

334 is a startling novel revealing the harsh New York City life of an all-too-near future. The novel is constructed from a series of connected short stories; each revolves around inhabitants of a massive, state-run housing project, 334 East 11th Street (which gives the book its title), and together they construct a matrix through which future city life can be viewed. In some respects the author seems optimistic. A relative equality between the sexes has been achieved, and homosexuality has become a socially respectable lifestyle. But for the most part, our contemporary urban problems have simply worsened. An exemplary treatment of this theme, Disch's novel shows the struggle of human beings, both as individuals and as members of family units, to survive in increasingly hostile urban conditions. Several of *334*'s characters are homosexual. The most significant are Shrimp Hanson and her black lesbian lover, January. Several of these short stories were initially published elsewhere.

Biographical Note

Thomas Michael Disch (b. 1940) is both a skilled science-fiction author and an accomplished poet. He is also the author of *The Brave Little Toaster* (New York: Doubleday, 1986).

Homosexuality often figures as an element within his work and all his writing should be examined closely. His Victorian historical novel, *Clara Reeve*, published under the pseudonym Leonie Hargrave (New York: Knopf, 1975), has major lesbian characters. Disch discusses science fiction and sexual politics in "Taking Flight with Thomas Disch: An Interview by David Galbraith and Alexander Wilson," in *Body Politic: A Magazine for Gay Liberation* (Toronto), no. 79 (December 1981). Biographical information on Disch may be found in Brian Ash's *Who's Who in Science Fiction* (New York: Taplinger, 1976) and in *Contemporary Authors*, vols. 23-24, ed. Barbara Harte and Carolyn Riley (Detroit: Gale, 1970).

---

266 DONNELLY, NISA. *The Bar Stories: A Novel after All*. New York: St. Martin's, 1989. [F]

Donnelly's *Bar Stories* is an entertaining series of short stories set in a popular California lesbian bar. The women of Babe's bar constitute the spectrum of the lesbian community. Babe Daniels, the bar's owner, is a strong business woman "who kept a dildo under the pillow and back issues of *Penthouse* under the bed." Her longtime lover, Sharon, is a lesbian mother. Matty, a customer, is a member of the Radical Womyn's Center. Kate is a photographer, searching for herself. These women, described with great warmth, build a community of love, passion, and survival. Toward the end of the novel, a lesbian vampire named Mara begins to frequent Babe's, but this element of fantasy seems incongruous with the rest of the novel.

267 DOUGLAS, LAUREN WRIGHT. *In the Blood*. Tallahassee, Fla.: Naiad, 1989. [F]

Biological warfare has devastated the United States. The nation has been put under quarantine by rest of the world and has broken into regional factions. A military unit comprised of lesbian soldiers is assigned to accompany virologist Dr. Ashe to the California border. Along the way, Ashe falls in love with a young corporal and they set off for a legendary women's community. Not very deep, but fun reading.

Biographical Note
Lauren Wright Douglas (b. 1947) is also the author of the lesbian-themed, non-science-fiction novels *The Always Anonymous Beast* (Tallahassee, Fla.: Naiad, 1987) and *Osten's Bay*, as Zenobia N. Vole (Tallahassee, Fla.: Naiad, 1988). She has plans to write a sequel to *In the Blood*.

268 DRAKE, DAVID. *Hammer's Slammers*. New York: Ace, 1979. [m]
A series of stories revolving around a group of intergalactic mercenaries. One of the paid soldiers is a psychopathic, vicious homosexual.

269 DUANE, DIANE. *Deep Wizardry*. New York: Delacorte, 1985. [m?]
In this sequel to *So You Want to Be a Wizard*, thirteen-year-old wizard Nita Callahan and her best friend Kit assist a kindly whale-wizard battle an evil power. As in Duane's earlier volume, they are aided by writer Tom Swale and media executive Carl Romero, two men who share a house in New York. Given the author's intended audience, there is no indication that Swale and Romero are gay, but the implication is obvious.

DUANE, DIANE. Epic Tales of the Five Series. [f, M]:

270 ▪ *The Door into Fire*. New York: Dell, 1979.

271 ▪ *The Door into Shadow*. New York: Bluejay, 1984.
An enjoyable fantasy utilizing a heroic quest, magic, and strong gay and lesbian characters. Herewiss Hearn's son is a sorcerer with a problem. He has been unable to tap the Power of the Flame that dwells within him. He is experienced enough in sorcery to rescue his lover, Prince Freelorn of Arlen, when Freelorn and his band get trapped in an old keep, but it is not until a chance meeting with the Goddess that Herewiss is offered the magical key to himself. Together Freelorn and Herewiss battle sorcery, armies, and dragons. Their relationship is a central component of the series, and same-sex love (both male and female) is common and approved of throughout Duane's fantasy world.

272 DUANE, DIANE. *So You Want to Be a Wizard*. New York: Delacorte, 1983. [m?]
The discovery of instructions to the ancient art of wizardry in the children's room of the public library propels Nita Callahan into adventure and danger. She is joined by her young Hispanic friend Kit, an impish white hole (the opposite of a black hole) named Fred, and senior wizards Tom and Carl (an older gay male couple). Duane "desexes" Tom and Carl for her younger readers.

Biographical Note
Diane Duane (b. 1952) is also the author of the following Star Trek novels: *The Wounded Sky* (New York: Pocket Books, 1983); *My Enemy, My Ally* (New York: Pocket Books, 1984); *The Romulan Way*, with Peter Morwood (New York: Pocket Books, 1987); and *Spock's World* (New York: Pocket Books, 1988). The third novel in her Wizard series, *High Wizardry*, is forthcoming. Duane discusses her writing and her sexuality in Jeffrey Elliot's "Interview: Diane Duane," in *Starship*, Fall 1980.

DUCASSE, ISIDORE LUCIEN. *See* LAUTRÉAMONT, Comte de (pseudonym)

273 DUNN, DENNIS. *The Big Trucker: A Magical Novel*. San Francisco: Dancing Rock Press, 1979. [M?]

The Big Trucker, a burly truck driver who rides the nation's highways seeking the "Big Load," gives a lift to a stranded college radical, known as Kid, who is hitching home from the 1968 March on Washington. Somewhere in the Midwest, the pair hit a timewarp and are transported into the fantastic world of Our Sweet Land. There, the garish excesses of American consumerism predominate. The Big Trucker and his young companion set off to meet the ruler of this wacky place: a giant talking hamburger named Big Mac. They meet up with Wanda and Johnny Apple and form a loving four-way relationship. Homosexuality is implicit in this domestic arrangement. On a more subtle level, the Big Trucker's search for the elusive Big Load easily can be seen as a homosexual metaphor.

274 DYKEWOMAN, ELANA. *They Will Know Me by My Teeth*. Northampton, Mass.: Megaera Press, 1976. [F]

This collection of lesbian short stories and poems contains three Amazon fantasies about tribes of women growing and loving together. "How We Got the Moon" and "Solstice Story" are lesbian creation myths. "The Journal She Kept" is a poem about a women's tribe in the distant past or far future.

Biographical Note
Elana Dykewoman is also the author of *Riverfinger Women* (Plainfield, Vt.: Daughters, 1974), a nonfantasy lesbian novel written under her former name, Elana Nachman, and a poetry volume, *Fragments from Lesbos* (Langlois, Oreg.: Diaspora Distribution, 1981). Since 1987 she has been the editor and publisher of *Sinister Wisdom*.

275 EAKINS, WILLIAM K. *Key West, 2720, A.D.* Pound Ridge, N.Y.:
Knights Press, 1989. [M]
      In Eakins's future vision, the United States has crumbled and the
continent is ruled by small, independent city-states. Gays are viciously
persecuted, sometimes exterminated, except in Key West, where Mayor
(and gay hero) Sam Phoe has established a sanctuary for homosexuals.
Things begin to heat up (in more ways than one) when Sam rescues a
gay teenager named Gibb, who is running away from homophobic
violence.

276 EDDINGS, DAVID. *The Elenium: The Diamond Throne.* New York:
Del Rey, 1989. [m]
      Beautiful Queen Ehlana is dying of a magically induced sickness
and lies frozen in a cube of crystal. The evil priest Annias rules the land.
The Queen's Champion, Sparhawk, returns from a ten-year exile, and
he joins forces with the sorceress Sephrenia and a psychically powerful
girl. They begin a quest to save the Queen. Among the evil priest's nasty
toadies is the "notorious pederast" Baron Harparin. Harparin wears
fancy clothes, fawns over his footmen, and helps Annias arrange a mass
rape and murder. Although Harparin is the only overtly homosexual
character, the tone of Elenian court life is foppish and effeminate. The
attitude of Sparhawk and his comrades toward the regal "butterflies" is
one of derision and ridicule. *The Diamond Throne* is the first of the
Elenium trilogy, to be followed by *The Ruby Knight* and *The Sapphire
Rose.*

EDGAR, ALFRED. *See* LYNDON, BARRE (pseudonym)

277 EDWARD, ALAN. "The Stake." *Panthology Two: Stories about Boy
Love.* Amsterdam: Coltsfoot Press, 1982. [M]
      A proper Englishman encounters a sexy and obliging thirteen-
year-old boy while traveling through Eastern Europe. As Edward's
humorous story recounts, the youngster turns out to be a vampire.

278 EFFINGER, GEORGE ALEC. *A Fire in the Sun.* New York:
Doubleday, Foundation, 1989. [m]
      Effinger sets his sequel to the exciting *When Gravity Fails* in the
same sleazy, decaying Arabic ghetto. Once again, detective Marid
Audran must investigate a crime. Several of the secondary characters
are gay men.

279 EFFINGER, GEORGE ALEC. *When Gravity Fails.* New York: Arbor
House, 1986. [m, X]
      Effinger's novel is an exciting mix of hard-boiled detective novel
and cyberpunk thriller. Marid Audran is a private eye who lives in a

sleazy, decaying Arabic ghetto. Audran's world is rife with designer drugs, computer crime, and prostitution, but the detective avoids the latest craze: surgical implantation of computer modules in order to experience new personalities. A series of brutal murders, apparently committed by a person under the influence of one of these personality modules, throws Audran into a net of corruption and violence. Audran's lover is a transsexual prostitute, and transsexual and gay male characters appear throughout the novel. Effinger combines a fast-paced plot with skillful writing to produce an atmospheric and effective novel.

280 EISENSTEIN, PHYLLIS. *Sorcerer's Son.* New York: Ballantine, Del Rey, 1979. [X]

The demon Gildrum is given different bodies to wear by its master, Smada Rezhyk. Around Rezhyk's castle Gildrum is a fourteen-year-old girl and Rezhyk's sexual partner. But Gildrum can also be male, and in a man's form the demon falls in love with a sorceress, Delivef Ormoza. In their own world demons have only one gender but mate and reproduce with each other. Ormoza has a very passive role as does the only other woman character, a seer who appears toward the end of the novel. It is interesting that Gildrum, the sex-changing demon, is by far the most human of all the characters.

281 EKLUND, GORDON. "The Anaconda's Smile." *Fantasy and Science Fiction*, May 1979. [F]

Two Americans are sent deep into the Amazon basin to investigate a U.F.O. sighting. There, they find a run-down home filled with strangely behaving children and an odd menagerie of animals. One of the Americans is a lesbian who is gruesomely eaten by a savage army of wild ants at the conclusion of the story.

282 EKLUND, GORDON, and BENFORD, GREGORY. "What Did You Do Last Year?" In *Universe Six*, edited by Terry Carr. Garden City, N.Y.: Doubleday, 1976. [f]

This rather bizarre satire on contemporary heterosexual marriages in which two couples hold annual reunions has marginal lesbian content: both women are bisexual and at one point have had an affair.

ELDRIDGE, PAUL. *See* VIERECK, GEORGE SYLVESTER (joint author)

283 ELLIOT, SUMNER LOCKE. *Going.* New York: Harper & Row, 1975. [m]

The United States has become an openly fascist state that mandates behavior modification as a means of social control and enforces euthanasia of older citizens who are considered a burden on society. An active and lucid older woman named Tess carefully reviews the passions and sorrows of her life as she accepts her impending death. The author portrays Tess with skill and compassion but is not as effective with his political prophecy, and his lack of social analysis weakens the story. The gay male minor character is portrayed sympathetically.

284 ELLISON, HARLAN. "Catman." In *Final Stage: The Ultimate Science Fiction Anthology*, edited by Edward L. Ferman and Barry N. Malzberg. New York: Charterhouse, 1974. [f, m]

Ellison depicts a future society in which most people are bisexual. The ultimate perversion in such a permissive environment is intercourse between human and robot. A young thief finds himself becoming attracted to this option. Most of the story's characters, other than the two primary ones, are gay or bisexual. Gay men are referred to as "twinkle boys."

285 ELLISON, HARLAN. "Enter the Fanatic, Stage Center." In *Gentleman Junkie; and Other Stories of the Hung-Up Generation*. Evanston, Ill.: Regency, 1961. [f]

A small town is wholly disrupted when a mysterious and sinister artist reveals the community's best-kept secrets by means of his paintings. Wilma Foltin, the town's librarian, is thus exposed as a lesbian. An interesting story.

286 ELLISON, HARLAN. "A Path through the Darkness." *Fling Magazine*, January 1963. Reprinted in *Love Ain't Nothing but Sex Misspelled*. New York: Trident, 1968. [F, m]

This short story concerns a homophobic author and his affair with a young lesbian named Stephie. Stephie is portrayed as a totally perverted and pitiful creature, likened to a cell of botulism, and the gay male minor characters fare little better.

287 ELLISON, HARLAN. "Sally in Our Alley." *Knave Magazine*, December 1959. Reprinted in *Gentleman Junkie; and Other Stories of the Hung-Up Generation*. Evanston, Ill.: Regency, 1961. [f]

A young woman is the victim in this murder story set in a beatnik neighborhood. An innocuous lesbian couple are incidental characters.

288 ELLISON, HARLAN. "World of Women." *Fantastic*, February 1957. [F?]

Until recently, a matriarchal world has been ruled by five benevolent sisters. However, one of the sisters has gone insane and executed nearly all the men on the planet. A man disguised as a woman is sent to stop her. Lesbianism is specifically mentioned in passing and referred to as a perversion.

289 ELLISON, HARLAN, and ZELAZNY, ROGER. "Come to Me Not in Winter's White." *Fantasy and Science Fiction*, October 1969. Reprinted in *Partners in Wonder*, edited by Harlan Ellison. New York: Walker & Co., 1971. [F]

Lesbianism is a major theme in this story about the nature of time and the consequences of fooling with it. A scientist, finding his beloved wife dying of an incurable disease, creates a room for her in which time becomes frozen. Thus, his wife can remain alive and unaged until a cure can be developed. Complications arise when the scientist hires a woman companion to keep his wife company and the two women fall in love.

Biographical Note

Harlan Ellison (b. 1934) has won six and a half Hugo awards and three Nebula awards for his often controversial science fiction. He discusses his opinions on homosexuality in Jeremy Hughes's article "Sex in the Year 2500," in *In Touch for Men*, July 1982.

---

290 ENGH, M. J. *Arslan*. New York: Warner, 1976. [M]

Arslan, a contemporary Alexander the Great, has come out of Turkistan and conquered the world at the young age of twenty-five. He turns established political and economic systems upside down, institutes a dictatorship, and rules the world from his headquarters in a small American town. Arslan rapes a schoolboy, Morgan Hunt, and forces him into an intimate and long-lasting sexual relationship. The quality of this novel's descriptions of Morgan's masochism and self-knowledge makes it a grade above conventional conqueror science fiction.

291 ENNIS, CATHERINE. *To the Lightning*. Tallahassee, Fla.: Naiad, 1988. [F]

This lesbian fantasy works as a mixture of soap opera and lesbian erotica. Chris, recovering from the death of her lesbian lover, and Meredith, a recent divorcee, get zapped by a flash of lightning while on a camping trip. They are transported to a prehistoric valley where they must become female Robinson Crusoes to survive. Between earthquakes, wild boar attacks, and assorted other primordial terrors, the two women discover their love and physical desire for each other. Descriptions of lesbian lovemaking are plentiful, but the author does not attempt an explanation for the time travel.

292 ERMAYNE, LAURAJEAN [pseudonym of Forrest J. Ackerman]. "The Radclyffe Effect." In *The Science Fiction Worlds of Forrest Ackerman and Friends*. Reseda, Calif.: Powell Publications, 1969. [F]

This amusing short story concerns the initial reactions to the disappearance of the Earth's male population by the world's women. The extreme brevity of the story allows for little exploration of the possibilities.

293 ESSER, KEVIN. *Dance of the Warriors*. Amsterdam: Acolyte Press, 1988. [M]

Dance of the Warriors is both an imaginative extrapolation and a clear warning. Esser envisions a brutal future in which a fundamentalist Christian dictatorship is destroying America with its proscriptive morality. Homosexuals, particularly intergenerational lovers, are being rounded up and exterminated. Thirteen-year-old Teddy and his slightly older Chicano lover Cisco join the "vags," a gang of vagabond youths living in the burnt-out cores of the cities, to battle the authorities and overthrow their oppressors. Esser builds his characters well and his novel is well-written. Some readers will be put off by the author's endorsement of intergenerational love. *Dance of the Warriors* is reminiscent of William Burroughs's "wild boys" fantasies.

294 ESSER, KEVIN. "The Dying of the Light." In *The First Acolyte Reader*. Amsterdam: Acolyte Press, 1986. [M]

In a sexually repressive, totalitarian future, a relationship between a precocious thirteen-year-old boy and an older man brings disastrous results. This story was written as a preparatory sketch for *Dance of the Warriors*.

Biographical Note

Kevin Esser (b. 1953) is also the author of *Streetboy Dreams* (New York: Gay Presses of New York, 1983) and *Mad to Be Saved* (New York: Gay Presses of New York, 1985). Both novels have significant gay male content. *Dance of the Warriors* is the first volume of a proposed trilogy.

---

295 ESTACADA, ALIX, and BONA DEA, MARIDES. "Excerpt from *Nozama*." *Women* (Baltimore) 5, no. 1 (1976). [F]

A short excerpt from an unpublished book about the planet Nozama, which is inhabited exclusively by lesbians. This taste details a farmer's dream of bringing the varying factions of Nozama together in harmony. No overt lesbianism is included in the excerpt.

ESTRIDGEL, ROBIN. *See* LORAINE, PHILIP (pseudonym)

296 EWERS, HANNS HEINZ. *Alraune*. Translated by Guy Endore. Illustrated by Mahlon Blaine. New York: John Day, 1929. Originally published as *Alraune; Die Geschichte eine lebenden Wesens*. Illustrated by Ilna Ewers-Wunderwald. Munich: G. Muller, 1911. [F, m]

Ewers's science fantasy may have rivaled Krafft-Ebing for sexual titillation in its day. Frank Braun, hero of several of Ewers's books, convinces his uncle to conduct a heinous experiment. They impregnate a prostitute with the sperm of a recently executed murderer. The prostitute dies giving birth to a baby girl who the two men name Alraune. Alraune is feminine evil incarnate; the lives of all whom she touches quickly fall to ruin. Her prostitute mother is but the first of her victims. She seduces both sexes, and two lesbians are among those drawn into her alluringly fatal web. It is not until she falls in love with Braun that the beautiful young villain is brought to her dramatic end. Ewers's comment on bourgeois morals is obvious: Alraune's victims are often more decadent and corrupt than she is and deserve what they get. Alraune's bisexuality, the lesbianism of her women lovers, and the pedophilia of Braun's pompous uncle are distinct components of Ewers's intentionally twisted fantasy. The kinky and sexist eroticism of the book reflects the sexual permissiveness and political air of Germany at the time, and the influence of the expressionist artistic aesthetic is noticeable.

297 FAIRBAIRNS, ZOË. *Benefits*. London: Virago, 1979. [F]

This strongly feminist British novel, spanning several decades, deals with the governmental manipulations of a feminist political demand. In 1976, radical feminists turn a run-down London housing project into a commune exclusively for the habitation of women and demand payment to all women who work in the home and rear children. This demand grows into a feminist platform, and the government ostensibly gives in, yet it uses these cash benefits to enforce traditional sex roles and to increase the oppression of women. When the government's racist experiment in eugenics accidentally causes serious birth defects in all newborns, British women begin their revolution in earnest. The author portrays women's sexual love for women in the two lesbian major characters and in the predominantly heterosexual feminist protagonist.

298 FALKON, FELIX LANCE [pseudonym]. "Good Eating." In *Hitchhiked and Other Stories*. San Diego: Phenix, 1969. [M]

Pornographic gay male science fiction.

299 FALKON, FELIX LANCE [pseudonym]. *Hung in Space*. San Diego: Phenix, 1969. [M]
Pornographic gay male science fiction.

300 FALKON, FELIX LANCE [pseudonym]. "Spaceport Pickup." In *Nine Easy Pieces*. San Diego: Greenleaf Classics, 1971. [M]
Pornographic gay male science fiction.

301 FALKON, FELIX LANCE [pseudonym]. "Vice-Versal." In *Nine Easy Pieces*. San Diego: Greenleaf Classics, 1971. [M]
Pornographic gay male science fiction.

302 FARMER, PHILIP JOSE. *Blown*. North Hollywood, Calif.: Essex House, 1969. [f, m, X]
Blown continues the semipornographic story the author began in *The Image of the Beast* (see citation below). Again, hero Herald Childe battles his bloodthirsty and sex-driven alien adversaries, this time aided by science-fiction writer, collector, and fan, Forrest J. Ackerman. The sexuality is as explicit as in the earlier book, and the majority of it is violent. Some lesbian and gay male sexual activity is included.

303 FARMER, PHILIP JOSE. *A Feast Unknown*. North Hollywood, Calif.: Essex House, 1969. [f, M]
Farmer's exploration of the connection between violence and sexual repression produces a near-pornographic novel of brutality and bloodshed. Lord Grandrith and Doc Caliban, Farmer's versions of the 1930s fantasy figures Tarzan and Doc Savage, find themselves affected by a strange force. They involuntarily become sexually aroused and ejaculate whenever they kill someone, which, in the course of Farmer's novel, is often. This bizarre curse has been brought about by the mysterious organization of immortals, known as the "Nine," who indulge in violent bisexual orgies, and who seek to pit Grandrith and Doc against each other. Overt homosexuality is viewed as neurotic compulsive behavior.

304 FARMER, PHILIP JOSE. *Flesh*. New York: Beacon, 1960. [m]
An astronaut returns home after 800 years of exploring the stars. The Earth he returns to has dispensed with science and technology and has again become a tribal agricultural society. The astronaut is renamed "Sunhero" because he came out of the sky. At one point, he is captured by a tribe of homosexual warriors who are depicted as swishy stereotypes despite their bravery.

305 FARMER, PHILIP JOSE. *The Image of the Beast*. North Hollywood, Calif.: Essex House, 1968. [m, X]

The brutal sex murder of his partner throws private detective Herald Childe into a series of sexually explicit encounters involving a vicious band of vampires, werewolves, and other alien sex fiends. Sections of the novel are as tasteless and raunchy as any found in a pornographic paperback, and the entire novel barely rises above this caliber. Some gay male sexual activity can be found among the excesses.

306 FARMER, PHILIP JOSE. "Riders of the Purple Wage." In *Dangerous Visions*, edited by Harlan Ellison. Garden City, N.Y.: Doubleday, 1967. [m]

In a future both better and worse than our present situation, a young male artist wins public acclaim despite his refusal to sleep with a renowned male art critic. The author depicts increasing violence, unemployment, overpopulation, environmental destruction, and bureaucratic overload. Sexual expression is a social expectation, beginning in the crib with socially approved incest and continuing through promiscuous adolescence into adulthood, when many become addicted to orgasm-inducing machines. Propagation is governmentally discouraged while homosexuality is regarded as just one more form of sexual expression. The author shows his male characters in conflict with, yet at home in, a chaotic and turbulent environment. The few female characters are sketched as angry lovers, sluggish mothers, or objects of desire and repulsion.

307 FAST, JONATHAN. *The Secrets of Synchronicity*. New York: Signet, 1977. [m]

Adolescent Stephin is lured away from his cozy home by an attractive job offer. The offer is a trick and Stephin becomes a slave in the mines of Slabour. By a series of fortuitous occurrences, he becomes the liberator of Slabour's slaves and eventually destroys the galactic capitalist system. His luck is caused by a mineral that, when eaten in small doses, connects seemingly random events in ways that benefit the consumer. The portrayals of women as either prostitutes (scrugals) or wives and of homosexuals as sexually abusive authority figures are clichéd treatments.

308 FAST, JULIUS. *The League of Grey-Eyed Women*. Philadelphia: Lippincott, 1970. [f]

All telepaths are grey-eyed women. There are no telepathic men because telepathy is a sex-linked genetic trait. In addition to causing grey eyes, regardless of race, this telepathic gift also causes extreme sensitivity, so very few of the telepathic women can tolerate the embraces of, let alone marriage with, nontelepaths. Consequently, most of them live a lesbian life-style with each other. The League's goal is to change *Homo sapiens* into *Homo telepathens*, a (heterosexual) species without war, racism, or deception. Once heterosexuality is an option, most of the women make that their preference but, with the dearth of grey-eyed men, not their practice.

309 FEINBERG, KAREN. "The Sender of Dreams." *Amazon Quarterly* (Berkeley, Calif.), July 1974. Reprinted in *The Lesbian Reader*, edited by Gina Covina and Laurel Galana. Oakland, Calif.: Amazon Press, 1975. [F]

In a small New England community, two women emerge as lesbians. One has the power to create and send dreams, a gift that runs in the female line of her family. The other has the power to plant thoughts and desires in other people's minds. They use their powers to attract each other without the notice of their conservative neighbors, finding an end to fear in each other's arms.

310 FINCH, SHEILA. *Infinity's Web*. New York: Bantam, 1985. [F]

Finch's award-winning first novel describes four women in four different realities, who are, in fact, all facets of one woman. Ann is an unhappy wife and mother; Val is a lesbian professor; Stacey is a free-loving heterosexual; and Tasha, a tarot card-reading sorceress. Similar to Russ's *The Female Man*, but with a stronger narrative and a less demanding style.

311 FISHER, M[ARY] F[RANCES] K[ENNEDY]. *Not Now, but Now*. New York: Viking, 1947. [f]

Fisher's novel, centering on an arrogant, bisexual, time-traveling woman who wrecks the life of everyone she meets, was considered witty, wicked, and indecent at the time of its publication. The sharp-tongued protagonist, Jeannie, effortlessly skips between the nineteenth and twentieth centuries by getting on a public train and magically getting off in a different time period. All of her romantic and financially rewarding affairs are short because, ironically, she condemns the conduct of her partners as sordid, simplistic, and beneath her scruples. In Illinois in 1947, she becomes attracted to a high school senior, Barbara. When Jeannie loses interest, she simply jumps to another time period, leaving Barbara to face her family's homophobia without support.

312 FISK, NICHOLAS. "Find the Lady." In *New Dimensions Five*, edited by Robert Silverberg. New York: Harper & Row, 1975. [M]

Two British homosexuals survive a worldwide alien invasion by selling dubious antiques to their mechanical conquerors. The two men are depicted as wimpy, fussy, and exceedingly camp, but also as stubborn survivors.

313 FITZGIBBON, CONSTANTINE. *When the Kissing Had to Stop.* London: Cassell, 1960. Reprint. New York: W. W. Norton, 1960. [m]

A cold-war prediction tells of Britain's fall into the hands of totalitarian socialists. As a result of this political disaster, England becomes a satellite of the Soviet Union and English citizens are imprisoned in Siberian work camps. A minor character is a simpering, traitorous homosexual. Women are unaware of their oppression, and their sexuality is determined by their equally unaware male lovers. The cold-war vision may seem all too familiar to contemporary readers.

314 FLETCHER, GEORGE U. [pseudonym of Fletcher Pratt]. *The Well of the Unicorn.* New York: William Sloane, 1948. [F?, m]

Readers may be unwilling to plow through the elaborate details in the construction of Pratt's remarkable fantasy world, but this epic is a classic. Five male homosexuals and two heterosexual women passing as men play a vital part in a subjugated people's revolt against their oppressors, the Vulks. The heterosexual protagonist looks down upon the male-male love that surrounds him, but the author has refrained from using solely homophobic stereotypes. The lisping, boy-loving Duke Roger is the first gay character introduced; the next is the arrogant and effeminate Prince Auraruis. The author balances the effeminate images with those of the strong Mikalegon and the brave Star Captain Pleiander and the lover they share, a gentle fisherman named Visto. The fantasy is interesting, if somewhat tedious, and is notable also for its headstrong, cross-dressing female characters. Later editions of the novel were printed under the author's real name.

315 FORBES, CAROLINE. "The Comet's Tale." In *The Needle on Full.* London: Onlywomen Press, 1985. [F]

The author is a British lesbian whose strong feminist politics are evident throughout her fiction. Her novella-length "The Comet's Tale" focuses on two women astronauts who develop a close personal relationship while on a twenty-year spaceflight.

316 FORBES, CAROLINE. "London Fields." In *The Needle on Full.* London: Onlywomen Press, 1985. [F]

A mysterious genetic mutation has caused the extinction of all human males. At the same time women have discovered "the power of women to control their fertility" and Britain is now populated entirely by lesbians. But suddenly a group of healthy young men are discovered, and the women must decide what to do.

317 FORBES, CAROLINE. "The Needle on Full." In *The Needle on Full.* London: Onlywomen Press, 1985. [F]

A married woman in a class-structured, gas-rationed future Britain escapes her confining marriage and discovers love and rebellion when an attractive young lesbian enters her life.

318 FORBES, CAROLINE. "Night Life." In *The Needle on Full*. London: Onlywomen Press, 1985. [F?]

The three women characters live in a bleak and oppressive future. One of them is eventually overcome by the hopelessness of her situation, but two survive, presumably by becoming lesbian lovers.

319 FORREST, KATHERINE V. *Daughters of the Coral Dawn*. Tallahassee, Fla.: Naiad, 1984. [F]

Forrest is one of the current stellar lights of lesbian fiction. Her "Kate Delafield" mysteries have acquired a devoted following who appreciate Forrest's use of exciting action and hot lesbian sexuality. In *Daughters of a Coral Dawn*, Forrest's first venture into science fiction, thousands of women, descendants of a single alien mother, flee Earth to colonize a women-only world. While the plot meanders a bit and is not as effective as some of Forrest's best mysteries, the novel shows its author to have great promise in the science-fiction field.

320 FORREST, KATHERINE V. "The Gift." In *Swords and Dreams*. Tallahassee, Fla.: Naiad, 1987. [F]

Two lesbian mothers must trust an alien species with their daughter's life to cure her of a disability.

321 FORREST, KATHERINE V. "Mother Was an Alien." In *Swords and Dreams*. Tallahassee, Fla.: Naiad, 1987. [F]

A female alien, smuggled to Earth by her male lover, begins a mysterious, psychic, all-female family. An excerpt from, and "prequel" to, *Daughters of the Coral Dawn*.

322 FORREST, KATHERINE V. "O Captain, My Captain." In *Swords and Dreams*. Tallahassee, Fla.: Naiad, 1987. [F]

A vampiritic lesbian space captain gets her nourishment from cunnilingus in this spicy combination of science fiction and horror.

323 FORREST, KATHERINE V. "The Test." In *Swords and Dreams*. Tallahassee, Fla.: Naiad, 1987. [F, M]

"The Test" offers a brief glimpse into a future in which homosexuality is recognized as humankind's next evolutionary step.

Biographical Note

Katherine V. Forrest (b. 1939) is a major voice in contemporary lesbian fiction. She is also the author of *Curious Wine* (Tallahassee, Fla.: Naiad,

1983), *Amateur City* (Tallahassee, Fla.: Naiad, 1984), *An Emergence of Green* (Tallahassee, Fla.: Naiad, 1986), *Murder at the Nightwood Bar* (Tallahassee, Fla.: Naiad, 1987), and *The Beverly Malibu* (Tallahassee, Fla.: Naiad, 1989). All are significantly lesbian in content.

See also McKINLAY, M. CATHERINE (pseudonym)

324 FORSTCHEN, WILLIAM R. *The Alexandrian Ring*. New York: Ballantine, 1987. [M?]

Alexander the Great and a huge, wolflike alien are illegally transported through time by gambler Corbin Goblona to lead opposing armies on the isolated ring-world of Kolbard. The rulers of this future civilization launch interplanetary war games and then speculate on the outcomes, but after centuries of violence these amusements have been banned. There is mention of Alexander's lifelong companion and his "strange" love for Bagoas, his eunuch lover, but Alexander's sexual identity is not the author's focus.

325 FORSTER, E[DWARD] M[ORGAN]. "The Classical Annex." In *The Life to Come, and Other Stories*. London: Edward Arnold, 1972. Reprint. New York: W. W. Norton, 1973. [M]

A lusty supernatural entity, having survived since ancient Grecian days, wreaks havoc on the Bigglemouth Municipal Museum by seducing the curator's son. Written around 1931.

326 FORSTER, E[DWARD] M[ORGAN]. "The Curate's Friend." In *The Celestial Omnibus and Other Stories*. London: Sidgwick & Jackson, 1911. Reprint. New York: Knopf, 1923. [M?]

A highly suggestive story about a bachelor curate and an impish faun who befriends him.

327 FORSTER, E[DWARD] M[ORGAN]. "Dr. Woolacott." In *The Life to Come, and Other Stories*. London: Edward Arnold, 1972. Reprint. New York: W. W. Norton, 1973. [M]

A young invalid, Clesant, is seduced by a handsome ghost in this haunting romantic fantasy, which was written in 1927.

Biographical Note

E. M. Forster (1879-1970) has been called one of Britain's leading twentieth-century novelists. He was a member of the artistically influential circle of upper-class friends known as the "Bloomsbury group," which included such writers as Virginia Woolf and Lytton Strachey. Much of Forster's short-story output was science fiction and fantasy, most of which is collected in *The*

Eternal Moment (New York: Harcourt, Brace & Co., 1928) and *The Celestial Omnibus and Other Stories* (New York: Knopf, 1923).

Virtually all of Forster's work that reflected his own homosexuality remained unpublished during his lifetime, including his major gay male novel *Maurice* (New York: W. W. Norton, 1971) and the stories collected in *The Life to Come, and Other Stories* (London: Edward Arnold, 1972). A gay male critique of Forster's work, including many of his fantasy tales, can be found in Jeffrey Meyer's *Homosexuality and Literature 1890-1930* (London: Athlone Press, 1977). *E. M. Forster: A Life*, by P. N. Furbank (New York: Harcourt Brace Jovanovich, 1978), is the most comprehensive of the many Forster biographies to date.

---

328 FRANKLIN, PATRICK. "Sea Gift." In *Shadows of Love*, edited by Charles Jurrist. Boston: Alyson, 1988. [M]

Well-written ghost story about a young gay man in an isolated beach house who finds a mysterious lover.

FRIEDMAN, JERROLD DAVID. *See* GERROLD, DAVID (pseudonym)

329 FRIEDMAN, SANFORD. "Lifeblood." In *Still Life*. New York: E. P. Dutton; Saturday Review Press, 1975. [M, X]

Friedman's novella tells of life among the great gods of Olympus and of the "beautiful boy" Attis, the son, lover, and eventual victim of the hermaphroditic Agdistis.

330 FRYER, DONALD S. *Songs and Sonnets Atlantean*. Sauk City, Wis.: Arkham House, 1971. [m]

This small volume contains poetry and prose that is purported to be translated from the original Atlantean text, which would be 15,000 years old. Male homosexual content rests entirely upon one poem entitled "To a Youth." The volume describes many facets of Atlantean life.

331 GADD, NEVILLE. "2032: A Gay Odyssey." *Gay News* (London), no. 3 (1972). [M]

In the year 2032, homosexuals are registered by the state and allowed limited freedoms in return for loyalty to the government, abstention from promiscuity and political activity, and willingness to convert to heterosexuality "should a reliable method be discovered." A love affair between two state-registered homosexuals breaks up when one of them strays from the prescribed models of behavior.

332 GARBER, ERIC. "Uranian Worlds: The Best of Gay Sci-Fi and Fantasy." *Out / Look* (San Francisco), no. 4 (Winter 1989). [Nonfiction]
A historical survey of lesbian and gay imagery in the science-fiction and fantasy fields; includes a bibliography of works published during the 1980s.

333 GARDNER, THOMAS. "The Last Woman." *Wonder Stories*, April 1932. Reprinted in *From off This World*, edited by Leo Margulies and O. J. Friend. New York: Merlin Press, 1949. [M?]
Gardner wrote "The Last Woman" to counter ideas proposed by Wallace West in "The Last Man" (see entry below). Earth has become almost entirely populated by males. A male explorer returns from a long voyage and immediately falls in love with the last woman alive on Earth, who is kept in a display case in a museum. Together they plot an escape from the planet but are caught. Gardner hints that the progenitor of this misogynist society was homosexual.

334 GARRETT, DAVE. *The Seedseekers*. Chatsworth, Calif.: GX, 1973. [M]
Pornographic gay male science fiction. Extremely misogynist.

335 GARRETT, RANDALL. "Spatial Relationship." *Fantasy and Science Fiction*, August 1962. [M?]
A spaceship returns to Earth carrying its two male crew members. The men have been hypnotically implanted with the suggestion that there were two women aboard with whom they had sex. Readers are left with a definite suggestion that the two men had slept with each other.

336 GARTON, RAY. *Live Girls*. New York: Pocket Books, 1987. [M?]
Both the sex and the violence are continuous and graphic in Garton's contemporary vampire novel *Live Girls*. Publishing executive Davey Owen tries to escape his depression over his love life by venturing into a seedy live sex show in the heart of Times Square – the "Live Girls" of the title. What Owen doesn't realize is that the sordid peepshow booths are the headquarters of a band of bloodthirsty vampires. These erotic dead are led by the beautiful, and bisexual, Shideh, and after a sexual encounter with one of the performers, Owen finds himself developing strange hungers.

337 GARTON, RAY. "Sinema." In *Silver Scream*, edited by David J. Schow. Arlington Heights, Ill.: Dark Harvest, 1988. [M]
Garton's nasty short story features a psychopathic pedophile who makes videotapes of his murderous orgies with young boys. Unnecessary and repellent.

338 GASKELL, JANE. *The Serpent*. London: Hodder & Stoughton, 1963. [m]

    Cija, Princess of Atlantis and the protagonist of this imaginative fantasy, has been kept secluded in a high tower by her mother, the Dictatress. Cija is released upon her seventeenth birthday and is utilized by her mother for a secret mission. She is sent to seduce and kill a half-human, half-lizard named General Zerd. *The Serpent* records Cija's journey to Atlan, the legendary lost continent. At one point, she meets a young male homosexual who is heavily into drag. He is sympathetically portrayed. This is the first in an enjoyable series of books revolving around Cija and Atlan.

339 GASKELL, JANE. *A Sweet, Sweet Summer*. London: Hodder & Stoughton, 1969. Reprint. New York: St. Martin's Press, 1972. [M]

    Aliens from outer space have isolated Britain from the rest of the world. Chaos is encouraged and the streets have become battlefields. Yet life continues. This is the story of three people trying their best to survive civilization's collapse: Pel, the narrator; Conner, his best friend; and Frijja, his cousin. Pel clearly has homoerotic feelings toward Conner, but they are never consummated.

340 GAWRON, JEAN MARK. *Algorithm*. New York: Berkley, 1978. [m]

    Algorithm is complex and dense and describes an Earth of the far future. A message has been received predicting an assassination, but neither the victim's nor the assassin's identities are made clear. The entire book consists of the unraveling of this ominous mystery. Several of the characters are presented as bisexual.

341 GEARHART, SALLY MILLER. *The Wanderground: Stories of the Hill Women*. Watertown, Mass.: Persephone Press, 1978. [F, m]

    Gearhart has written a feminist future vision that complements her radical lesbian political stance. Male violence has driven women away from the male-controlled city to seek refuge in the hills. There, they have developed their own culture, based largely on psychic awareness and nature worship. *The Wanderground* recounts with a touch of magic various tales of these women. The stories are filled with warm, positive lesbian images. What few heterosexual images appear are condemnatory, but the author has some hope for the male "Gentles," a vision of what feminist-oriented gay men may eventually become. Selections from this book have appeared in *WomanSpirit*, *Ms.*, *The Witch and the Chameleon*, and *Quest: A Feminist Quarterly*. Several authors have constructed similar lesbian utopias since *The Wanderground*'s publication but rarely as well as Gearhart.

Biographical Note

Sally Miller Gearhart (b. 1931) is a well-known author, scholar, and lesbian feminist who has contributed extensively to the lesbian, feminist, and gay presses. She is the coauthor, with Susan Renne, of *The Feminist Tarot: A Guide to Intrapersonal Communication* (Watertown, Mass.: Persephone Press, 1977) and the coauthor, with William R. Johnson, of *Loving Women / Loving Men: Gay Liberation and the Church* (San Francisco: Glide, 1974).

Gearhart has written two Wanderground-related stories: "Flossie's Flashes," in *Lesbian Love Stories*, ed. Irene Zahara (Freedom, Calif.: Crossing Press, 1989), and "Roxie Raccoon," in *Through Other Eyes: Animal Stories by Women*, ed. Irene Zahara (Freedom, Calif.: Crossing Press, 1988).

Supplemental information on Gearhart can be found in the following sources: in Nancy and Casey Adair's *Word Is Out* (San Francisco: New Glide; New York: Delta, 1978); in "Sally Gearhart: Spirituality vs. Politics," by Jill Clark in *Gay Community News* (Boston, Mass.), 15 December 1979; in "Sally Gearhart: Wandering–And Wondering–on Future Ground," by M. A. Karr in the *Advocate* (San Mateo, Calif.), no. 286 (21 February 1980); and in "Interview with Sally Gearhart," by Leila Klasse in *Lesbian Insider / Insighter / Inciter* (Minneapolis, Minn.), no. 1 (August 1980).

---

342 GENTLE, MARY. "Anukazi's Daughter." In *Isaac Asimov's Tomorrow's Voices*. New York: Dial, 1984. [M]

Rax Keshanu, a woman warrior in a feudal, patriarchal culture, finds her long-standing loyalties shifting after meeting a young, gay prisoner of war from a neighboring society.

GENTLE, MARY. The Orthe Novels. [X]:

343 ■ *Golden Witchbreed*. London: Gollancz, 1983. Reprint. New York: Morrow, 1983.

344 ■ *Ancient Light*. London: Gollancz, 1987. Reprint. New York: New American Library, 1989.

In *Golden Witchbreed*, and in its sequel *Ancient Light*, Gentle skillfully constructs an imaginative and alien fantasy with a strong female protagonist that is similar in many respects to Ursula Le Guin's *The Left Hand of Darkness*. The inhabitants of the distant planet of Orthe are human in appearance, except that they remain genderless until they enter puberty. Because of their unique biology, Ortheans have developed a culture that is free of sexual roles. In both of Gentle's lengthy and richly constructed novels, Terran diplomat Lynne Christie is sent to Orthe and gets embroiled in local politics.

345 GERROLD, DAVID [pseudonym of Jerrold David Friedman]. "How We Saved the Human Race." In *With a Finger in My I*. New York: Ballantine, 1972. [M]

Composed of various bureaucratic records and items from the news media, "How We Saved the Human Race" tells of a brilliant homosexual chemist who martyrs himself to save humanity from overpopulation. He has created a highly contagious venereal disease that causes infertility. As the disease is spread throughout the world, the birthrate plummets. Developed nations seek a vaccine to distribute among their select white populations, and mass accusations of genocide by people of color result. Interoffice memos and media excerpts show that attitudes toward the gay chemist change from hatred to hero worship, but his homosexuality is covered up by the previously tolerant society.

346 GERROLD, DAVID [pseudonym of Jerrold David Friedman]. "In the Deadlands." In *With a Finger in My I*. New York: Ballantine, 1972. [M]

A prose poem form is used to create an eerie feeling of desolation, fear, and homoeroticism. Homosexuality is an integral part of the lives of soldiers who are assigned to patrol lands that have been devastated by radiation.

347 GERROLD, DAVID [pseudonym of Jerrold David Friedman]. *The Man Who Folded Himself*. New York: Random House, 1973. [f, M]

In this snake-eating-its-own-tale time-travel story, a young man inherits a belt that can transport him into either the past or the future. With each use of the belt, however, the wearer is duplicated. Soon there is a large group of identical men who find each other to be ideal homosexual lovers. Their lives center solely on each other until one of them goes far back in time and meets a lesbian version of himself. The two fall in love, have children, and then break up. She returns to her version of the future and to her lesbian lovers (all, of course, copies of herself), and he returns to his. Both the lesbianism and the heterosexuality are marginal to the plot and seem to be a literary device to explain the origin of the time traveler's situation. More convincing is the protagonist's narcissistic love for the older and younger versions of himself. The novel is written as a journal by more than one of the men, and in places it is hard to determine who is who, but this only adds to the sense of paradox.

348 GERROLD, DAVID [pseudonym of Jerrold David Friedman]. *Moonstar Odyssey*. New York: Signet, 1977. [m, X]

On Satlik, children grow without a specific gender learning the myths, legends, and ways of Reethe, their Mother Goddess, and Dakka, their Father and Son God. During adolescence they must choose to become either female or male, and once they make their choice they must assume the sex role ascribed by their gender. For most, the choice is easy, but for Jobe, the protagonist, the choice is virtually impossible. It is not until disaster hits Satlik that Jobe learns to accept her gender. (Throughout the novel, even though Jobe technically has no sex, feminine pronouns are used.) A major thread involves two people, Lono and Rurik, who become lifelong lovers even though both are male. An interesting treatment of sex roles influenced by Le Guin's pioneering *The Left Hand of Darkness*.

Biographical Note

David Gerrold (b. 1944), author and scriptwriter, often utilizes variant forms of sexuality within his science-fiction stories. His novel *When Harlie Was One* (New York: Ballantine, 1972) includes mention of homosexuality, too brief for annotation here. Gerrold discusses his sexual politics and his feelings about homophobia in the essay "At War with the Trolls," in *Future Life*.

Gerrold published a brief autobiographical narrative in *The Trouble with Tribbles* (New York: Ballantine, 1973). Biographical information is also included in Brian Ash's *Who's Who in Science Fiction* (New York: Taplinger, 1976), and in *Contemporary Authors*, vols. 85-88, ed. Frances Carol Locher (Detroit: Gale Research, 1980).

---

349 GIBSON, WILLIAM. "Johnny Mnemonic." In *Burning Chrome*. New York: Arbor House, 1986. [f]

A cyberpunk story, by a noted author of the genre, which includes a minor reference to transsexual lesbian bar bouncers.

350 GILMAN, CHARLOTTE PERKINS. *Herland. Forerunner*, serialized January-December 1915. Reprint. New York: Pantheon, 1979. [F?]

This is a self-published, strongly feminist utopian novel. Three American men, exploring Africa, discover an isolated land where there are white women but no men. As guests / prisoners, the men stay with the women and learn their language and cultural values. In this feminist utopia, the women work collectively to make an idyllic life for their parthenogenetic daughters. Their small territory is a beautiful garden; their lives are filled with nurturance and intellectual pursuits. The women are not lesbians; sexual feelings of any sort are considered atavistic and aberrational. The novel shows the different ways each of the men reacts to this peaceful culture.

Biographical Note

Charlotte Perkins Gilman (1860-1935) was an early American feminist and socialist who was noted for her writing and lecturing. She is perhaps best known for her short story "The Yellow Wallpaper" (Boston: Small, Maynard, & Co., 1899) and her massive *Women and Economics* (Boston: Small, Maynard, & Co., 1898). She published two other feminist utopian fantasies: *Moving the Mountain*, serialized in the *Forerunner* in 1911, and *With Her in Our Land*, *Herland*'s sequel, which was serialized in the *Forerunner* in 1916. Both have been excerpted in *The Charlotte Perkins Gilman Reader; The Yellow Wallpaper and Other Fiction*, edited by Ann J. Lane (New York: Pantheon, 1980).

Throughout her life Gilman maintained close political and emotional bonds with other women, gaining strength and support from what one historian has called "the female world of love and ritual." Autobiographical information on Gilman can be found in *The Living of Charlotte Perkins Gilman: An Autobiography* (New York: D. Appleton-Century, 1935). The most comprehensive biographical information available is in Mary A. Hill's *Charlotte Perkins Gilman: The Making of a Radical Feminist, 1890-96* (Philadelphia: Temple University Press, 1980).

Margaret Miller compares *Herland* with Charnas's *Motherlines* in "The Ideal Woman in Two Feminist Science-Fiction Utopias," *Science Fiction Studies* (Montreal), no. 10 (July 1983).

---

351 GLENN, NANCY TYLER. *Clicking Stones*. Tallahassee, Fla.: Naiad, 1988. [F]

Clicking Stones is an amusing piece of lightweight science fantasy. While a child, Erica Demar is given a mysterious stone by a friendly old crone. When "clicked" against another rock, the stone magically emits a powerful light. She is enchanted with this special stone, and it remains important to Erica as she enters her teens, comes out as a lesbian, and moves into the twenty-first century. The Clicking Stone eventually develops a cult following of devotees. Lightweight fiction.

352 GLOECKNER, CAROLYN. "Andrew." In *Future Corruption*, edited by Roger Elwood. New York: Warner, 1975. [M]

A young boy is slowly but surely corrupted by a predatory older starship commander.

353 GOLDIN, STEPHEN. *Mindflight*. Greenwich, Conn.: Fawcett, 1978. [F, m]

A telepathic Terran secret agent, Alain Cheney, has entered "telepause," a condition found only in the most proficient telepaths, which causes severe mental disturbances. Telepausal agents are routinely assassinated by their employer, the Terran Intelligence Agency, because they are potential security risks. *Mindflight* concerns the persecution of Cheney by the TIA. The author's use of sexual variation is homophobic. Both male and female homosexuals are depicted as unpleasant and predatory, which contrasts sharply with the happy and successful heterosexual relationship of the novel's conclusion. Goldin effectively builds suspense throughout.

354 GOMEZ, JEWELLE. "Joe Louis Was a Heck of a Fighter." *The Village Voice (Voice Literary Supplement)*, December 1986. [F]
Gomez transforms the clichés of the horror genre into a powerful woman-identified voice with her Gilda stories, in which Gilda, an African-American, escapes slavery in the 1850s by becoming an immortal vampire. In "Joe Louis," Gilda is attacked by a would-be rapist while walking home to her lesbian lover.

355 GOMEZ, JEWELLE. ". . . Night." *The American Voice*, no. 4 (Fall 1986). [F]
An excerpt from a longer piece, "What Is Night?", which won the Beard's Fund Award for fiction. By 2084, Earth's ecological and immunological systems have collapsed and vampires are hunted for their blood. In this short piece, Gilda saves a woman's life while planning her own escape off-world.

356 GOMEZ, JEWELLE. "No Day Too Long." In *Lesbian Fiction: An Anthology*, edited by Elly Bulkin. Watertown, Mass.: Persephone Press, 1981. [F]
Gilda becomes involved with a group of black New Jersey lesbian feminists and finds a lover much older than she.

Biographical Note
Jewelle Gomez (b. 1948) is a noted poet, essayist, and short-story writer. Her work has appeared in *Conditions, Essence, On Our Backs, The Body Politic*, and *Out / Look*. She is the author of a volume of poetry titled *Flamingoes and Bears* (Jersey City, N.J.: Grace, 1986). The stories listed above are all part of *The Gilda Stories* scheduled for publication by Firebrand Press in 1991.

---

357 GOSSETT, HATTIE. "21st century black warrior wimmins chant." In *Presenting . . . Sister No Blues*. Ithaca, N.Y.: Firebrand, 1988. [f]
Gossett's poem is set in the twenty-first century and celebrates the empowerment of African-American women, including lesbian women.

358 GOSSETT, HATTIE. "womanmansion / to my sister / mourning her mother." In *Presenting . . . Sister No Blues*. Ithaca, N.Y.: Firebrand, 1988. [f]

"Womanmansion" is a poetic exploration of life after death that imagines a women-only heaven where all kinds of racial, economic, and sexual oppression (including heterosexism) has disappeared.

359 GOULART, RON. *After Things Fell Apart*. New York: Ace, 1970. [F, M?]

This lightweight science-fiction novel satirizes the follies and foibles of northern California living. A futuristic detective attempts to track down a gang of man-killing lesbians called "the Lady's Day Gang." The investigator must visit numerous gay bars and resorts during the course of his zany misadventures, and both lesbian and gay male characters abound. Goulart's silly satire is sometimes directly on target, but his characterizations of women and homosexuals are inept.

360 GOULART, RON. *Cowboy Heaven*. Garden City, N.Y.: Doubleday, 1979. [m]

A wacky science-fiction comedy in which a troubleshooter for a Hollywood talent agency finds his hands full keeping an ailing cowboy star and his android twin out of trouble. Homosexual elements are minor: an actor loses a job for posing in a nightgown with his lover, and two gay androids run off together.

361 GOULD, LOIS. *A Sea Change*. New York: Simon & Schuster, 1976. [F]

There is a sea creature, the *Labroides dimidiatus*, that can change sex. When the male of a group dies, the strongest female metamorphoses into a male and dominates the females. Gould draws a stunning, eloquent, and highly controversial human parallel to this creature. The novel is not intended to be a prescription for feminist behavior but is instead an examination of intensely emotional states. The feminist antihero, Jessie, is an indecisive, feminine, white, middle-class fashion model, who begins to change into a man after experiencing rape at gunpoint. The author uses the only black character as Jessie's rapist, but issues surrounding racism are not dealt with. Men's motivations for rape, parent-child incest, power inequalities in relationships between women, and feminine aspects of nature are the subjects of *A Sea Change*. The lesbian imagery, like the other sexual aspects of the novel, is infused with violence. Critical opinion is sharply divided on this book, and most readers find it to be unsettling.

362 GRAVERSEN, PAT. *The Fagin*. New York: A & W, 1982. [m]

Recently divorced Felice Allan and her young son, Jason, hope to find peace and tranquillity when they move to Blue Hill, Virginia. Instead, Jason is kidnapped by boy-sacrificing Satan worshipers. He is forced to submit to an institutional regime with five other imprisoned youths. There is plenty of male bonding and devoted friendship among the captive boys, but using a logic not uncommon in horror fiction, Graversen equates homosexuality (as personified in this case by pedophiliac rape) with the nefarious evils of the Devil.

363 GRAY, JOHN. *Park: A Fantastic Story*. London: Eric Gill, 1932. [M]
    A fantastic future vision by the reputed model for Oscar Wilde's brilliant *The Picture of Dorian Gray*. In John Gray's surrealist fantasy, a man dies and reawakens in a future inhabited by technologically advanced black Catholics and degenerate white Englishmen who live underground. As might be expected from a close friend of Oscar Wilde, there are many homosexual overtones in the plot.

364 GRINNELL, DAVID [pseudonym of Donald A. Wollheim]. "The Feminine Fraction." *Magazine of Horror*, November 1964. Reprinted in *Two Dozen Dragon Eggs*, edited by Donald Wollheim. Reseda, Calif.: Powell Publications, 1969. [X]
    Based on the assumption that every person has components of both sexes, this story concerns Louis Tyler, an American G.I., who is captured by the Nazis during World War II and subjected to horrendous torture. The Nazis succeed in totally destroying 90 percent of Louis's personality, the masculine part; all that remains is the small portion of him that is feminine. The fifty-year-old Louis has been transformed into a five-year-old girl named Louise.

365 GUNTER, ARCHIBALD C[LAVERING], and REDMOND, FERGUS. *A Florida Enchantment*. New York: Home Publishing, 1892. [F?, X]
    A Florida Enchantment, a fascinating nineteenth-century novel, humorously explores gender and transsexuality. Young New York socialite Lillian Travers, while vacationing in Florida, buys an old box in a tourist shop that contains four seeds from an extinct "tree of sexual change." The socialite swallows one of the seeds to take revenge on her deceiving fiancé. Initially, her gender changes, and she becomes a man in a woman's body. She falls in love with her best friend, Bessie, and attends a ball where she dances only with women; both situations have overt lesbian overtones. Later, she physically becomes a man, takes the name Lawrence Talbot, and marries Bessie. During the story, she transforms Jane, her black maid (a racist stereotype typical of the period), into a man, steals her ex-fiancé's new lover from him, and forces a seed down his throat, changing him into a masculine woman. No explicit lesbian love is portrayed, but the many transsexual changes lead to farcical complications.

366 HACKER, MARILYN. "Prayer for My Daughter." In *Millennial Women*, edited by Virginia Kidd. New York: Delacorte, 1978. [F]

A joyous poem of a women-only New York City celebrating the end of the War between the Sexes.

Biographical Note

Marilyn Hacker (b. 1942) is an award-winning poet who has been peripherally involved with science fiction for some time. In 1970 and 1971 she coedited, with Samuel R. Delany, the influential *Quark: A Quarterly Journal of Speculative Fiction*. Hacker has contributed to such journals as *Chrysalis, Ms.*, and *Christopher Street*, and a lesbian feminist sensibility is apparent within her work, particularly in the collections *Taking Notice* (New York: Knopf, 1980), *Assumptions* (New York: Knopf, 1985), and *Love, Death, and the Changing of the Seasons* (New York: Arbor House, 1986).

An intimate portrait of Hacker is provided in Samuel R. Delany's memoir *The Motion of Light in Water: Sex and Science Fiction Writing in the East Village, 1957-65* (New York: Arbor House, 1988). Other biographical and critical information is available in *Contemporary Authors*, vols. 77-80, ed. Frances Carol Locher (Detroit: Gale, 1979) and in "À La Recherche de Marilyn Hacker," by Thomas Disch in *Little Magazine* 9, no. 3 (1975).

See also RUSS, JOANNA (joint author)

367 HAGGARD, H[ENRY] RIDER. *Allan's Wife*. New York: George Munro's Sons, 1887. [F, m]

In this nineteenth-century fantasy adventure, Allan Quatermain, a British imperialist in South Africa and a frequent Haggard hero, sets off in search of adventure with his companion, an African witch doctor named Indaba-zimbi. In the middle of the African veld, he finds and falls in love with the only white woman within hundreds of miles, Stella Carson. Stella has an African companion, Hendrika, who was raised by the baboons and seems part simian herself. Hendrika is also in love with Stella, and it is around this love triangle that the plot develops. The novel is remarkable for its two-page discussion of lesbian relationships and includes a minor reference to gay male relationships as well. Racist references and assumptions regarding African peoples are frequent.

368 HAIMSON, MAUD. "Hands." *Amazon Quarterly* (Berkeley, Calif.), no. 2 (July 1974). Reprinted in *The Lesbian Reader*, edited by Gina Covina and Laurel Galana. Oakland, Calif.: Amazon Press, 1975. [F]

A lightweight fantasy about a woman who finds a female alien in a cave and invites her home. The alien tells her new Earth friend of the many planets she has visited by sitting on her feet and "moving." By the end of the story the two have made love, and the alien discovers that this is an even better kind of "moving" than travel between planets.

HAKIM. *See* BEY, HAKIM

369 HALDEMAN, JOE W. "Counterpoint." In *Orbit Eleven*, edited by Damon Knight. New York: Putnam, 1972. [m]

Two men from opposite backgrounds have destinies that are mysteriously linked from the moment of their births. Michael Kidd is the son of a millionaire, and Roger Wellings is the son of a prostitute. Their lives counterpoint each other as Wellings becomes a successful mathematician and Kidd slowly sinks into destitution. Wellings's homosexual activity as a youth is associated by the author with his deplorable childhood situation.

370 HALDEMAN, JOE W. *The Forever War*. New York: St. Martin's Press, 1974. [F, M]

The protagonist of this novel is sent from Earth on a military mission only to find upon his return that, because of the nature of faster-than-light travel, 2,000 years have elapsed. During this period, homosexuality has become the norm. There are numerous gay and lesbian characters throughout the novel, and the book implies that the reason human civilization has become homosexual is that the "real" men and women (i.e., heterosexuals) have all left for war. The book contains sexist passages, traditional homosexual stereotypes, and a conclusion in which the primary lesbian and gay male characters "reorient" their sexuality to become heterosexual. The book won both the Hugo and Nebula awards. Portions of this novel appeared in *Analog*, 1972-74.

371 HALDEMAN, JOE W. "The Moon and Marcek." *Vertex*, August 1974. [F, M]

An unconventional three-act science-fiction play. Marcek is stranded on the moon with no money to buy a return ticket to Earth. He soon teams up with a bisexual prostitute, Wise Martha, to exploit a wealthy, cliché-ridden homosexual.

372 HALFHILL, ROBERT. "My Alien Lover." *In Touch for Men* (Hollywood, Calif.), no. 144 (November 1988). [X]

A gay man describes his sexual relationship with a catlike alien prince named Kontar.

373 HALL, RADCLYFFE. "Miss Ogilvy Finds Herself." In *Miss Ogilvy Finds Herself*. New York: Harcourt, Brace, 1934. [F]

The author of the classic lesbian novel, *The Well of Loneliness*, takes a brief excursion into the fantastic. Hall paints the portrait of a lesbian in conflict with her socially sanctioned role as a feminine, submissive woman. Only during World War I, while working as a nurse on the front lines, is Miss Ogilvy able to feel comfortable. When peace comes she is shuffled back into a role she finds restrictive. Years later, she travels to a small island off the coast of Britain to spend her dying days. There, Miss Ogilvy's soul is transported back in time to where it belongs – in the body of a simple, sturdy cave man. The cave man takes for "his" mate a Neanderthal woman who grovels at "his" feet. The story reveals the author's belief that lesbians are actually men in women's bodies, an ideology that was widely accepted at the time and that still prevails to a lesser degree.

374 HALL, SANDI. *Godmothers*. London: Women's Press, 1982. [F]
Hall's political allegiance to lesbian feminism is evident throughout *Godmothers*, a manifesto of solidarity with women throughout time. The narrative follows four women from different times. In colonial America, a young woman is burned at the stake for being a witch. In contemporary Canada, a feminist political collective confronts the treachery of modern corporate capitalism. In an all-women future society, pairs of lesbians create video art. And in the Overtime, a spiritual dimension existing simultaneously with all these realities, all these women meet and merge with their "Godmothers." Although similar in some ways to Russ's *The Female Man*, Hall uses her own voice and vision to explore the meaning of the female experience.

375 HALL, SANDI. *Wingwomen of Hera*. San Francisco, Calif.: Spinsters / Aunt Lute, 1987 [F]
The foci of *Wingwomen of Hera* are two very different planets, Hera and Maladar. Hera supports an all-female population that reproduces by parthenogenetic manipulation. Maladar has a cosexual population and a mechanized, authoritarian government. Each culture develops problems, and eventually contact between the two worlds becomes necessary. The novel was originally intended as the first part of a trilogy, but the second volume, *The Newchild of Maladar*, has been cancelled.

376 HALPERN, JAY. *The Jade Unicorn*. New York: Macmillan, 1979. [F, m]
In this intriguing horror novel, a powerful group of Manhattan satanists supernaturally unleash a monstrous demon. Typically, a homosexual is one of its victims. Kermitt is a African-American gay man, cruising in the Village, when he meets a delectable teenage runaway. But the young fifteen-year-old turns out to be more than the predatory older man had bargained for, and Kermitt becomes a gruesome victim of the bloodthirsty satanists. In contrast, two of the novel's main characters are lesbian lovers; their love remains constant from the novel's first murders through its dramatic finale at a Black Mass.

HAMILTON, EDMOND. *See* WENTWORTH, ROBERT O. (pseudonym)

377 HARIS, MARSH. "The Escape." In *Overture in G Minor*, edited by James Ramp. San Francisco: Pan-Graphic, 1964. [M]
A few of the remaining Earth people escape the dying planet and journey to another world. They soon learn that their new home is unable to support female life of any kind, which forces the male survivors to accept homosexuality. The author presents primary gay male characters in a positive light while showing little compassion for the female characters.

378 HARNES, PETER. "The Arms of Arum." In *The Arms of Arum*. San Rafael, Calif.: Frenchy's Gay Line, 1970. [M]
Pornographic gay male science fiction.

HARRIS, JOHN WYNDHAM PARKES LUCAS BEYNON. *See* WYNDHAM, JOHN (pseudonym)

HARRIS, MERIL. *See also* MUSHROOM, MERRIL

379 HARRISON, HARRY. "The Final Encounter." *Galaxy*, April 1964. Reprinted in *The Eighth Galaxy Reader*, edited by Frederik Pohl. Garden City, N.Y.: Doubleday, 1965. [M]
By describing humanity's first contact with what is believed to be an intelligent alien life-form, the author of "The Final Encounter" evokes the awe and mystery inherent in such a meeting; the story serves as an effective reminder of our lonely status in the universe. Considering the year of publication, the use of a heterosexual woman and a gay man as two of the three primary characters seems progressive. However, this perspective is tempered by their characterizations (hers being conventionally self-effacing and his arrogantly misogynistic).

380 HARRISON, HARRY. *Great Balls of Fire: An Illustrated History of Sex in Science Fiction*. London: Pierrot, 1977. [Nonfiction]
In this history of sex in science fiction, Harrison touches briefly on sexuality in the early science-fiction pulp magazines and goes on to discuss topics such as sadomasochism and human-alien sexuality. His writing showcases the multitude of colorful (and usually sexist) illustrations. Harrison's chapter on homosexuality covers Superman and Wonderwoman comic books and speculates about Robert E. Howard's sexual orientation.

381 HARRISON, HARRY. *Star Smashers of the Galaxy Rangers*. New York: Putnam, 1973. [m]

A campy satire of the Flash Gordon school of space opera. Chuck and Jerry, two handsome and inventive college students, team up with their bubbly cheerleader, Sally Goodfellow, to explore other worlds. They fight off all kinds of strange and bizarre creatures, quickly making the universe safe for democracy. At the novel's conclusion, Sally kisses the two men, and then the men begin kissing each other passionately.

382 HARRISON, HARRY, and STOVER, LEON. *Stonehenge*. London: Peter Davies, 1972. Reprint. New York: Scribner's Sons, 1972. [M]

Set in 1473 B.C., *Stonehenge* involves a Mycenaean prince, Ason, and his voyages and adventures. Atlantis has attacked his homeland and Ason has been captured. Narrowly eluding death, he escapes imprisonment with the help of his Egyptian companion, Inteb. In the course of this epic tale, Ason takes a female mate, but Inteb's love for Ason remains an integral part of the story. The book's misogyny and bloodshed may limit its appeal.

383 HARTWELL, SHIRLEY. "Itu's Sixth Winter Festival." In *Memories and Visions: Women's Fantasy and Science Fiction*. Freedom, Calif.: Crossing Press, 1989. [M]

This lesbian feminist fantasy, set in a prepatriarchal, all-women culture, is an excerpt from Hartwell's forthcoming novel *Daughters of Gelasia*.

384 HAYS, WENDY. "The Giant Person and Her Hell-Hound." *Sisters* (San Francisco), February-March 1974. [M]

A romantic fairy tale about a giant lesbian and her enchanted dog. Cute.

385 HEARD, [HENRY FITZ]GERALD. *Döpplegangers: An Episode of the Fourth, the Psychological, Revolution, 1997*. New York: Vanguard, 1947. [M?]

A heady tale set near the end of this century. A seemingly benign world dictator maintains control by keeping the population as placid as cows. Dissidents are quickly disposed of and people are regulated into subservient roles. Alpha is worshiped as a deity. Omega, or the Mole, heads an underground movement to oppose Alpha's domination. The Mole forces a young man to undergo radical plastic surgery, transforming him into an Alpha doppelganger. This ersatz Alpha is then introduced into Alpha's court where the dictator, intrigued rather than wary, makes the duplicate his masseur and companion. The love-hate relationship that develops between these two men is loaded with homosexual overtones – a "queer sort of muscular intimacy" – but Heard avoids describing explicit ramifications of the ripe situation. Heard's tendency toward intellectualism makes for wordy reading.

Biographical Note

Henry Fitzgerald Heard (1889-1971) was a British philosopher, spiritual teacher, and science-fiction author. In the late 1930s he emigrated to the United States where he became involved in Vedanta with Christopher Isherwood and Aldous Huxley. In addition to the novel listed above, his fantasy and science-fiction works include *The Great Fog and Other Weird Tales* (New York: Vanguard, 1944), *The Lost Cavern and Other Tales of the Fantastic* (New York: Vanguard, 1948), and *Gabriel and the Creatures* (New York: Vanguard, 1952).

Heard was homosexual, and during the early 1950s he became actively involved in the efforts of the Mattachine Society. He wrote several pieces of speculative philosophy, under the pseudonym D. B. Vest, which were published in *ONE Magazine* and the *ONE Institute Quarterly*. He appeared three times as a lecturer at the ONE Institute, and he later conducted a private invitational seminar for ONE members at his Santa Monica home. His subject was his theory that the homosexual was humanity's next evolutionary step, a concept at the heart of the pseudonymously written science-fiction novel, *AE: The Open Persuader* (see Ignotus, Auctor).

Biographical and critical information about Heard can be found in *Twentieth Century Authors*, ed. Stanley J. Kunitz and Howard Haycraft (New York: Wilson, 1955), in "Shiel and Heard: The Neglected Thinkers of SF," by Sam Moskowitz in *Fantastic*, August 1960, and in David Dunaway's *Huxley in Hollywood* (New York: Harper & Row, 1989). A more personal view of Heard can be found in Christopher Isherwood's memoir *My Guru and His Disciple* (New York: Farrar, Straus & Giroux, 1980).

---

386 HEINLEIN, ROBERT A. "'–All You Zombies–.'" *Fantasy and Science Fiction*, March 1959. Reprinted in *The Unpleasant Profession of Jonathan Hoag*. Hicksville, N.Y.: Gnome Press, 1959. [X]

By utilizing sex changes and time travel, an individual manages to become both mother and father of her/himself. The seminal treatment of this paradoxical situation.

387 HEINLEIN, ROBERT A. *Friday*. New York: Holt, Rinehart & Winston, 1982. [F]

Friday is a beautiful and intelligent courier employed by a secret intelligence agency. Although her adventures on near-future Earth and far-off planets are action-packed, Friday is not particularly believable. Like Heinlein's Lazarus Long novels, the protagonist is a mouthpiece for the author's political and social musing. While Friday sleeps with women as well as with men, she is not perceived to be gay; the "real" homosexuals are stereotypic "bull-dykes" and "girl boys."

388 HEINLEIN, ROBERT A. *I Will Fear No Evil*. New York: Putnam, 1970. [F, M?]

Gender and sexual preference are important concerns of Heinlein's novel about the first successful brain transplant. Johann Smith, old, rich, and unwilling to die, looks to surgery as a means to immortality. His brain is transplanted into the first available donor – just coincidentally, his classically beautiful secretary, Eunice Branca. Even though her brain is replaced by Johann's, her memories and personality remain in the body as an entity separate from Johann's (does a woman's consciousness reside in her ovaries?). Johann and Eunice carry on a constant stream of chatter; Eunice advises, and Johann controls the body's movements and speech. Johann / Eunice Smith is his / her conception of the ideal woman: seductive, conniving, simpering, intuitive, and illogical, yet quite intelligent and powerful. Smith takes full advantage of renewed youth to seduce several women and many men, though s/he is unclear about which of these acts are homosexual.

389 HEINLEIN, ROBERT A. *Stranger in a Strange Land*. New York: Putnam, 1961. [f, m]

This was a 1960s underground classic. Valentine Michael Smith is the first human raised by Martians. He is brought to Earth and eventually founds a religion that teaches the Martian techniques of teleportation and telepathy. The cult advocates love, affection, nudity, and all sorts of sex – of the heterosexual variety. The communal spirit it provides is in counterdistinction to the individualistic society surrounding it. Women are used in the novel as sexy appliances; female bisexuality is added for titillation, and male homosexuality is mentioned as a "wrongness in the poor in-betweeners."

390 HEINLEIN, ROBERT A. *Time Enough for Love*. New York: Putnam, 1973. [f, m]

This massive book is the first installment of the Journals of Lazarus Long. The background is set in *Methuselah's Children* (New York: Putnam, 1958), which tells of the extremely long-lived Howard family members who have practiced selective eugenics for centuries. Their oldest family member, Lazarus Long, is alive by fluke after several hundred years. The loose plot of this novel concerns Lazarus's descendants' tenacious efforts to record the old man's memories, philosophy, and favorite quips. Frequent sexist and racist passages portray Lazarus the slave owner, Lazarus the slave liberator, and in particular, Lazarus the patriarch. Many of the family members are bisexual, and a few are homosexual, even though the family considers sex for the purpose of reproduction as the highest expression of love. Women, often professionals and competent people, are always beautiful and always subservient.

391 HEINLEIN, ROBERT A. *To Sail beyond the Sunset*. New York: Putnam, 1987. [F]

The autobiography of Lazarus Long's bisexual mother. Long-winded and confusing novel that serves primarily as a mouthpiece for the author's libertarian views.

Biographical Note

Robert A. Heinlein (1907-88) has been a primary figure within the science-fiction genre since his first story was published in 1939.

An important theme that recurs throughout his work is the exploration of sex roles and sexuality. In addition to the items mentioned above, this thread has been noted in "If This Goes On–" in *Astounding*, February 1940, reprinted in *The Past through Tomorrow* (New York: Putnam, 1967); *Beyond This Horizon* (New York: Fantasy Press, 1942); "The Year of the Jackpot," in *Galaxy*, March 1952, reprinted in *The Menace from Earth* (Hicksville, N.Y.: Gnome Press, 1958); and *Starship Troopers* (New York: Putnam, 1960). Discussion of Heinlein's use of sexuality can be found in "The Embarrassments of Science Fiction," by Thomas M. Disch in *Science Fiction at Large*, ed. Peter Nicholls (New York: Harper & Row, 1976); in "Variations on a Theme: Human Sexuality in the Work of Robert A. Heinlein," by Ronald Sarti in *Robert A. Heinlein*, ed. Joseph D. Olander and Martin H. Greenberg (New York: Taplinger, 1978); in Baird Searles's *Heinlein's Work* (Lincoln, Nebr.: Cliff's Notes, 1975); and in Leon Stover's *Robert Heinlein* (Boston: Twayne, 1987). Also of interest is Samuel R. Delany's essay, "Heinlein," in *Starboard Wine* (Pleasantville, N.Y.: Dragon Press, 1984).

Biographical information on Heinlein is available in *Twentieth Century Authors: First Supplement*, ed. Stanley J. Kunitz (New York: Wilson, 1955), and in Sam Moskowitz's *Seekers of Tomorrow* (New York: World, 1967).

---

392 HERBERT, FRANK. *The Dosadi Experiment*. New York: Berkley Medallion, 1978. [f, m]

On the poison-infested planet of Dosadi, life is almost untenable, yet the inhabitants have developed an uncanny knack for survival – so uncanny, in fact, that they are considered a threat to the rest of the galaxy and are therefore restricted to the one planet. Jorj X. McKie, the Bureau of Sabotage's best agent, is sent to Dosadi to impede their plans for space travel, but once on Dosadi he switches allegiances and teams up with Keila Jedrik, a forceful woman who has just gained control of her planet's government. The novel is well plotted, and it depicts several female characters in positions of power. Homosexuality is discussed briefly with a negative bias: of all Dosadi, only homosexuals lack the Dosadi will to survive. They are used by Keila Jedrik in battles where suicide is necessary.

393 HERBERT, FRANK. *Dune*. New York: Chilton, 1965. [m]

Dune has developed from a cult best-seller into a science-fiction classic, and with good reason. The desert planet of Arrakis (or Dune) is being held in a vise grip between the corrupt House of Harkonnen and the equally corrupt Imperial forces. Both desire Arrakis's harvest of "spice," a highly addictive drug that retards aging, and neither side cares one iota for the abused Arrakians. It remains for Paul Atreides, *Dune's* hero, to mobilize the planet's population and to become Arrakis's savior. The archvillain, Baron Harkonnen, is portrayed as a sleazy, obese pederast, wholly despicable, who continually victimizes young boys. Additionally, the author portrays women in a narrow context. Herbert handles his pacing, characterization, and description with finesse.

394 HERBERT, JAMES. *The Dark*. London: New English Library, 1980. Reprint. New York: Signet, 1980. [m]

Most of Herbert's popular horror stories rely on a strict formula. A valiant heterosexual man fights a literal manifestation of evil while rescuing (and seducing) a helpless woman in distress. In this case, a professional "ghost hunter" fights an inky supernatural fog that overpowers the citizens of London and drives them to frenzied violence while rescuing a blind scientist's daughter. The action in a Herbert novel is fast-paced and usually is intercut with graphic scenes of violence: grisly rapes, mutilations, and murders. *The Dark* hosts several references to homosexuality: the most substantial being a young fag-basher struggling with his own gayness who in turn becomes a victim of the unearthly fog.

395 HERBERT, JAMES. *The Fog*. London: New English Library, 1975. [f, m]

A typical Herbert chiller in which a freak earthquake devastates a small British town and accidentally releases a top-secret, biologically lethal organism. Feeding on airborne industrial waste, the microorganism rapidly grows, eventually encompassing all of London in its poisonous fog. Breathing the toxic air turns humans into raving animals, and they kill and maim everything around them. At least half of the novel is devoted to graphic depictions of violence and carnage. Minor characters include a masochistic gay man and a suicidal lesbian.

396 HERBERT, JAMES. *The Rats*. London: New English Library, 1974. [m]

In Herbert's first published novel, mutated rats begin to attack human beings across Britain, and the hero must find a solution. As in much of Herbert's subsequent fiction, the violence is graphic and bloody. An early victim of the rodent rampage is a self-hating, alcoholic homosexual. Sequels include *Lair* (London: New English Library, 1979), and *Domain* (London: New English Library, 1984).

397 HERBERT, JAMES. *Sepulchre*. London: New English Library, 1987. Reprint. New York: Putnam, 1988. [m]

Liam Halloran, a trained operative and skilled bodyguard, is hired to protect Felix Kline, a reclusive employee of a multinational company. Kline turns out to have unusual psychic powers and to practice ancient, nefarious Sumerian rituals. Among Kline's assistants are two sadistic Arabs who are homosexual lovers.

398 HERBERT, JAMES. *The Shrine*. London: New American Library, 1983. [f]

When a young girl begins seeing visions and healing the sick, many believe that it is a miracle from God. But, predictably, she is actually possessed by an ancient, evil, bisexual demon.

399 HERBERT, JAMES. *The Spear*. London: New English Library, 1978. Reprint. New York: Signet, 1980. [X]

Private detective Harry Steadman's investigation into the disappearance of a foreign agent uncovers an international neo-Nazi conspiracy that is threatening world order by its use of occult powers. Steadman must battle the fascists, overcome supernatural forces, and rescue freelance writer Holly Miles. At one point, the hero is sexually tempted by an alluring hermaphrodite – an overture he soundly rejects.

400 HERBERT, JAMES. *The Survivor*. London: New English Library, 1976. [m]

An airline pilot miraculously survives a horrible plane crash that has killed everyone else. Obsessed by guilt, the pilot soon realizes that he has been chosen for a special supernatural task. Minor gay male content.

Biographical Note

James Herbert (b. 1943) is a noted horror writer who regularly includes secondary lesbian and gay characters in his work, and all his writing should be examined carefully. He is interviewed in Douglas E. Winter's *Faces of Fear* (New York: Berkley, 1985).

---

401 HESSE, HERMANN. "Faldum." In *Strange News from Another Star*, translated by Denver Lindley. New York: Farrar, Straus & Giroux, 1972. Originally published in *Marchen*. Berlin: S. Fisher, 1919. [M?]

A young violinist and his devoted friend are each granted one wish by a mysterious stranger. The wishes happen to separate the two men for many years until they are supernaturally reunited. Their love is clearly specified, although sexuality is never implied. Several other stories in this fantasy collection contain suggestive male-male friendships, particularly "Strange News from Another Star" and "A Dream Sequence."

402 HESSE, HERMANN. *Magister Ludi*. Translated by Mervyn Savill. New York: Henry Holt, 1949. Reprinted as *The Glass Bead Game*, translated by Richard and Clara Winston. New York: Holt, Rinehart & Winston, 1969. Originally published as *Das Glasperlenspiel*. Berlin: Suhrkamp, 1943. [M?]

Like all good literature, *Magister Ludi* can be read in several ways. It is a biography of twenty-fifth-century intellectual Joseph Knecht, an examination of a future utopia in which spiritual values are kept alive through the cultivation of the disciplined mind, and a treatise on Hesse's philosophical beliefs. He creates an aristocratic, sexist hierarchy of male intellectuals known as the Castalian Order. Its purpose is to coordinate all of the arts and sciences into a balanced whole. In *Magister Ludi*, as in much of Hesse's fiction, highly charged, emotional male-male friendships are a strong, consistent theme, and many critics have interpreted these relationships as homosexual. The book won Hesse the 1946 Nobel Prize for Literature.

403 HESSE, HERMANN. *Steppenwolf*. Translated by Basil Creighton. New York: Henry Holt, 1929. Originally published as *Der Steppenwolf*. Berlin: S. Fisher, 1927. [F, M?]

Hesse uses a psychological interpretation of the werewolf legend to deliver a scathing indictment against bourgeois society. The protagonist, Harry Haller, typical of Hesse's self-reflective heroes, is a man in conflict with both himself and his environment. He perceives himself as part man and part wolf. His existence is isolated and unhappy until he meets by chance a woman named Hermine. By introducing Harry to the sensuous and decadent delights of the physical world, Hermine becomes a catalyst for spiritual growth and human development in Haller. Dramatic events culminate in a hallucinatory "Magic Theatre." Hermine is lesbian, and several male characters, including the protagonist, appear to have homosexual tendencies.

404 HOFFMAN, NINA KIRIKI. "Works of Art." *Year's Best Horror: 17*, edited by Karl Edward Wagner. New York: DAW, 1989. [F]

Eerie horror story about art, love, and death, featuring a lesbian couple.

405 HOLLAND, CECELIA. *Floating Worlds*. New York: Knopf, 1976. [f, M?]

In *Floating Worlds*, Holland transfers the same superb skill with which she writes historical fiction to a futuristic motif. She creates a tangle of politics: fascists control Mars; black, slave-owning imperialists of Neptune and Uranus are moving into new territory; and the anarchists are attempting to maintain a grip on Earth. The anarchist hero, Paula Mendoza, is placed in the impossible position of being responsible for the enforcement of a peace treaty between these divergent political entities. Holland intentionally creates a noticeable distance between the reader and her protagonist, a distance that somewhat limits empathy; nevertheless, Mendoza's bravery and her devious strategies are poignant. Halfway through this thick novel, Paula Mendoza initiates an affair with a black woman from the outer planets. The two black male major characters are extremely intimate, but their relationship is never defined as homosexual. There are overtly gay male minor characters.

406 HOLMES, OLIVER WENDELL. *Elsie Venner*. Boston: Ticknor & Fields, 1861. [F?]

Elsie Venner is one of the earliest examples of American occult fiction. The protagonist, Elsie Venner, has acquired occult powers because her mother suffered a rattlesnake bite during pregnancy. As a result of this prenatal influence, Elsie has grown up with a strong will, an uncanny ability to communicate with snakes, and an even more uncanny ability to mesmerize certain individuals by her gaze. Among those who fall under Elsie's control is her unmarried schoolteacher, and their relationship has often been noted as lesbian.

407 HOPPE, STEPHANIE T. *The Windrider*. New York: DAW, 1985. [F]

Oa, the bisexual heir to the throne of the Empire, is given an impossible choice: either kill the woman she loves or lose her chance for the throne. Rather than make a decision, Oa flees, and after a dangerous voyage she finds herself among a tribal people who ride magical horses. The rest of the story takes place among these Windriders, as Oa rises to become their leader. Lesbian sexuality is portrayed positively in an otherwise unexciting novel.

408 HOWARD, ROBERT E. "Red Nails." *Weird Tales*, July-October 1936. Reprinted in *The Sword of Conan*. Hicksville, N.Y.: Gnome Press, 1955. [F]

In the last Conan fantasy Howard wrote, his barbarian hero, Conan, is traveling with Valeria, a woman who is fairly liberated compared with Howard's typical treatment of female characters. Fleeing a dragon, the two discover an ancient walled city. They find the city inhabited by people split into warring clans. Conan assists in the destruction of one faction, but his efforts are not rewarded. Instead,

Valeria is abducted by the lesbian villain, Tascela. In the end, Conan wins back Valeria. The tale includes a rather racy lesbian whipping scene.

409 HOWARD, ROBERT E. "The Vale of Lost Women." *Magazine of Horror*, Spring 1967. Reprinted in *Conan of Cimmeria*. New York: Lancer, 1969. [F]

Written in the 1930s, this story was not published until much later, most likely because of its explicit lesbian content. Conan comes upon a young white woman captive of a tribe of black Africans. Conan rescues the woman, but when he comes to collect her as his reward she has other ideas. Rejecting the brutality of men, she flees to the Vale of Lost Women, an idyllic all-women society. She finds, to her dismay, that the valley is filled with lesbian natives who seduce her despite her fears. Again, Conan rescues her, and he chivalrously allows her to retain her virginity. Sexist and racist.

Biographical Note

Robert E. Howard (1906-36) virtually created the Sword and Sorcery genre of fantasy fiction. His work, noted for its sexism, racism, and violence, has been repeatedly imitated, usually without any higher degree of awareness.

Hints of lesbianism occur often in his work but always as a way to titillate his male readers. Howard stories that contain lesbian overtones too minor to annotate here are "The Black Stranger," *Fantasy Magazine*, February-March 1953; "The Slithering Shadow," *Weird Tales*, September 1933; and "A Witch Shall Be Born," *Weird Tales*, December 1934.

Howard never married and there has been speculation about his sexual orientation. For example, see Harry Harrison's *Great Balls of Fire: An Illustrated History of Sex in Science Fiction* (London: Pierrot, 1977).

---

410 HOWES, KEITH. "Echoes of Tomorrow." *Gay News* (London), no. 143 (18-31 May 1978). [Nonfiction]

Written from a gay point of view, this article analyzes several contemporary science-fiction novels that to some degree deal with lesbianism and male homosexuality. Included is an interesting interview with Michael Moorcock on gay liberation.

411 HUFF, TANYA. *Gate of Darkness, Circle of Light*. New York: DAW, 1989. [M]

Huff's novel is a good-natured fantasy with an unusual group of heroes and a positive attitude toward same-sex love. Amid the back alleys and trash bins of contemporary Toronto, a young mentally retarded woman, a street musician, a bag lady, and a sympathetic social worker battle the magical forces of Darkness for the destiny of the

Earth. Their ally is a handsome Adept of the Light named Evan, whom they all find sexually attractive. This proves particularly difficult for Roland, the musician, who is not used to desiring male beauty. The two men never consummate their passion, but Roland comes to realize "what difference does the plumbing make" when you're in love.

412 HUGHART, BARRY. *The Story of the Stone*. New York: Doubleday, 1988. [m]

In a wineshop in an alternate world's ancient Beijing, the sage Master Li and his able assistant Number 10 Ox are confronted with a mystery. At the monastery in the Valley of Sorrows, a monk has been murdered and an ancient manuscript stolen. Master Li and Number 10 investigate the crimes, aided by a beautiful prostitute, Grief of Dawn, and a handsome homosexual, Moon Boy. A sequel to the award-winning *Bridge of Birds*, this fantasy offers fast-paced adventure and some very humorous moments, but some readers will doubt the veracity of Hughart's Asian culture.

413 HUGHES, JEREMY. "Sex in the Year 2500." *In Touch for Men* (Hollywood, Calif.), no. 69 (July 1982). [Nonfiction]

Five professional science-fiction authors – Poul Anderson, Alfred Bester, Arthur C. Clarke, Harlan Ellison, and Frederik Pohl – participate in a roundtable discussion about the future of homosexuality, possible alternative sexualities, and gay imagery in the science-fiction genre.

414 HUGHES, PETER TUESDAY [pseudonym]. *Alien*. San Diego: Greenleaf Classics, 1972. [M]

Pornographic gay male science fiction.

415 HUGHES, PETER TUESDAY [pseudonym]. *Daemon*. Santee, Calif.: Blueboy Library, 1977. [M]

Pornographic gay male horror story.

416 HUGHES, PETER TUESDAY [pseudonym]. *Remake*. San Diego: Greenleaf Classics, 1971. [M]

Pornographic gay male science fiction.

417 HUYSMAN, JORIS KARL. *Down There*. Translated by Keene Wallis. New York: Boni, 1924. Originally published as *Là Bas*. Paris: Plon-Nourrit, 1891. [m]

Là Bas follows a nineteenth-century French Catholic named Durtal through the hellish world of satanism in his quest for spiritual understanding. As part of this search, Durtal becomes obsessed with the infamous bisexual child-murderer, Gilles de Rais. He cannot understand how de Rais, comrade of Joan of Arc, could become such a loathsome, Satan-worshiping monster. It is to answer this question that Durtal begins investigating contemporary satanism. The novel culminates with Durtal's attendance at a Black Mass. As in some other French literature of the period, Huysman goes out of his way to give his readers explicit descriptions of both de Rais's atrocities and the repugnant activities of his contemporary satanists. Male homosexuality, usually involving young children, is clearly associated with satanism and depravity. The book is intended to revolt its readers and as such it is a classic.

418 IGNOTUS, AUCTOR [pseudonym]. *AE: The Open Persuader*. Los Angeles: ONE, 1969. [M]

This novel is both an involved philosophical tract and a gay male utopian fantasy. Ulick Stackpole, a young reporter, is investigating a utopian society secreted somewhere in South America. The utopia comprises exclusively gay men who are developing the "next step" in the evolution of the human race. The "next step" in this case has male sex organs, female breasts and figure, and equine hooves. Stackpole tours the fantastic premises, while the designer of the experiment explains the concepts behind this new race, concepts that range from the inventive to the ridiculous, from the sexually radical to the overtly misogynistic. Ulick rapidly embraces this society's philosophy and life-style. The plot is minimal, and it is made virtually incomprehensible by the bizarre vocabulary and stilted writing style employed by the author. The fantasy is intriguing for its exposition of the eccentric ideas of philosopher / science-fiction author Gerald Heard, an early mentor of the Mattachine Society. Whether Heard had a hand in writing the novel is debatable, but his influence can be found within every paragraph.

See also HEARD, GERALD

419 ING, DEAN. "Fleas." *Destinies* 1, no. 3 (April-June), edited by Jim Baen. New York: Ace, 1979. [M]

A bisexual male vampire finds himself the quarry of a predatory female of another species. Just as vampires feed on humans, this other species feeds on vampires. Homosexual content is explicit.

420 ING, DEAN. *Soft Targets*. New York: Ace, 1979. [m]

In this suspense thriller set in the very near future, a plan is devised to thwart the activities of an international terrorist, Hakim Arif. A gay man who plays a substantial role in the intrigue is characterized by stereotypic mannerisms and appearance. He is killed off in a particularly revolting and unnecessary manner.

421 INOUYE, JON. "Last Man." In *A Night Tide*. Culver City, Calif.: Randen, 1976. [M]

In the year 2180, women are exterminated in an effort to control population growth. Male homosexuality becomes natural. Inouye's tale revolves around the last heterosexual male.

422 JACKSON, SHIRLEY. *Hangsaman*. New York: Farrar Straus, 1951. [F?]

Like all Shirley Jackson novels, this one is composed of horror, suspense, mystery, and a touch of the occult. Natalie is a young woman living away from her oppressive family while she attends college. She meets a woman, Toni, who lures her to a deserted spot. An attempted seduction follows, but since Natalie is portrayed as slightly schizophrenic, it is never certain whether Toni is an actual person or a fragment of Natalie's personality. Interesting reading.

423 JACKSON, SHIRLEY. *The Haunting of Hill House*. New York: Viking, 1959. [F]

Four psychic individuals are invited to spend a summer at a reputedly haunted house in order to conduct a scientific experiment. Eleanor, the one whom the house has chosen as its victim, displays overt lesbian tendencies when she falls in love with Theodora. Theodora is also a lesbian and has come on the summer trip after fighting with her previous lover. This very spooky story is recommended.

424 JACKSON, SHIRLEY. *We Have Always Lived in the Castle*. New York: Viking, 1962. [F?]

This is one of those subtle mysteries that should not be spoilt by someone explaining it all. Two sisters have secluded themselves in the old family mansion, away from the prying and curious public. They are the survivors of a long-ago mass family murder for which the older sister is blamed. Events occur that force them into the public eye and then further into isolation. The lesbian components are tied to the mystery of their seclusion and to the question of "whodunit." The lesbian content is allegorical, but it is major and basic to the plot. Recommended.

425 JAKUBOWSKI, MAXIM. "Essex House: The Rise and Fall of Speculative Erotica." *Foundation*, no. 14 (September 1978). [Nonfiction]

A thought-provoking article on the speculative erotica published by Essex House between 1968 and 1970. Several of the works examined are included in this bibliography.

426 JAMES, HENRY. "The Turn of the Screw." In *Two Magics*. New York: Macmillan, 1898. [F?, M?]

"The Turn of the Screw" is a strange and enigmatic ghost story by one of America's foremost nineteenth-century novelists. A young governess travels to a remote British estate to take charge of two orphaned youngsters, a boy and a girl. She soon glimpses a sinister-looking woman and an equally foreboding man lurking around the premises. She learns that they are the children's former governess and her lover, the estate's former groom, both of whom are now dead. The pair has been responsible for the absolute corruption of the children, and they desire to continue their domination even after death. The new governess battles these unearthly apparitions for the souls of the children. James never clarifies how the children were actually corrupted, but both lesbian and gay male elements can be easily interpreted. Even more intriguing, albeit sexist in the adherence to the "hysterical female" theme, are the questions that arise as to whether the events recounted actually happened or are simply a figment of the governess's fervid imagination. Either way, the story is compelling and mysterious, and it has become a true classic of psychological horror.

Biographical Note

Henry James (1843-1916), one of America's greatest novelists and short-story writers, wrote numerous fantasy and science-fiction pieces throughout his career. Many of these have been collected in the anthology *Henry James: Stories of the Supernatural*, ed. Leon Edel (New York: Taplinger, 1970). Several of his works touch on both male and female homosexuality, and there is reason to suspect that James was homosexual. Critical exploration of "The Turn of the Screw" specifically discussing the lesbian and gay male implications of the plot can be found, among other places, in Jeanette Foster's *Sex Variant Women in Literature* (New York: Vantage, 1956) and in Maureen Duffy's *The Erotic World of the Faery* (London: Hodder, 1972). Biographical information on James is plentiful, but by far the most comprehensive source is the five-volume Leon Edel biography collectively called *The Life of Henry James* (New York: Lippincott, 1953-72). H. Bruce Franklin discusses James in relation to other nineteenth-century science-fiction authors in his *Future Perfect: American Science Fiction of the Nineteenth Century* (New York: Oxford University Press, 1966, rev. ed. 1978).

427 JANIFER, LAWRENCE M. *Bloodworld*. New York: Lodestone Books, 1968. [f, m]

The free members of Bloodworld's society are organized and governed by a repressive code of ethics that specifies their position of power within their hierarchical nuclear families. The frustrations of these citizens are channeled into the torture of an enslaved caste, the descendants of criminals, who are kept bound in socially condoned "remand houses." Male homosexuality is considered taboo, but the activities of women are apparently not important enough to merit censure, and sexual violence by women toward other women is considered natural. As the culture destroys itself, the narrator, atypical in that he feels guilty for beating his bound female slave, liberates her from the remand house and they escape from the planet. Although at odds with his culture's brutal excesses, the protagonist never questions his absolute domination of his partner in all other aspects of their relationship. One of the most ghastly books cited in this bibliography.

428 JANIFER, LAWRENCE M. "The Gift." In *Dystopian Visions*, edited by Roger Elwood. Englewood Cliffs, N.J.: Prentice-Hall, 1975. [M]
      Alan and Paullson, two male lovers, acquire a new adult novelty item called a Being. The Being gradually becomes central to the couple's life. Although homosexuality is ostensibly accepted in this future society, the author depicts the couple as unfulfilled, self-destroying, and misogynistic.

429 JAY, VICTOR. *The Gay Haunt*. New York: Olympia, 1969. [M]
      Pornographic gay male ghost story.

430 JERSILD, P. C. *After the Flood*. New York: William Morrow, 1986. [M?]
      This novel, by a noted Swedish author, takes place in a bleak, postapocalypse future. The protagonist, the youngest survivor of a global war, is the lover of an oceangoing ship's captain.

431 KALMANSOHN, [M]AVID. "Brave New Worlds." *Frontiers* (West Hollywood) 7, no. 20 (25 January 1989). [Nonfiction]
      An examination of the gay appeal in science fiction.

432 KANE, DANIEL. *Power and Magic*. London: GMP, 1987. [F, M]
      Adopted at birth, Adam is a repressed homosexual living in a drab, oppressive, feudal village in an alternative universe where magic and sorcery are real. He discovers that he is actually Ethonian, a despised race of homosexual people thought to be wicked by the rest of the world; his destiny is to battle the fearsome Demon King who threatens all human life. Paul, a gay man in our contemporary London, suddenly finds himself transported to Adam's world to help the fight of good against evil. Adam and Paul learn a great deal from each other. An important character is Obsidian, an amazon Ethonian. A bit silly perhaps, but well-developed and wholly good-natured. All royalties for the sale of this book are donated to the Terence Higgins Trust to help in its work for people with AIDS.

433 KARLINS, MARVIN, and ANDREWS, LEWIS M. *Gomorrah*. Garden City, N.Y.: Doubleday, 1974. [m]
   This extremely violent and bloody detective story is set in a future crime-ridden New York. During the course of the story, Victor Slaughter, the aptly named protagonist, enters a bisexual "pleasure dome" and proceeds to act bisexually.

434 KATZ, JUDITH. "The Amazing Disappearing Girl." *Sinister Wisdom* (Berkeley, Calif.), no. 34 (1988). Reprinted, slightly altered, in *Memories and Vision: Women's Fantasy and Science Fiction*, edited by Susanna J. Sturgis. Freedom, Calif.: Crossing Press, 1989. [F]
   Lesbian feminist horror / fantasy of a literal underground of women fighting the Patriarchy.

435 KAYE, MELANIE. "Amazons." *Conditions 2* (1978). Reprinted in *Amazons!* edited by Jessica Amanda Salmonson. New York: DAW, 1979. [F?]
   Fantasy poem recounting a young girl's first glimpse of a troupe of presumably lesbian women warriors.

436 KEENE, DAY, and PRUYN, LEONARD. *World without Women*. Greenwich, Conn.: Fawcett, 1960. [f, m]
   Connie and Matt Renner return from a long seafaring vacation to find that almost all the women in the United States have died from a strange illness and that men have become sex-starved animals. During their first day back, the Renners encounter a predatory drag queen; later, Matt discovers that an old friend, one of the few surviving women, has become a lesbian. The lesbian is portrayed as so self-destructive that she voluntarily submits to a mob of raving heterosexual men and is subsequently raped and killed.

437 KELLER, DAVID H. "The Feminine Metamorphosis." *Science Wonder Stories*, August 1929. Reprinted in *When Women Rule*, edited by Sam Moskowitz. New York: Walker, 1972. [F?]
   A group of rich, talented businesswomen band together to take over America's economy and to dispense with men. The women are quite clear about their preference for their own sex. By injecting themselves with male hormones (obtained by the castration of Chinese men) they are able to adopt the external characteristics of men. Thus disguised, they set about changing the bias of our culture from masculine to feminine. Their plans are thwarted by a male detective who infiltrates their forces while posing as a Chinese woman. By utilizing his wife's intuition, he uncovers the women's plot, destroys their plans, and informs them that the Chinese hormones they have been

using have given them syphilis and will drive them insane. The story is so bad that it's good.

438 KELLER, DAVID H. "The Revolt of the Pedestrians." *Amazing Stories*, February 1928. Reprinted in *Beyond Time and Space*, edited by August Derleth. New York: Pellegrini & Cudahy, 1950. [f]

Keller depicts a nightmare world of the future in which human society has been totally altered by the use of the automobile. People spend their entire lives within their cars, and their legs have atrophied into useless appendages. The "Automobilist" society has waged a war of extermination against the few remaining individuals with functional legs ("Pedestrians"), and the mechanized culture now believes that the entire Pedestrian species is extinct. Hidden away in the Ozark Mountains, however, is a small band of Pedestrians who have kept the puritan work ethic alive and are plotting their eventual return from exile. An interesting twist is added to the plot with the introduction of an overtly lesbian character. Although she is perceived as "pathologically soul-sick," her inclusion in the story is remarkable for the period.

KELLER, DENISE. *See* CLARK, KEITH (joint author)

439 KELLEY, LEO P[ATRICK]. *Mythmaster*. New York: Dell, 1973. [M]

A fast-paced science-fiction adventure with a major male homosexual theme. John Shannon, an embittered space pirate, is without scruples. His income is derived from stealing human fetuses and selling them to the highest bidder. Shannon is threatened by the equally slimy villain, Oxon Kaedler. A strong motivational factor throughout the story is Shannon's involvement with two very different individuals. One is the exotic female courtesan, Reba Charlo; the other is a handsome gay "astrogator," Starson. A bisexual triangle develops among the three, with Shannon at the apex. Ultimately, Shannon is forced to confront the ambivalence of his sexuality. The author opts for a traditional tragic ending.

KETTLE, LEROY. *See* KNIGHT, HARRY ADAM (pseudonym)

440 KETTLE, PAMELA. *The Day of the Women*. London: Leslie Frewin, 1969. [F?]

Eve Datchard returns to Britain after her husband's accidental death to find her old friend, Diana Druce, has launched a national feminist political movement called Impulse. Eve becomes an enthusiastic Impulse supporter and helps Diana run for prime minister, but she soon has second thoughts. The women's movement, initially designed to foster equality between the sexes, begins to support radical separatism and eventually becomes totalitarian. There is considerable man-hating in Kettle's fictional plea for moderate feminism but little overt lesbianism.

441 KILLOUGH, LEE. *A Voice out of Ramah*. New York: Ballantine, Del Rey, 1979. [f]

On Marah, an isolated planet once colonized by a Terran religious sect, most males die before reaching maturity. Generally thought to be the result of a mysterious virus, these male fatalities are actually caused by a poison ritually administered by the male religious establishment. It is not until the arrival of an off-worlder, a woman, that this long-established custom is discovered and challenged. With such a large female population and so few men, Marah's culture quite naturally accepts lesbianism, but Killough plays down this aspect of her story to concentrate on the males. Easy and entertaining reading.

442 KING, STEPHEN. *It*. New York: Viking, 1986. [m]

An effective supernatural thriller about a horrible shape-changing monster that terrorizes a small New England town. A secondary incident is based on the actual murder of a gay man in Ancor, Maine. The gay man is portrayed as being a rather pathetic drag queen.

443 KING, STEPHEN. *The Shining*. Garden City, N.Y.: Doubleday, 1977. [m]

This highly effective horror thriller takes place in a haunted resort hotel in the Rocky Mountains. A young married couple and their psychic five-year-old son move to the hotel when the father accepts a position as the isolated resort's winter caretaker. As the winter progresses, the family finds itself becoming increasingly aware of the loathsome evil the hotel contains. The tension builds to a riveting climax. There are several mentions of gay and bisexual male characters, none of which is presented positively. A vivid and frightening book.

444 KING, STEPHEN. "Sneakers." *Night Visions 5*, edited by Douglas E. Winter. Arlington Heights, Ill.: Dark Harvest, 1988. [M]

A young recording executive becomes aware of a haunted restroom in his office building. While the executive is not gay, there are several significant gay male characters.

445 KING, STEPHEN. *The Stand*. Garden City, N.Y.: Doubleday, 1978. [f, m]

The Stand is a tension-packed novel of epic proportions that chronicles a postapocalyptic future. At least 95 percent of the world's population has died from a flu virus accidentally released from a United States military laboratory. The survivors, guided by paranormal dreams, migrate to Boulder, Colorado, to rebuild on the remnants of their former world. They soon find that their troubles have just begun. Another cluster of people, ruled by a despotic nonhuman entity named Randall Flagg, is rising in the West. Flagg is bent on destroying what good remains in the world, and the Boulder settlement must soon prepare for battle. Two of King's evil characters are gay men; one of the heroes turns out to be a lesbian.

446 KNIGHT, HARRY ADAM [pseudonym of John Brosnan and Leroy Kettle]. *The Fungus*. London: W. H. Allen, 1985. [F?]

The Fungus is a fairly standard horror novel, gory and action-packed, in which a lethal fungus attacks the citizens of London. The novel has merit, but the vivid characterizations and flashes of humor that punctuate it are not enough to overcome the underlying misogyny of the text. The plague has been unleashed by a group of repellent man-hating female separatists, out to destroy the human species. Ironically, among the first victims of this gruesome killer are two lesbians.

447 KONVITZ, JEFFREY. *The Guardian*. New York: Bantam, 1978. [M]

Written as a sequel to *The Sentinel* (see citation below), *The Guardian* takes up where the earlier novel left off. Again, the immortal hordes of hell are rising to take over the Earth. The hierarchy of the Catholic Church must find another replacement for God's sentry at hell's gate. A young couple find themselves in the middle of this apocalyptic battle between good and evil. Homosexuality is introduced in a contrived manner: the couple turn out to be gay male lovers, passing for heterosexual, but this ending is without enough foreshadowing to be credible.

448 KONVITZ, JEFFREY. *The Sentinel*. New York: Simon & Schuster, 1974. [f, m]

A young model, Alison Parker, returns to New York to find herself trapped in an age-old battle between the Catholic Church and Satan's loathsome evil. After renting an apartment in a peculiar brownstone, strange and terrifying things begin happening to her, and Alison discovers that her apartment building is actually the gateway between Earth and hell. Two of Alison's neighbors are abusive and obscene lesbians, who turn out to be part of Satan's legions of hell. An effeminate homosexual makes a brief appearance.

KORNBLUTH, C[YRIL] M. *See* POHL, FREDERIK (joint author)

449 KOSTER, R. M. *Mandragon*. New York: Morrow, 1979. [f, m, X]

A small dark-skinned child is born in the imaginary South American republic of Tinieblas. The child is hermaphroditic and is raised by a black voodoo woman as if it were a monster. Considered to be little more than a chattel, the sensitive and intelligent child is sold to a traveling circus, where the youngster is viciously exploited in the freak show. Suddenly, an irresistible and unexplained Power takes hold of the young hermaphrodite, and from that moment on, s/he becomes Mandragon, an instrument wielded by some mysterious force for its own purposes. There are several overtly gay male characters depicted and a suggestion of lesbian activities among Mandragon's followers. Perhaps more intriguing is Mandragon's own sexuality, which shifts with the changes in Mandragon's gender identity. This is the third volume in the author's Tinieblas trilogy, preceded by *The Prince* (New York: Morrow, 1971) and *The Dissertation* (New York: Harper's Magazine Press, 1975).

450 KREISLER, KURT. "Star Stud: Part One." *Him*, November 1969. [M]
Gay male science-fiction erotica.

451 KREISLER, KURT. "Star Stud: Part Two." *Him*, December 1969. [M]
Gay male science-fiction erotica.

452 KUBE-McDOWELL, MICHAEL P. *Empery*. New York: Berkley, 1987. [F]
The third book of Kube-McDowell's acclaimed Trigon Disunity trilogy, *Empery* takes place 60,000 years after the first human interstellar civilization was destroyed by the Mizari, an alien species from another star. Another advanced human civilization has arisen and now the question arises: Should humanity aggressively attack the Mizari? On opposite sides are Defense Director Harmack Wells, a member of the elitist secret society known as the Nines, and Chancellor Janell Sujata, a pacifist and a lesbian. Sujata is competent, caring, and pivotal to the plot. The first two books in the trilogy are not relevant to this bibliography.

453 KURAS, PAT M., and SCHMIEDER, ROB. "When It Changed: Lesbians, Gay Men, and Science Fiction Fandom." *Gay Community News* (Boston) 8, no. 10 (27 September 1980). [Nonfiction]
Report on the Thirty-eighth World Science Fiction Convention, focusing specific attention on gay and lesbian fans. Includes comments by Elizabeth Lynn, Samuel R. Delany, and Frank M. Robinson.

454 KUSHNER, ELLEN. "Red Cloak." *Whispers* (Binghamton, N.Y.) 5, no. 1-2 (August 1982). [M]
Set in the same locale as *Swordspoint*, this story again features Richard St. Vier and his lover, Alec. This tale adds sorcery to Kushner's fast paced sword adventure. Excellent.

455 KUSHNER, ELLEN. *Swordspoint*. New York: TOR, 1989. [M]

Set in a medieval time and a place where nobles hire swordsmen to fight their duels, this adult fairy tale is diamond-brilliant. It combines superb writing, great adventure, and a most enticing romance between two male characters. Young Richard St. Vier, the best swordsman of them all, and his lover Alec, the gangly scholar dressed in black rags, get caught in a net of political intrigue of the nobles across the river. Two of the other male characters are bisexual. A "really gotta read."

456 LACENAIRE, PETER FRANCIS. "They Came in Outer Space." *Mandate* 10, no. 8 (November 1984). [M]

An advanced species known only as The Intelligence has conquered an all-male planet and enslaved its people. Their domination is assisted by "clonoidals," artificial men with enormous sexual organs. Lacenaire's story concerns a rebellious human who is captured and raped by a trio of clonoidals. He eventually falls in love with his captors.

LACKEY, MERCEDES. The Books of the Last Herald Mage. [M]:

457 ▪ *Magic's Pawn*. New York: DAW, 1989

Lackey sets *Magic's Pawn* in her mythical kingdom of Valdemar. Valdemar is a feudal world, ruled by a benevolent monarchy, where magic and chivalry exist side by side. Vanyel is a young man with artistic dreams whose hopes are crushed by his strict, almost abusive father. Sent in disgrace to live with his aunt, Vanyel falls in love with another student and is drawn into a dangerous family fight. When his lover uses magic to open a mystic Gate, Vanyel's Mage powers are awakened. Lackey handles Vanyel's awakening sexuality with skill and compassion. The trilogy will be completed in 1990 with the publication of *Magic's Promise* and *Magic's Price*.

458 LACKEY, MERCEDES. *Burning Water*. New York: TOR, 1989. [m]

A series of brutal, occult-linked murders brings romance novelist and practicing witch Diana Tregarde to Dallas to battle an ancient Aztec spirit. Diana is intelligent and resourceful. She is heterosexual, but a very close friend, Lenny, is gay and is ill with AIDS. Lenny is sensitively portrayed. A prequel, entitled *Children of the Night*, also featuring Lenny, is scheduled for publication in 1990 by TOR.

459 LACKEY, MERCEDES. "A Different Kind of Courage." In *Free Amazons of Darkover*, edited by Marion Zimmer Bradley. New York: DAW, 1985. [F]

Lackey borrows Marion Zimmer Bradley's world of Darkover to tell the inspiring story of Rafiella, a Free Amazon. Rafiella's self-confidence wanes when the Guild House sends her traveling with an older, more experienced lesbian couple.

LACKEY, MERCEDES. The Heralds of Valdemar Trilogy. [f]:

460 ▪ *Arrows of the Queen*. New York: DAW, 1987.

461 ▪ *Arrow's Flight*. New York: DAW, 1987.

462 ▪ *Arrow's Fall*. New York: DAW, 1988.
    An enjoyable trilogy that perceptively examines both child abuse and male chauvinism within Lackey's mythical kingdom of Valdemar. Talia, a thirteen-year-old girl from the puritanical and patriarchal Borderlands, is on the verge of despair when she is chosen by Rolan, a magical horselike being called a Companion, to become a Herald for the Queen. Together they travel to a nonsexist culture where Talia must train, learn of her unique psychic gifts, and overcome the effects of her abusive childhood. Talia is heterosexual, but one of her closest friends and mentors is a loving lesbian.

Biographical Note

Mercedes Lackey (b. 1950) frequently includes gay and lesbian characters in her fantasy writing. She is also the author of *Oath Bound* (New York: DAW, 1988) and *Oath Breakers* (New York: DAW, 1989), two Valdemar novels featuring a pair of women who travel together and eventually establish a family (they are not specifically defined as lesbians). Her forthcoming fantasy, *Knights of Ghosts and Shadows*, written with Ellen Guon, has significant gay male content.

Lackey's novels are very popular; an organization of her readers and fans is called "Queen's Own," P.O. Box 43143, Upper Montclair, NJ 07043.

---

463 LAIDLAW, MARC. *Dad's Nuke*. New York: Donald I. Fine, 1985. [m]
    Dad's Nuke is a darkly humorous satire about contemporary suburban competition and neosurvivalists set in the near future. "Dad" Johnson believes in protecting his family. Paranoid to an extreme, he has gone so far as to build a nuclear reactor in his fortified garage to make his family self-sufficient. Unfortunately, the family he cherishes is rapidly falling apart. His son, for example, genetically programmed by Dad to be gay in order to balance the family unit, has rebelled against his father's authority and escaped the family compound. His wife begins an affair, and his daughter becomes a terrorist. Soon events are spiraling out of control.

LAMBERT, WILLIAM J., III. Adonis Trilogy. [M]:

464 ▪ *Adonis*. San Diego: Pleasure Reader, 1969.

465 ▪ *Adonis at Actum*. San Diego: Pleasure Reader, 1970.

466 ▪ *Adonis at Bomasa*. San Diego: Pleasure Reader, 1970.
Pornographic gay male fantasy trilogy.

LAMBERT, WILLIAM J., III. Demon Series. [M]:

467 ▪ *Demon's Stalk*. San Diego: Pleasure Reader, 1970.

468 ▪ *Demon's Coronation*. San Diego: Pleasure Reader, 1971.
Pornographic gay male science-fiction series.

469 LAMBERT, WILLIAM J., III. *Male Sex Idol*. San Francisco: Parisian Press, 1972. [M]
Pornographic gay male fantasy.

LAMBERT, WILLIAM J., III. Tlen Series. [M]:

470 ▪ *Five Roads to Tlen*. San Diego: Greenleaf Classics, 1970.

471 ▪ *The Gods of Tlen*. San Diego: Greenleaf Classics, 1970.
Pornographic gay male science-fiction series.

472 LAMBERT, WILLIAM J., III. *Valley of the Damned*. San Diego: Greenleaf Classics, 1971. [M]
Pornographic gay male fantasy.

473 LAMONT, GIL. *Roach*. North Hollywood, Calif.: Essex House, 1969. [M?]
The author of this near-pornographic novel uses an experimental writing style to depict the horrifying, mechanized Los Angeles of the future. The protagonist eventually turns to drugs and a transvestite lover to escape his miserable existence.

474 LAPIDUS, JACQUELINE. "Design for the City of Women." *Heresies*, no. 3 (Fall 1977). [F]
A common lesbian feminist fantasy, that of a woman discovering a culture of parthenogenetically reproducing lesbians, is skillfully molded by poet Jacqueline Lapidus into an affirmation of lesbian selfhood and sexuality.

LANE, MARY E. *See* ZAROVITCH, Princess VERA (pseudonym)

475 LaPORTE, RITA. "A Document." *Ladder* (San Francisco), February-March 1971. Reprinted in *The Lavender Herring*, edited by Barbara Grier and Coletta Reid. Baltimore: Diana Press, 1976. [F]

"A Document" is written as if it were an official report from a Martian sociologist to the people of Earth. The Martian has been studying the cultures of our globe for years, and the report concludes that lesbian feminists exhibit the most advanced thinking.

476 LaTOURETTE, AILEEN. *Cry Wolf*. London: Virago, 1986. [F]

LaTourette's intriguing, but slow-paced, feminist extrapolation is set in the far future, following a nuclear holocaust that has destroyed most of the world's population. Five lesbian survivors have built a struggling new cosexual society that they have protected from any knowledge of the past. Eventually only one of the founders remains, and she finds herself in conflict when her new society demands some answers.

477 LAUMER, KEITH, and BROWN, ROSEL GEORGE. *Earthblood*. Garden City, N.Y.: Doubleday, 1966. [m]

The galaxy, 11,000 years from now, is so overrun by aliens and mutants that the few genetically pure humans who have survived are considered freaks. The youthful Roan, one of these rarities, manages to hijack a spaceship. Space opera adventures follow as Roan and his crew of aliens (one of whom is homosexual) bash their way through the galaxy seeking the legendary planet Earth, home of "True Men." Roan expects the native Earth men to be tough and arrogant, the way the ancient legends have depicted them, but to his disgust, they turn out to be extremely effeminate. This effeminacy is never equated with homosexuality.

478 LAUTRÉAMONT, Comte de [pseudonym of Isidore Lucien Ducasse]. *The Lay of Maldoror*. Translated by John Rodker. London: Casanova Society, 1924. Reprinted as *Maldoror (Les Chants de Maldoror)*, translated by Guy Wernham. Mt. Vernon, N.Y.: Golden Eagle Press, 1943. Originally published as *Les Chants de Maldoror*. Brussels: A. Lacroix, Verboeckhoven & Co., 1869. [M, X]

Lautréamont paints a nightmare landscape inhabited by demons, hermaphrodites, murderers, and fallen angels. His novel centers upon a hopelessly damned individual who wanders restlessly through his grotesque, shadowy world driven by two passions: his hatred of God and his disgust with humankind. Maldoror, the central character, indulges in explicit sadistic and masochistic fantasies, often homosexual and pederastic. Wordy meditations alternate with brutal scenes of carnage, torture, and death. On occasion, Lautréamont achieves an almost hypnotic beauty, riveting his readers' consciousness on his fantastic and repugnant subjects, yet for the most part *Les Chants de Maldoror* remains an attempt to disgust readers. This work is a representative example of seventeenth-century French romanticism that only a few will appreciate, but it had a strong influence on symbolists and, through them, on twentieth-century surrealists. There have been numerous editions of this book.

479 LEATHERWOOD, HANK. *Startail.* San Diego: Greenleaf Classics, 1969. [M]
Pornographic gay male science fiction.

LEE, GENTRY. *See* CLARKE, ARTHUR C. (joint author)

480 LEE, RAND B. "Full Fathom Five My Father Lies." *Isaac Asimov's Science Fiction Magazine*, February 1981. Reprinted in *Worlds Apart: An Anthology of Lesbian and Gay Science Fiction and Fantasy*, ed. Camilla Decarnin, Eric Garber, and Lyn Paleo. Boston: Alyson, 1986. [M]
Lee's "Full Fathom Five" is an intelligent, thought-provoking fantasy of an all-male world in which ritualized incest is of sacred importance. Tragedy results when a son resists his father's sexual advances because he is in love with a beloved friend.

481 LEE, RAND B. "The Sound of His Wings." *Isaac Asimov's Science Fiction Magazine*, August 1982. [M]
Two older gay men, longtime lovers, are the central characters in Lee's exploration of the far future. Strange, ominous dreams of a golden seagull come to members of a small colony of psychic and nonpsychic refugees, struggling to survive in a hostile United States. The gay men are respected throughout their society.

482 LEE, TANITH. *Anackire.* New York: DAW, 1983. [M]
Lee skillfully combines kinky sex, vivid characterizations, and swift-paced action to create her popular fantasy stories and novels. In *Anackire*, a sequel to *The Storm Lord*, she entwines an incestuous passion between a royal brother and sister and the adventures of a gay man, once a warrior for a king. Most of Lee's adult fiction revels in this kind of erotic decadence, often developing homosexual, incestuous, transsexual, and sadomasochistic themes. But her treatment of same-sex love remains ambivalent. In *Anackire*, for example, the gay soldier is "properly" converted to heterosexuality by the end of the novel.

483 LEE, TANITH. *Death's Master.* New York: DAW, 1979. [f, M?, X]

Death's Master follows the related stories of Simmu and Zhirem, two superhuman beings, as they wander across the flat, demon-infested Earth of long ago. Simmu, who has the ability to change sex at will, is the demon child of a powerful lesbian queen who was magically inseminated by a dead gay man. Zhirem is the immortal son of a nomadic king. The two meet when Simmu is a male, and a loving, erotically tinged relationship develops between them. It is desire for Zhirem that awakens Simmu's ability to change sex, and as a female Simmu seduces Zhirem. Zhirem is repulsed by what they have done, and from that time on the two are enemies. Interwoven throughout the narrative are numerous subplots involving characters such as the Master of Death, the Master of Night, and Simmu's regal lesbian mother. Although not the focus of the novel, women – particularly the lesbian queen – play a strong role within the story. Lee's use of the erotic is explicit and often kinky.

484 LEE, TANITH. *Don't Bite the Sun*. New York: DAW, 1976. [f, m, X]

In the bizarre culture in the distant future, society is managed by a massive computer complex. Human beings are kept in a prolonged state of adolescence and are expected to be reckless, impulsive, and hedonistic. Virtually every means of sensory stimulation is available to them, from Dream Rooms to Weather Synthesizers, and if for some reason the teenagers happen to kill themselves, computers will rescue them and refurbish them with bodies of their choosing. Although sex-changing is taken for granted in this future world, nearly all the sex portrayed is heterosexual and traditionally role-defined. The plot involves a rebellious individual, usually female, who finds a spoon-fed existence unfulfilling and attempts to do something about it.

485 LEE, TANITH. *Drinking Sapphire Wine*. New York: DAW, 1977. [f, m, X]

A sensuously written sequel to *Don't Bite the Sun* (see citation above) in which Lee's plucky, sex-changing protagonist commits the computerized society's one crime – murder. For this offense, s/he is banned forever from the mechanized utopian cities and is forced to find her/his own way in the uninhabited desert wilderness. Sex-changing is again a focus of the author's attention, but as in her previous book, there is little homosexual activity.

486 LEE, TANITH. "Love Alters." In *Despatches from the Frontiers of the Female Mind*, edited by Jen Green and Sarah Lefanu. London: Women's Press, 1985. [F, m]

A young woman living in a society in which homosexuality is the norm finds heartbreak when her latent heterosexuality surfaces.

487 LEE, TANITH. *Night's Master*. New York: DAW, 1978. [f, m]
     This series of interconnected fables revolves around the Demon
King, Azhrarn. The magical ruler governs an enchanted and frightening
world beneath our own. Being of demonkind, he is immortal and has
little care for mortal humans. To him they are simply playthings who,
when they dabble in sorcery, are likely to burned. There is much
sensuality and sexuality in the story, and several times same-sex intimacy
arises. At one point, Azhrarn takes a youth as his lover, and later, in a
scene laden with sapphic overtones, a woman falls in love with her
mirror-reflected image. Like all of the other mortal characters in the
novel, both Azhrarn's male lover and the narcissistic woman suffer as a
result of dealing with the Night's Lord, but this seems characteristic of
the author's subtle sense of humor rather than homophobia.

488 LEE, TANITH. "Nunc Dimittis." In *The Dodd, Mead Gallery of Horror*,
     edited by Charles L. Grant. New York: Dodd, Mead, 1983. [M]
     An ancient vampire princess recruits a young bisexual petty
criminal to assist her when her longtime human companion begins to
die.

489 LEE, TANITH. "The One We Were." In *Elsewhere Three*, edited by
     Terri Windling and Mark Alan Arnold. New York: Ace, 1984. [F]
     Claira Von Oeau, a popular historical novelist, adopts the dress
and conduct of a heterosexual eighteenth-century French male poet
after consulting a medium about her past lives.

490 LEE, TANITH. *Quest for the White Witch*. New York: DAW, 1978. [f,
     M?]
     A tightly woven tapestry of adventure and sorcery. Vazkor, son of
a warrior father and a goddesslike mother, dons the supernatural
powers that are his birthright and ventures forth seeking his mother. His
journey takes him to the great city of Bar-Ibithni whose "fancy boys,"
painted male courtesans, are numerous and often visited. He joins
forces with a disfavored prince, Sorem, and together they wage a battle
against the city's king. Sorem falls in love with Vazkor, but the magical
hero is resolutely heterosexual, so the prince sadly carries his
unrequited passion to a premature grave. Vazkor becomes the lover of
Sorem's bisexual mother. With Sorem's death, Vazkor leaves the city to
continue searching for his mother. Lee's bold writing intricately depicts
the exotic lands of her barbaric world. The novel is the third in a Sword
and Sorcery trilogy that begins with *The Birthgrave* (New York: DAW,
1975) and continues with *Son of Vazkor* (New York: DAW, 1978).

491 LEE, TANITH. "Southern Lights." In *Amazons II*, edited by Jessica
     Amanda Salmonson. New York: DAW, 1982. [F?]

Cross-dressing amazon warrior Jaisel becomes involved with a mysterious older man and his beautiful daughter. The story becomes complicated when the daughter becomes enamored with the amazon. Jaisel also appears in Lee's "Northern Lights," in *Amazons!* edited by Jessica Amanda Salmonson. (New York: DAW, 1979).

492 LEE, TANITH. "Under the Hand of Chance." In *Tamastara*. New York: DAW, 1984. [m]

A beautiful Hindu boy spurns the men whom he attracts, but he falls prey to misfortune and magic.

493 LEE, VERNON [pseudonym of Violet Paget]. "Fourth Unlikely Story: Winthrop's Adventure." In *For Maurice; Five Unlikely Stories*. London: John Lane, 1927. [M]

Julian Winthrop uncovers the antique portrait of a young singer who had been scandalously murdered many years earlier. The young man in the portrait is so lovely that Winthrop immediately becomes enamored of him, and for several years he searches for more information about the long-dead youth. The story reaches its climax at the deserted villa where the young singer had been murdered. It is there that Winthrop confronts the beautiful man's ghost. The homosexual elements of the story are subtle but clear.

Biographical Note

Vernon Lee (1856-1935) was the pseudonym of lesbian Violet Paget, who was well known for her literary output, a substantial portion of which was considered either "weird fiction" or ghost stories. Biographical information on Lee is available in Michael Ashley's *Who's Who in Horror and Fantasy Fiction* (New York: Taplinger, 1977) and in *Lesbian Lives*, ed. Barbara Grier and Coletta Reid (Baltimore: Diana Press, 1976).

---

494 LEFANU, [JOSEPH] SHERIDAN. "Carmilla." In *In a Glass Darkly*. London: R. Bentley, 1872. [F]

A historically important lesbian fantasy. The young, innocent Laura lives with her father and governess in an isolated European castle. Chance, as it often will, brings her a visitor in the form of a lovely woman named Carmilla. Laura and Carmilla form a tight romantic relationship, yet soon Laura begins to grow ill. Carmilla is a vampire and is drawing nourishment from young Laura. It is likely that the author's equation of lesbianism with evil vampirism enabled him to treat this subject more explicitly than other authors of the day.

495 LEFANU, SARAH. *In the Chinks of the World Machine: Feminism and Science Fiction*. London: Women's Press, 1988. Reprinted as *Feminism*

and Science Fiction. Bloomington, Ind.: Indiana University Press, 1989. [Nonfiction]

Lefanu argues that science fiction is the ideal form for the fusion of feminist politics with imagination in this interesting analysis of contemporary science fiction written by women. The author pays special attention to the works of James Tiptree, Jr., Ursula Le Guin, Suzy McKee Charnas, and Joanna Russ.

496 Le GUIN, URSULA. *The Dispossessed*. New York: Harper & Row, 1974. [m]

Le Guin contrasts two political / social systems in this brilliant novel. Annares has an anarchist-syndicalist system based on the philosophy of mutual aid. It is a desert world with scarce resources, barely enough to feed and clothe its people. Neighboring Urras, on the other hand, is abundant with decadence, and its political system is imperialistic. In her contrast, Le Guin pays particular attention to class divisions and the subjugation of women. *The Dispossessed* is, however, a novel, not a political treatise. Shevek, a physicist from the anarchist planet, despairs as he realizes that Annares's once-revolutionary society is stagnating and is becoming entrenched in rule by bureaucracy. Shevek must deal with conflicting emotions as he moves between the two societies. Homosexuality is dealt with on a superficial level although the anarchists purport to accept all sexual variations. The writing is superb, and the novel won both the Hugo and Nebula awards.

497 Le GUIN, URSULA. *The Left Hand of Darkness*. New York: Ace, 1969. [X]

The Left Hand of Darkness examines a culture without sex roles. Winter's inhabitants are neuter except for a few days each month. During these periods, known as kemmer, they randomly become either female or male. Genly Ai, a man from Earth, is on the icy planet of Winter to establish diplomatic relations. He becomes entangled in a form of politics unfamiliar to him, and he is thrown into a concentration camp. Estraven, a prime minister, rescues him, and the two escape across Winter's icy landscape. Even though they must depend upon each other, Ai finds that he cannot trust "a man who is a woman, a woman who is a man." When Estraven goes into a feminine cycle during kemmer, Ai's distrust and confusion intensify, but he knows this is his neurosis, rather than a behavior he considers appropriate. His respect for Estraven grows into nonsexual love. Le Guin chooses to refer to the genderless people as "he," which may make it difficult for readers to imagine Winter's inhabitants as anything but male; it remains, however, a powerful and absorbing book. This novel won both the Hugo and Nebula awards and has been very influential throughout the science-fiction field; note in particular Bradley's *The World Wreckers*, Gerrold's *Moonstar Odyssey*, and Gentle's Orthe novels.

498 Le GUIN, URSULA. "Nine Lives." *Playboy*, November 1969. Revised and reprinted in *Best SF 1969*, edited by Harry Harrison and Brian Aldiss. New York: Putnam, 1970. [f, M?]

A team of ten clones arrives at a space station to help with a mining crisis. The two male residents are at first threatened by the clones' efficient teamwork, their similar thinking patterns, and particularly their bisexuality. A tunnel caves in, killing nine of the clones. The survivor experiences nine deaths almost as if they were his. One of the original residents helps the clone survive the shock of separation and shares a touching moment with the survivor by telling the clone that he (the resident) loves his partner. A beautiful "what if" story. Various versions of the story are in circulation; the author's personal favorite is the one printed in *The Wind's Twelve Quarters* (New York: Harper & Row, 1975).

499 Le GUIN, URSULA. *Planet of Exile*. New York: Ace, 1966. [m]

A rapidly dwindling Terran colony has been isolated for 600 years on the planet Eltanin. The Terrans seek support from their indigenous Eltanian neighbors in their struggle against invading nomadic tribes. Jakot Agat, a Terran leader, and Rolery, a native woman, fall in love. Their marriage has serious repercussions. A close friend of Jakot, Huru Pilotson, is homosexual.

500 Le GUIN, URSULA. "Winter's King." In *Orbit Five*, edited by Damon Knight. New York: Putnam, 1969. [X]

This short story, which apparently sparked *The Left Hand of Darkness*, was not published until after the novel's success. Le Guin uses the masculine pronoun to describe the genderless people of Winter.

501 Le GUIN, URSULA. "The Word for World Is Forest." In *Again Dangerous Visions*, edited by Harlan Ellison. Garden City, N.Y.: Doubleday, 1972. [m]

This story is a statement about imperialism and a bitter examination of patriarchy's indifference to nature. Men, having depleted the Earth of its natural resources, have begun to exploit those of other worlds. The planet of Athshe, a lush, densely forested world, has been recently colonized: the timberlands are being stripped; the native population is becoming enslaved. The planet's delicate ecological chain, undisturbed for a millennium, will soon be destroyed. The Athsheans finally realize the situation and an uprising begins. Le Guin brings the Athshean's peaceful culture to life and sharply contrasts it to the violent, male-dominated culture of the humans. It is briefly noted that homosexuality is both common and condoned within the human settlements. The story won the 1973 Hugo Award for best short story, and it was later published in a single volume by Putnam.

Biographical Note

Ursula K. Le Guin (b. 1929) has achieved acclaim both outside and within the science-fiction genre. She is also the author of *The Lathe of Heaven* (New York: Scribner, 1971), *The Eye of the Heron* (New York: Harper & Row, 1978), *Malafrena* (New York: Berkley, 1979), *The Beginning Place* (New York: Harper & Row, 1980), *Compass Rose: Short Stories* (New York: Harper & Row, 1982), and *Always Coming Home* (New York: Harper & Row, 1985).

Le Guin is an outspoken feminist and she often includes variant sexuality and androgyny within her stories. She discusses the development of her novel *The Left Hand of Darkness* in "Is Gender Necessary?", in *Aurora: Beyond Equality*, ed. Vonda N. McIntyre and Susan Janice Anderson (Greenwich, Conn.: Fawcett, 1977). She is also the author of *The Language of the Night: Essays on Fantasy and Science Fiction* (New York: Berkley, 1979) and *Dancing at the Edge of the World: Thoughts on Words, Women, Places* (New York: Grove, 1989). Feminist discussion of Le Guin's work is plentiful. See in particular "Androgyny, Ambivalence, and Assimilation in *The Left Hand of Darkness*," by N. B. Hayles, in *Ursula K. Le Guin*, ed. Joseph D. Olander and Martin Harry Greenberg (New York: Taplinger, 1979) and Sarah Lefanu's *In the Chinks of the World Machine: Feminism and Science Fiction* (London: Women's Press, 1988). Samuel R. Delany offers a valuable critical perspective in "To Read *The Dispossessed*," in *The Jewel- Hinged Jaw: Notes on the Language of Science Fiction* (Elizabethtown, N.Y.: Dragon Press, 1977). See also Barbara J. Bucknall's *Ursula K. Le Guin* (New York: Ungar, 1981) and Charlotte Spivack's *Ursula K. Le Guin* (Boston: Twayne, 1984).

Biographical information on Le Guin is available in *Contemporary Authors*, vols. 21-22, ed. Barbara Harte and Carol Riley (Detroit: Gale, 1969), and in Brian Ash's *Who's Who in Science Fiction* (New York: Taplinger, 1976).

502 LEIBER, FRITZ. "Dark Wings." In *Heroes and Horrors*, edited by Stewart Schiff. Chapel Hill, N.C.: Whispers Press, 1978. [F]

This forceful, erotic horror fantasy touches on a wide range of social / sexual dynamics including incest, lesbianism, sadomasochism, and rape. Two women, Rose and Violet, meet by chance and discover that they are identical twins separated during their infancy. They go to Rose's apartment to explore their physical similarities in detail and wind up engaging in sex. It is implied that during the sexual act Violet metamorphoses into a big, black male bird or demon and rapes Rose, but these elements are open to interpretation. Aspects of Violet and Rose's love are validating and realistic; however, the story implies that lesbianism is a result of child abuse.

503 LEIBER, FRITZ. *Our Lady of Darkness*. New York: Berkley, 1977. [f, m]

Franz Westen, a fantasy writer living in San Francisco, is plunged into a mystery that involves events that took place more than 100 years earlier. Westen uncovers ancient sorcery in his inquiry into the secrets of Thibaut de Castries. It seems that de Castries, an acquaintance of fantasy author Clark Ashton Smith, left some kind of curse that comes back to haunt Westen. There are two minor lesbian characters of the sex-kitten variety, and several intimations of male homosexuality, specifically in reference to Gun and Saul, two of Westen's friends.

504 LEIBER, FRITZ. "The Ship Sails at Midnight." *Fantastic Adventures*, September 1950. Reprinted in *The Outer Reaches*, edited by August Derleth. New York: Pellegrini & Cudahy, 1951. [F]

While visiting Earth, a beautiful female alien falls in love with four people, one of whom is a woman. The author handles bisexuality explicitly.

505 LEIBER, FRITZ. "The Two Best Thieves in Lankhmar." In *Fantastic*, August 1968. [F]

Leiber has fashioned a series of Sword and Sorcery stories around a swashbuckling duo named Fafhrd and the Grey Mouser. In this story, Leiber's dashing heroes are taken for all they are worth by a pair of lesbians more roguish than the men.

506 LEIBER, FRITZ. *The Wanderer*. New York: Ballantine, 1964. [F]

Hugo Award-winning novel about a mysterious planet that suddenly appears in close proximity to the Earth. Because of its enormous size and gravitational pull, the new planet causes tidal waves and earthquakes. A forerunner of the disaster genre of fiction and film. One incidental character is an unpleasant lesbian, Colonel Mabel Wellington.

Biographical Note

Fritz Leiber (b. 1910) has won five Hugo awards, three Nebula awards, and the Gandalf Award. Other Leiber stories that include possible lesbian or gay male content too minor to annotate are: "The Frost Monstreme," in *Flashing Swords Three: Warriors and Wizards*, ed. Lin Carter (New York: Dell, 1976); "Nice Girl with Five Husbands," in *Galaxy*, April 1951; and "Rime Isle," in *Cosmos 1*, nos. 1-2 (1977).

---

507 LEIBSCHER, WALT. "Do Androids Dream of Electric Love?" In *Strange Bedfellows*, edited by Thomas Scortia. New York: Random House, 1972. [M]

A homosexual sex offender finds his court-appointed psychodroid more sympathetic to his plight than he had initially expected. The psychodroid is apparently also gay. The title refers to a famous science-fiction novel of the same period. An amusing short story.

508 LEVENTHAL, STAN. "The Crystal Storm." In *A Herd of Tiny Elephants*. Austin, Tex.: Banned Books, 1988. [M]

In the far-distant future, a mighty warrior king finds his personal problems answered with the arrival of a handsome young scholar to his private chambers.

509 LEVENTHAL, STAN. "The Star of David." In *A Herd of Tiny Elephants*. Austin, Tex.: Banned Books, 1988. [X]

A chance encounter in a gay bar leads to sexual interaction between a young gay man and an ancient Jewish vampire.

510 LEVENTHAL, STAN. "Telesex." In *A Herd of Tiny Elephants*. Austin, Tex.: Banned Books, 1988. [M]

Two gay male lovers renew their sexual relationship after a cure for AIDS has been discovered.

511 LEWIS, C[LIVE] S[TAPLES]. *That Hideous Strength; A Modern Fairy-Tale for Grown-Ups*. London: John Lane, 1945. Reprint. New York: Macmillan, 1946. [f]

A quiet British college town is disrupted and partially destroyed by the bureaucratic National Institute of Co-ordinated Experiments. The N.I.C.E. is actually a front for the forces of evil that, with callous disregard for human values, plan to conquer Earth using technological skills. It is up to Lewis's hero, Ransom, aided by the legendary sorcerer, Merlin, to fight this pernicious threat to humanity. One of the villains is a mannish, sadistic lesbian whose real name is Miss Hardcastle, but who is known as the Fairy. The book is the third in a fantasy trilogy. The first novel in the series, *Out of the Silent Planet* (London: John Lane, 1940), and the second, *Perelandra* (London: John Lane, 1943), are not relevant to this bibliography. All three books are strongly Christian allegories and moralistic in tone.

512 LEWIS, SINCLAIR. *It Can't Happen Here*. Garden City, N.Y.: Doubleday, 1935. [m]

Sinclair Lewis, well-known liberal and American man of letters, issued this dire warning to a Depression-torn country after observing the victory of totalitarianism in Germany and Italy. Lewis feared similar developments within the United States, and this novel extrapolates the frightening rise of a fascist dictatorship in this country. The new regime institutes martial law and concentration camps. Democratic processes are dissolved, women are coerced back into the home, and the official persecution of racial and religious minorities is begun. Chief among the villains is Senator Berselius Windrip, modeled on the Louisiana senator Huey Long, but it is his top aide, Lee Sarason, that is of interest to this bibliography. Sarason is a slimy, manipulative, repugnant homosexual, who recruits a small group of handsome young men for his elite, private guard. His career and subsequent murder appear to be based on the life of a German Nazi, Ernest Roem. Lewis's antitotalitarian message can still be heard today; unfortunately, so can his homophobic one.

513 LICHTENBERG, JACQUELINE. *House of Zeor*. Garden City, N.Y.: Doubleday, 1974. [m, X]

Earth of the future is populated by two mutant human races: the vampiristic "simes" and the victimized "gens." The novel describes the struggle of a newly formed fringe group, composed of both simes and gens, to establish a symbiotic relationship between the two races. Undertones of homosexuality are present in this new group, but these allusions are never made explicit. However, among the old-fashioned, death-dealing simes, obvious homosexuality does arise when a particularly cruel male sime buys male gens for sexual torture. This mediocre mix of postholocaust science fiction and vampirism uses female characters in extreme moderation and for the purpose of romantic interest.

LINEBARGER, PAUL M. A. *See* SMITH, CORDWAINER (pseudonym)

514 LINSSEN, JOHN. *Tabitha fffoulks: A Love Story about a Reformed Vampire and His Favorite Lady*. New York: Arbor, 1978. [f, m, X]

Tabitha fffoulks, a bored office worker, finds the quality of her life greatly enhanced when she becomes lovers with the suave, sophisticated vampire, Georg Szegi. She becomes caught in a battle between good and evil when Georg's daughter, a terrifying lesbian vampire named Nicola, begins to pursue her relentlessly. Vampires are divided into two groups: the reformed, law-abiding, good citizens such as Georg, who get blood from volunteer donors using sterile hospital techniques, and the unreformed, inhumane vampires, such as Nicola, who attack and terrorize their victims. Among the unreformed, predominantly homosexual vampires, terror, death, and sex merge into one form of expression. The equation of homosexuality with evil could point to a homophobic theme, but this idea is largely dispelled by the novel's surprise ending.

515 LITTELL, JONATHAN. *Bad Voltage*. New York: Signet, 1989. [M]
Littell's *Bad Voltage* is a fast-paced cyberpunk novel about Lynx, the founder of a roving band of high-tech, drugged-out street kids called the Livewires. Lynx and his addicted male lover Mara wander the riot-torn underworld of a future Paris craving adventure until their madcap lives are disrupted by an heiress from Uptown. The entire novel is prefaced with quotes from Genet and Baudelaire and is concluded with a list of music played while the novel was being written (Bronski Beat, Miles Davis, Lou Reed). Kinky, dangerous territory that the author handles delightfully.

516 LIVIA, ANNA. *Bulldozer Rising*. London: Onlywomen Press, 1987. [F]
Anna Livia is a noted British author of *Relatively Norma*, *Accommodations Offered*, and *Incidents Involving Warmth*. She consistently incorporates explicitly lesbian and feminist themes in her work. In *Bulldozer Rising*, Livia again explores these concerns, this time setting them in a fast-paced, media-conscious, patriarchal, recreationally drugged, and violently youth-oriented future, where aging is a crime. A secret movement of old women – all lesbian – plot to overthrow the system. Discarding conventional narration, Livia uses a series of expressionist scenes to convey her stylistically complex future vision.

517 LOGAN, GREG. "An Alien Heat." *Honcho* (West Hollywood), August 1987. [M]
Gay male science-fiction erotica.

518 LOGAN, GREG. "Space Pup." *Stallion* 6, no. 8 (March 1987). [M]
Gay male science-fiction erotica.

519 LORAINE, PHILIP [pseudonym of Robin Estridgel]. *Voices in an Empty Room*. New York: Random House, 1973. [M]
The sordid past of the Spencers, an old San Franciscan family, literally comes back to haunt them. A major character, Richard Owen Spencer, is homosexual. He is a sympathetic character throughout. An effective genre novel of possession and the supernatural.

520 LOUISE, VIVIENNE. "Ayemu's Children." *Sinister Wisdom* (Berkeley, Calif.), no. 34 (1988). [F]
In a nightmarish future world, many women have joined the Cortrona, a colony of women who can change from women to spiders. These magical spider-women hide from, and feed off, men. "Ayemu's Children" concerns one spider-woman's return to human form and society to help her mother.

521 LUCIAN. "True History." In *The Works of Lucian of Samosata*. Oxford: Clarendon Press, 1905. [M]

This is the oldest citation listed in this bibliography. A pure fantasy tale written by the notable Greek satirist, Lucian, around A.D. 200. The involved narrative recounts the marvelous journey of Lucian and his men. It contains one of the earliest literary travels to the moon. The adventurers find the moon inhabited entirely by men who mate with each other and give birth to their young through their calves.

522 LUMLEY, BRIAN. "Aunt Hester." In *The Horror at Oakdeene, and Others*. Sauk City, Wis.: Arkham House, 1977. [f]

Aunt Hester has the uncanny ability to exchange bodies with her twin brother. As a young girl, Hester manages to force the switch several times. Her twin eventually moves to Australia to escape her horrifying powers. When Aunt Hester is an old spinster spiritualist she again attempts the process. One of the body exchanges results in a short lesbian sequence that Hester finds repugnant.

523 LUPOFF, RICHARD A[LLEN]. *A Crack in the Sky*. New York: Dell, 1976. [f, m]

It is sometime in the maybe-not-so-distant future. The Earth is polluted beyond recognition, and the few humans who are left live in domed cities scattered far apart. In the midst of all the chaos, while the rest of the population hangs onto the slim hope of contact with another planet that could restore their lost technology, the Order of St. Jerome is plotting to take over the world. When word does come from outside, the Jerome Order commandeers the computer center, and war breaks out. Bisexual content is minor but explicit, taking the form of group marriages.

524 LUPOFF, RICHARD A[LLEN]. "Stroka Prospekt." Illustrated by Ann Mikolowski. West Branch, Iowa: Toothpaste Press, 1982. [M, X]

Lupoff has outdone himself (and everyone else) with this story about the future Soviet Union. Six workers from Planetoid Mining Station No. 18 take a holiday in the resort town, Novaya Zevezdograd. One of the six is able to fulfill his dreams of engaging in sex with a member of the officially nonexistent alien race, Polnyiki. Apparently, all planetoid miners are homosexual, as shown when two of them discuss what their families think of them. Lupoff writes convincingly of Soviet future daily life, male bonding, and sexual variance. This story is a part of the publisher's Singularities series of illustrated letterpress limited editions edited by Thomas Disch.

LUPOFF, RICHARD A[LLEN]. Sun's End Trilogy. [f]:

525 ■ *Sun's End*. New York: Berkley, 1984.

526 ■ *Galaxy's End*. New York: Berkley, 1988.

Sun's End and Galaxy's End are two parts of a trilogy revolving around astronaut Daniel Kitajima. Kitajima is slammed by a crane while orbiting in space and awakens eighty years later to find himself medically reincarnated as a cybernetic experiment. Two of his closest friends and lovers are a lesbian couple, Lydia Haddad and Tovah Decertes. The third book in the trilogy, *Time's End*, is forthcoming.

527 LYNDON, BARRE [pseudonym of Alfred Edgar], and SANGSTER, JIMMY. *The Man Who Could Cheat Death*. London: Ace, 1959. Reprint. New York: Avon, 1959. [f]

Based on the screenplay of a film by the same name, this story is about a man who finds a way to live forever by receiving glandular transplants. During his adventures he meets a lesbian. He first converts her to heterosexuality, then he marries her, and finally he murders her.

LYNN, ELIZABETH A[NNE]. The Chronicles of Tornor Trilogy. [F, M]:

528 ■ *Watchtower*. New York: Berkley, 1978.

529 ■ *The Dancers of Arun*. New York: Berkley, 1979.

530 ■ *The Northern Girl*. New York: Berkley, 1980.

Elizabeth Lynn's Chronicles of Tornor comprise a fine fantasy trilogy with some of the best gay and lesbian images in science fiction. The three novels detail the gradual changes wrought throughout a rigid feudal society when a powerful, humanistic philosophy is introduced into the social weave. This philosophy, the chea, is spread by the nonsexist dancer / warriors, the chearis. All three novels contain considerable gay male and lesbian content. *Watchtower* deals with the loyal but chaste relationship between young Prince Errel and his military commander Rilke, and it features a pair of lesbians who are mistaken for hermaphrodites. The main character of the second volume, *The Dancers of Arun*, has three concerns: he is disabled (his right arm was severed at the shoulder); he has telepathic seizures; and he is in love with his brother. The trilogy climaxes with *The Northern Girl*, which is primarily lesbian in content. There is a 100-year lapse between each novel. The trilogy is loving and positive; highly recommended.

531 LYNN, ELIZABETH A[NNE]. "Circus." In *Chrysalis Three*, edited by Roy Torgeson. New York: Zebra Books, 1979. [m]

An eerie fantasy story about a raggle-taggle traveling circus and its magical ringleader. A minor character, Tony, is homosexual.

532 LYNN, ELIZABETH A[NNE]. *A Different Light*. New York: Bantam, 1978. [f, M]

Jimson is a talented young artist with incurable cancer. To survive he must remain confined to his planet; a journey to the stars soon would kill him. Nevertheless, he makes the decision to seek outer-space adventure and to search for his former male lover, the wild and headstrong Russell. Once off-world, Jimson becomes romantically involved with a female space pilot named Leiko, but their affair abruptly ends when Russell shows up on the scene. The two men resume their stormy and sometimes painful relationship. Russell must learn to deal with Jimson's impending death, and Jimson must work out his feelings of resentment over Russell's abandonment. They embark upon an adventure with Leiko and a telepathic alien. Love between women is presented positively in the form of a youthful-looking older starship captain who reminisces about a former lover.

533 LYNN, ELIZABETH A[NNE]. "The Gods of Reorth." In *The Berkley Showcase Volume 1: New Writings in Science Fiction*, edited by Victoria Schochet and John Silbersack. New York: Berkley, 1980. [F]

Using a mythological style, Lynn issues a harsh condemnation of male violence and warfare. A lesbian scientist from an advanced civilization is revered as a god by the people of a peaceful planet. When the aggressive tactics of other "gods" unleash chaos and bloodshed, the Goddess fights back.

534 LYNN, ELIZABETH A[NNE]. "Jubilee's Story." In *Millennial Women*, edited by Virginia Kidd. New York: Delacorte, 1978. [F]

A traveling group of amazon women come upon a run-down farmhouse and inside find a woman in labor. They help the woman give birth to her child and choose not to interfere as her brother-in-law murders her husband in a fight over fatherhood rights. In an effort to save her newborn daughter from her own horrible situation, the mother gives the baby to the amazons as they leave. One of the amazons vows to return to help the mother.

535 LYNN, ELIZABETH A[NNE]. "The Man Who Was Pregnant." In *Chrysalis One*, edited by Roy Torgeson. New York: Zebra Books, 1977. [m]

One morning, a man awakens to find himself pregnant. When his lovers (one female and one male) are unable to help him deal with his unique predicament, he turns to his sisters for help. The story challenges traditional sex roles yet steers clear of polemics.

536 LYNN, ELIZABETH A[NNE]. "The White King's Dream." In *Shadows Two*, edited by Charles L. Grant. Garden City, N.Y.: Doubleday, 1979. [m]

An evocative horror story set in a contemporary geriatric ward. A comatose patient and a young alcoholic orderly find themselves ominously dreaming about their deaths. A minor character is a sympathetically described gay man.

537 LYNN, ELIZABETH A[NNE]. "The Woman Who Loved the Moon." In *Amazons!* edited by Jessica Amanda Salmonson. New York: DAW, 1979. [F]

Lynn creates an enchanting myth / fantasy from the imaginary County of Issho. Kai Talvela and her two sisters anger the moon with their fame as warriors. An old woman named Sedi, a manifestation of the moon, challenges the sisters to combat, and she slays first one, then another. Kai, the remaining sister, vows to avenge these deaths, and she travels to the Cave of the Moon at the world's edge, seeking the elusive Sedi. When the time comes for the women to fight, Kai finds Sedi too beautiful to kill, and for many seasons they live together as lovers. This moving and magical lesbian tale won the 1980 World Fantasy Award.

Biographical Note
Elizabeth A. Lynn (b. 1947) consistently combines her talent for storytelling with a positive feminist / gay perspective. She is also the author of *The Sardonyx Net* (New York: Putnam, 1981) and *The Silver Horse* (New York: Bluejay, 1984). All of the above-mentioned short stories have been reprinted in *The Woman Who Loved the Moon* (New York: Berkley, 1981).

Lynn is aware of other social issues too and incorporates this awareness into her work. Many of her characters are lesbians or gay men. Another strong influence on her writing is the Japanese martial art, Aikido, in which the author holds a black belt.

Supplemental information on Lynn can be found in "Tales of Gay Tomorrow: Elizabeth Lynn," by Elenore G. Pred in the *Advocate* (San Mateo, Calif.), no. 253 (1 November 1978).

---

538 MacARTHUR, ARTHUR. *After the Afternoon*. New York: D. Appleton-Century, 1941. [M]

After the Afternoon is a historical fantasy set in ancient Greece that follows the loves and adventures of Lykos, a Cretan faun. Lykos is granted immortality and superpowers by the gods and goddesses of Olympus, and he has the ability to make men, as well as women, fall in love with him. This is clearly illustrated in his relationship with his brother-in-law, Alcmaeon. Lykos also has a racy sadomasochistic affair with another Greek youth while visiting Egypt. The homosexual elements are unmistakable.

539 MacBETH, GEORGE. *The Transformation*. London: Gollancz, 1975. [F, M, X]
A bizarre short fantasy that concerns a protagonist who indiscriminately changes from male to female without any apparent rhyme or reason. The story is narrated in the first person as the sex-changing protagonist experiences her/his metamorphoses and has several sexual encounters with individuals of both sexes. Intentionally obscure, this is a compelling book.

540 McCAFFREY, ANNE. "Changeling." In *Get Off the Unicorn*. New York: Ballantine, Del Rey, 1977. [M]
A heterosexual woman and a gay man, both involved in a four-way marriage, decide to have a child via artificial insemination. The author's attitude toward this arrangement, and especially toward the father's sexuality, is puzzling. Although she professes sympathy and friendship with gay men in her brief introduction to "Changeling," the personality of her gay male character is arrogant, misogynistic, and cruel.

541 McDONALD, JOHN D. "The Big Contest." *Worlds Beyond*, December 1950. Reprinted in *Human?*, edited by Judith Merril. New York: Lion, 1954. [m]
An entertaining story about an old man recalling an encounter with an alien at a small-town spitting contest. An extreme "sissy" stereotype is used to identify one of the minor characters as homosexual.

McDOWELL, MICHAEL. Blackwater Series. [f, m]:

542 ▪ *The Flood*. New York: Avon, 1983.

543 ▪ *The Levee*. New York: Avon, 1983.

544 ▪ *The House*. New York: Avon, 1983.

545 ▪ *The War*. New York: Avon, 1983.

546 ▪ *The Fortune*. New York: Avon, 1983.

547 ▪ *Rain*. New York: Avon, 1983.
In Michael McDowell's six-part Blackwater series, the residual evil of a mysterious 1919 flood in Perdido, Alabama, disturbs the Caskeys, a large backwater family, for generations. This evil takes the

form of Elinor Dammert, who exerts a supernatural influence over the family ... *and* the river. McDowell includes both gay male and lesbian characterizations in this sprawling family saga.

548 McDOWELL, MICHAEL. *The Elementals*. New York: Avon, 1981. [M]
A funeral brings the far-flung members of the McCrays and the Savages, two respected Mobile families, to a summer reunion on the family beachfront property on the Gulf. As the hot summer wears on, the skeletons in the familial closet literally begin to haunt the party. Suspenseful and well-drawn horror fiction, enhanced with significant and positive gay male content.

549 McDOWELL, MICHAEL. "Miss Mack." In *Halloween Horrors*, edited by Alan Ryan. Garden City, N.Y.: Doubleday, 1986. [F]
Miss Mack, a grade-school teacher in a small Southern town, finds her lesbian romance thwarted by the sinister occult manipulations of a heterosexual rival.

Biographical Note

Michael McDowell (b. 1950) has a talent for combining imagination, suspense, and horror, yet he avoids the gratuitous violence so common in the horror field. He is also the author of *The Amulet* (New York: Avon, 1979), *Cold Moon over Babylon* (New York: Avon, 1980), *Gilded Needles* (New York: Avon, 1980), and *Katie* (New York: Avon, 1980), and he was the scriptwriter for the film *Beetlejuice*.

McDowell is openly gay. His *Gilded Needles*, a mystery novel, has significant lesbian content. McDowell is half of the writing team responsible for the delightful gay Nathan Aldyne mysteries.

He is interviewed in Douglas E. Winters's *Faces of Fear* (New York: Berkley, 1985). Additional biographical information can be found in *Contemporary Authors*, vols. 93-96, ed. Francis C. Locher (Detroit: Gail, 1988).

---

550 McGREGOR, LOREN. *The Net*. New York: Berkley, 1987. [F, m]
The Net by up-and-coming writer Loren McGregor is a finely wrought adventure in which the risks are high and the stakes are great. Wealthy space captain Jason Horiuchi is offered a challenge: to steal a priceless ruby from a well-guarded museum. Horiuchi's pride and curiosity are stimulated and she accepts. The ensuing caper is fast and exciting. McGregor's future is extremely high-tech, and body alterations are common. The captain's lesbian lover, for example, has a pelt of fur implanted on her shoulders.

McILWAIN, DAVID. *See* MAINE, CHARLES ERIC (pseudonym)

551 McINTYRE, VONDA N. *The Exile Waiting.* Garden City, N.Y.: Doubleday, 1975. [M?]

Mischa is a wonderful adolescent hero living in a vast enclosed city of rock and steel on a future Earth. In her struggle to escape poverty and abuse, she boldly appeals to two alien pirates named Sub-One and Sub-Two who, although emotionally bound together, have come to despise each other. Mischa has a powerful and often painful telepathic communication with her siblings and with some of the mutant humans who are forced to live in underground caverns as outcasts of the dominant "normal" culture. The mutants have developed an egalitarian and supportive society in contrast to the sexual and class exploitation of the dominant culture. There is minor mention of homosexuality among the ruling class and their slaves. The author celebrates the strength of differences in people and writes a fast-paced, feminist novel.

552 McINTYRE, VONDA N. "Looking for Satan." In *Thieves' World III: Shadows of Sanctuary*, edited by Robert Lynn Asprin. New York: Ace, 1981. [F]

McIntyre uses a lesbian character of Marion Zimmer Bradley's to spin a delightful love story. Lythande, Bradley's cross-dressing sorcerer with a mysterious blue star on her forehead, helps three travelers rescue their enslaved friend and falls in love with one of them. The travelers, two women and two men, have all slept together at various times.

553 McINTYRE, VONDA N. "Screwtop." In *The Crystal Ship*, edited by Robert Silverberg. New York: Nelson, 1976. [M?]

A hot jungle planet is used as a prison where convicts are forced into hard labor. A woman and two men form a strong emotional and sexual bond until the cruel head guard interferes. A painful and absorbing story.

554 McINTYRE, VONDA N. *Starfarers.* New York: Ace, 1989. [M]

The *Starfarer* is a gigantic interstellar research ship in the last stages of construction. The international crew of scientists is on board when the United States attempts to take control of the ship for nationalistic defense purposes. Alien Contact Team Leader Victoria Fraser MacKenzie and her partners, Satoshi and Stephen Thomas Gregory, need to convince the other members of the ship's community to go ahead with the research mission. Victoria MacKenzie is an African-Canadian, and Satoshi is an American of Japanese and Hawaiian descent. With Gregory, they form a professional / familial / sexual partnership. McIntyre pays close attention to cultural heritage, intergenerational family relations, and the sexual identity of her characters.

555 McINTYRE, VONDA N. "Wings." In *The Alien Condition*, edited by Stephen Goldin. New York: Ballantine, 1973. [M?, X]

McIntyre creates a beautiful and sad story about a race of winged people on a dying world. While children, these people are androgynous; they choose their gender at puberty. A keeper of a temple whose god has long since fled nurtures a broken-winged androgynous youth while struggling to repress his sexual attraction by conceiving of it as a boy. When the youth heals, it leaves to avoid becoming a lover of the crippled temple keeper. A year later the youth, now a man, returns to the temple to express his love for the dying keeper.

556 McKAY, CLAUDIA. *Promise of the Rose Stone*. Norwich, Vt.: New Victoria, 1986. [F]

McKay's implausible plot makes for weak science fiction, but readers may enjoy her positive depiction of lesbianism. When the traditions of her mountain village are threatened, Isa, a young woman warrior, travels to the ruling Federation for help. Established after a terrible war, the Federation insures peace by enforcing rigid conformity. The warrior becomes acquainted with Federation mores, but is suddenly captured and banished to the satellite Olyeve, which circles her planet. Within Olyeve, she discovers wondrous secrets and finds a beautiful, dark-skinned lover.

557 McKINLAY, M. CATHERINE [pseudonym of Katherine V. Forrest]. "Xessex." *Fantasy and Science Fiction*, February 1983. Reprinted in *Swords and Dreams*. Tallahassee, Fla.: Naiad, 1987. [M, X?]

An intriguing story about an alien's sexual contact with two human males. The alien physically resembles a human female but is actually a male. One human rejects sexual involvement, and the other human welcomes it.

See also FORREST, KATHERINE V.

558 McMAHAN, JEFFREY N. "The Dark Red Day." In *Somewhere in the Night*. Boston: Alyson, 1989. [M]

McMahan delivers a powerful horror story in which a successful urban gay man returns to his backward hometown to visit his first male lover and to wreak a horrible revenge on his youthful tormentors.

559 McMAHAN, JEFFREY N. "Fantasyland." In *Somewhere in the Night*. Boston: Alyson, 1989. [M]

An unhappy gay teenager escapes into a world of fantasy until his male sweetheart is threatened by fag-bashers.

560 McMAHAN, JEFFREY N. "Hell Is for Children: Cruising with Andrew–Again." In *Somewhere in the Night*. Boston: Alyson, 1989. [M]

McMahan's vampire, Andrew Lyall, is an out-of-the-closet version of Anne Rice's renowned vampire, Lestat. He works the night shift in a boutique and cruises the gay bars for his meals. His character is an excellent study in the complexities of vampire life: he is civilized, wry, and urbane, yet a vicious man-killer; compellingly erotic, yet fatally dangerous; human, yet alien. In "Hell Is for Children," Andrew finds a serial killer cramping his style.

561 McMAHAN, JEFFREY N. "Somewhere in the Night: Cruising with Andrew." In *Somewhere in the Night*. Boston: Alyson, 1989. [M]

Another Andrew Lyall story in which the erudite vampire questions his solitary existence when he is pursued by a handsome young Adonis.

562 McMAHAN, JEFFREY N. "This Apartment Possessed." In *Somewhere in the Night*. Boston: Alyson, 1989. [M]

After a young gay man moves into a haunted apartment, he experiences blackouts and finds his behavior dramatically changing.

563 McMAHAN, JEFFREY N. "Two-Faced Johnny." In *Somewhere in the Night*. Boston: Alyson, 1989. [M]

Johnny and Robert, two gay men in search of a Halloween party, find more than they ask for when one of them undergoes a macabre transformation.

564 McMAHAN, JEFFREY N. "Who Could Ask for Anything More?" In *Somewhere in the Night*. Boston: Alyson, 1989. [M]

Ethan, a middle-class suburban gay man, discovers a strange, ominous weed slowly taking over his garden.

Biographical Note

Jeffrey N. McMahan (b. 1954) is also the author of *Vampires Anonymous*, a novel featuring Andrew Lyall, to be published by Alyson Press.

---

565 McOY. "Living Legend." *Mandate* (New York), August 1989. [M]

Two starship captains meet in a space station bar and have an erotic encounter.

566 MADSON, CATHERINE. "Commodore Bork and the Compost." *Women* (Baltimore) 5, no. 1 (1976). [F]

The *Ark* is a funky but homey spaceship inhabited by a feminist, matriarchal crew composed of both women and men. Crew members from the *Invictus*, a sterile, patriarchal spaceship, board the *Ark* in a cultural exchange. The story presents a fun and positive lesbian image.

567 MAINE, CHARLES ERIC [pseudonym of David McIlwain]. *Alph*. Garden City, N.Y.: Doubleday, 1972. [F]

In the lesbian society of future Earth, men have been extinct for 500 years. When a baby boy is created in a laboratory from the sperm of a frozen male corpse, the government orders his extermination. A revolution erupts to protect the boy, and the new "Reversionist" (also totalitarian) government takes steps to create more males. Yet another group springs up to oppose the Reversionists' eugenic plan. This group of lesbians equate heterosexuality with rape; "simulo," one of their guerrilla tactics, involves the rape of a lesbian by a "simulated man" (another lesbian) combined with a speech saying that rape is the new government-supported form of sexual expression – get used to it. Although disgusted by the "party game" the victims frequently return again and again.

568 MAINE, CHARLES ERIC [pseudonym of David McIlwain]. *World without Men*. New York: Ace, 1958. [F]

The first section of this reactionary book shows the future lesbian society as perverted and women as emotionally disturbed. The second section of the book jumps back in time to describe how men became extinct, and it becomes a diatribe on birth control pills. The wide use of the Pill causes moral values and social institutions to deteriorate. Women become promiscuous; nuclear families are abandoned. The birthrate plummets, and (for unexplained reasons) the few children born are usually female. This situation leads to worldwide censorship of news media, compulsory fertilization of women, and state institutions to rear and condition children since women are no longer willing to perform this function. The concluding section is identical to the first few chapters in *Alph*, published fourteen years later with a two-page racy lesbian scene omitted.

569 MAINS, GEOFF. *Gentle Warriors*. Pound Ridge, N.Y.: Knights, 1989. [f, M]

Mains sets his bitter and pessimistic AIDS fantasy in the very near future. In an effort to "clean up" America, a diabolic conspiracy between right-wing and Fundamentalist forces, a fascist president, and the CIA has engineered the AIDS virus and planted it in the gay community. The San Francisco gay and lesbian community, led by a gay man with AIDS, resorts to guerrilla warfare. The vision can be compared to similar ones by Barrus, Birdstone, Bryan, and Welles.

570 MALZBERG, BERRY N[ORMAN]. *Beyond Apollo*. New York: Random House, 1972. [m]
   The space program attempts to land two men on Venus, but the landing never takes place. When the ship returns to Earth, the authorities find that the captain was murdered and that the crew member, Evans, is crazy. They question what, or who, is responsible – something alien on Venus or the conditions to which astronauts are subjected during their training? Evans was in love with the captain, and *Beyond Apollo* includes a violent sex scene between the two men.

571 MALZBERG, BERRY N[ORMAN]. "Culture Lock." In *Future City*, edited by Roger Elwood. New York: Trident, 1973. [M]
   Two men, Burt and Kenny, find their homosexual relationship threatened by the loveless, promiscuous, but socially acceptable gay life of the future in this bleak and depressing story. The couple is consciously role-defined.

572 MALZBERG, BERRY N[ORMAN]. "Going Down." In *Dystopian Visions*, edited by Roger Elwood. Englewood Cliffs, N.J.: Prentice-Hall, 1975. [M]
   A troubled clerk enters "The Institute," a psychiatric treatment center where patients are hypnotically enabled to live out their private sexual fantasies. The treatment, however, reveals far more than the clerk's latent homosexuality. Frightening and powerful.

573 MALZBERG, BERRY N[ORMAN]. "In the Stocks." In *New Dimensions Seven*, edited by Robert Silverberg. New York: Harper & Row, 1977. [M]
   A sequel to "Culture Lock" (see citation above) in which Burt has a sexual encounter with a woman who may, or may not, be real. This brief lapse into possible heterosexuality causes estrangement from Burt's male lover and eventually causes Burt's expulsion from his all-male community. Male homosexuals are again portrayed as role-defined and misogynistic.

574 MALZBERG, BERRY N[ORMAN]. *On a Planet Alien*. New York: Pocket Books, 1974. [M]
   An interesting look at a space mission to colonize an alien planet. The story unfolds through the eyes of the commander of the mission in a stream of consciousness-style of writing. The crew of the mission includes two gay men, Closter and Stark.

575 MALZBERG, BERRY N[ORMAN]. *The Sodom and Gomorrah Business*. New York: Pocket Books, 1974. [M]

The Sodom and Gomorrah Business depicts a New York of the future entirely devoid of human compassion. The majority of the population lives in a desperate urban jungle known as the Network, where wild gangs roam the streets looking for trouble. Life within the Network is controlled by the fascist Institute for Urban Control. An Institute student and his male lover set out to terrorize the Network's inhabitants. They are, however, captured by Network revolutionaries and forced to lead an assault against the Institute. Women are oppressed both within the Institute and within the Network. Homosexuality is clearly linked with perversion and decadence.

576 MALZBERG, BERRY N[ORMAN]. "State of the Art." In *New Dimensions Four*, edited by Robert Silverberg. New York: Signet, 1974. [F]

At some unspecified time in the future, several famous literary figures attend a gathering with the narrator in a decaying Paris. Among the notables (including Shakespeare, Hemingway, and Ezra Pound) are Gertrude Stein and Alice B. Toklas. The women's lesbianism embarrasses the narrator, and their characterizations are neither convincing nor sympathetic.

577 MALZBERG, BERRY N[ORMAN]. *Tactics of Conquest*. New York: Pyramid, 1974. [M]

In this bizarre novel, the Overlords of the universe require two Earth men – David, the first-person narrator, and Louis, his lifelong chess opponent – to play a chess tournament for the fate of the galaxy. Much of the novel's meaning is revealed in the complicated chess game. Both of the players are megalomaniacs who are extremely guilt-ridden about their occasional homosexual involvement with each other. Except for one prostitute, the novel contains no women.

578 MANDEVILLE, Sir JOHN [pseudonym]. *Voiage and Travayle of Syr John Maundeville, Knight*. New York: Dutton, Everyman's Library, 1928. [Note: This edition is a reprint of the texts of 1568 and 1887, with certain passages that the Elizabethan printers omitted in error restored.] [F, X]

Various editions of this fantasy began circulating as early as 1499. The epic poem from the Middle Ages recounts the amazing voyage of Sir John Mandeville. Among the many uncharted islands that Mandeville and his crew discover are an amazon island and an island inhabited by members of a "third sex."

579 MARAH, JASMINE. "Catching a Spirit." *Sinister Wisdom* (Berkeley, Calif.), no. 34 (1988). [F]

Two young Jewish girls, exploring the woods outside of Prague, encounter an ancient spirit who encourages them to become lesbians.

580 MARION. *Spiderwomon's Lesbian Fairy Tales*. Stanford, Conn.: New Moon Communications, 1977. [F]

The short fables in this small-press book consist of more than familiar fairy tales simply revised for lesbian readers. They are free-flowing verses concerning nature, spirituality, and women loving women that utilize traditional fantasy characters. The calligraphy by Mary Lee Lemke enhances the book.

581 MARSHANK, SONDRA, and CULBRETH, MYRNA. *The Price of the Phoenix*. New York: Bantam, 1977. [M?]

Like much "Star Trek" apocrypha, this novel centers on the intense emotional relationship between Captain Kirk and Mr. Spock. The relationship is complicated by the introduction of a second Kirk, designated "James." Created by the diabolic Omne as part of a plot to force Spock to betray the Federation, James has all of Kirk's memories, loyalties, and virtues. The intensity and complexity of the shifting emotional commitments make clear the implicit homoeroticism of the male characters – including Omne, who pauses only slightly this side of overt sexual intentions toward the "original" Kirk. Sadomasochistic erotic content is strong, though unacknowledged.

582 MARTIN, GEORGE R. R. *Dying of the Light*. New York: Simon & Schuster, 1977. [M?]

A great Festival of the Worlds has been held on the mysteriously wandering planet of Worlorn. As Worlorn moves further away from its temporary orbit around a group of suns, the Festival celebrators depart, leaving fantastic, deserted cities behind. Among the few who remain are two males from Kaval, Jaan and Janacek. The two men are bound together in a traditional Kavallan relationship called "teyn," meaning "the chosen-brother and soulmate and lover and warrior twin." The men share a woman, Gwen, in a bond of "obligation and possession. No love." Gwen's old lover, Dirk, shows up on the planet to release her from this trapped situation but finds Gwen satisfied with her lot. Although the teyn relationship is intriguing, the sexual aspects are entirely ignored. The descriptions of abandoned ghost cities and deserted amusement parks are memorable.

583 MARTINI, VIRGILLIO. *The World without Women*. Translated by Emile Capouya. New York: Dial, 1971. Originally published as *Il Mondo Senza Donne*. Iesolo, Italy: Tritone, 1969. [M]

An early version of this novel was published by the author in Ecuador in 1936, and the final version has been reprinted several times. In the year 2000, a mysterious disease, *falloppitis*, proves lethal for millions of women. Finally, only one of childbearing age remains, Rebecca Levy, who is sold by her father to serve as the world's whore. One of her daughters, Eve, heralds the dawn of a transitory matriarchy. All of Martini's characters are stereotypes: the miserly Jew, the primitive black, and the whoring woman. His homosexual characters are depicted as misogynistic queens who are responsible for the invention and propagation of *falloppitis* to attain the "divine" state of worldwide homosexuality.

584 MASON, DAVID. *Kavin's World*. New York: Lancer, 1969. [m]

An interesting Sword and Sorcery novel detailing the adventures of the barbaric Kavin, Prince of Dorda, and his battle against the powers of evil. Toward the end of the novel, an androgynous male villain claims that Kavin's attraction to his female lover is tinged by homoerotic feelings towards the villain, since the lover and the villain look alike. ("You knew men, in her, and you were drawn . . . .") The interchange ends with Kavin calling the epicene villain a sailor's wench. As in most Sword and Sorcery fantasies, there are sexist elements.

585 MATHESON, RICHARD [BURTON]. *Hell House*. New York: Viking, 1971. [f, m]

During the 1920s, Emeric Belasco's house was known for the decadence and debauchery of its inhabitants. Even after Belasco's death, the malevolence clung to the building, earning it the title, "The Mount Everest of Haunted Houses." Five psychic investigators endeavor to exorcise the house, with frightening results. In one instance, a woman becomes possessed and attempts to molest another woman. There is a brief mention of Belasco being sexually abused as a youngster by an older homosexual teacher.

586 MATHESON, RICHARD [BURTON]. *The Shrinking Man*. Greenwich, Conn.: Fawcett Gold Medal, 1956. [m]

A classic science-fiction story about a man who suddenly begins to shrink in size. Specialists are unable to aid him, and eventually he is battling spiders as if they were enormous monsters. At one point, when he is just over four feet tall, a sleazy pederast mistakes him for a young boy and makes a pass at him. This derogatory homosexual image was eliminated from the motion picture version of the story (though probably for all the wrong reasons).

587 MATHEWS, PATRICIA. "Camilla." In *Sword of Chaos*, edited by Marion Zimmer Bradley. New York: DAW, 1982. [F?]

Camilla, a Free Amazon character from Marion Zimmer Bradley's popular Darkover series, becomes a Terran agent to rescue a stranded female scientist. Although Camilla is an open lesbian in several of Bradley's most popular novels, her sexuality can only be inferred from Mathews's short story; there is no overt mention of her lesbianism.

588 MAXIM, JOHN R. *Platforms*. New York: G. P. Putnam's Sons, 1980. [m]

After a freak accident at a railway station, advertising executive Peter Halloran begins seeing ghosts while waiting for his morning train. A team of trained parapsychologists, concerned about the psychic energy emanating from the station, rushes to help. Among the ghost hunters is gay Alex, a contradictory character of both evil and good.

MELTZER, DAVID. The Agency Trilogy. [f, m]:

589 ■ *The Agency*. North Hollywood, Calif.: Essex House, 1968.

590 ■ *The Agent*. North Hollywood, Calif.: Essex House, 1968.

591 ■ *How Many Blocks in the Pile?* North Hollywood, Calif.: Essex House, 1968.

This pornographic trilogy describes a secret, sexually reactionary government agency with almost omnipotent international power. The trilogy is an intentional experiment in the use of pornography as a means of social satire and political dissent. Lesbian and gay male sequences are scattered throughout the three novels.

MELTZER, DAVID. The Brain Plant Tetralogy. [f, m]:

592 ■ *Lovely*. North Hollywood, Calif.: Essex House, 1969.

593 ■ *Healer*. North Hollywood, Calif.: Essex House, 1969.

594 ■ *Out*. North Hollywood, Calif.: Essex House, 1969.

595 ■ *Glue Factory*. North Hollywood, Calif.: Essex House, 1969.

In this pornographic tetralogy, Meltzer again experiments with using erotica for social comment on the Vietnam War. The four novels episodically reveal a nightmarish future ruled by the Military Industry with undeclared military conflict, sexual anarchy, and rebellion. Lesbian, gay male, and bisexual situations occur throughout.

596 MELUCH, R[EBECCA] M. "Conversation with a Legend." In *Memories and Visions: Women's Fantasy and Science Fiction*, edited by Susanna J. Sturgis. Freedom, Calif.: Crossing Press, 1989. [M]

A young American woman, apparently the reincarnation of Alexander the Great's beloved companion Hephaistion, visits the Garden of Midas while touring Greece. Drawn to a particular spot by a stream, she (he?) encounters the soul of his lover.

597 MELUCH, R[EBECCA] M. *Sovereign*. New York: Signet, 1979. [M, f]

The protagonist in Meluch's *Sovereign*, Teal Ray Stewert, is the thirty-third generation of a long genetic experiment. The planet of Arana is breeding a new race – the Royalists – and Teal is a key figure in its evolution. But fate has greater things in store for Teal, and he becomes a player in a galaxy-wide war between Earthlings and Uelsons for the domination of the universe. Teal is bisexual; his relationships with men are primary to the plot. There is also a minor lesbian character.

598 MELUCH, R[EBECCA] M. *Wind Child*. New York: Signet, 1982. [M, X]

Meluch's main character, Daniel East, is the son of an Earth man and a Kistraalian woman. Kistraal is in danger, and East must save his mother's people. His companion during the adventures is an androgyne named Tavi. Tavi is perceived by East as a man, and they eventually sleep together. There is also mention of a gay male ballet dancer. Sequel to *Wind Dancers* (New York: Signet, 1982).

Biographical Note

Rebecca M. Meluch (b. 1956) is also the author of *Jerusalem Fire* (New York: Signet, 1985). Her science-fiction novel *Chicago Red* (forthcoming) contains significant gay male content but will be published too late for inclusion in *Uranian Worlds*.

---

599 MERLE, ROBERT. *The Virility Factor*. Translated by Martin Sokolinsky. New York: McGraw-Hill, 1977. Originally published as *Les Hommes Protégés*. Paris: Éditions Gallimard, 1974. [F]

A fatal plague hits the United States and affects only virile men. Women assume power, and business continues as usual. The new fascist government, headed by a lesbian separatist, turns society upside down. Women are expected to engage exclusively in lesbian sexual activity; men are expected to be subservient and pay penance for their virility. Dr. Martinilli, a scientist researching a cure for the virility-attacking disease, joins an underground movement (comprising both women and men) to overthrow the government and to replace it with a tolerant, heterosexual matriarchy. Dr. Martinilli apologizes for his misogyny, accepts his lower social position, and acquiesces to a passive sexual role – all in a way that reads like a masochistic male fantasy. Lesbians in the book are despotic, and only two are developed—a sadist and a masochist. The former is murdered; the latter commits suicide.

600 MERRICK, CURT. "Half a World." *ONE Magazine* (Los Angeles), December 1954. [M]

A gay man, Dick Lovett, has a dream of the future in which homosexuals have found total integration into "normal" society. A very idealistic and enjoyable 1950s gay vision.

601 MERRIL, JUDITH. *The Tomorrow People*. New York: Pyramid, 1960. [m]

A two-man expedition to Mars returns with only one member. The returning astronaut, Johnnie Wendt, refuses to talk about the events on Mars that led to the disappearance of his copilot, Laughlin. As a result, there are massive efforts on the part of psychiatrists to figure out what happened. The primary theory is that "for a time before Laughlin's disappearance, a strong homosexual attraction had apparently been developing between the two men." This theory is later proved false.

602 MERRITT, A[BRAHAM]. *The Metal Monster. Argosy—All Story*, 1921. Reprint. New York: Avon, 1946. [F]

While exploring the innermost recesses of the mighty Himalayas, Dr. Walter T. Goodwin and his brave band of adventurers discover a civilization of extraterrestrial beings. These awesome creatures, enormous in size, are shaped in metallic geometric forms and live on electrical energy. Their ruler is a strange, magnetically beautiful woman named Norhala who takes a liking to Goodwin's expedition—and particularly to the solitary female explorer, Ruth. After many harrowing adventures, Norhala, now clearly in love with Ruth, abducts the young woman. When Ruth is finally returned to Goodwin, she can only remember how much Norhala had loved her. Merritt writes with a lush and florid style several steps above most pulp writers of his period. His depiction of lesbian love is remarkable. The novel is a sequel to *The Conquest of the Moon Pool* (New York: Putnam, 1919).

603 MERWIN, SAM, Jr. *Chauvinisto*. Canoga Park, Calif.: Major, 1976. [F?, M?]

Women have ruled the world for centuries and have eliminated racism, sexism, and all vestiges of patriarchal culture. But there remain social malcontents. A small band of butch "Neo-Feminists" are bent on ridding the planet of all men. (These pseudolesbians, however, are actually a front for a male-run conspiracy to alter the Earth's economic base.) The straight male protagonist has a sex change, is zapped into another dimension, is forced into prostitution, and then is gang-raped.

The events are as confusing to the reader as they are to the protagonist, and any interesting sexual identity questions remain unaddressed.

604 MERWIN, SAM, Jr. *The White Widows*. Garden City, N.Y.: Doubleday, 1953. Reprinted as *The Sex War*. New York: Beacon, 1960. [F]

A young male scientist unwittingly stumbles upon a worldwide lesbian conspiracy to eliminate all men. The plot hinges on a mutant strain of women who are telekenetic and attempting to reproduce by parthenogenesis. However, not a single "amazon" has any recognizable emotional or physical desire for other women. They are lesbians in name only.

605 MICHAELS, WARD. "Bobby's Friend." *In Touch for Men* (Hollywood, Calif.), no. 34 (March-April 1978). [M]

An amusing fantasy about a young man's sexual encounter with a handsome merman.

606 MICHAELS, WARD. "The Moons of Sirus." *In Touch* (Los Angeles), no. 39 (January-February 1979). [F?, M]

An intriguing story about a society structured around the total isolation of the sexes. The only contact between women and men is for reproductive purposes. All the males in the story are homosexual, and it can be assumed that the one female character is lesbian.

607 MILLER, P[ETER] SCHUYLER. "Status Quondam." In *New Tales of Space and Time*, edited by Raymond J. Healy. New York: Henry Holt, 1951. [m]

The hero of this story is Simon MacIvor, a heterosexual 1950s man who gets transported from the United States to the Golden Age of Greece by means of a time belt. It does not take long before the morals of Grecian life begin to bother Simon. His tolerance finally snaps when he runs into a bunch of effeminate Grecian gay men. Homosexuality is referred to as a "festering sore" and all gay men are depicted as effeminate.

608 MILLER, WALTER M[ICHAEL], Jr. "The Lineman." *Fantasy and Science Fiction*, August 1957. Reprinted in *A Wilderness of Stars*, edited by William F. Nolan. Nashville: Sherbourne, 1969. [f, m]

Moon settlement has begun. For complex biological reasons, moon bases are required to be single-sexed. "The Lineman" concerns the arrival of an interplanetary brothel on an all-male moon base and the resulting chaos. Homosexuality is mentioned as a result of this sexual segregation.

609 MITCHELL, LORNA. *The Revolution of Saint Jone*. London: Women's Press, 1988. [F]

British feminist and religious scholar Lorna Mitchell creates an unusual saga about a young woman's emotional and sexual awakening. In a postholocaust world, "Krischan" missions preach a rational (and antisexual) way of life to pagans across the world. Recently sanctified Reverend Jone Grifan arrives at her first assignment in the northern Yukey Islands expecting difficulties, but she has no idea that her faith will be so challenged. First, she discovers the immoral, yet beautiful, music of the androgyne singer, Yalida. Worse, she finds a heathen woman, Luner, mysteriously attractive. The author's eclectic spelling becomes irritating, but this is a fine first novel with a strong, prosex, feminist message.

610 MITCHISON, NAOMI [MARY MARGARET]. *Memoirs of a Spacewoman*. London: Gollancz, 1962. Reprint. New York: Berkley, 1973.

The narrator's occupation as an intergalactic communications specialist brings her into close contact with numerous alien species. Each species has its own unique perception and thought pattern, and so it takes a great deal of psychic adjustment on the part of Mary, the narrator, to communicate. The Martians are of particular interest to this bibliography: they have reproductive organs of both sexes, and they become single-sexed only during certain biological cycles. *Memoirs of a Spacewoman* is one of only a handful of pre-1970s science-fiction novels to feature a woman as the main character, and the author makes Mary a dynamic and believable one.

611 MITCHISON, NAOMI [MARY MARGARET]. *Solution Three*. New York: Warner, 1975. [F, M]

When overpopulation threatens to destroy the human race, society finds an answer: homosexuality. Heterosexuals are treated as perverted deviants; their children are "surplus population." To stop war and aggression, the government tries another solution: cloning the perfect black man and the perfect white woman. Their thousands of asexually produced clones, revered by the nonclone population, are sensitive, brilliant, and homosexual. The world seems like a paradise. But underneath this veneer of social equity lies a police state. The several lesbian and gay male relationships depicted have an aura of naïveté and superficiality. In contrast, the solitary heterosexual couple is represented with depth. By the end of the novel, society veers away from mandated homosexuality and begins to accept all forms of sexual expression.

Biographical Note

Naomi Mary Margaret Mitchison (b. 1897) is a skilled novelist, playwright, and poet, who occasionally turns her talents to the science-fiction field. In addition to the novels mentioned above, several of her science-fiction short stories have been published (the first in 1929). None are relevant to this bibliography.

Much of Mitchison's non-science-fiction historical work is of interest to studies of both lesbian and gay male literature. *The Corn King and the Spring Queen* (New York: Harcourt Brace, 1931) and *Black Sparta: Greek Stories* (New York: Harcourt, 1928) are particularly notable from a gay male viewpoint, and the short story "The Delicate Fire," in *The Delicate Fire* (London: Jonathan Cape, 1931), has a major lesbian theme.

Biographical information on Mitchison is available in *Twentieth Century Authors*, ed. Stanley J. Kunitz and Howard Haycraft (New York: Wilson, 1942), and in *Contemporary Authors*, vols. 77-80, ed. Frances Carol Locher (Detroit: Gale, 1979).

---

612 MITZEL, JOHN. "The Last Piece of Trade in America." In *On the Line: New Gay Fiction*, edited by Ian Young. Trumansburg, N.Y.: Crossing, 1981. [M]

Gay journalist John Mitzel offers an amusing satirical look at a future in which effeminate behavior is in vogue. Stanley "Butch" Markman, raised by a hermit in a midwestern state, is courted by many when he brings his masculine ways into perfumed, effete city life.

613 MONTGOMERY, REX. *Man-Made Stud*. Santee, Calif.: Surree, 1977. [M]

Pornographic gay male science fiction.

614 MONTGOMERY, ROD. "Succubus." *In* (Los Angeles), no. 1 (July 1969). [M]

A young man, staying in an old mansion in the bayou country, receives nightly visitations from a beautiful youth, only to find out that the visitor is actually a demon. Cute and mildly pornographic.

615 MOORCOCK, MICHAEL [JOHN]. *The Adventures of Una Persson and Catherine Cornelius in the Twentieth Century*. London: Quarter, 1976. [F]

Two women, Una Persson and Catherine Cornelius, who make frequent appearances within Moorcock's science fiction, travel back and forth through time involving themselves in a wide variety of historical and political events. Far from being traditional helpless heroines, they are independent, capable, and politically inclined. They are both friends and lovers, and their bisexuality, though conspicuously colored by the author's male imagination, is prominently displayed. Scenes of heterosexual activity include rape.

616 MOORCOCK, MICHAEL [JOHN]. "Ancient Shadows." *New Worlds Quarterly*, September 1975. Reprinted in *New Worlds Nine*, edited by Hilary Bailey. London: Corgi, 1975. Reprinted in *Legends from the End of Time*. New York: Harper & Row, 1976. [F, X]

Prudish time traveler Dafnish Armatuce and her son, Snuffles, find themselves transported to Moorcock's amusing and amoral world at The End of Time. People can eat whatever they want, do whatever they please, and change sex at will. Snuffles soon learns to love the hedonistic pleasures of the future society, but his mother pines for the rigid morals of her own time. When Miss Ming, a resident of The End of Time, begins to court Dafnish unabashedly, the situation reaches a crisis. A minor character, Sweet Orb Mace, randomly switches sex and assumes rather effeminate affectations.

617 MOORCOCK, MICHAEL [JOHN]. *Breakfast in the Ruins*. London: New English Library, 1972. Reprint. New York: Random House, 1974. [M]

This episodic, almost plotless novel examines the life of a familiar Moorcock character, Karl Glogauer, and raises some existential questions. The novel's central sequence of events takes place in the rooftop garden of a London department store, Derry and Tom's, a locale Moorcock uses often in his science fiction. The protagonist is approached by a black Nigerian. The cruising and seduction that goes on between the two men becomes a framework through which the rest of the novel is seen.

MOORCOCK, MICHAEL [JOHN]. The Cornelius Chronicles. [f, M, X]:

618 ■ *The Final Programme*. Illustrated by Malcolm Bean. New York: Avon, 1968.

619 ■ *A Cure for Cancer*. Illustrated by Malcolm Bean. London: Allison & Busby, 1971. Reprint. New York: Holt, Rinehart & Winston, 1971.

620 ■ *The English Assassin*. London: Allison & Busby, 1972. Reprint. New York: Harper & Row, 1974.

621 ■ *The Condition of Muzak*. Illustrated by Richard Glyn Jones. London: Allison & Busby, 1977. Reprint. Boston: Gregg Press, 1978.

A fascinating tetralogy that, though often hilariously loony, is nonetheless both serious and structurally complex. All the novels revolve around the mythic figure of Jerry Cornelius and should be read in order of publication. *The Final Programme* introduces Jerry Cornelius and sets the stage for the rest of the tetralogy. In the course of the novel's surreal plot, Jerry flies from London to Lapland. Along the way, he transforms into a hermaphroditic messiah of the New Age, and in the process he kills his brother, his incestuously beloved sister, and several thousand other people. In volume two, Jerry is resurrected as a negative image of himself – black skin and white hair. He is reduced to a catatonic state and spends the majority of *The English Assassin* rotting inside a coffin, which floats in and out of the plot as life continues for Jerry's siblings, the predominantly lesbian Catherine and the bisexual Frank. *The Condition of Muzak* wraps up the saga of Jerry Cornelius. There is male homosexuality and lesbianism throughout the tetralogy, which was issued as a single volume by Avon Books in 1977.

622 MOORCOCK, MICHAEL [JOHN]. *Glorianna; Or the Unfulfill'd Queen: Being a Romance*. London: Allison & Busby, 1978. Reprint. New York: Avon, 1979. [F, m]

The magnificent Queen Glorianna rules the mighty empire of Albion with a firm but just hand. She is beloved by her subjects, and peace, prosperity, and happiness have thrived since her coronation. But the country's stability is a facade, precariously held together by the unceasing efforts of Glorianna and her ministers. The good queen has a deeply personal problem: she is unable to attain orgasm. Despite her valiant and sometimes unique efforts, sexual satisfaction eludes her. The queen is bisexual, and numerous lesbian and gay male minor characters appear within the book's pages. These sexual aspects are handled matter-of-factly, simply incorporated into the weave of an already highly textured book. Although the queen remains in a traditional "princess" mold throughout, never transcending sexist limitations like other Moorcock females, *Glorianna* is one of the author's most clever and best-written pieces.

623 MOORCOCK, MICHAEL [JOHN]. "Waiting for the End of Time." *Visions of Tomorrow*, 1970. Reprinted in *Moorcock's Book of Martyrs*, London: Quartet, 1976. Reprinted in *Dying for Tomorrow*, New York: DAW, 1978. [X]

This wonderful short story is set in a time when the entire galaxy is rapidly condensing into a single mass: the doom of all civilization. The approaching holocaust is watched by two hermaphroditic lovers whose love for each other keeps them brave. A bittersweet and beautiful depiction of their relationship.

Biographical Note

Michael Moorcock (b. 1939) is a highly prolific author who is most often identified with the New Wave science-fiction movement of the 1960s. It was during this period that Moorcock edited the influential British science-fiction magazine *New Worlds*, which published avant-garde pieces by himself, Thomas Disch, Samuel Delany, Charles Pratt, and others.

Moorcock's science-fiction novels, as opposed to his heroic fantasy novels, often contain sexual variations of all kinds and deserve close examination. Information on Moorcock can be found in Peter Nicholls's *The Science Fiction Encyclopedia* (Garden City, N.Y.: Doubleday, 1979). Moorcock discusses his attitudes toward gay liberation in "Echoes of Tomorrow," by Keith Howes in *Gay News* (London), no. 142 (May 1978): 18-31.

624 MOORE, C[ATHERINE] L. "Black Thirst." *Weird Tales*, April 1934. Reprinted in *Shambleau, and Others*. Hicksville, N.Y.: Gnome, 1953. [M?, X]

The Alendar, the evil and mysterious lord of the legendary Venusian harem, is a collector of feminine beauty. Our hero, Northwest Smith, follows one of the Alendar's women into the harem and becomes trapped when the Alendar develops a taste for the "beauty of men." Because the Alendar is decidedly nonhuman, and because his desires are ultimately vampiritic rather than sexual, it is difficult to define "Black Thirst" as a truly homosexual tale. However, considering the Alendar's male persona, it is easy to interpret the story in this way. Great atmosphere development.

625 MOORE, RAYLYN. *What Happened to Emily Goode after the Great Exhibition*. Norfolk, Va.: Donning, Starblaze, 1978. [f]

A very proper Victorian woman is transported through time into the twentieth-century United States and sets off to explore her new terrain. She stumbles across some interesting characters along the way, among them a lesbian named Barry. Barry is an amalgam of derogatory lesbian stereotypes. With such an example, it is no wonder that Emily Goode finds she prefers the sexually repressed Victorian culture. The novel is sexist.

626 MORAN, DANIEL KEYS. *The Armageddon Blues*. New York: Bantam, 1988. [f, m]

Jalian of the Fires Clan, a silver-eyed bisexual amazon from a barbarious future, and Georges Mordeaux, an immortal Frenchman, team up to save the Earth from nuclear Armageddon in this inventive novel by newcomer Moran. Using a stolen time-traveling device, Jalian and Georges return to 1962 to manipulate the time line and to alter destiny. Despite her independence, Jalian is not wholly admirable. To ensure passage of an important appropriations bill, she blackmails, then murders, a closeted top-level Defense Department bureaucrat.

627 MORDDEN, ETHAN. "The Ghost of Champ McQuest." In *Everybody Loves You*. New York: St. Martin's, 1988. [M]
Several gay men find their summer on Fire Island disturbed by a pesky ghost.

628 MORE, MEREDITH [pseudonym]. *October Obsession*. Tallahassee, Fla.: Naiad, 1988. [F]
Laura Westmoreland discovers a hidden diary while investigating the mysterious disappearance of her beloved Aunt Josie. The diary reveals that Laura's aunt has run off with her longtime lesbian lover, an immortal moon-goddess named Selene. The diary speaks directly to Laura, since she is wrestling with her own emerging lesbian passions. A silly, but good-natured, read.

MORRIS, JANET. The Kerrion Trilogy. [M]:

629 ■ *Dream Dancer*. New York: Putnam, 1980.

630 ■ *Cruiser Dreams*. New York: Putnam, 1981.

631 ■ *Earth Dreams*. New York: Putnam, 1982.
Morris's space opera trilogy reads like a science-fiction version of "Dallas." Beautiful Shebat is both an experienced psi-pilot and an erotic, illusion-producing "dream dancer," skilled in a powerful and ancient art. She becomes involved with two feuding brothers, the power-driven Marada and the bisexual Chearon, who are struggling for control of the interstellar Kerrion trading empire. Their changing relationships, and the passions thereof, are the focus of the trilogy.

MORRIS, JANET. The Silistra Series. [f, m]:

632 ■ *High Couch of Silistra*. New York: Bantam, 1977.

633 ■ *The Golden Sword*. New York: Bantam, 1977.

634 ■ *Wind from the Abyss*. New York: Bantam, 1978.

635 ■ *The Carnelian Throne*. New York: Bantam, 1979.
This series is notable for its tedious prose and proliferation of rape fantasies. It revolves around Estri, a courtesan on a planet where courtesans are supposedly powerful. One of her masters, Sereth, forces her to have sex with another powerful woman, and, though forced into

it, the women later admit to each other that they enjoy it. In the second book, Estri teams up with a man, Chayin, as half-partner, half-slave. Her former master Sereth and Chayin become lovers, acceptable since they prove their masculinity by knocking all other men in the book senseless. The last novel of the Silistra series is by far the most readable. Chayin, Sereth, and Estri arrive in a new country where they are assailed by animals controlled by a community of minds called "wehrs." The wehrs, who engage in loathsome practices such as murdering children, are under the command of the Imca-Sorr-Aat. The main object of this book's plot is the throne, with a subplot involving the fate of the human beings.

636 MOSKOWITZ, SAM. "When Women Rule." *If Science Fiction*, August 1967. Reprinted in *When Women Rule*. New York: Walker, 1972. [Nonfiction]
  This article discusses the use of the "woman dominant" theme in science fiction and presents a great deal of fascinating material, some of which is particularly relevant to lesbianism.

637 MOYLAN, TOM. *Demand the Impossible: Science Fiction and the Utopian Imagination*. New York: Methuen, 1986. [Nonfiction]
  Critical work that includes detailed discussion of Russ's *The Female Man*, Le Guin's *The Dispossessed*, Piercy's *Woman on the Edge of Time*, and Delany's *Triton*.

638 MUSHROOM, MERRIL. *Daughters of Khaton*. Denver: Lace, 1987. [F, m]
  A cosexual space exploration team lands on Khaton, a utopian all-lesbian planet where a mystical cogent tree is worshiped. In this world, there is an absence of power imbalances, money, violence, and male aggression. As the patriarchal and lesbian-separatist cultures interact, the crew members find themselves changing. Mushroom works her plot well, but the details and dimensions of Khaton are sketchy. A selection of *Daughters of Khaton* was originally published as "Excerpt from *Sisterworld*," by Meril Harris in *Sinister Wisdom* (Charlotte, N.C.), no. 3 (July 1976).

Biographical Note
Merril Mushroom is a frequent contributor to the lesbian press. She has contributed to *We Are Everywhere: Writings by and about Lesbian Parents*, ed. Harriet Alpert (Freedom, Calif.: Crossing, 1987); *The Leading Edge: An Anthology of Lesbian Sexual Fiction* (Denver, Colo.: Lace, 1987); and *Lesbian Love Stories*, ed. Irene Zahava (Freedom, Calif.: Crossing, 1989).

NACHMAN, ELANA. *See* DYKEWOMAN, ELANA (name change)

639 NADER, GEORGE. *Chrome*. New York: Putnam, 1978. [M]
As the first science-fiction novel published by a major house specifically geared towards the gay male market, *Chrome* is significant but disappointing. It delivers in thrills and explicit homosexuality, but the author's awareness of sexual politics is limited. The story centers on space cadet Chrome and his love affair with the alien warrior king, Vortex. Chrome is a "robot," a genetically engineered human, and the difficulties Chrome and his lover encounter within the future society are the crux of Nader's novel. The love that the two men have for each other is portrayed with honesty, and the entire novel sparkles with homoerotic tension rare in science fiction. The novel displays antifeminist, and sometimes overtly misogynistic, attitudes. Few of the female characters escape traditional women's roles, and as women become more powerful, they correspondingly become more evil. The author attributes the Earth's degeneration into a totalitarian state as intrinsically tied to women's refusal to be mothers, their hunger for power, and their domination of men.

Biographical Note
George Nader (b. 1921) is a former film actor who has recently turned to writing science fiction. Information on Nader can be found in David Galligan's "Chrome Finish: George Nader as Novelist," in the *Advocate* (San Mateo, Calif.), no. 284 (10 January 1980).

---

640 NEWELL, STEVEN WAYNE. *Dreams of Allon*. New York: Carlton, 1987. [M]
This vanity press science-fiction novel contains major gay male content and some interesting ideas, but it is virtually unreadable. The basic plot revolves around the love affair between Jim Drennen, a young college student, and his friend, Mike Staurland. Staurland, it turns out, is actually an enlightened being named Vonius of Allon from an alternative universe, who has opinions on virtually everything, including the environment, nuclear warfare, and even the proper way for two men to make love. (Mutual masturbation is good, Vonius assures us, but oral and anal sex are bad.) The result is a confusing mix of eclectic philosophy, similar in ways to Ignotus's *AE: The Open Persuader*. The author's emphasis on mutual masturbation over anal sex may be in response to the AIDS epidemic.

641 NICKELS, THOM. "After All This." In *Two Novellas*. Austin, Tex.: Banned Books, 1989. [f, M]

After an unexplained flash of lightning kills most of the population of the earth, Toma, a gay man, his friend Julius, and a few other survivors receive a series of bizarre spiritual revelations and found a new culture.

642 NICKELS, THOM. How I Became a Vampire, Anita Bryant." *In Touch for Men* (Los Angeles), no. 32 (November-December 1977). [M, X]
Gay male vampire story.

643 NICKELS, THOM. "Walking Water." In *Two Novellas*. Austin, Tex.: Banned Books, 1989. [M]
A young gay man journeys across an enigmatic river where he happens onto a monastery and begins a metaphysical voyage.

644 NIK [pseudonym]. "The Prince's Predicament." *Ladder* (San Francisco) 4, no. 3 (December 1959). [F, M]
Subtitled "A Fairy Story," this tale concerns Prince Gaylord, who is turned into a woman by a wicked fairy. The new Princess Gay, forced to marry by her parents, opts for convenience and marries Prince Alexander, a man who at one time was a woman. It is obvious that it is all meant in fun.

645 NISSENSON, HUGH. "The Mission." *Playboy*, December 1964. Reprinted in *The Playboy Book of Science Fiction and Fantasy*. Chicago: HMH Publishing, 1966. [m]
Atomic warfare has destroyed Earth's civilization. The planet is inhabited by mutated human beings. A few nonmutant men have survived in a protected military silo; their main problem is an extreme lack of nonmutant women. One result of this shortage is that the men go out on missions to kidnap the few remaining nonmutant women. Another result is an increase in male homosexuality. The depiction of women is abusive.

646 NIVEN, LARRY, and POURNELLE, JERRY. *Inferno*. New York: Pocket Books, 1976. [m]
Niven and Pournelle have written a contemporary updating of Dante's classic descent into hell. A man dies and suddenly finds himself traveling through the inferno. Like Dante's hero, he encounters numerous people, lost and tormented souls, on his journey. Several gay men are among the sinners. Lesbian feminist Monique Wittig uses the same material in her *Across the Acheron* with wildly different results.

647 NORDEN, ERIC. "The Gathering of the Clan." *Fantasy and Science Fiction*, February 1979. [M]

A highly disreputable family gathers for the reading of a dead relative's will only to find that the recently deceased has played a trick on them. The author adds an unexpected twist to this well-used scenario by using a science-fiction ending. Among the disreputable clan members, and the most sympathetic, is a gay man.

648 NORDEN, ERIC. *The Ultimate Solution*. New York: Warner, 1973. [m]
If Hitler had won the war, the world would be a living nightmare. Norden violently shows this nightmare through the eyes of a New York City police officer who, with the Gestapo, is leading a manhunt for the last surviving Jew. In Nazi America, people of color are treated as dogs, and the torture of women is considered a healthy release for white male frustration. Male homosexuality is the state-sanctioned form of sexual expression, and sexual enjoyment is a male prerogative. Abusive scenes picturing women and men in pain fill the pages and leave an acid taste that is not alleviated by the solitary freedom-seeking character who shows up in the final scene.

649 NOVITSKI, PAUL DAVID. "Nuclear Fission." In *Universe Nine*, edited by Terry Carr. Garden City, N.Y.: Doubleday, 1979. [F, M]
This story is set in Oregon after the social / technological revolution, and it looks at social dynamics. In child rearing and family life, gay people play as vital a role as heterosexuals. The story focuses on a woman's lesbian relationship and the growing ambivalence of her feelings towards her deaf son and homosexual husband. Another theme of this fine story is the struggle of their six-year-old boy to accept his deafness and gender.

NUTT, CHARLES. *See* BEAUMONT, CHARLES (pseudonym)

650 [O'BRYAN, MILES.] "Tales of Gay Tomorrow: Miles O'Bryan." Interview by James M. Saslow. *Advocate* (San Mateo, Calif.), no. 253 (1 November 1978). [Nonfiction]
An interview with Miles O'Bryan, author of the unpublished science-fiction trilogy, *The Journals of Kalia-Zann*. The trilogy recounts the many adventures of two male lovers from a distant planet.

651 OFFUTT, ANDREW J[EFFERSON], and BERRY, D. BRUCE. *Genetic Bomb*. New York: Warner, 1975. [f, M]
Someone, or something, is causing an epidemic of insanity among the world's women. Young girls are writhing in the streets, and Doctor Wesley Harmon must find a solution. The explanation turns out to be a genetic time bomb that was implanted thousands of years ago in our cave-dwelling ancestors by more evolved aliens. The future culture envisioned embraces bisexuality as its norm, yet the lesbian characters

are either villains or become heterosexual, and the gay males are either incidental characters or so marginally bisexual as to be indistinguishable from heterosexuals.

652 OSBURN, JESSE. "Peppermint Kisses." In *Shadows 6*, edited by Charles L. Grant. Garden City, N.Y.: Doubleday, 1983. [M]

Homosexuality is used to heighten the horror in Osburn's creepy thriller. A deadly kissing disease is epidemic and civilization is collapsing. Characterized by peppermint-flavored breath, the disease causes a fatal, zombielike condition. Osburn's protagonist is a teenage boy who must avoid the kisses of a repellent older man while searching for food.

PAGET, VIOLET. *See* LEE, VERNON (pseudonym)

653 PAIN, BARRY. *An Exchange of Souls*. London: Eveleigh Nash, 1911. [F?, X]

A British gentleman recounts his friendship with an eccentric scientist, Daniel Myas, who is conducting metaphysical investigations into the nature of death. Myas uses his devoted young assistant, Alice Lade, for a dangerous experiment involving the transmigration of the soul. When the experiment fails, the body of Myas is left lifeless while his soul remains in the body of his female assistant. (Her soul is gone.) The new "Alice" must adapt as best "she" can by living as a woman disguised as a man. The British narrator believes that "Alice" is a man trapped in a woman's body, but a physician gives an alternate explanation for the persistent masquerade. He believes that Alice Lade is a woman who has suffered from a peculiar (and perhaps sexually related) mental disorder. This novel is an early literary example of the use of psychoanalytic theory to explain gender anomalies.

654 PAINE, MICHAEL. *Cities of the Dead*. New York: Charter, 1988. [m]

Set in early twentieth-century Egypt, Michael Paine's novel concerns Howard Carter, a former Inspector of Monuments for Upper Egypt, who acts as a guide for visiting tourists. While traveling across the country, sleeping in tombs, and running into some very sinister Catholic nuns, Carter suddenly begins finding mummies for sale on the black market. He becomes suspicious and his investigation involves him in frightening occult rituals. One of Carter's clients, a German baron, is homosexual. A fairly compelling horror novel.

655 PANATI, CHARLES. *The Pleasuring of Rory Malone*. New York: St. Martin's, 1982. [f, m]

Rory Malone is a sexually repressed seventeen-year-old boy who is gifted with psychokinetic powers. Dr. Elizabeth Hartman, a scientist at Columbia University, is curious about Malone's case and decides to investigate, but she accidentally releases a sexual poltergeist from the young man's psyche. After feeding this spirit by reading pornographic literature, Malone begins to psychically assault women he encounters on Manhattan streets, eventually coming into contact with sleazy gay men, lesbians, and transsexuals.

656 PANGBORN, EDGAR. "The Children's Crusade." *Continuum One*, edited by Roger Elwood. New York: Putnam, 1974. [M?]

A devastating twenty-minute nuclear war has wiped technological civilization from the face of the Earth. Survivors of this holocaust live in an often harsh and brutal feudalistic society. "The Children's Crusade" concerns a messiah figure who gathers a small band of followers to search for a New Jerusalem. Strong male-male love is shown between Malachi, the messiah figure, and his young friend, Jesse, but their special love is nonsexual.

657 PANGBORN, EDGAR. *The Company of Glory*. *Galaxy*, August-September 1974. Reprint. New York: Pyramid, 1975. [F, M]

The Company of Glory is set in the same postholocaust world as "The Children's Crusade." An aged storyteller named Demetrios can still remember the Old Time, our own twentieth century, and he amuses his listeners with his tales of technological marvels. The storyteller, however, can also remember other tales that the ruling class of Demetrios's homeland would rather not have repeated. When Demetrios defies their wishes and tells the forbidden stories, he is arrested. He must gather his friends, his Company of Glory, and search for a new, more hospitable home. Pangborn's personal values are strongly present in this wonderful novel. Repressive, evangelical religions are condemned, the author's pacifism and opposition to war are apparent, and open expression of all forms of sexuality is given approbation. The warm and humanistic outlook of the story makes reading it enjoyable. The novel is the winner of the International Fantasy Award.

658 PANGBORN, EDGAR. *Davy*. New York: St. Martin's Press, 1964. [F?, m]

Davy is the first novel Pangborn located in his feudal, postholocaust New England future. It is written as a first-person narrative of Davy Loomis, an adolescent growing up 300 years after the destruction of twentieth-century civilization. The plot follows Davy through his various loves and exploits, and Pangborn is perhaps at his best when depicting the bubbly, fun-loving nature of his hero. Although Davy is strictly heterosexual, at one point he disguises himself in women's clothing and falls in love with a woman, one who has first appeared in male attire. Two women are mentioned who have a "rare sort of friendship that no man could ever break up," and there are scattered references to male homosexuality throughout. There is also a marriage between a man and two women, with the implication that the women may be lovers.

659 PANGBORN, EDGAR. "Harper Conan and Singer David." In *Tomorrow Today*, edited by George Zebrowski. Santa Cruz, Calif.: Unity Press, 1975. [M?]

Again, Pangborn's postholocaust world provides the setting for the romance between Harper Conan, a blind youth, and his friend, Singer David. Their love for each other is depicted with warmth and is accepted as natural. Recommended.

660 PANGBORN, EDGAR. *A Mirror for Observers*. Garden City, N.Y.: Doubleday, 1954. [M?]

A Mirror for Observers is a pre-*Davy* novel, yet the themes Pangborn later develops are distinctly foreshadowed here. The plot concerns a split among the refugee Martians who mingle secretly with humanity. Most are "Observers" benevolently awaiting humanity's eventual maturation. A few Martians, however, hate the Earth's native population and seek its downfall. This conflict is played out against the backdrop of contemporary urban life. The book climaxes with a man-created holocaust, similar to the one in the *Davy* novels and stories, which sets "progress" back far enough that we can start over. The strong male-male love that flourishes in Pangborn's later work is also evident in muted form. The author describes two relationships (one an evil domination and one a positive Platonic love) that are suggestive, but not explicitly sexual, examples of strong male bonding. A lovely story that won the International Fantasy Award.

661 PANGBORN, EDGAR. "The Night Wind." In *Universe Five*, edited by Terry Carr. New York: Random House, 1974. [M]

This wonderful story is again set in Pangborn's *Davy*-cycle world. Benvenuto, a slight fifteen-year-old lad, has been caught making love with another youth. Forced to leave his village, he flees, confused and suicidal. A meeting with a loving old witch gives him a feeling of strength and pride in himself.

662 PANGBORN, EDGAR. "Tiger Boy." In *Universe Two*, edited by Terry Carr. New York: Ace, 1972. [M?]

A haunting and tragic tale of a young man, known as the Tiger Boy, who roams Pangborn's *Davy*-cycle world searching for a special friend. Although accompanied by his faithful tiger, it is not until he meets Bruno, a young mute, that the Tiger Boy finds the friendship he has been seeking. Their blissful idyll ends suddenly when hunters, pursuing the tiger, find the three together.

663 PANGBORN, EDGAR. "The Witches of Nupal." In *Continuum Three*, edited by Roger Elwood. New York: Berkley, 1974. [M?]

"The Witches of Nupal" revolves around a charismatic young man, Rudi Zavier, and his small band of adolescent admirers. Rudi organizes a small coven of witches, but his hunger for power leads to his death. Two male coven members, minor characters, are homosexual. More important to the story is the nonsexual love of the narrator for Rudi.

Biographical Note

Edgar Pangborn (1909-76) was an extremely talented author who was fascinated by same-sex love, and all his work should be examined carefully for variant content. His science-fiction novel *West of the Sun* (Garden City, N.Y.: Doubleday, 1953) is one of the earliest sympathetic (if somewhat naive) male-authored visions of a matriarchal culture. His non-science-fiction novel, *The Trial of Callista Blake* (New York: St. Martin's, 1961), is of both lesbian and gay male interest. His novel *The Wilderness of Spring* (New York: Rinehart, 1958) is a historical story of major importance to gay male literature.

Biographical information on Pangborn can be found in "The County Called Edgar," by Spider Robinson in the collection of Pangborn short stories titled *Still I Persist in Wondering* (New York: Dell, 1978). Further information can be located in *Contemporary Authors*, vol. 1, ed. James M. Ethridge (Detroit: Gale Research, 1962).

PANSHIN, ALEXEI. The Anthony Villiers Trilogy. [f, m]:

664 ■ *Star Well*. New York: Ace, 1968.

665 ■ *The Thurb Revolution*. New York: Ace, 1968.

666 ■ *Masque World*. New York: Ace, 1969.

A delightful trilogy about Anthony Villiers, galactic remittance man, and his traveling companion, Torve the Trog. In the first novel, a group of teenage girls en route to a finishing school become involved with the smugglers who run the port of Star Well. In one minor incident, a room service attendant mistakenly assumes that the girls and their chaperon are having sadomasochistic sex together. In the second novel, Villiers's old school friend, Fred, instructs a local youth, David Clodfelter, in the basics of woodcraft so that he may start a Big Beaver chapter on Cinkin Island. The previously heterosexual Fred becomes magnetically attracted to young David, and he confesses his love to

Villiers in a scene of notable sophistication for 1968. The last of the Villiers romps has Panshin's hero looking for his remittance, as usual, this time in the palatial (if dimly lit) residence of his uncle, Lord Semichastny. All become involved in a long night of Wonders and Marvels. Mr. McBe, a customs official, fends off the wet nose of his superior, Slyne, who has fallen in love with McBe's smell. Other homoerotic relationships include that of Lord Semichastny with both his robot butler (who deep, deep within him enjoys groveling just the least little bit) and Harbourne Firnhaber, whom he passes off as his nephew – one of a succession of "nephews."

667 PAXSON, DIANA L. "A Gift of Love." In *Sword of Chaos*, edited by Marion Zimmer Bradley. New York: DAW, 1982. [F]

In this story, set in Marion Zimmer Bradley's Darkover universe, a man brings his mistress home to meet his wife and a ménage à trois develops.

668 PAXSON, DIANA L. "The Song of N'sardi-el." In *Millennial Women*, edited by Virginia Kidd. New York: Delacorte, 1978. [X]

Superbly told from a woman's point of view, this short story involves the tragic death of a little girl at the hands of the Xicitholi, a nurturing, five-gendered alien race.

669 PERRY, STEVE. *The 97th Step*. New York: Ace, 1989. [M?]

In order to escape an abusive family situation, sixteen-year-old Mwili sells himself to a spaceship First Officer. Once safely off his home planet, Mwili spends a sexual apprenticeship with a crusty petty criminal. Mwili later becomes exclusively heterosexual, but he tells a female lover, "Benjo [the First Officer] was the first person, save for my mother, who had even demonstrated any real affection for me. Even a perverse love is better than no love at all."

670 PHELPS, ELIZABETH STUART. "Since I Died." *Scribner's Monthly*, February 1873. Reprinted in *Sealed Orders*. Boston: Houghton, Osgood, 1879. [F]

The departed spirit of a New England woman passionately remembers her beloved woman friend in this remarkable nineteenth-century ghost story. The erotic overtones of the story are exceptionally overt.

671 PICANO, FELICE. *An Asian Minor: The True Story of Ganymede*. New York: Seahorse Press, 1981. [M]

A delightful retelling of the ancient Greek myth of Zeus and Ganymede. Sexy and enjoyable.

672 PICANO, FELICE. "Hunter." In *On the Line: New Gay Fiction*, edited by Ian Young. Trumansburg, N.Y.: Crossing, 1981. [M]

An aspiring young writer encounters a ghostly male lover while summering at a New England artist's colony.

673 PICANO, FELICE. *To the Seventh Power*. New York: Morrow, 1989. [m]

Picano delivers what he is well known for: a gripping mainstream occult thriller with strong characterizations and compelling suspense. Barry Brescia runs a popular occult shop in Boston's trendy Back Bay district. When a strange teenage girl appears in the store with an uncanny familiarity with his past, Barry is thrown into intrigue and adventure. Teaming up with a former lover (and ex-Soviet agent) named Anna Kuragin, Picano's protagonist discovers a secret plot involving children with advanced psychic powers. Picano includes several minor gay male characters, notably Anna's business partner, but the most substantial is the evil CIA agent, Alex Land.

Biographical Note

Felice Picano (b. 1944) is a poet, novelist, and publisher. He is the author of numerous horror novels: *Smart as the Devil* (New York: Arbor House, 1975), *Eyes* (New York: Arbor House, 1976), and *The Mesmerist* (New York: Delacorte, 1977). His short story "One Way Out" was published in Ramsey Campbell's *New Terrors Two* (London: Pan, 1980). "Absolute Ebony" appeared in *Masters of Modern Horror*, ed. Frank Coffrey (New York: Coward, McCann, & Geoghegan, 1981), and "Spices of the World" appeared in Graham Masterton's *Scare Care* (New York: TOR, 1989). He is the author of the following nonfantasy works: *The Deformity Lover and Other Poems* (New York: Sea Horse Press, 1977); *The Lure* (New York: Delacorte, 1979); *Late in the Season* (New York: Delacorte, 1981); *House of Cards* (New York: Delacorte, 1981); *Slashed to Ribbons in Defense of Love, and Other Stories* (New York: Gay Presses of New York, 1982); and *Window Elegies* (Tuscaloosa, Ala.: Close-Grip Press, 1985).

Picano is openly gay, and male homosexuality is a major theme throughout his work. *The Lure* is a suspense novel set in Manhattan's gay world, and male homosexuality is central to *Late in the Season* and *Slashed to Ribbons*. Also note his poems in *The Deformity Lover* and *Window Elegies* and in the collections *Penguin Book of Homosexual Verse*, ed. Stephen Coote (London and New York: Penguin, 1983), and *Poets for Life*, ed. Michael Klein (New York: Crown 1989). He is the founder of the Sea Horse Press, and he joined forces with two other small-press owners in 1981 to set up Gay Presses of New York. He has been a contributing editor of *Christopher Street*, the *New York Native*, and the *Advocate*. He is the editor of *A True Likeness: An Anthology of Lesbian and Gay Writing Today* (New

York: Sea Horse, 1980). His as-yet-unpublished science-fiction novel, *Dryland's End*, has major lesbian and gay male content.

Autobiographical information on Picano can be located in his memoirs *Ambidextrous: A Memoir in the Form of a Novel* (New York: Gay Presses of New York, 1985) and *Men Who Loved Me: A Memoir in the Form of a Novel* (New York: New American Library, 1989). Biographical information on Picano can be found in *Contemporary Authors; New Revision Series*, vol. 11, ed. Ann Evory and Linda Metzger (Detroit: Gale, 1984).

---

674 PIERCY, MARGE. *Woman on the Edge of Time*. New York: Knopf, 1976. [f, m]

Piercy writes a brilliant, if somewhat didactic, novel about Consuelo Ramos, a Latina incarcerated in a New York City mental institution. Piercy's extensive research into the abuse suffered by inmates is incorporated into the narrative and makes for painful reading. Despite her situation, Consuelo has the will to live and to strike back at the authorities. As a sharp contrast to Consuelo's incarceration, descriptions of relations and rituals in a future utopia are interfaced throughout the novel. Luciente, a member of the future utopia, time-travels to the past (Consuelo's present) and is able to transport Consuelo for visits to this future. The feminist and ecologically conscious utopian culture accepts homosexuality, although the two gay relationships depicted are more problematic and less stable than the heterosexual ones. Recommended.

Biographical Note

Marge Piercy (b. 1936) is a noted author, poet, and feminist. She has written numerous volumes of poetry, including *Available Light* (New York: Knopf, 1988). She has also written the non-science-fiction novels *Small Changes* (Garden City, N.Y.: Doubleday, 1973), *The High Cost of Living* (New York: Harper & Row, 1979), *Vida* (New York: Summit, 1980), *Braided Lives* (New York: Summit, 1982), *Fly Away Home* (New York: Summit, 1984), *Gone to Soldiers* (New York: Summit, 1987), and *Summer People* (New York: Summit, 1989). Many of these deal in varying degrees with the contemporary lesbian feminist experience. The second is also of gay male interest.

---

675 PISERCHIA, DORIS. "Naked and Afraid I Go." In *Orbit 13*, edited by Damon Knight. New York: Berkley, 1974. [Note: this story is not included in the paperback edition of the anthology.] [f, m]

When women unite in rage and organize massive marches in the streets, a genetic mutation is triggered. The masculine gender becomes no longer essential to the human race. Pregnant virgins, including at least one lesbian, begin showing up at medical clinics all over the world.

Male medics encourage the abortion of these parthenogenetic fetuses. They also campaign to give the women's liberation movement everything it demands (including equal rights for all other disadvantaged groups) in the hope that the mutations will cease if there is no female rage. But it becomes evident that women are reproducing baby girls on a large scale. The narrator, a male medic, is balanced between the doom of his gender and love for his wife and daughters. The writing style and the presentation of politics in this story are superb.

676 PLATT, CHARLES. *The Gas*. New York: Ophelia, 1970. [f, m]
A pornographic science-fiction novel in which both male and female bisexual activity is explicitly depicted.

677 POHL, FREDERIK. "Day Million." *Rogue*, February 1966. Reprinted in *Day Million*. New York: Ballantine, 1970. [M]
Two genetic males far in the future marry. The story is farcical, and the author's heterosexual bias is pronounced.

678 POHL, FREDERIK. *Gateway*. New York: St. Martin's, 1977. [M]
By all rights, Robinett Broadhead should be limitlessly happy. He has survived a dangerous expedition to an ancient alien Heechee spaceship and has become one of the richest men alive. Yet he is miserable; among other things his repressed homosexuality causes him pain and guilt. Pohl intersperses throughout Broadhead's adventures detailed accounts of the protagonist's therapy sessions with Sigfrid, a computerized analyst. Since several other homosexual minor characters are presented as being without guilt feelings or stereotypic manners, and since the society is depicted as being basically not homophobic, it is difficult to understand why Broadhead agonizes so much over admitting his mild attraction to men. Also weak is the cause of Broadhead's repressed homosexual components: his beloved mother gave him a feminine name, and she had a penchant for rectal temperature taking. *Gateway* won both the Nebula and Hugo awards.

679 POHL, FREDERIK, and KORNBLUTH, C[YRIL] M. *The Space Merchants*. Boston: Houghton Mifflin, 1953. [m]
Mitchell Courtenay, a first-rate advertising executive, lives in a future in which commercialism and hard-sell advertising techniques pervade the world. He is assigned to the "Venus Account"–an attempt to con consumers into establishing a settlement on the inhospitable planet of Venus. But before he can begin, he is kidnapped and forced into labor on a plantation. Eventually he comes in contact with the "Consies," an underground organization of conservationists attempting to prevent the destruction of the Earth, and his worldview alters. Although he used homosexually oriented advertising techniques in the

past, it is not until he actually meets a male homosexual after his abduction that Courtenay begins to question this practice. The nontraditional role that Courtenay's wife plays in the action is surprising, considering the date of publication. The authors lay the satire on thick, and the novel has become an amusing classic within the genre. A condensed version of *The Space Merchants* initially appeared in *Galaxy*, June-August 1952, under the title *Gravy Planet*, but the references to homosexuality were not included.

Biographical Note

Frederik Pohl (b. 1919) is also the author of *The Age of the Pussyfoot* (New York: Trident, 1969) and *Man Plus* (New York: Random House, 1976). He discusses his opinions on homosexuality in Jeremy Hughes's article "Sex in the Year 2500," *In Touch for Men*, July 1982.

---

680 POLIDORI, JOHN [WILLIAM]. *The Vampyre: A Tale. New Monthly Magazine* (London), April 1819 [incorrectly attributed by the publisher to Byron]. Reprint. London: Sherwood, Neely & Jones, 1819. Reprint. New York: Dover, 1966. [M?]

    The Vampyre is a brief Gothic novel that has the distinction of being the first full-fledged vampire story written in English. Lord Ruthven, a mysterious nobleman, develops a supernatural hold over the young protagonist, Aubrey. Ruthven turns out to be a vampire, and inevitably both Aubrey and his sister fall prey to the vampire's powers. Homosexual elements are subjective but may become clearer when the reader realizes that Aubrey is based on the author himself, and Lord Ruthven is modeled on Lord Byron, Polidori's bisexual employer and traveling companion.

681 POLLACK, RACHEL. "Black Rose and White Rose." *New Worlds Quarterly*, June 1974. Reprinted in *New Worlds Six*, edited by Charles Platt and Hilary Bailey. New York: Avon, Equinox, 1974. [F]

    White Rose, sold as a lowly kitchen maid by her poverty-stricken parents, sneaks out to see the carnival one night and meets Black Rose, a beautiful dancer under the control of a wicked magician. The two women become lovers until the magician discovers them and sends Black Rose back to the shadows from whence he had summoned her. White Rose searches throughout the world until she finds her beloved again. This magical gem of a lesbian fantasy is wonderful reading.

682 POLLACK, RACHEL. "Burning Sky." In *Semiotext(e): SF*, edited by Rudy Rucker, Peter Lamborn Wilson, and Robert Anton Wilson. Brooklyn, N.Y.: Autonomedia, 1989. [F]

Pollack pens a compelling fantasy that speaks to issues of lesbianism and sexual freedom. Two related stories entwine. In the first, a woman leaves her husband for a woman lover on the first steps of her journey to self-discovery. At the same time, a lesbian photographer uncovers a mysterious cabal of blue-clad feminist vigilantes. A well-crafted mixture of lesbian feminist vision and cyberpunk style.

POURNELLE, JERRY. *See* NIVEN, LARRY (joint author)

PRATT, FLETCHER. *See* FLETCHER, GEORGE U. (pseudonym)

683 PRESTON, JOHN. *The Heir*. Austin, Tex.: Caliente, 1986. [f?, M]
Preston's *The Heir* is set in the far future, but it is more sadomasochistic erotica than science fiction. After nuclear war has destroyed the Earth's civilization, a handful of men construct an all-male society based on bondage and sexual slavery. Everyone is happy with the arrangement; the slaves service the masters, the masters protect the slaves. The author explores the erotic potential between masters and slaves in explicit detail. Since all of the male characters are homosexual, the few female characters in the novel presumably are, too. Preston touches some of Delany's territory but not nearly as well.

PRUYN, LEONARD. *See* KEENE, DAY (joint author)

684 PUGMIRE, W. H., and SALMONSON, JESSICA AMANDA. "'Pale Trembling Youth.'" In *Cutting Edge*, edited by Dennis Etchison. New York: Doubleday, 1986. [m]
Eerie ghost story about the suicide of a young punk rocker. The narrator clearly identifies with gays and other social outsiders but is not homosexual. A secondary character is an older gay man.

QUICK, W[ILLIAM] T. Dream Trilogy. [M]:

685 ■ *Dreams of Flesh and Sand*. New York: Signet, 1988.

686 ■ *Dreams of Gods and Men*. New York: Signet, 1989.
Quick mixes the old-fashioned espionage thriller with a high-tech cyberpunk style in his enjoyable Dream trilogy recounting the mighty Matrix Wars between Earth and the Moon. Master computer programmer Iceberg Berg and his ex-wife Icebreaker Calley discover a new universe *inside* a vast computer network when they are hired by Shag Nakamura of Nakamura-Norton, the most powerful corporation in the world. Nakamura's partner, Bill Norton, has literally wired himself into the company's computer network and Berg and Calley are hired to get him out. Homosexual content is substantial in all three novels;

Nakamura, who rises from corporate president to become the ruler of both worlds, is a connoisseur of vintage brandies and handsome waiters. There is also mention of the Blades, genetically altered warriors who usually are homosexual. The third volume in the trilogy, *Singularities*, is forthcoming.

687 QUICK, W[ILLIAM] T. *Systems*. New York: Signet, 1989. [f, m]

Science-fiction thriller in which a twenty-first-century computer expert and former intelligence agent Joshua Tower is thrust into a world of espionage and violence when his wife is killed in a mysterious air-taxi accident. Several nonjudgmental scenes involving gay men take place in San Francisco's gay Castro Street district. Less charitable is Quick's depiction of a lesbian nurse who wears a crew cut and chases the candy stripers.

688 QUICK, W[ILLIAM] T. *Yesterday's Pawn*. New York: Signet, 1989. [m]

Garry Hamersmidt accepts an alien artifact while working in his father's pawnshop, and within days the artifact is stolen, the shop destroyed, and Garry's father dead. Garry teams up with a Terran intelligence operator to avenge his father's murder. Among the characters Garry meets during his many adventures is Candy, a mildly dirty, but very, *very* old, man. *Yesterday's Pawn* takes place in the same universe as Quick's Dream trilogy, but thousands of years in the future.

689 QUINN, SEABURY. *Alien Flesh*. Illustrated by Stephen Fabian. Philadelphia: Oswald Train, 1977. [f, X]

Brilliant archeologist Hugh Arundel is attracted to the beautiful Egyptian, Ismet Foulik. But Ismet remains aloof, as if she were afraid. Finally, in a burst of confidence, Ismet divulges her dread secret: she is actually Hugh's trusted friend and renowned male colleague, Lynne Foster, who has been transformed by Oriental sorcery into a woman. After the transformation, Lynne/Ismet had been sold into slavery and forced to marry. The marriage raised to-be-expected sexual identity confusion. She escaped and became a wealthy woman, still confused about her sexuality. She is repulsed by the sexual advances of both men and women until she rejoins Hugh and tries to forget that she was ever a man. As with much transsexual fantasy, *Alien Flesh* assumes that a change in sex would necessitate a change in sexual preference, gender identity, and social / sexual role. The novel was written in the late 1940s but remained unpublished until after the author's death.

690 QUINN, SEABURY. "Clair de Lune." *Weird Tales*, November 1947. Reprinted in *The Ghoul Keepers*, edited by Leo Margulies. New York: Pyramid, 1961. [F]

Much of Seabury Quinn's note as a fantasy author rests on his long series of short stories featuring the feisty (and misogynistic) psychic detective, Jules de Grandin. In "Clair de Lune," de Grandin struggles with the lovely, but vaguely repellent, actress Madelon Leroy over the life of an innocent twenty-year-old woman. Madelon is actually an ageless vampire who survives through the centuries by sucking the youth and vitality from "fair, fresh maidens." Lesbianism is perceived as a loathsome evil, capable of destroying any young woman drawn into its web.

691 QUINN, SEABURY. "The Poltergeist." *Weird Tales*, October 1927. Reprinted in *The Horror Chambers of Jules de Grandin*, edited by Robert Weinburg. New York: Popular Library, 1977. [F]
Quinn's psychic detective Jules de Grandin battles a lesbian ghost who is trying to prevent her beloved sister's impending marriage.

692 QUIRK, LAWRENCE J. *Some Lovely Image*. New York: Quirk Publishing, 1976. [M]
The narrator of this enjoyable ghost story first encounters handsome nineteenth-century aristocrat Tom Lanning while searching through microfilm at the Boston Public Library. Soon Lanning becomes an obsession with him. He becomes convinced that he and Lanning are supernaturally fated to be lovers. Similar to Vernon Lee's "Winthrop's Adventure," the narrative is perhaps too old-fashioned for readers accustomed to contemporary horror's graphic overkill, but the author's wholesome approach to male homosexuality is refreshing.

693 RABINOWITZ, JACOB. "Louie, Louie." In *Semiotext(e): SF*, edited by Rudy Rucker, Peter Lamborn Wilson, and Robert Anston Wilson. Brooklyn, N.Y.: Autonomedia, 1989. [M]
"Louie, Louie" is an unusual mix of werewolf horror and sweaty erotic meditation that explores the sometimes thin line between fantasy and reality.

694 RANDALL, MARTA. *A City in the North*. New York: Warner, 1976. [f, m]
Alin Kennerin and Toyon Sutak own an interplanetary empire. Their marriage is on the rocks, and they journey to Heop-Henninah ostensibly to explore ancient ruins but actually to try to mend their relationship. Once on the planet, they are guided by an indigenous people called the Henninah and by a bisexual woman, Quellan, to the archeological site. Quellan is an outstanding example of competency; it is she, not Alin's husband, who saves Alin from the addicting drugs secretly fed to Alin by the Henninah for their mysterious purposes. A sadistic pederast villain is a minor character.

695 RANDALL, MARTA. *Dangerous Games*. New York: Pocket Books, 1980. [f, m]

A sequel to Randall's popular *Journey, Dangerous Games* continues the saga of the Kennerin family. Their domestic peace is threatened by Parallax, a giant, galaxy-wide corporation that has designs on the Kennerins' planet. As in her earlier novel, women play strategic roles in the action, and several of the novel's varied characters are gay or bisexual.

696 RANDALL, MARTA. *Islands*. New York: Pyramid, 1975. [F?, m]

Tia is a freak, born into the wrong time. In the future society in which she lives, all humans have attained immortality ... except Tia. For some reason the treatments that stop aging in others have not worked on her. She is destined to grow old in a youth-oriented society. For years she dashes from place to place, from lover to lover, searching for the meaning of her singular situation. While on an archeological expedition under the ocean, Tia finds what she has been seeking. Bisexuality is a tolerated, and perhaps a preferred, form of sexual expression in Tia's world. The novel is enjoyable, and the female protagonist is a strong and developed character.

697 RANDALL, MARTA. *Journey*. New York: Pocket Books, 1978. [M]

Randall's beautiful saga details thirty years of the Kennerin family. They are wealthy enough to buy a planet and compassionate enough to then hold open their arms to a large group of refugees from another world. For twelve years the Kennerins have been the only humans on their world, so the sudden influx of 200 humans causes major changes in the family's dynamics. The relationships in the book are intense, and the struggle for physical and emotional survival motivates most of the action. The women in the book are decisive, competent, and warm. They are respected by their lovers and husbands. Three of the male characters are bisexual, and each incorporates male love into his life in a different way. Recommended.

698 RAVEN, SIMON. *Doctors Wear Scarlet; A Romantic Tale*. London: A. Blond, 1960. Reprint. New York: Simon & Schuster, 1961. [M?]

An intriguing vampire thriller that successfully mingles supernatural horror with psychological insight. Richard Fountain, a young British scholar, travels to Greece to work on his doctoral thesis. While there, Fountain gets involved in some very mysterious business, and several of his close friends must travel to Crete to retrieve him. They are shocked when they find that Fountain has become the victim of a female vampire, a remnant of an ancient pagan culture. Fountain's rescuers must destroy the villainous creature before they can return her victim to Britain. Even with the vampire's destruction, however, her repulsive curse lives on. The feeling that Fountain's rescuers have for him borders on the homosexual. An older homosexual "auntie" is an important character, and despite his stereotypic fussing and fluttering he is a likable figure. There is a noticeable chauvinistic, upper-class, sexist tone throughout the novel.

699 REAMY, TOM. "The Detweiler Boy." *Fantasy and Science Fiction*, April 1977. Reprinted in *San Diego Lightfoot Sue, and Other Stories*. Kansas City, Mo.: Earthlight, 1979. [m]

A private detective investigating a series of brutal murders finds himself drawn into a strange and fantastic mystery. He is looking for a handsome hunchback named Andrew Detweiler, and his search leads him, among other places, to a gay apartment complex. When he finally locates Detweiler, the detective finds more than he bargained for. Several well-drawn gay male characters are introduced. A frightening and effective tale.

700 REAMY, TOM. "San Diego Lightfoot Sue." *Fantasy and Science Fiction*, August 1975. Reprinted in *Nebula Award Stories Eleven*, edited by Ursula K. Le Guin. New York: Harper & Row, 1977. [m]

A young boy, recently orphaned, moves to Los Angeles. There he is befriended by two flamboyant gay men. Through the pair, he meets a magical artist named San Diego Lightfoot Sue, and they begin an affair. Reamy draws his characters with exceptional love and care, and his gay characters are no exception. A Nebula Award-winning story.

701 REAMY, TOM. "Under the Hollywood Sign." In *Orbit Seventeen*, edited by Damon Knight. New York: Harper & Row, 1975. [M]

A Los Angeles police officer notices a beautiful, red-haired young man at the scene of several violent deaths. At first the officer finds it only curious, but soon he is actually looking for the man, following him into gay bars and becoming enamored of him. He slowly realizes that there are many of these stunningly attractive men, eerily all look-alikes and all drawn to violent deaths. The officer's emotional and sexual confusion becomes too difficult to handle, and he breaks. Gripping horror brings the story to an end. The officer's emerging homosexuality is handled well.

Biographical Note

Tom Reamy (1935-77) was a very talented author who, while remaining closeted professionally, was open about his homosexuality among his close friends. He discusses his own career, as well as homosexuality and gay fandom, in "Shayol Interview: Tom Reamy," in *Shayol*, no. 1 (November

1977). Biographical information on Reamy can be found in Peter Nicholls's *The Science Fiction Encyclopedia* (Garden City, N.Y.: Doubleday, 1979).

REDMOND, FERGUS. *See* GUNTER, ARCHIBALD C. (joint author)

REED, LILLIAN CRAIG. *See* REED, KIT (pseudonym)

702 REED, KIT [pseudonym of Lillian Craig Reed]. "Songs of War." In *Nova Four*, edited by Harry Harrison. New York: Walker, 1974. [F]
       Women in a small town build an army and attempt to wage a war for women's liberation. Government forces remain unrealistically unconcerned about the armed takeover of the town, yet because the women cannot decide on a unanimous policy toward men, their guerrilla-warfare tactics fail and one by one most of the women return to their families. The story explores the ambivalent feelings of heterosexual women toward men and portrays the castrating "butch sisters" (lesbians) as exceedingly shallow and violent. The story satirizes the problem of establishing unity among all women when each has a different goal level of commitment to revolution. It is a pessimistic view.

703 REID, FORREST. *Demophon: A Traveller's Tale*. London: Collins, 1927. [M?]
       Demophon is the first instance in which Reid blends his favorite theme of devoted male friendships with the fantastic. Demophon, a young boy living in ancient Greece, is befriended as a child by the goddess Demeter. Through her, he meets the young god Hermes, and they develop a divine friendship: chaste but intensely passionate. Demeter, the Earth Goddess, attempts to immortalize Demophon, but his mother interrupts the ritual, leaving Demophon only touched by the divine. As Demophon grows older he finds himself missing his beloved companion Hermes, and he soon sets off on an amazing adventure to search for his lost friend. Demophon's love for Hermes is rich in homosexual implications.

704 REID, FORREST. *Uncle Stephen*. London: Faber & Faber, 1931. [M?]
       Young Tom Barber finds himself orphaned and forced to live with his unloving stepmother. He runs away to his Uncle Stephen, a mysterious, eccentric old man who has secluded himself on his estate. A rapport immediately develops between the uncle and nephew. While Uncle Stephen is away, Tom discovers another runaway, Phillip Coombe, hiding in his uncle's carriage house. The two boys fall in love and then discover that Phillip is actually Uncle Stephen. He has been transformed by dream magic into the boy of his youth. Their

relationship, conflicting with an intense friendship Tom has already developed with a neighboring lad, is resolved when Phillip is transformed back into Uncle Stephen. In the final scene Tom is adopted by his uncle and the two set off to Italy for a happy life together. Reid was later to write two sequels to *Uncle Stephen*: *The Retreat; or, the Machinations of Henry* (London: Faber & Faber, 1936); and *Young Tom: or, Very Mixed Company* (London: Faber & Faber, 1944). These novels also contain similar homosexual overtones and peripheral fantasy elements that are too weak for annotation here.

Biographical Note
Forrest Reid (1875-1947) was an important Anglo-Irish novelist who occasionally made the supernatural the focus of his stories. *Pender among the Residents* (London: Collins, 1922), a ghost story, is a good example. More often, however, supernatural elements were used to accentuate his plots, making all his fiction marginally fantastic.

Reid invariably chose young boys as the protagonists in his novels, and intense male-male (often boy-boy) friendships are a predominant theme throughout his work. Aside from the novels mentioned above, homoemotional characters and situations appear in *The Garden God: The Tale of Two Boys* (London: David Nutt, 1905), *Pirates of the Spring* (London: T. Fisher Unwin, 1919), and *Denis Bracknel* (London: Faber & Faber, 1947). Reid also published a translation of Greek love poetry entitled *Poems from the Greek Anthology* (London: Faber & Faber, 1943), which is primarily of gay male interest.

Autobiographical information on Reid can be found in *Apostate* (London: Constable, 1926) and *Private Road* (London: Faber & Faber, 1940). Biographical and critical information is in Mary Bryan's *Forrest Reid* (Boston: Twayne, 1976) and Russell Burlingham's *Forrest Reid: A Portrait and a Study* (London: Faber & Faber, 1953).

---

705 REYNOLDS, MACK. *Commune 2000 A.D.* New York: Bantam, 1974. [f, m]

A utopia of the future is threatened by a mass migration to communes outside of the large cities. Among the communes the author examines are a lesbian commune called Lesbos, a gay male commune called New Tangier, and a bisexual commune called Gomorrah.

RICE, ANNE [O'BRIEN]. Chronicles of the Vampires. [M]:

706 ▪ *Interview with a Vampire.* New York: Knopf, 1975.

707 ▪ *The Vampire Lestat.* New York: Knopf, 1985.

708 ■ *Queen of the Damned*. New York: Knopf, 1988.

It isn't surprising that Anne Rice's undead leap out of their closet doors. Her nonvampire fiction, sometimes written under the name A. N. Roquelaure, is rich in eroticism and sensuality. In *Interview with a Vampire*, Rice's first vampire novel, Louis is made a vampire by Lestat, a handsome aristocratic Frenchman. And this begins a saga that leads the reader from a pre-Civil War Southern plantation to nineteenth-century Paris. Louis and Lestat fall in love and form a three-way relationship with a young girl vampire. Lastat leaves Louis and in the subsequent volume and becomes a rock star living in San Francisco's Castro Street district. Here, Rice makes the underworld of the vampires (they congregate secretly in vampire bars) a metaphor for the contemporary gay community. In the third volume, when Akasha, the Queen of the Vampires, is awakened from her eternal slumber and begins attacking the vampire bars–watch out! Like many horror novelists before her, Rice uses vampirism to describe erotic passions, but her novels are much kinkier than their nineteenth-century predecessors. Her Chronicles of the Vampires are great fun and have developed a devoted following. Watch for further sequels.

709 RICE, ANNE [O'BRIEN]. *The Mummy*. New York: Ballantine, 1989. [m]

Once he was Ramses the Great and walked the streets of ancient Cairo, but now he has drunk the elixir of life and has become Ramses the Damned, an undead mummy. Reawakened in Edwardian London, Ramses assumes the identity of Dr. Ramsey, an expert in Egyptology. As in most of Rice's fiction, kinky eroticism plays an essential role in *The Mummy*. In this case, the sex between Ramses, heiress Julie Stratford, and the long-dead Queen Cleopatra borders on the necrophiliac. Elliot Savarell, once a lover of Julie's brother, is a pivotal character.

Biographical Note

Anne Rice (b. 1941) is an exciting and prolific writer of horror fiction. She is also the author of *The Feast of All Saints* (New York: Simon and Schuster, 1979); *Cry to Heaven* (New York: Knopf, 1982); the three A. N. Roquelaure erotic novels, *The Claiming of Beauty* (New York: Dutton, 1983), *Beauty's Punishment* (New York: Dutton, 1984), and *Beauty's Release* (New York: Dutton, 1985); and the Anne Rampling books, *Exit to Eden* (New York: Arbor House, 1985) and *Belinda* (New York: Arbor House, 1986). Many of these novels have significant gay and lesbian content.

Biographical and critical information on Rice can be found in *Contemporary Authors, New Revision Series*, vol. 12, ed. Linda Metzger (Detroit: Gale, 1984); in Robert Atkins's "Interview with the Vampire," the

Advocate, no. 234 (8 February 1978); in Kenneth Holditch's "Old Haunting Grounds," in *Lambda Rising Book Report* (Washington, D.C.), no. 7 (1988); and in "Do the Rice Thing," by David Perry, in *Omni*, October 1989.

There is a strong following for Rice's Vampire Chronicles and the next installment, *The Body Thief*, is eagerly awaited. Information about the Vampire Lestat Fan Club can be obtained from P.O. Box 58277, New Orleans, LA 70158-8277.

---

710 RIMMER, ROBERT H[ENRY]. *Love Me Tomorrow*. New York: Signet, 1978. [f]

In this limited vision of a future sexual utopia, Christina North, a promiscuous, suicidal, ex-porno star turned millionaire, becomes the involuntary subject of a scientific experiment. Put into a state of suspended animation, Christina awakens in 1996 to a society that has been radically altered both economically and socially. Most of the population now belongs to the Church of United Love, which embraces a very open attitude toward sexuality . . . at least toward heterosexuality. Mate swapping and group encounters are encouraged, but there is little place in Rimmer's utopia for same-sex love. Lesbianism is mentioned in passing, usually as sexual foreplay between marginally bisexual women, and gay male sexuality is not mentioned at all. The result is a mildly pornographic novel written for the titillation of heterosexual males and pretentiously packaged as science fiction.

711 RIVERS, DEANA. *Journey to Zelindar: The Personal Account of Sair of Semasi*. Denver: Lace, 1987. [F]

Rivers sets her fantasy in a brutal, feudal society where women are considered male property. When Sair refuses her husband's advances, she is raped, abandoned, and left for dead. She is rescued by the Hadra women, lesbian warriors with potent psychic powers. At first, the amazons frighten Sair, but soon she grows to love them and to become one of them. The plot could be tighter, but Rivers makes up for it with considerable imagination and detail. Similar to Gearhart's *The Wanderground*.

RIVKIN, J. F. [pseudonym]. Silverglass Series. [F, m]:

712 ▪ *Silverglass*. New York: Ace, 1986.

713 ▪ *Web of Wind*. New York: Ace, 1987.

714 ▪ *Witch of Rhostshyl*. New York: Ace, 1989.

In her Silverglass series, J. F. Rivkin has taken the conventions of the Sword and Sorcery novels and turned them inside out: Corson, her dashing, lusty mercenary protagonist, is a bisexual woman, as comfortable bedding the serving girl as bedding the stableman. In *Silverglass* she is hired to assassinate the Lady Nystasia, a noblewoman of Rhostshyl and a reputed sorceress, but Nystasia proves too beautiful for the mercenary to kill. Instead, the two women flee Nystasia's enemies. *Web of Wind* continues the couple's fast-paced adventures as they search for hidden treasure, and in *Witch of Rhostshyl* Nystasia and Corson return home. Swashbuckling good fun!

Biographical Note
J. F. Rivkin is the pseudonym of two American women writers, both born in 1951. The fourth novel in the Silverglass series, entitled *Mistress of Ambiguities* (New York: Ace, forthcoming), will be published too late for inclusion in this bibliography.

---

715 ROBERTS, KEITH. "The Beautiful One." *New Worlds Quarterly*, May 1973. Reprinted in *New Worlds Five*, edited by Michael Moorcock and Charles Platt. New York: Avon, Equinox, 1973. [f, M]

A fable of greed and corruption set in a future postapocalyptic stone age. A stunningly beautiful young man is rescued from slavery and death by a priestess of the Corn God, and he soon becomes her lover. Initially, he is grateful to his rescuer, but later his gratitude turns into self-indulgence and he begins to sow the seeds of his own destruction. Bisexuality, both male and female, is threaded throughout the story, and male homosexuality provides the pivot for the conclusion. A simple and well-written tale.

716 ROBINS, PETER. "Cheriton." In *On the Line: New Gay Fiction*, edited by Ian Young. Trumansburg, N.Y.: Crossing, 1981. [M]

Robins creates an evocative tale of lust and lycanthropy. As a young man, just before shipping off to fight the Great War, Curtis Hodges spends an eerie evening on the grounds of Cheriton, a regal British estate. He meets the mansion's handsome young heir and their interaction is charged with erotic promise, but their planned rendezvous is interrupted by a large wolf.

ROBINSON, FRANK M. *See* SCORTIA, THOMAS N. (joint author)

ROBINSON, JEANNE. *See* ROBINSON, SPIDER (joint author)

717 ROBINSON, SPIDER. *Telempath*. New York: Berkley, 1976. [m]

Someone has developed a new chemical that has caused the sensitivity of the human sense of smell to increase a thousandfold. Humans have become unable to tolerate the multitude of odors within urban areas, and cities have been abandoned. A determined young

African-American man sets off for New York to find the chemical's inventor and to take revenge for the destruction of civilization. The youth's harrowing adventures are recorded in the fast-paced novel. For some unexplained reason, homosexuality no longer exists in this world, but a sympathetic minor character states that he was gay before the cities were abandoned.

718 ROBINSON, SPIDER, and ROBINSON, JEANNE. *Stardance*. New York: Dial, James Wade, 1979. [m]

In the Robinsons' first collaboration, Shara Drummond, considered to be too large to perform dances on Earth, develops a new form of creative expression–zero-gravity dance. When she is killed while trying to communicate with a frightening alien life-form, Charlie Armstead, the story's narrator, and Norrey Drummond, Shara's sister, must develop their zero-gravity dance troupe without her. An eventual encounter with the alien being responsible for Shara's demise causes the troupe to experience a breakthrough in human consciousness. Homosexuality is introduced when Raoul and Harry, two troupe members, become lovers. They are both likable characters, but because they are homosexual in a social vacuum their credibility as homosexuals is considerably diminished. Even so, *Stardance* remains a book with strong, independent women characters and a positive gay image. "Stardance," the novella that comprises the first third of *Stardance*, won both the Hugo and Nebula awards.

719 ROSINSKY, NATALIE M. *Feminist Futures: Contemporary Women's Speculative Fiction*. Ann Arbor, Mich.: UMI Research Press, 1984. [Nonfiction]

Rosinsky compares a variety of contemporary speculative fictions written by women to explore the ways in which a feminist theoretical framework has been used within the science-fiction genre. Many of the novels examined are cited in *Uranian Worlds*, including Gould's *A Sea Change*, Carter's *The Passion of New Eve*, Woolf's *Orlando*, Bryant's *The Kin of Ata Are Waiting for You*, Le Guin's *The Left Hand of Darkness*, Russ's *The Female Man*, Gearhart's *The Wanderground*, and Piercy's *Woman on the Edge of Time*.

720 RUBIN, MARTY. *The Boiled Frog Syndrome*. Boston: Alyson, 1987. [f, M]

Rubin's compelling thriller, *The Boiled Frog Syndrome*, is a near-future warning. Rubin envisions a future United States overrun with religious fascism. The election of right-wing preacher Peter Wickerly to the presidency has resulted in mass censorship and concentration camps for lesbians and gay men. Leatherman Stephen Ashcroft escapes the homophobic roundups and joins the Resistance to free his incarcerated lover.

721 RUNYON, CHARLES W[EST]. *Pigworld*. Garden City, N.Y.: Doubleday, 1971. [f, m]

A violent novel about the near future. A group of revolutionaries plot to take over the world. They are thwarted and succeed only in creating total chaos. Homosexuality is referred to briefly. Near the end of the novel, the revolutionary leader visits a community that is trying to rebuild itself. In doing so, community members have established a strict authoritarian morality in which homosexual emotions but not physical expression are allowed. The novel denigrates leftist politics.

722 RUSS, J. J. "Aurelia." In *Future Corruption*, edited by Roger Elwood. New York: Warner, 1975. [M]

Russ portrays a world in which all the women have died from a viral epidemic ... except Aurelia. She strips nightly before what is left of the heterosexual male population. Most men have given up and become gay, even though homosexuality is viewed as a second-rate substitute for "normal" sex.

723 RUSS, JOANNA. *And Chaos Died*. New York: Ace, 1970. [m]

A spaceship crashes on a planet; the two survivors are a passenger named Jai Vedh and the ship's captain. They find the planet inhabited by telepathic, telekinetic people who lead a utopian existence free of material wants, war, government, racism, and sexism. The captain's personality is too rigid to be influenced by either the ESP or the cultural values of the people, but Jai Vedh is transformed. One of the planet's women, Evne, becomes Jai's mentor, "cures" him of homosexuality (which in him was linked with misogyny), and trains him in a range of supernatural powers. Two years later, a rescue party lands and brings Jai and the captain back to Earth. Jai's new psychic talents make him physically invulnerable to, yet extremely aware of, the violence of his native culture. Although no longer homosexual, Jai retains the capacity to love men as shown in his filial relationship with a boy. Russ's experimental writing style is effective, and the novel suggests how it might feel to be telepathic in a society in which the expression of feelings is limited.

724 RUSS, JOANNA. "Bodies." In *Extra(Ordinary) People*. New York: St. Martin's Press, 1984. [F, M]

A gay adolescent boy from London circa 1930 and the narrator, a real estate entrepreneur from Portland circa 1970, are transported 2,000 years into the future. The boy is initially delighted with the utopian New Mexico society where he can engage in fantasy fulfillment and sex with adult men. But he is angry when the postsexist men do not act like "real" men. The bisexual narrator accepts the utopia more gracefully, but she has her own problems in a society where everyone is so very nice. Like all Russ stories, this one is highly recommended.

725 RUSS, JOANNA. "The Clichés from Outer Space." In *Despatches from the Frontiers of the Female Mind*, edited by Jen Green and Sarah Lefanu. London: Women's Press, 1985. [F]

Hilarious and angry satire on the various negative stereotypes of women in the science-fiction genre. Russ includes sadistic lesbians and man-hating amazons in her critique.

726 RUSS, JOANNA. "Corruption." In *Aurora: Beyond Equality*, edited by Vonda McIntyre and Susan Anderson. Greenwich, Conn.: Fawcett, 1976. [m]

A man leaves a loving and egalitarian culture to exist as a subversive among his enemies in their monolithic city / building. He exiles himself for twenty years to an all-male, rigidly structured hierarchic society where luxury and (homosexual) sex are privileges. His intelligence, coupled with years of hard work, gain him the authority and knowledge necessary to destroy the building and its inhabitants, but by the time he signals to his people to come and take him home, alienation and power have corrupted him. An evocative story.

727 RUSS, JOANNA. *The Female Man*. New York: Bantam, 1975. [F]

Using an experimental style, Russ captures the feelings and problems that are inherent in the relationships between women and women and between women and men. Her hard-hitting approach reveals the frustration, guilt, repression, and murderous rage in women. The humor throughout the novel is dry and spares no one for the sake of politeness. Russ presents four characters in different universes: Janet, on Whileaway where men are extinct; Joanna, struggling to have her intellect acknowledged by her male academic colleagues; Jeannine, caught in the social trap of husband hunting; and Jael, who brings the other three together on her Earth in order to settle her planet's very literal War between the Sexes. Lesbianism occurs on the women-only world of Whileaway and in a marvelous coming-out scene on Joanna's Earth. The author's feminist consciousness is pervasive as each of the characters decides whether to support Jael's battle against men. The novel is one of the most important to this bibliography.

728 RUSS, JOANNA. "Gleepsite." In *Orbit Nine*, edited by Damon Knight. New York: Putnam, 1971. [F?, X]

A short, evocative story told in a surrealistic, dreamlike style. With sulfuric winds raging outside, a hermaphroditic, batlike peddler enters a building to demonstrate an illusion-creating device to two fiftyish female twins who work the night shift as janitors. Implications of lesbianism are subtle.

729 RUSS, JOANNA. *Kittantinny: A Tale of Magic.* New York: Daughters, 1978. [F?]

This enchanting fantasy novel for young people concerns an eleven-year-old girl named Kit who sets off one day on a quest for adventure. While on the road, she meets a dragon, monsters, and storybook figures such as the Woman Warrior and Sleeping Beauty. She returns home matured, but she finds that she can no longer live in her valley's sexist culture and once again sets off. This time, however, she is accompanied by a beloved girlfriend. An excerpt was first published in *Sinister Wisdom* (Fall 1977).

730 RUSS, JOANNA. "Mr. Wilde's Second Chance." *Fantasy and Science Fiction*, September 1966. Reprinted in *The Hidden Side of the Moon.* New York: St. Martin's Press, 1987. [M]

Oscar Wilde, noted poet, dramatist, and homosexual, is caught in a strange limbo after his death. He is thought "too sad for heaven and too happy for hell." An opportunity is given to him to rearrange his past life's pattern into a beautiful and ordered picture. If he accomplishes this task, he will be free to live again. The picture that Wilde completes is a respectable, prosperous, and heterosexual one, but the poet ultimately realizes that he prefers his own life, whatever its unconventionalities and subsequent misfortunes, to the mock one he has invented. Short and delightful.

731 RUSS, JOANNA. "The Mystery of the Young Gentleman." In *Speculations*, edited by Isaac Asimov and Alice Laurance. New York: Houghton Mifflin, 1982. [M, X]

This is a quintessential gender-confusion tale such as only Russ can write. The narrator, "Joe Smith," who is perceived to be a cross-dressing woman (but isn't), accompanies an adolescent girl (who is neither of these) from nineteenth-century London to New York on an ocean liner. Joe Smith convinces a passenger that Joe is actually a homosexual man to divert suspicion away from the narrator's true identity. A "must read" story.

732 RUSS, JOANNA. "Nobody's Home." In *New Dimensions Two*, edited by Robert Silverberg. Garden City, N.Y.: Doubleday, 1972. [f]

On the future Earth, people can travel to any place on the globe by stepping into a booth and stepping out of it at their destination. Society and economics have radically changed and the average IQ has skyrocketed. In this world of no material scarcity, bisexual group marriages are common. The story explores one of these families and examines what it might feel like to be of singular intelligence. A finely wrought story.

733 RUSS, JOANNA. *The Two of Them*. New York: Berkley, 1978. [F?, m]
Irene Waskiewicz and Ernst Neumann, agents for the mysterious TransTemp organization (a recurrent element throughout Russ's science-fiction work), are assigned to the planet Ka'abah where women are veiled and kept confined at home. They meet a thirteen-year-old girl facing life imprisonment (like her aunt before her) because she prefers to be a poet rather than a mother and is therefore considered mad by her culture. Irene and Ernst have worked together for fifteen years. He was her mentor, and she loves him. But when Ernst attempts to prevent Irene from rescuing the young poet, she realizes that even the best of men like Ernst cannot escape all of their biases against women. Homosexuality and lesbianism come up in a variety of ways in the novel. Male homosexuality is expected in the poet's culture, and while Irene identifies herself as heterosexual, she acknowledges the possibility of becoming a lesbian. Ka'abah's culture is based on Suzette Haden Elgin's beautiful feminist short story, "For the Sake of Grace," in *At the Seventh Level* (New York: DAW, 1972), with the author's permission. A brilliant and challenging novel.

734 RUSS, JOANNA. "When It Changed." In *Again, Dangerous Visions*, edited by Harlan Ellison. Garden City, N.Y.: Doubleday, 1972. [F]
An incredible story that takes the not-uncommon (and usually prurient) men-land-on-planet-inhabited-by-all-women plot and turns the tables. Narrated by Janet Evason, who later appears in *The Female Man* (see citation above), it describes the arrival of men as an inevitable occurrence but, nonetheless, as a shock. The lesbians neither need nor want the men and know that their arrival will bring massive changes to the woman-identified culture. Funny, sad, and beautifully written, this story won the Nebula Award.

Biographical Note

Joanna Russ (b. 1937), highly acclaimed writer and academic, is the person most directly responsible for the introduction of radical lesbian feminism into contemporary science fiction. Throughout her work, both an awareness of power and oppression and an appreciation of women's feelings, needs, and potentials are central. In addition to the works listed above, see "Daddy's Girl," in *Epoch* (Winter 1975); *Alyx* (Boston: Gregg Press, 1976); and *We Who Are about To . . .* (New York: Dell, 1977).

Russ has also held science fiction up to feminist analysis: "Images of Women in Science Fiction," in *Image of Women in Fiction: Feminist*

Perspectives, ed. Susan Koppelman Cornillon (Bowling Green, Ohio: Popular Press, 1973) and *"Amor Vincit Foeminam*: The Battle of the Sexes in SF," in *Science Fiction Studies*, March 1980. See also "Reflections on Science Fiction: An Interview with Joanna Russ," in *Quest: A Feminist Quarterly* (Washington, D.C.), Summer 1975. She has contributed to lesbian, feminist, and gay journals including *Sinister Wisdom, Frontiers: A Journal of Women's Studies, Quest: A Feminist Quarterly, The Witch and the Chameleon*, and *Christopher Street*. Her non-science-fiction novel, *On Strike against God* (New York: Out and Out, 1980), is a marvelous lesbian coming-out novel. See also her *Magic Mommas, Trembling Sisters, Puritans, and Perverts*. (Trumansburg, N.Y.: Crossing Press, 1985).

Marilyn Hacker's "Science Fiction and Feminism: The Work of Joanna Russ," in *Chrysalis* (Los Angeles), no. 4 (1977), and "No Docile Daughters: A Study of Two Novels by Joanna Russ," by Marilyn J. Holt in *Room of One's Own* (Vancouver, B.C.), nos. 1-2 (1981), offer feminist perspectives on Russ's work.

Autobiographical material by Russ can be found in "Not for Years but for Decades," in *The Coming Out Stories*, ed. Julia Penelope Stanley and Susan J. Wolfe (Watertown, Mass.: Persephone Press, 1980). Biographical information can be found in *The Science Fiction Encyclopedia*, ed. Peter Nicholls (Garden City, N.Y.: Doubleday, 1979), and in *Contemporary Authors*, vols. 25-28, rev. ed., ed. Christine Nasso (Detroit: Gale, 1977).

---

735 RUSSELL, RAY. *Incubus*. New York: Morrow, 1976. [f, m]

The female population of a small California town is terrorized by a supernatural demon who literally rapes women to death. The author writes explicit scenes of violence against women. In the final pages of the book, the supernatural rapist is revealed to be a woman. A brief display of lesbian sexuality and an even more brief depiction of a gay male character are included.

736 RYMAN, GEOFF. "O Happy Day!" In *Interzone (The First Anthology)*. London: Dent, 1985. [f, M]

Feminists have rounded up all heterosexual men and sent them to extermination camps. Two men, tired of the oppression, begin a revolution.

737 SABERHAGEN, FRED. *Love Conquers All*. *Galaxy*, November 1974- January 1975. Reprint. New York: Ace, 1979. [m]

Rita and Arthur Rodney live in a future in which indiscriminate sexual promiscuity is the socially mandated norm. The government allows no deviation from this norm, and chastity has become the new curse word. Strict zero population growth is maintained, and no women may give birth to more than two children. Rita Rodney is pregnant with her third. In order to escape forced sterilization, she goes underground to join the "Young Virgins," a procelibacy Christian group. The author perceives a sexually loose society as tyrannical, oppressive, and totally opposed to a woman's right to her own body. He equates the gay liberation movement with this tyranny, and he portrays gay men as desiring to be the opposite sex. Lesbians, though mentioned as being part of the "Homo League," are never seen.

738 SACKERMAN, HENRY. *The Love Bomb*. New York: Bantam, 1972. [M]

Kaslan Codrimex, an anthropology student from the distant planet of Krushk, arrives on Earth to study the primitive customs of its people. He quickly runs afoul of the law, is mistaken for a Soviet spy, and is thrown into jail. He is rescued by a fledgling attorney, Miss Fay Cory. She and Kaslan incite desire in each other, but on Krushk, mating is done in trios. It is impossible for any Krushkan male to complete the act without intimate assistance from another male, called a co-hab. It is difficult for Kaslan to convince Fay's fiancé to be his co-hab. The homosexual implications of the plot are played down; Kaslan's bisexuality is portrayed as an alien social quirk rather than as a viable alternative life-style. *The Love Bomb* is primarily a heterosexual farce that uses sexist role definition and objectification for much of its humor.

739 SALMONSON, JESSICA AMANDA. "The Prodigal Daughter." In *Elsewhere*, edited by Terri Windling and Mark Allan Arnold. New York: Ace, 1981. [F]

An enchanting fantasy about a lesbian knight-errant named Dame Unise McKenzie of Morska-on-the Tarn and her battle with a terrifying demon.

SALMONSON, JESSICA AMANDA. The Tomoe Gozen Saga. [F]:

740 ▪ *Tomoe Gozen*. New York: Ace, 1981.

741 ▪ *The Golden Naginata*. New York: Ace, 1981.

742 ▪ *Thousand Shrine Warrior*. New York: Ace, 1984.

Salmonson spins a fantasy trilogy revolving around a female samurai warrior named Tomoe Gozen. Set in an alternative world based on medieval Japan, Tomoe Gozen is forced by fate and duty to lead armies, to slaughter demons, and sometimes to love beautiful women. The action is swift, and it may be a bit bloody for some tastes.

Biographical Note
Jessica Amanda Salmonson (b. 1950) is a noted feminist and martial arts expert. Of related interest are her novels *The Swordswoman* (New York: TOR, 1982) and *Ou Lu and the Beautiful Madwoman* (New York: Ace, 1985). She is the editor of the award-winning *Amazons!* (New York: DAW, 1979), *Amazons II* (New York: DAW, 1982), and *What Did Miss Darrington See? An Anthology of Feminist Supernatural Fiction* (New York: Feminist Press, 1989).

See her "Science Fiction: A Woman's Literature," *Lesbian Voices* (San Jose, Calif.), February 1976, and her "Fantastic Feminist Sci-Fi Adventures," *Lesbian Tide* (Los Angeles), May-June 1980.

For biographical information see *Contemporary Authors*, vol. 114, ed. Hal May (Detroit: Gale, 1985).

See also PUGMIRE, W. H. (joint author)

743 SANDERS, LAWRENCE. *The Tomorrow File*. New York: Putnam, 1975. [f, M]

The near-future society values efficiency and technological progress over human life. "Obsolete" ideals (as well as "obsolete" humans) are rapidly discarded to make way for such things as televised executions, genetic engineering, and the dictatorship of a scientific / bureaucratic elite. Within this scientific elite where disregard for human values is most apparent, protagonist Nicholas Flair travels. In his quest for a position of power, Flair contends with a Machiavellian labyrinth of intrigue and treachery. Homophobia, like sexism and racism, is considered inefficient, and for the most part it has been eliminated. Flair is openly bisexual; his male "user" (lover) is a major character. Other bisexual and homosexual characters are scattered throughout. Additionally, the author places several women in positions of power. The novel clearly equates sexual freedom with a mechanistic lack of humanity.

SANGSTER, JIMMY. *See* LYNDON, BARRE (joint author)

744 SANTOMARTINO, THOMAS. "Sex in Space." *Honcho* 9, no. 9 (December 1986). [M]

Sexually explicit gay male science fiction.

745 SARGENT, PAMELA. *The Shore of Women*. New York: Crown, 1986. [F, m]

Pamela Sargent, editor of the noted Women of Wonder series, presents a critical picture of a sexually segregated society. Following a nuclear conflict, women have rebuilt a new society. Living in isolated, walled cities, they control all knowledge and technology. Men are kept ignorant and are forced to live outside the cities in nomadic tribes. All people are homosexual; reproduction is performed through insemination. Against this harsh backdrop, Sargent draws interwoven plots. A young lesbian begins to question the sexual apartheid surrounding her, and a young man finds a lone woman outside the city's walls. Sargent does not succumb to all the tired clichés of the world-without-men stories; she leaves her lesbian world intact at the end of the novel.

SASLOW, JAMES M. *See* O'BRYAN, MILES

746 S[CHNEIDER], I[SADOR]. *Doctor Transit*. New York: Boni & Liveright, 1925. [m, X]

John and Mary, a young married couple, are each dissatisfied with their gender. Their dissatisfaction gives rise to lengthy arguments, but nothing can be resolved until they meet Doctor Transit. Doctor Transit is an archetypal mad scientist who agrees to switch their sexes. The resulting couple, Joan (John) and Marlowe (Mary), promptly fall in love. Marlowe finds contentment in his new situation, but Joan remains unfulfilled. Eventually she returns to Doctor Transit for another sex change, becoming Jeremiah. The experience of having been both sexes gives Jeremiah a higher understanding of humanity, and the book ends with Jeremiah becoming a new messiah. *Doctor Transit* was daringly avant-garde when first published; its style and its explicit sexuality were considered quite scandalous. The author makes only slight allusion to homosexuality; apparently he was more concerned with philosophical concepts. His use of transsexual changes, however, remains remarkable to this day.

747 SCHULMAN, J. NEIL. *The Rainbow Cadenza*. New York: Simon & Schuster, 1983. [f, m]

Schulman offers a humorous satire of contemporary sexual and social mores. Joan Darris lives in a future where males outnumber females seven to one, a permanent underclass is hunted for sport, and young women are conscripted by the government for sexual service. When Joan gets her induction notice, she revolts against her plight. One of her allies is her uncle, the lavender-attired "Gaylord" Wendell Darris. There are lesbian and gay situations scattered throughout the novel.

748 SCORTIA, THOMAS N[ICHOLAS]. *Earthwreck!* Greenwich, Conn.: Fawcett, Gold Medal, 1974. [M]

Two orbiting space stations, one Soviet and one American, are spectators as Earth is destroyed through nuclear warfare. The only chance for the survival of the human race is through cooperation between the two crews, but long-standing conflicts naturally emerge. A crew member's homosexual past proves crucial to the plot and is handled with compassion. The American crew contains only one woman, a doctor, while the Soviets' is sexually balanced.

749 SCORTIA, THOMAS N[ICHOLAS]. "Flowering Narcissus." In *Eros in Orbit*, edited by Joseph Elder. New York: Trident Press, 1973. [M]

A motorcyclist survives a worldwide plague and awakens in the distant future. The world is now populated entirely by androids; the motorcyclist is the only remaining human being. The androids supply him with a woman, but he is revolted when she turns out to be a feminine clone of himself. The human refers to the androids as "pansies" and "faggots." An unpleasant protagonist, but an interesting story.

750 SCORTIA, THOMAS N[ICHOLAS]. "Old, Old Death in New, New Venice." In *Caution! Inflammable!* Garden City, N.Y.: Doubleday, 1975. [M]

Conrad, a poet, arrives on a colonized Mars that has been built to imitate twelfth-century Venice. Amid the canals and plazas, he meets the Contessa de Almade, a woman he finds personally repugnant yet exceedingly useful for the attainment of his aspirations. Conrad's affairs become more complicated when Demetrios, the Contessa's servant, falls in love with him. Bizarre.

751 SCORTIA, THOMAS N[ICHOLAS]. "The Worm in the Rose." *Swank*, May 1972. Reprinted in *Caution! Inflammable!* Garden City, N.Y.: Doubleday, 1975. [M]

A young enlisted man, frustrated with his girlfriend, allows an older man to fellate him in a public restroom, only to be trapped by the vice squad. A good portrayal of a man trapped by circumstances, but a seedy representation of homosexuality.

752 SCORTIA, THOMAS N[ICHOLAS], and ROBINSON, FRANK M[ALCOLM]. *The Glass Inferno*. Garden City, N.Y.: Doubleday, 1974. [M]

Disaster strikes when a sixty-six-story high rise begins to burn uncontrollably while hundreds of people are trapped within. The authors follow the lives of a representative sample of those people suddenly forced by circumstances to take control of their destinies. They offer a new twist to the standard disaster theme by making their heroes a homosexual, a black man, and an older woman. The homosexual, Ian Douglas, is a paunchy, forty-five-year-old interior decorator who is losing both his business and his lover. Although at the end of his rope, Douglas shines when forced into action. His heroic contribution makes a skillfully written novel even more enjoyable. Borderline science fiction.

753 SCORTIA, THOMAS N[ICHOLAS], and ROBINSON, FRANK M[ALCOLM]. *The Nightmare Factor*. Garden City, N.Y.: Doubleday, 1978. [m]

Suppose a nation were experimenting with a 100-percent-fatal virus and something were to go wrong. . . . Such is the premise of *The Nightmare Factor*, a suspenseful novel set in San Francisco. When the unknown virus begins killing the city's tourists, it becomes the job of one hapless doctor to figure out what the deadly disease is and who is responsible for its outbreak. The authors do not ignore San Francisco's sizable gay population and one scene takes place in a crowded Castro Street restaurant. A fast-paced presentation of a frightening and very possible kind of experiment.

754 SCOTT, JODY. *I, Vampire*. New York: Ace, 1984. [F, m]

I, Vampire is a hilarious fantasy in which a bisexual Transylvanian vampire, working as a dance teacher in Chicago, falls in love with a reincarnation of Virginia Woolf. Woolf, it turns out, is in fact a dolphinlike alien, part of a team trying to save humanity from itself. Wacky, witty, feminist, and even erotic.

755 SCOTT, JODY. *Passing for Human*. New York: DAW, 1977. [f]

This is a satiric novel of intergalactic travel and adventure. Denaroyal, the heroine, is a thirty-six-foot extraterrestrial dolphinlike being who dons "Earthie" bodies to exist on our planet. Thus, in the course of her continuing battle with Scaulzo, the Prince of Darkness, she becomes Brenda Starr, Mary Worth, Emma Peel, and Virginia Woolf. The cast of characters also includes Abe Lincoln, General Patton, Sam Spade, and several thousand Richard Nixons. A minor character, a jail matron, is a lesbian.

756 SCOTT, MELISSA. *A Choice of Destinies*. New York: Baen, 1986. [M]

In an alternative universe, Alexander the Great abandons his invasion of India to return to Rome with his armies, rewriting the subsequent history of the Earth. There are several secondary gay male characters among Alexander's trusted Sacred Band of Theban warriors. His friendship with his beloved Hephaestion is a motivating force throughout the story.

757 SCOTT, MELISSA. *The Kindly Ones*. New York: Baen, 1987. [M?]

Science-fiction novel set on an icy, rigidly caste-based world. A pivotal character, the Medium, sleeps with men, but since the author never specifically identifies the Medium's gender, these relationships could be either homosexual or heterosexual.

758 SCOTT, MELISSA. "The King Who Was Summoned to Damascus." In *Arabesques: More Tales of the Arabian Nights*, edited by Susan Shwartz. New York: Avon, 1988. [M]

Male homosexuality plays a red herring role in this Arabic fantasy tale. A young male slave, thought by most to be a king's "catamite," is actually a supernatural healer.

759 SCOTT, MELISSA. "The Merchant." In *Arabesques 2*, edited by Susan Shwartz. New York: Avon, 1989. [M]

Two friends try to save a boy-loving merchant who lies dying of a rival's curse.

SCOTT, MELISSA. The Silence Series. [f, M]:

760 ▪ *Five-Twelfths of Heaven*. New York: Baen, 1985.

761 ▪ *Silence in Solitude*. New York: Baen, 1986.

762 ▪ *The Empress of Earth*. New York: Baen, 1987.

In Scott's universe, the art of alchemy has been refined and it is metaphysics rather than electronics that drives starships. Silence Leigh is a young female pilot in a misogynistic universe. She joins two male crew members in what starts as a marriage of convenience, only to find that they work for a pirate's syndicate. They, and about half the known universe, seek the path to the possibly mythical Earth. But none succeed until Silence discovers unique metaphysical abilities and develops her talents under the tutelage of a magus. The sexual elements are kept concise in all three volumes, but references make clear her husbands' attraction for each other. The only female pilots other than Silence are all from a lesbian planet, and women from this planet are respected and befriended by Silence and her husbands.

763 SCOTT, MELISSA, and BARNETT, LISA. *The Armor of Light*. New York: Baen, 1988. [M]

Scott and Barnett place their compelling and thoroughly researched alternative-world fantasy in Elizabethan England. James VI rules the throne in Scotland, but political forces have resorted to sorcery to destroy him. Playwright (and secret queen's agent) Christopher Marlowe is sent to rescue James from treachery and witchcraft. The homosexuality of both James and Marlowe is accurately represented, though sexuality *per se* is not central to the plot. The novel is enjoyable reading.

764 SEARLES, BAIRD. "The Wilis." *Fantasy and Science Fiction*, May 1968. [m]

The company manager of the Gotham Ballet Company relates the eerie and riveting tale of a very special performance of the ballet *Giselle*. The performance marks the final stage appearance of prima ballerina Lyda Volpe. The real and the supernatural mix subtly throughout. Male homosexuality is casually accepted within the ballet troupe.

765 SHECKLEY, ROBERT. "In a Land of Clear Colors." In *New Constellations*, edited by Thomas Disch and Charles Naylor. New York: Harper & Row, 1976. [m]

A volunteer in the First Extraterrestrial Exploration Corps is sent as a Terran emissary to the planet Kaldor V. He finds himself rapidly assimilating into the ever-changing culture of the alien planet and eventually feels more Kaldorian than Terran. This assimilation is further enhanced by his acceptance into a Kaldorian friendship group that includes both heterosexual and homosexual relations. Not until he begins a journey with his new friends does he realize that he never will be truly Kaldorian. A beautiful short story with an open attitude toward same-sex love.

SHELDON, ALICE. *See* JAMES TIPTREE, Jr., and SHELDON, RACCOONA (pseudonyms)

766 SHELDON, RACCOONA [pseudonym of Alice Sheldon]. "Your Faces, O My Sisters! Your Faces Filled with Light." In *Aurora: Beyond Equality*, edited by Vonda McIntyre and Susan Anderson. Greenwich, Conn.: Fawcett, 1976. [F?]

Sheldon presents one woman's fantasy world with skill and sympathy. The nameless main character, who has been violated by both unwanted motherhood and shock treatments, escapes a mental institution and lives under the delusion that she exists in the far future. In her private world the cities are in ruins, there are no men, and she is safe. She naively greets men and women in the same friendly way, believing them all to be women. Unfortunately, her defenseless attitude leaves her even more vulnerable to the male violence that in reality surrounds her. A beautiful, but tragic, feminist story.

767 SHERMAN, DELIA. *Through a Brazen Mirror*. New York: Ace, 1989. [M]

The medieval kingdom of Albia has been free of formal sorcery for generations, though every village has a woman with skills sufficient to perform the basic healing arts. Into this pastoral calm rages the sorceress, Margaret. The sorceress's unerring mirror has foretold her execution at the hand of her daughter, Elinor. Margaret attempts to undo her grim demise by destroying Elinor through the use of plague-infested winds that sweep the kingdom. The author makes it easy for the reader to hold in high estimation both the "bad" Margaret and the "good" Elinor as the two women counter each other's magic (and generally run or ruin the lives of men around them). Elinor dresses as a man and ascends to the position of the young King Lionel's chamberlain. The king's awareness of his homosexuality is awakened through association with his cross-dressing chamberlain. His resolution to the perceived conflict of being both a good king and a homosexual is integral to the plot. An exceptionally well-crafted high sorcery fantasy.

768 SHWARTZ, SUSAN. "In the Throat of the Dragon." In *Sword of Chaos*, edited by Marion Zimmer Bradley. New York: DAW, 1982. [F]

A lesbian Free Amazon and a heterosexual Comyn lord come to a hard-won alliance in this entertaining story set in Marion Zimmer Bradley's popular Darkover universe.

769 SIDDON, ANNE RIVERS. *The House Next Door*. New York: Ballantine, 1982. [m]

A well-written haunted house story in which a strange supernatural building brings out the "worst" in the people who live in it. One of those affected is a young husband whose latent homosexuality is awakened.

770 SILVERBERG, ROBERT. *The Book of Skulls*. New York: Scribner's, 1972. [M]

The discovery of an ancient manuscript leads four male college students into the wilds of the Arizona desert in search of immortality. There they find a secret monastery run by an age-old religious sect called the Keepers of the Skull. The youths decide to become disciples of the sect while knowing that for two to become immortal two must die. Of the four, two are homosexual, and both characters are well developed. An intriguing book.

771 SILVERBERG, ROBERT. *Dying Inside*. New York: Scribner's, 1972. [m]

David Selig is a psychic receptor. He has heard other people's thoughts and emotions all his life and has had to make significant adjustments to his unusual gift. But things are changing for Selig; his remarkable talent is disappearing. The experience is subjectively like dying, and this novel records Selig's understanding and acceptance of his "death." Silverberg writes with remarkable insight into the mind of a heterosexual telepathic male, but his characterization of the novel's gay male is weak.

772 SILVERBERG, ROBERT. "Hawksbill Station." *Galaxy*, August 1967. Expanded and reprinted as *Hawksbill Station*. Garden City, N.Y.: Doubleday, 1968. [M]

An oppressive future government has found shuffling troublemakers through a time transporter the easiest way to deal with dissent, hence a penal colony has been established in the Paleozoic Age specifically for political prisoners. "Hawksbill Station" concerns the arrival of a new inmate in this isolated prison. Homosexuality exists among the colony's entirely male population, but it is viewed as situational, as a second-rate substitute for women. There are no self-defined gay men in the story.

773 SILVERBERG, ROBERT. "In the House of Double Minds." *Vertex*, June 1974. Reprinted in *The Feast of St. Dionysus*. New York: Scribner's, 1975. [F]

The House of Double Minds is a training school for young oracles-to-be. "Double minds" refers to the surgery severing the two hemispheres of the brain, which all oracle students must undergo. Silverberg's short story concerns a young oracle trainee, his developing psychic powers, and his friendship with a lesbian guide and counselor at the House of Double Minds. Her lesbianism is portrayed very positively.

774 SILVERBERG, ROBERT. "Passengers." In *Orbit Four*, edited by Damon Knight. New York: Putnam, 1968. [M]

The society that Silverberg writes about is much like our own but with one major difference. Imagine an invisible parasite that can unexpectedly take over the consciousness of a human. During the time a human is playing host to one of these invisible "passengers," she or he can be driven to any pleasure or any pain, but when the "passenger" leaves the human has no recollection of what has transpired. Society has had to adapt to these body-borrowing parasites, and as a result, trust between people has virtually disappeared. Male homosexuality is used as a cruel game by a passenger laughing at love. An excellent story. A Nebula Award winner.

775 SILVERBERG, ROBERT. "Ringing the Changes." In *Alchemy and Academe*, edited by Anne McCaffrey. Garden City, N.Y.: Doubleday, 1970. [f]

Silverberg imagines a device that transports a person's mind out of her or his body and into someone else's. This has become a popular form of recreation, but occasionally technical foul-ups occur. "Ringing the Changes" concerns such a foul-up. A transmission error has placed several minds temporarily in limbo while awaiting return to their initial homes. During this period, a "changer" is placed in several bodies not his own, including that of a lesbian named Vonda Lou. Although she appears only briefly, Vonda Lou is a sympathetically drawn character.

776 SILVERBERG, ROBERT. *Son of Man.* New York: Ballantine, 1971. [X]

An interesting experiment that reads much like an acid trip or a wet dream. A man caught in a time flux is transported far into the future. The Earth he finds is populated by "humans" who have bright red eyes, immense psychic powers, and the ability to change sex at will. There are also other species that have descended from the narrator's human form. The narrator befriends them all and makes love to most of them. In fact, this all-encompassing love that he feels for his fellow "humans" takes on almost religious significance by the end of the novel. The sensual, kaleidoscopic writing style is intriguing, but the author's overpowering phallic fantasies may weaken the novel's appeal.

777 SILVERBERG, ROBERT. *The World Inside.* Garden City, N.Y.: Doubleday, 1971. [f, m]

In Silverberg's world of 2381, the expansion of the Earth's population has caused people to build up rather than out, to create enormous buildings that reach into the sky. People live out their entire lives within these massive structures, and society has had to adapt accordingly. People, usually men, wander around at night and randomly select an apartment to enter. It is bad form to refuse sex with a night guest. Although the majority of the sexuality presented is heterosexual, several characters express bisexual inclinations.

778 SINGER, ROCHELLE. *The Demeter Flower.* New York: St. Martin's, 1980. [F]

Singer examines life in a lesbian-separatist utopia secluded in the valley of Demeter in the mountains of California. Refugees of the chaos of the 1980s, which destroyed American life, the women of Demeter have developed a self-sustaining farming community. They are all lesbian, and reproduce by drinking a special herb tea that induces parthenogenesis. Conflict arises when a heterosexual couple arrives in the valley. An interesting speculation, comparable to Bradley's *The Ruins of Isis* and Gearhart's *The Wanderground.*

779 SKIPP, JOHN, and SPECTOR, CRAIG. *The Light at the End.* New York: Bantam, 1986. [m]

Skipp and Spector have crafted a chilling and grisly vampire story that begins as an ancient vampiric predator slaughters the passengers of a New York City subway train. Police assume that there is a new mass murderer lose, but a handful of people realize the threat's true supernatural nature and attempt to vanquish the danger. Among this small group of heroes are two gay men. Their depiction is ostensibly sympathetic, but their ultimate purpose in the story is questionable. One is a swishy black bicycle messenger and the other is a sexually repressed movie buff (who feels a little lust for the vampire). There is a graphically depicted homosexual rape, complete with chains and torture. Many readers will be put off by the homophobic epithets that pepper the novel.

780 SLEASAR, HENRY. "Ersatz." In *Dangerous Visions*, edited by Harlan Ellison. Garden City, N.Y.: Doubleday, 1967. [M]

After months of wandering through a North America decimated by nuclear war, a soldier joyously stumbles across a "Peace Station," a fallout-proof oasis for the few surviving enlisted men. There, his hosts offer him synthetic meat made of wood bark and ersatz tobacco made of wool fiber. He meets a beautiful woman to whom he is sexually attracted, but his attraction turns to horror when he realizes that the woman is actually a man in woman's attire. This gay man is referred to as "the creature" and "it"; as the title suggests, gay men are equated with synthetic women.

781 SLONCZEWSKI, JOAN. *A Door into Ocean*. New York: Arbor House, 1986. [F]

Author and biologist Slonczewski uses her scientific knowledge to depict Shora, a planet completely covered by water. The all-female inhabitants of Shora live ecologically balanced lives within enormous floating rafts. When the patriarchal planet of Valedon attacks the watery world, the Shorian women, psychologically and ethically incapable of fighting, must confront the invaders in their own fashion.

782 SMITH, CORDWAINER [pseudonym of Paul M. A. Linebarger]. "The Crime and Glory of Commander Suzdal." *Amazing*, May 1964. Reprinted in *Seven Trips through Time and Space*, edited by Geoff Conklin. Greenwich, Conn.: Fawcett, Gold Medal, 1968. [M]

Suzdal, commander of a solo intergalactic flight, receives a distress signal from the planet of Arachosia where, years before, the mysterious death of all women created a race of jaded homosexual men. Knowing "what they were," the Arachosians hated themselves and the larger universe. The SOS is a trap, set to capture their enemies. Homosexuals are viewed as "terrible people," "monsters," somehow not even human.

783 SMITH, THORNE. *Turnabout*. Garden City, N.Y.: Doubleday, 1931. [f, M?]

In this light and humorous novel, an ancient Egyptian idol, irritated by the constant bickering of a stereotypic heterosexual married couple, plays a dirty trick on them. One morning Sally and Tim Willows awaken to find that they have exchanged bodies. Complications ensue as Sally is forced to go to Tim's job, and Tim becomes pregnant. Quasi-homosexuality runs throughout (e.g., Sally flirts with a male friend and the friend assumes that Tim has gone gay). This witty and urbane comedy, very 1930s in style and pacing, relies heavily on sexist conventions for its humor. The book was considered quite racy when first published.

784 SPERRY, RALPH A. *Status Quotient: The Carrier*. New York: Avon, 1981. [M]
Gay male protagonist Ancil's world has destroyed itself through war, but he is immortal and is condemned to solitude for centuries. To mark the time he keeps a journal, recounting his experiences and memories. How much of the journal is reality and how much is Ancil's fantasy?

785 SPINRAD, NORMAN [RICHARD]. "The Age of Invention." *Fantasy and Science Fiction*, July 1966. Reprinted in *The Best from Science Fiction and Fantasy: Sixteenth Series*, edited by Edward Ferman. Garden City, N.Y.: Doubleday, 1967. [M]
A story about the invention of art, art criticism, and other artifacts of civilization during the Stone Age. Peacock and Cuckatoo, two swishy Neolithic buddies, invent a form of behavior that leads to another invention . . . the vice squad. The story relies heavily upon stereotypic homosexual mannerisms.

786 SPINRAD, NORMAN [RICHARD]. "Blackout." *Cosmos*, September 1977. Reprinted in *The Star Spangled Future*. New York: Ace, 1979. [M]
A Defense Department investigation into the flying-saucer phenomenon causes a two-day blackout of the news media, which panics the nation. Archie and Bill, two Manhattan homosexuals, are among those frightened by the lack of news. Their characterizations are warm and amusing.

787 SPINRAD, NORMAN [RICHARD]. *The Iron Dream*. New York: Avon, 1972. [M?]
In Spinrad's alternative universe, the German National Socialist Party died in 1923. Its leader, Adolf Hitler, did not become führer of the Third Reich but instead achieved fame by writing American pulp science fiction. In *The Iron Dream*, one of his best-known novels, a future fascist, Feric Jaggar, finds his "racial destiny" by destroying all mutated humans. When it becomes apparent that radiation will continue to produce mutations despite Jaggar's efforts, he orders his followers to develop cloning techniques to perpetuate "true" human

males. Although there is no overt homosexuality within Jaggar's narrative, an intriguing afterword analyzes Hitler's phallic obsession, fetishism, and repressed homosexuality.

788 SPINRAD, NORMAN [RICHARD]. "Journals of the Plague Years." In *Full Spectrum*. New York: Bantam, 1988. [m]
Spinrad seems to enjoy imagining a future of sexual and religious fascism where a complete quarantine of HIV-positive people is mandated by the government and a cure for AIDS is repressed by corporate greed.

789 SPINRAD, NORMAN [RICHARD]. *Little Heroes*. New York: Bantam, 1987. [m]
Spinrad constructs a nasty and homophobic novel set in a desperate future Manhattan of psychedelic drugs, music videos, and advanced computer technology. One of the novel's primary characters, a Puerto Rican drug addict, spends his time fag-bashing gay "leathermen." Male homosexuality is portrayed as dangerous and sleazy.

790 SPINRAD, NORMAN [RICHARD]. *A World Between*. New York: Pocket Books, 1979. [f, m]
Pacifican culture holds two values as all-important: sexual equality and electronic democracy. On this planet, lesbians and gay men are matter-of-factly accepted until Pacifica's political harmony is upset by involvement with the galaxy-wide Pink and Blue War, a battle between the sexes. The Transcendental Scientists, a rigid, logical, and extremely male-dominated group challenges the Femocrats, lesbian supremacists from Earth. The novel's examination of sexual politics is weak because its analysis of misogyny and patriarchy is superficial and its portrayal of lesbianism is stereotypic.

791 STAPLEDON, [WILLIAM] OLAF. *Odd John; A Story between Jest and Earnest*. New York: Dutton, 1936. [M?]
Stapledon's *Odd John* is perhaps one of the finest science-fiction novels utilizing the superhuman theme. John Wainwright is born into a staid British family several years before World War I. From the start, there is something special about him, something odd. John masters geometry and physics by the age of eight, and by inventing clever household gadgets and intelligently investing in the stock market, he is independent at sixteen. He locates others of his species, *Homo superior*, and they form a colony on an isolated Pacific island. The moral and philosophical questions inherent in human interaction with a superior species are explored with a depth rare to science fiction. Homosexuality is introduced when John enters puberty and goes through a homosexual phase and then a heterosexual one. He finds, however, that sex with

humans is bestiality, and his period of sexual experimentation quickly ends. More important to the story is the nonsexual devotion the narrator has for John. There are inferences of racism and sexism scattered throughout, but Stapledon makes it clear that these attitudes are the human narrator's, not John's.

792 STAR. "Foreheads Forever." In *A Woman's Touch: An Anthology of Lesbian Eroticism and Sensuality for Women Only*, edited by Cedar and Nelly. Eugene, Oreg.: Amazon Reality, 1979. [F]
Sexually explicit lesbian science-fiction erotica. Written and published by lesbian feminists.

793 STEAD, CHRISTINA. "Sappho." In *The Salzburg Tales*. London: Peter Davies, 1934. [F]
Surrealistic fantasy tale in which the Greek poet Sappho lusts after Eve after she arrives in heaven.

794 STEELY BLUE, JOSH. "Star Hawk: Discipline and Rehabilitation." *Advocate Men*, August 1989. [M]
Gay male science-fiction erotica.

795 STENBOCK, STANISLAUS ERIC, Count. "The True Story of a Vampire." In *Studies of Death: Romantic Tales*. London: David Nutt, 1894. [M]
In Stenbock's marvelous and melancholy tale of homoerotic vampirism, an old woman recounts a tale of her youth. Her family had been visited by a mysterious Count Vardalek. Vardalek fell in love with the narrator's brother, Gabriel, and they were soon inseparable. Predictably, Gabriel fell ill and died as a result of this friendship. The author, Stenbock, was one of the many gay men involved in the flowering of openly homosexual creativity that took place in Britain during the late 1800s.

STEVENS, BARBARA. The Martos Series. [F]:

796 ▪ "A Night at Riley's." *Ladder* (San Francisco), March 1958.

797 ▪ "A Martian View." *Ladder* (San Francisco), April 1958.

798 ▪ "The Coming Out of Martos." *Ladder* (San Francisco), May 1958.
A humorous science-fiction series of stories about Martos the Martian anthropologist and his wonderful friends from Riley's Pub, a lesbian bar. Martos is taught the importance of camouflage and learns a great deal about butch-femme role-playing.

799 STEVENS, BARBARA. "1974: An Orwellian Fantasy." *Ladder* (San Francisco), April 1963. [F]
An imaginative story set in a Big Brother future of 1974. The plot concerns an underground revolutionary group of green-haired lesbians.

800 STEWART, DESMOND. *The Vampire of Mons*. New York: Harper & Row, 1976. [m, X]
Three boys enter an English boarding school just as World War II breaks out. Two of them, Theo and Darwin, become the faithful companions of a reclusive schoolmaster, Dr. Vitaly. The third, Clive, is in love with the other two. Clive desperately tries to undermine the boys' loyalty to Vitaly by convincing them that he is a vampire. They in turn accuse Vitaly of being a pederast, and the three boys burn the doctor to death. Since Vitaly shows none of the traditional signs, it is not clear whether he is in fact a vampire, but the two boys are convinced that they are now homosexual vampires. In addition to the complex triangles of love, there are two minor characters who are sent home at midterm because of homosexual indiscretions. A bit dry.

801 STEWART, FRED MUSTARD. *Star Child*. New York: Bantam, 1975. [M]
Helen Bradford, a resident of the quiet New England town of Shandy, finds herself dreaming of a beautiful boy who calls himself the Star Child and who promises to help save the world. Concurrently, several other townspeople, including Helen's husband, Jack, have equally vivid dreams involving another personage named Raymond. Raymond professes to be a god and incites those who dream of him to bisexuality, violence, and murder. Shandy's residents soon become the pawns in a battle between the good Star Child and the evil Raymond. The two dream-beings are eventually revealed to be visitors from our own future who have traveled back to our own time. Homosexuality, bisexuality, and the breakdown of traditional sex roles are linked with Raymond and his decadent, inhuman world of the future.

802 STINE, HANK. *Season of the Witch*. North Hollywood, Calif.: Essex House, 1968. [X]
A pornographic novel in which a man, as punishment for murdering a woman, is biologically transformed into his female victim.

803 STIRLING, S. M. *Snowbrother*. New York: Signet, 1985. [F]

804 STIRLING, S. M., and MEIER, SHIRLEY. *The Cage*. New York: Signet, 1989.

805 STIRLING, S. M., and MEIER, SHIRLEY. *The Sharpest Edge.* New York: Signet, 1986.

The beautiful, sword-bearing, bisexual barbarian Shkai'ra is the focus of the first volume of this page-turning fantasy trilogy. In the distant future after the great holocaust, Shkai'ra and her soldiers battle for possession of a small village. In the first pages of *The Sharpest Edge*, the amazon meets Megan Thansdoom, her companion and lover through the next two novels. The action throughout is swift and bloody, and the primary characters are not always admirable, but the series is entertaining and has earned a strong following.

806 STONE, MERLIN. "The Plasting Project." In *Hear the Silence: Stories by Women of Myth, Magic, and Renewal,* edited by Irene Zahava. Trumansburg, N.Y.: Crossing Press, 1986. [F]

Two lesbians, longtime lovers and members of an alien race, strive to prevent Earth from destroying itself. They eventually decide they must speak specifically to Earth's women, who seem better able to hear the alien culture's message of peace and harmony.

STOVER, LEON. *See* HARRISON, HARRY (joint author)

807 STRAUB, PETER. "The Juniper Tree." In *Prime Evil,* edited by Douglas E. Winter. New York: New American Library, 1988. [M]

In this haunting tale, Straub delicately tackles the horrors of sexual abuse and its lifelong consequences. A young boy finds his carefree afternoons in the local movie theater forever ruined after he develops a sexual relationship with an older man. This well-written and powerful story is only marginally fantasy, but it was published in a horror genre collection.

808 STRAUB, PETER. *Koko.* New York: Dutton, 1988. [M]

Straub again uses the consequences of child abuse as the underlying horror in this brilliant suspense thriller. At the unveiling of the Vietnam War Memorial in Washington, D.C., four veterans reminisce about the time they spent together in the jungles of Southeast Asia. When they hear of a series of horrible random murders taking place throughout Asia, in which a playing card is found in the mouth of each of the mutilated victims, the four men realize that the murderer must be another member of their platoon, a friend of theirs. They agree to return to Asia and find the killer. Thus begins a nerve-wracking journey halfway around the world, with stops in several Bangkok gay bars and sex shows. Chilling and recommended. The story contains only marginal fantasy elements, but it won a World Fantasy Award for best novel.

809 STRICKLAND, BRAD. *To Stand beneath the Sun*. New York: Signet, 1986. [f]

Tomas Perion, an interstellar geologist, awakens to find himself on a world where women are warriors and men (in short supply) are fought over. Sexual activity between women is considered "recreational," but male homosexuality is a strong social taboo.

810 STRIEBER, WHITLEY. *The Hunger*. New York: Morrow, 1981. [F]

The sexuality implicit in vampirism is made overt in this flashy contemporary vampire tale. Miriam is beautiful, sophisticated, and centuries-old. Continually lonely, she finds suitable human lovers, male and female, with whom to share her blood and her life. Unfortunately, these companions are not real vampires and cannot survive forever. Miriam's current lover, John Blaylock, is decaying and Miriam chooses Sarah, a research scientist, as her next companion.

811 STURGEON, THEODORE. "Affair with a Green Monkey." *Venture*, May 1957. Reprinted in *A Touch of Strange*. Garden City, N.Y.: Doubleday, 1958. [M]

A human-appearing alien is rescued from a band of marauding thugs by a top government official and his wife. Because of the alien's soft and gentle manner, the official mistakenly assumes that he is a human gay man; this assumption proves to have far-reaching consequences. An amusing and insightful look at society's oppressive gay and straight stereotypes. Recommended.

812 STURGEON, THEODORE. "If All Men Were Brothers, Would You Let One Marry Your Sister?" In *Dangerous Visions*, edited by Harlan Ellison. Garden City, N.Y.: Doubleday, 1967. [m]

This short story confronts the incest taboo by positively portraying a culture despised by the rest of the galaxy for its validation of incest. A Terran male, motivated by greed, makes contact with these wealthy outcasts and goes to their world. He is at first repulsed by their sexual morals but later becomes convinced that they are emotionally healthy, sane, and loving. Corrupt instances of homosexuality are used to show that the taboo against incest is more deeply ingrained (and perhaps less valid) than taboos against other forms of sexual expression. The story challenges the argument that inbreeding automatically produces mentally retarded children, but it does not touch on issues of unequal power frequently found in parent-child sexual relationships.

813 STURGEON, THEODORE. "Rule of Three." *Galaxy*, January 1951. Reprinted in *Galaxy Reader of Science Fiction*, edited by Herbert Gold. New York: Crown, 1952. [F?, m]

This story is chock-full of homosexual implications. The plot revolves around a virus that causes neurosis. Aliens who merge and communicate in triads take over the bodies of various Earthlings and attempt to force their human hosts to do the same. Characters include two devoted spinsters and a person with a homosexual past.

814 STURGEON, THEODORE. "Scars." *Zane Grey's Western Magazine*, May 1949. Reprinted in *E. Pluribus Unicorn*. New York: Abelard-Schuman, 1953. [M?]

A strangely beautiful Western story. An aging cowboy relates to his partner an anecdote that he has kept secret for years, a tale concerning a nonsexual experience he once had with a woman. Sturgeon's story subtly touches on homosexuality. The piece clearly foreshadows the work Sturgeon was later to do that would introduce frank sexuality into science-fiction genre writing.

815 STURGEON, THEODORE. "The Sex Opposite." *Fantastic* (Fall 1952). Reprinted in *E. Pluribus Unicorn*. New York: Abelard-Schuman, 1952. [X]

Two friends, a female reporter and a male mortician, each meet and fall in love with the same being who appears to each of them as a member of the opposite sex. Unbeknownst to humans, this being, and others of its race, is in a symbiotic relationship with the human species. The beings benefit from humans' aptitude at building things, and in exchange they are the inspiration of love and understanding among humans. The being shows the two humans how to dissolve the isolation of each person from the next.

816 STURGEON, THEODORE. *Venus Plus X*. New York: Pyramid, 1960. [X]

In a future utopia people are neither male nor female but rather one neuter gender. Sex as we know it does not exist, yet these special beings court and marry. An ordinary human male, brought into this society to test his reactions, becomes revolted at their way of life when he discovers that they have intentionally altered themselves. "Men marrying men. Incest, perversion, there isn't anything you don't do. . . . A mutation would have been natural [and more acceptable]. . . . We'd exterminate you down to the last queer kid . . . and stick that one into a sideshow. . . . Get me out of here." His hatred and disgust are contrasted with the genderless people's gentleness and wisdom.

817 STURGEON, THEODORE. "The World Well Lost." *Universe*, June 1953. Reprinted in *E. Pluribus Unicorn*. New York: Abelard-Schuman, 1953. [M]

"The World Well Lost" is often credited with having introduced the subject of homosexuality into the genre. A pair of androgynous aliens land on Earth. Unaware that the two lovers are of the same sex, the Earth's population becomes enchanted with the pair and dubs them the "lovebirds." When it is learned that the pair are fugitives, public opinion turns against them. They are arrested, put on a spaceship, and sent back to their home world to be executed. While on the spaceship their survival is uncertain until the crew person, Grunty, helps them to escape because he realizes that they are homosexual. Grunty, a closet homosexual, identifies and sympathizes with the lovebirds' feeling for each other.

Biographical Note

Theodore Sturgeon (1918-85) was highly influential in opening the science-fiction genre to exploration of sexual themes. His stories often touch upon questions of sexual variation and social prejudice, usually from a sympathetic and well-thought-out viewpoint. A Sturgeon short story marginally relevant to this bibliography, but too minor to warrant annotation, is "Who?" in *Galaxy*, March 1955; retitled and reprinted as "Bulkhead" in *SF: The Year's Greatest Science Fiction and Fantasy*, ed. Judith Merril (New York: Dell, 1956).

Biographical and critical information on Sturgeon can be found in Peter Nicholls's *The Science Fiction Encyclopedia* (Garden City, N.Y.: Doubleday, 1979) and in Sam Moskowitz's *Seekers of Tomorrow* (Cleveland: World Publishing, 1966).

---

818 SUNDANCE, BONNIE. "An Elder Womon's Tale from the Year 2000." *WomanSpirit* (Portland, Oreg.) 3, no. 11 (Spring Equinox 1977). [F]

An idealistic vision of a land-based lesbian utopia, which was written for the Washington Womyn's Land Project Meeting on Visions, December 1976.

819 SUNLIGHT. *Womonseed.* Little River, Calif.: Tough Dove Books, 1986. [F]

On the eve of the turn of the next century, the women and children of Womonseed, an all-women's culture, gather and share their stories. Snowbird recounts the founding of Womonseed. Woodwomon remembers her heterosexual past and her discovery of the women's movement. Night describes her experiences as an African-American lesbian. And as the women tell their tales and sing their songs, a picture of this idyllic, woman-centered society emerges. Portions of this novel first appeared in *WomanSpirit* and *Common Lives / Lesbian Lives*.

820 SUTHERLAND, JOHN. *Unnatural Father*. San Diego, Calif.: Greenleaf Classics, 1973. [M]
   Pornographic gay male vampire story.

821 SWANN, THOMAS BURNETT. *Green Phoenix*. New York: DAW, 1972. [F?, M?]
   Swann draws upon the classic Greco-Roman legend of Aeneas to construct this light fantasy. Aeneas, the son of Aphrodite and the Prince of Troy, has escaped the fallen city and wandered for many years seeking to establish a new home. He has been accompanied on the journey by his aging father, his young son, and several ships bearing Trojan settlers. After many misfortunes they have found a satisfactory spot, the place where Rome will someday stand. Conflict arises immediately between the Trojans and the nonhuman races who populate the area. The Dryads, an entirely female race of forest dwellers, resolve to kill the intruders whom they perceive as rapists and killers. A forbidden love affair between Aeneas and a Dryad ultimately leads to cooperation between the races. There is explicit (and positive) homosexual mention of a pair of shipboard lovers; further, the relationship between the boyish Aeneas and his son is very suggestive of homoeroticism in its intensity.

822 SWANN, THOMAS BURNETT. *How Are the Mighty Fallen*. New York: DAW, 1974. [M]
   This is a magical retelling of the tragic biblical love story of Jonathan and David. It is obviously intended to validate homosexual love. When David and Jonathan meet, Jonathan is the prince of Israel and David is the armsbearer for Jonathan's legendary father, King Saul. After David slays the cyclops Goliath, the two young men fall in love. They are joyous as lovers, but they must shield their love from public view because the god who rules Israel, Yahweh, frowns on such passions. The only support the lovers get is from Jonathan's mother, Ahinoam, who worships the Great Mother Goddess rather than the patriarchal Yahweh. The death of Jonathan brings the story to its tragic conclusion, but the author makes it clear that the lovers will meet again in the "Celestial Vineyard." Minor positive mention of love between women.

823 SWANN, THOMAS BURNETT. *Moondust*. New York: Ace, 1968. [f, M?]
   This is an extrapolation of another biblical story, the Battle of Jericho. Rehab, or Moondust, is an ugly young woman who suddenly appears at Bard the Potter's home in a mysterious exchange for his beloved brother. Bard grows to love Moondust and is shocked when one day she transforms into a strikingly beautiful winged woman. She is of a

race that is enslaved by fennecs – small foxlike animals who control their slaves with their minds. There is mention of same-sex sexuality in Sodom and in Gomorrah, and the love between Bard and his best friend, Zen, is intense but unconsummated.

824 SWANN, THOMAS BURNETT. "The Murex." *Science Fantasy*, February 1964. Reprinted in *The Dolphin and the Deep*. New York: Ace, 1968. [F?]

"The Murex" concerns the conversion of an amazon, Daphne, into a heterosexual. The process is assisted by a Myrmidon insect boy named Tychon. The evil, war-loving amazons are not defined as lesbian.

825 SWANN, THOMAS BURNETT. *Queens Walk in the Dusk*. Illustrated by Jeff Jones. Forest Park, Ga.: Heritage Press, 1977. [M?]

Again Swann utilizes the mythical figure of Aeneas for his literary inspiration, this time drawing from an earlier portion of the epic hero's life. A supernatural storm has tossed Aeneas's boat across the Mediterranean Sea to Carthage. There, accompanied by his loyal friend, Achates, and his delightfully boisterous son, the hero meets and falls in love with Dido, the country's queen. Dido, a mother figure, becomes an important character in the drama. But Dido and Aeneas's love affair is opposed by the Elephant King who jealously covets Dido for his own. On the most overt level, male homosexuality is sentimentally displayed in Achates, Aeneas's gay friend who is designed to elicit sympathy rather than self-assertion and pride. Yet Aeneas, despite his heterosexual nature, returns Achates's love in a nonsexual way, and his love for his young son is even more suggestive of homoeroticism. This nonsexual male-male love triangle between Aeneas, his son, and his best friend survives the calamity that destroys the more physical, heterosexual bond between Aeneas and Dido.

826 SWANN, THOMAS BURNETT. *The Tournament of Thorns*. New York: Ace, 1976. [M?]

A delightful fantasy tale that takes place in the Middle Ages in a magical forest inhabited by unicorns and mandrakes. Three young people, two boys and a girl, find adventures galore as they explore the enchanted woods. A subtle but unmistakable gay relationship exists between the two boys.

827 SWANN, THOMAS BURNETT. *Wolfwinter*. New York: Ballantine, 1972. [f, M?]

The wisdom and experience of an old tree-dwelling sybil named Erinna is called into play when a broken-hearted young man seeks her help. The lad is grieving over the death of a beloved male friend. To console him, Erinna tells the story of her life. She was born on the island of Lesbos, where as a youngster she played and sang with the great poet Sappho (who is depicted as bisexual). A homely girl, Erinna was never chosen at the fertility festivals until she met a charming satyr, half-goat and half-man. The two had a brief and passionate affair that ended only when Erinna's father married her to a stuffy husband from another island. After giving birth to a son with horns, the mother had to flee with her child to establish a new life among the satyrs. The message of the story, and of the novel, is that love of any variety is worth cherishing no matter how quickly it may disappear.

Biographical Note
Thomas Burnett Swann (1928-76) was an author, critic, scholar, and poet. His fantasy works often use classical myths and legends as their basis and frequently have been characterized as sentimental.

The theme of male homosexuality occurs repeatedly throughout his work, and there can be little doubt that Swann was homosexual. In addition to his fantasy work, all of which should be examined for variant elements, two of his nonfantasy books of literary criticism concern poets who are reputed to have been lesbians: *Wonder and Whimsy: The Fantastic World of Christina Rossetti* (Francestown, N.H.: Jones, 1960) and *The Classical World of H. D.* (Lincoln: University of Nebraska Press, 1962).

Biographical information on Swann is available in *Contemporary Authors*, vols. 5-6, ed. James M. Ethridge (Detroit: Gale Research, 1963). A more personal view of Swann can be found in "Remembering Tom Swann," by Gerold Page, printed as an afterword to *Queens Walk in the Dusk* (Forest Park, Ga.: Heritage Press, 1977).

---

828 THOMAS, THEODORE L. "Broken Tool." *Astounding*, July 1959. [M]
A homosexual member of the Deep Space Command finds his emotions and loyalties in conflict when the young cadet whom he has raised as a son fails the final test to become a deep-space pilot. Walter Carter, the homosexual, is completely closeted about his emotions to even the closest of friends, yet the author steers clear of stereotype and Carter is a sympathetic, realistic character. The author is cryptic in his presentation of homosexuality.

829 TIMLETT, PETER VALENTINE. *The Seedbearers*. London: Quartet, 1974. [m]
The people of Ruta are descendants of the inhabitants of Atlantis. Three times evil has destroyed civilization; three great Ages of Man have passed. A new evil is now rising, in the form of the barbaric Vardek, the lord commander of Ruta's army. Vardek holds in open contempt the priesthood, the sole protector of the ancient and mystic secrets of the Atlanteans. The priesthood, reading the omens of the Sun

God, prepares new "seedbearers" to flee Ruta and to carry the secret knowledge to a new shore. Timlett spins his tale amid a backdrop of explicitly depicted violence, warfare, torture, and rape. While the bloodthirsty villain is truly disgusting, the priesthood is little better: it valiantly protects a strictly caste-oriented system that embraces not only sexism but fervent racism as well. Blacks are portrayed as savage, cannibalistic, death-worshiping slaves. Homosexuality also is presented in a contrived manner: only the artisan caste practices male-male love. The novel's primary purpose is to promote the author's personal doctrine of occult science.

830 TIPTREE, JAMES, Jr. [pseudonym of Alice Sheldon]. "Filomena and Greg and Rikki-Tikki and Barlow and the Alien." In *New Dimensions Two*, edited by Robert SILVERBERG, Garden City, N.Y.: Doubleday, 1972. Reprinted as "All Kinds of Yes." In *Warm Worlds and Otherwise*. New York: Ballantine, 1975. [X]

A rich and desperate alien is deterred from her mission on Earth by four young teenagers. The teens know that she is an alien, despite her human appearance, and they are attracted to her foreignness. They think she is a male; they all have sex with her. Later they find out the alien's horrifying true identity and mission on Earth.

831 TIPTREE, JAMES, Jr. [pseudonym of Alice Sheldon]. "Houston, Houston, Do You Read?" In *Aurora: Beyond Equality*, edited by Vonda McIntyre and Susan Anderson. Greenwich, Conn.: Fawcett, 1976. [F]

This Hugo Award-winning story is a valuable portrayal of how deeply men learn misogyny. Three American astronauts make an accidental jump into the future. In the future society, men have died off centuries before. The remaining women have adapted by developing extensive cloning techniques and, quite naturally, by becoming lesbians. The astronauts are unable to cope with these drastic social changes. Tiptree handles the resulting tension with a great deal of perception. Powerful and well worth reading.

832 TIPTREE, JAMES, Jr. [pseudonym of Alice Sheldon]. "I'll Be Waiting for You When the Swimming Pool Is Empty." In *Protostars*, edited by David Gerrold and Stephen Goldin. New York: Ballantine, 1971. [f]

A satiric tale of a "nice boy" who discovers a world of "barbarians" while on his graduation-present space voyage. Although professing to respect their unique cultural identity and values, he pushes his "superior" technology on the inhabitants, completely changing the structure of their society. The indigenous people try a number of tactics to rid themselves of their imperialistic invader; at one point they send him twelve women with murderously erotic skills. Minor mention of lesbianism is included in this scene.

833 TIPTREE, JAMES, Jr. [pseudonym of Alice Sheldon]. "The Milk of Paradise." In *Again, Dangerous Visions*, edited by Harlan Ellison. Garden City, N.Y.: Doubleday, 1972. [m]

Timmer, son of a famous space explorer, cannot forget his childhood home of Paradise, even though he has gone through drastic personality reconstruction since his rescue from the alien planet. So wonderful, to Timmer, were the inhabitants of Paradise that he is repulsed by sex with either men or women. Shock comes when he is tricked into returning to the planet of his youth.

834 TIPTREE, JAMES, Jr. [pseudonym of Alice Sheldon]. "A Momentary Taste of Being." In *The New Atlantis*, edited by Robert SILVERBERG, New York: Hawthorn, 1975. [m]

Earth needs a release from overpopulation, so a team is sent into space to find another inhabitable world. After years of searching, the group thinks it has found the choice spot for colonization. What they have really found is human destiny: to act as sperm to fertilize the vegetablelike race on the new planet–to be nothing more than insignificant parts in the reproduction of an unimaginable species. One character is subtly portrayed as a homosexual, though his sexual orientation has little impact on the story.

835 TIPTREE, JAMES, Jr. [pseudonym of Alice Sheldon]. "Painwise." *Fantasy and Science Fiction*, February 1972. Reprinted in *The Best Science Fiction of the Year #2*, edited by Terry Carr. New York: Ballantine, 1973. [M]

A man surgically altered to feel no pain is on a solo space mission. After wandering between stars attempting to return to Earth, he is found by three joy-loving empaths: a butterfly, a boa constrictor, and a young boy. The man becomes lovers with the empaths; they give him every pleasure. Despite their affections, he insists that there is no reality without pain, and he demands to be shipped back to Earth where he will again experience hurt.

836 TIPTREE, JAMES, Jr. [pseudonym of Alice Sheldon]. *Up the Walls of the World*. New York: Berkley Medallion, 1979. [f]

Tiptree brings three very different kinds of beings together on a journey that could span infinity. She creates a fascinating culture in which the inhabitants float on strong wind currents and never touch their planet's surface. Traditional sex roles are reversed in this culture; the fathers raise the children while the mothers fly off on wild adventures. Their world is being burned by the mysterious Destroyer, so several of the aliens physically search the galaxy for suitable bodies to take over, and they make mental contact with a group of Earth's telepaths. Two of the human telepaths, Fredericka and Valeria, are lesbian lovers.

837 TIPTREE, JAMES, Jr. [pseudonym of Alice Sheldon]. "With Delicate Mad Hands." In *Out of the Everywhere*. New York: Ballantine, 1981. [F?]
    Another powerful story by Tiptree. Carol Page's life is miserable. Because of her piglike appearance (she has a "huge, fleshy, obscenely pugged nose") she grew up without friends and is considered a "human waste can" by her coworkers. Her only companion is an inner Voice that calms her and keeps her happy. When a violent rape shatters Carol's sanity, she flees across outer space and discovers the alien source of her Voice. The lesbian elements of the story are open to interpretation.

Biographical Note

Alice Sheldon (1915-87) unintentionally provided intrigue in the science-fiction community when she began writing in 1967 under the name of James Tiptree, Jr. When Tiptree's frequently feminist stories won acclaim people began actively to seek information on the reclusive author. (For a time there was much speculation about Tiptree's gender.) When writing with a more emotional style, Sheldon began using the pseudonym Raccoona Sheldon. She is also the author of *Brightness Falls from the Air* (New York: TOR, 1985) and *The Starry Rift* (New York: TOR, 1986).

Sheldon discusses her feminism in "A Woman Writing Science Fiction and Fantasy," in *Women of Vision: Essays by Women Writing Science Fiction*, ed. Denise DuPont (New York: St. Martin's, 1988). Feminist exploration of her work includes a detailed analysis of "Your Faces, O My Sisters! Your Faces Filled with Light"; "Method in her Madness: Feminism in the Crazy Utopian Vision of Tiptree's Courier," by Caroline Rhodes, in *Women and Utopia: Critical Interpretations*, ed. Marleen Barr and Nicholas D. Smith (Lanham, Md.: University Press of America, 1983); and Marleen Barr's "'The Females Do the Fathering': James Tiptree's Male Matriarchs and Adult Human Gametes," *Science Fiction Studies* (Montreal) 13 (March 1986), which is an examination of Tiptree's female characters.

For further information on Sheldon/Tiptree, see Ursula K. Le Guin's introduction to Tiptree's third collection of short stories, *Star Songs of an Old Primate* (New York: Ballantine, 1978); R. Reginald's *Science Fiction and Fantasy Literature: A Checklist*, vol. 2 (Detroit: Gale Research, 1980); and *The Fiction of James Tiptree, Jr.*, by Gardner Dozois (New York: Algol Press, 1977).

See also SHELDON, ALICE

838 TOWNSEND, LARRY. *Beware the God Who Smiles*. San Diego: Greenleaf Classics, 1971. [M]

Pornographic gay male science fiction.

839 TOWNSEND, LARRY. *Jovencachoteca*. San Diego: Greenleaf Classics, 1970. [M]
Pornographic gay male science fiction.

840 TOWNSEND, LARRY. *The Scorpius Equation*. New York: Traveler's Companion, 1971. [M]
Pornographic gay male science fiction.

TOWNSEND, LARRY. 2069 Series. [M]:

841 ▪ *2069*. San Diego: Greenleaf Classics, 1969.

842 ▪ *2069 + 1*. San Diego: Greenleaf Classics, 1970.

843 ▪ *2069 + 2*. San Diego: Greenleaf Classics, 1970.
The underlying theme of this pornographic gay male science-fiction trilogy is the sociopolitical development of a gay subculture within a tolerant future society.

844 TRACHTMAN, PAULA. *Disturb Not the Dream*. New York: Crown, 1981. [m]
Dr. Bertram Bradley, his wife Alice, their children, and their sexy au pair move into the foreboding Mulberry house. Soon, the family begins to see terrifying ghostly manifestations, and Bradley, a noted psychiatrist, begins to look for an explanation in the house's sinister past. He eventually finds his answer, but not until several grisly murders have occurred. Part of the supernatural evil that clings to the house is the result of incestuous sexual abuse of a young boy many years previously.

845 TRENFIELD, KAREN. "Feminist Science Fiction: Reality or Fantasy? A Review of Some Recent Science Fiction by Women." *Hecate: A Women's Interdisciplinary Journal*, February 1978. [Nonfiction]
A feminist appraisal of women science-fiction writers and their work. Trenfield touches briefly on homosexuality.

846 TREVANION, ADA. "A Ghost Story." In *National Magazine*, January 1858. Reprinted in *What Did Miss Darrington See? An Anthology of Feminist Supernatural Fiction*, edited by Jessica Amanda Salmonson. New York: Feminist Press, 1989. [F]
Subtle ghost story about the romantic friendship between a young girl and a special teacher.

847 TURNER, FREDRICK. *A Double Shadow.* New York: Berkley, 1978.
[F, M, X]
　　Stylistically similar to a classical Greek tragedy, *A Double Shadow*
takes place on a terraformed Mars of the far future. The
hermaphroditic Narcissus and her / his sister and lover, Cleopatra,
challenge another young couple to a "status-war." The narrative follows
the two couples through their various travels, from the canals of Mars to
the mountainous home of the goddess, and culminates in an epic duel in
the Great Canyon of Coprates. The exotic sexuality displayed is directly
linked to the general decadence of the planet. Narcissus's
hermaphroditic nature remains for the most part underdeveloped; s/he
is little more than a male persona with breasts. Turner's use of the
mythical mode and his writing style create a fascinating novel.

848 TURNER, GEORGE. *Beloved Son.* London: Faber & Faber, 1978.
Reprint. New York: Pocket Books, 1979. [m]
　　A five-day holocaust has radically reduced the population of
Earth. Entire countries have disappeared, and political systems have
been rearranged. An ineffectual world government and a strict moral
ethic barely hold the struggling citizenry together. Into this developing
world comes an interstellar spaceship that was launched prior to the
cataclysm, and it is around the returning ship that the plot revolves.
Homosexuality is introduced through a set of gay male clones, designed
as an experiment to see whether sexual orientation is genetic. Although
the clones are quite bitchy, they are noticeably unstereotypic in other
ways, and they are well-developed characters. Within the 400 pages of
this novel there are only two female characters: a sexy kitten and a
senile old woman who serves as a warped mother figure. Bleak and
sexist.

TURTLEDOVE, HARRY. The Videssos Cycle. [m]:

849 ▪ *The Misplaced Legion.* New York: Ballantine, 1987.

850 ▪ *An Emperor for the Legion.* New York: Ballantine, 1987.

851 ▪ *The Legion of Videssos.* New York: Ballantine, 1987.

852 ▪ *Swords of the Legion.* New York: Ballantine, 1987.
　　Turtledove's four-volume Videssos Cycle details the trials and
adventures of members of an unfortunate Roman legion who find
themselves miraculously transported to a magical alternative empire.
Among the soldiers is a Greek physician, Gorgidas, who is homosexual.

853 TUTTLE, LISA. "Mrs. T." *Amazing*, September 1976. Reprinted in *A Spaceship Built of Stone*. London: Women's Press, 1987. [f]

A woman reporter makes a remarkable discovery while investigating an eccentric old woman: the sexes are crossing over and becoming each other. An interesting exploration of sex and sex roles with significant lesbian context.

854 TUTTLE, LISA. "Stone Circle." *Amazing*, March 1976. [F]

An explicitly lesbian story of love, betrayal, and remorse set in a cruel and hopeless future. Neither of the characters is portrayed in a stereotypic manner, but the ending is tragic.

855 TUTTLE, LISA. "The Wound." In *Other Edens*, edited by Christopher Evans and Robert Holdstock. London: Unwin, 1987. [M, X]

A well-written and eerie short story about two male schoolteachers who develop a friendship and eventually fall in love in a gender-shifting, far-future world.

Biographical Note

Lisa Tuttle (b. 1953) is the author of *A Spaceship Built of Stone* (London: Women's Press, 1987) and *A Nest of Nightmares* (London: Sphere, 1986), and she is the coauthor (with George R. R. Martin) of *Windhaven* (New York: Timescape, 1981). A noted feminist, Tuttle is also the author of *Encyclopedia of Feminism* (New York: Facts on File, 1986).

UPCHURCH, BOYD B. *See* BOYD, JOHN (pseudonym)

856 UPTON, MARK. *Dark Summer*. New York: Pocket Books, 1979. [F]

When Colonel Benjamin D. Coulter and his beautiful daughter, Diane Cheney, move into the wealthy New England town of Penlow Park, they are treated with friendliness and curiosity. The Colonel's aptitude for magic tricks and Mrs. Cheney's mind-reading ability are sparkling new ingredients to the small town's social gatherings. But the mysterious pair soon begin making their presence felt in more destructive ways. Mrs. Cheney becomes an instrument of evil, and she uses her psychic talents and sexual allure to seduce both male and female residents of Penlow Park. These supernatural seductions lead to marital discord, madness, and murder. The occult elements are left without motivation, and there is little to distinguish *Dark Summer* from the multitude of extramarital melodramas.

857 UTLEY, STEPHEN. "The Man at the Bottom of the Sea." *Galaxy*, October 1976. [F, m]

The female protagonist of this story lives on a distant planet where bisexuality is fully accepted. She is a space traveler, and her woman lover is worried that she may not return alive from her next space voyage. The story's narrative is weak, but the author's depiction of the women's love for each other is supportive. A minor mention is made of a gay man.

VAN FELIX-WILDE, LUCY. *See* VAN FELIX-WILDE, MARTHA (joint author)

858 VAN FELIX-WILDE, MARTHA, and VAN FELIX-WILDE, LUCY. "Anastasia." In *The Ripening Fig: Tales of Emerging Womanhood*. West Hampstead, N.Y.: Porpoise Press, 1975. [F]

An occult story written by lesbian separatists. Anastasia, a young lesbian, finds her psychic powers and spirituality enhanced by her association with an older woman.

859 VAN FELIX-WILDE, MARTHA, and VAN FELIX-WILDE, LUCY. "Sunshine and Margarita." In *The Ripening Fig: Tales of Emerging Womanhood*. West Hampstead, N.Y.: Porpoise Press, 1975. [F]

Several lesbians, whose mothers were involved in the women's liberation movement of the 1960s and 1970s, meet to discuss their shared values and their mothers' hardships. One of the women has recently emerged as a lesbian. This story, by itself, could stand as an example of feminist political fiction, but when placed in the context of the entire collection its message becomes clear: that women who are not in a monogamous lesbian relationship are emotionally dysfunctional.

VARLEY, JOHN. The Gaean Trilogy. [F, m, X]:

860 ■ *Titan*. Illustrated by Freff. New York: Berkley, 1979.

861 ■ *Wizard*. New York: Berkley, Putnam, 1980.

862 ■ *Demon*. New York: Putnam, 1984.

Science-fiction trilogy with major lesbian content. The primary character, Cirocco Jones captains an exploratory space probe investigating Saturn's moons. She and her crew discover a twelfth satellite, previously unknown, which they name Themis and begin routinely to explore. Suddenly, they are attacked, and they find themselves inside Themis, naked and disarmed. This begins Cirocco's rollicking adventures as she meets the centaurs (an ingenious race of beings possessing three sex organs), angels, and a cocaine-snorting goddess who inhabit Varley's imaginative world. At times *Titan* resembles a science-fiction version of the classic fantasy *The Wizard of*

Oz. As in many other Varley stories, virtually all of the trilogy's characters are to some degree self-consciously bisexual, and the captain's evolution toward lesbianism is pivotal to the plot.

863 VARLEY, JOHN. "Lollipop and the Tar Baby." In *Orbit Nineteen*, edited by Damon Knight. New York: Harper & Row, 1977. [F]
An intriguing story with a strong lesbian protagonist. It has been discovered that black holes are a source of tremendous energy, but finding them is expensive and chancy. While hunting, one must live in virtual solitude for up to twenty years at a time. To relieve her boredom, Zoe, one of the future "gold diggers," has cloned herself; the adolescent clone, Xanthia, functions as both daughter and lover for Zoe. Xanthia's complete trust in Zoe breaks down when a self-aware black hole manipulates the two women for its own greedy purpose.

864 VARLEY, JOHN. *The Ophiuchi Hotline.* New York: Dial, James Wade, 1977. [F]
The Ophiuchi Hotline, like many of Varley's stories, takes place in his Eight Worlds' future, when technology is quite sophisticated. Interplanetary space travel is commonplace, and body alterations (particularly sex changes) are as simple as visiting the beautician. "Invaders," large gaseous beings, have taken over the Earth and humans have been forced to colonize the other airless planets that circle the sun. Lilo, a criminal convicted of tampering with genetics, escapes from prison and is cloned, creating several Lilos all having exactly the same personality. Lilo is bisexual, and this quality is believably integrated into her character. A fun adventure.

865 VARLEY, JOHN. "Options." In *Universe Nine*, edited by Terry Carr. Garden City, N.Y.: Doubleday, 1979. [f, m]
A simple and inexpensive way to change sex has become possible through cloning techniques and brain transplants, and a significant portion of Luna's population switches sex frequently. Cleo, working woman and mother of three, becomes curious about this social trend. Her interest brings into focus the way in which sex roles come into play in her marriage. She adopts the life-style of a sex-changer while her husband does not. At first this makes for a stormy relationship, but the two show respect for each other's decisions, enabling their love to continue. Open relationships and bisexuality are fully accepted options within Varley's Eight Worlds society. Recommended.

866 VARLEY, JOHN. "The Persistence of Vision." *Fantasy and Science Fiction*, March 1978. Reprinted in *The Persistence of Vision*. New York: Dial, James Wade, 1978. [f, m]

In "The Persistence of Vision," Varley has created a truly innovative utopia. Early in the 1990s, while the rest of America is in an economic depression, a courageous band of people who are both blind and deaf build a commune in New Mexico. It is named after Helen Keller, and within its boundaries the deaf and blind can create an environment designed entirely for their own needs. Among their developments is a radically new form of communication evolving American Sign Language to something beyond telepathy. It is this new form of communication that leads to the story's startling conclusion. Varley treats the Keller community's physical differences as well as their pansexuality with integrity and intelligence. A Nebula and Hugo award-winning story.

Biographical Note

John Varley (b. 1947) is a skilled writer of science fiction and has been strongly influenced by feminist thought. Strong, independent female protagonists appear regularly in his work, as do a wide variety of variant sexualities, and his work should be watched for lesbian and gay male characterizations. Other Varley stories that include some mention of same-sex love (though too brief to warrant full annotation here) are "Picnic on Nearside," in *Fantasy and Science Fiction*, August 1974, and "In the Bowl," in *Fantasy and Science Fiction*, December 1975, reprinted in *The Best Science Fiction of the Year #5*, ed. Terry Carr (New York: Ballantine, 1976).

---

867 VICKI. *Sleeping Beauty*. Atlanta: Sojourner Truth Press, 1971. [F]
The classic fairy tale is delightfully retold; this time it is a woman's kiss that awakens the sleeping princess.

868 VIDAL, GORE. *Kalki*. New York: Random House, 1978. [F]
A death-worshiping religious cult arises in Nepal run by a man who claims to be the reincarnation of Kalki, destroyer and savior of Hindu mythology. It has been foretold that when Kalki returns the world will come to an end, yet skepticism develops when it turns out that "Kalki" is an American ex-GI who is quite possibly fronting a drug ring out of his ashram in Katmandu. Pilot and journalist Teddy Ottinger is commissioned to get to the bottom of the mysterious holy man, and from the moment she accepts her new assignment her life is a blur of espionage and intrigue. Teddy is a feminist and predominantly a lesbian throughout the novel. Although the reader never forgets that a male wrote this image of a woman's sexuality, it is neither prurient nor sensational. Vidal's sharp criticism of the CIA, heterosexism, and most components of Western society not only gives this end-of-the-world vision its humor but also provides the book with its brilliance. Portions of this novel originally appeared in *Playboy*.

869 VIDAL, GORE. *Myra Breckinridge*. Boston: Little, Brown, 1968. [F, M]
Myra Breckinridge is a 1960s amazon of heroic proportions who has spent her entire existence uncomfortably submerged within the body of a rather insipid homosexual named Myron. Released from her imprisonment via plastic surgery and hormone treatments, Myra sets off to fulfill her true destiny: to realign the sexes through "the destruction of the last vestigial traces of traditional manhood." Near the end of the novel, Myra turns away from men and becomes a lesbian. Vidal articulates a conflicted sexual politics that is opposed to socially defined sex roles, yet condescending in its attitude toward women. Since transsexuality is an actual medical procedure, it is hard to categorize *Myra Breckinridge* as science fiction, but the superhuman persona of the title character, the overall fantastic "high camp" quality of the writing, and the highly relevant nature of the book's sequel (*Myron: A Novel*) make *Myra Breckinridge* worthy of annotation here.

870 VIDAL, GORE. *Myron: A Novel*. New York: Random House, 1974. [M]
Myron, the sequel to *Myra Breckinridge*, is not as successful a novel. Myra returns to plague the now-heterosexual Myron by pushing him through his television screen and onto the 1943 Hollywood film set of *Siren of Babylon*, a Maria Montez vehicle. Myra is still determined to realign the sexes, this time by altering men into beautiful sterile amazons, but she is repeatedly interrupted by Myron's persistent reappearances in his body. She remains undaunted, however, and with the help of a male homosexual hairdresser named Maude she again indulges in her penchant for raping heterosexual males. Vidal's arrogant attitude toward women is again displayed and the satire in *Myron*, as funny as it is, lacks the focus of the author's earlier book. But he manages to ridicule brilliantly the United States Supreme Court's 1973 ruling on pornography.

Biographical Note

Gore Vidal (b. 1925) is a noted essayist and novelist who occasionally uses science fiction to illustrate his outspoken ideas. His play *Visit to a Small Planet* (Boston: Little, Brown, 1956) involves an alien's visit to the Earth, and his novel *Messiah* (New York: Dutton, 1954) is a science-fiction classic. Vidal is openly bisexual and has been interviewed extensively within the gay press. Much of his fiction has touched on homosexual situations. *The City and the Pillar* (New York: Dutton, 1948) was one of the first American novels to deal explicitly with the theme, and as a result, Vidal was blacklisted for some time after the book's first publication. Other works notable for gay content include *A Thirsty Evil* (New York: Zero, 1956), *The Best Man* (Boston: Little, Brown,

1960), and *Two Sisters: A Memoir in the Form of a Novel* (Boston: Little, Brown, 1970).

Vidal articulates his sexual politics in *Views from a Window: Conversations with Gore Vidal*, ed. Robert J. Stanton (New York: Lyle Stuart, 1980), and in an interview in *Gay Sunshine Interviews*, vol. 1, ed. Winston Leyland (San Francisco: Gay Sunshine Press, 1979). *Myra and Gore*, by John Mitzel and Steven Abbott (Dorchester, Mass.: Manifest Destiny, 1974), includes an extensive radical gay examination of *Myra Breckinridge*. Further biographical and critical information on Vidal can be found in *Contemporary Authors*, vols. 5-8, rev. ed., ed. Barbara Harte and Carolyn Riley (Detroit: Gale, 1969).

---

871 VIERECK, GEORGE SYLVESTER. *Gloria: A Novel.* London: Duckworth, 1952. Reprinted as *The Nude in the Mirror.* New York: Woodford Press, 1953. [F?, M?]

Doctor Adam Greenleaf, while on a trans-Atlantic ocean cruise, falls head over heels in love with the attractive Stella de la Mar. Ms. de la Mar, it turns out, is an incarnation of Lakshmi, the Hindu goddess of love, and she has searched for centuries for a sexually adequate lover. She recounts her stories for Adam, weaving such notables as Socrates, Julius Caesar, and Sappho of Lesbos into her tales. Viereck uses his recurring themes of immortality and sexual freedom common in his Wandering Jew trilogy, but *Gloria: A Novel* is a weaker work. However, the author was able to expand upon his belief in the universality of bisexuality and the natural superiority of women, which were given only muted expression in his previous volumes.

872 VIERECK, GEORGE SYLVESTER. *The House of the Vampire.* New York: Moffat, Yard & Co., 1907. [M?]

A then-contemporary interpretation of the traditional vampire legend. A young and delicate writer, Ernest Fielding, falls into the clutches of an older and more sophisticated artist, Reginald Clarke. Soon their relationship becomes all-consuming for Ernest; it even overshadows his highly emotional friendship with his college companion, Jack. As his unnatural obsession for Clarke grows, Ernest finds his creative spirit diminishing. Clarke, it is discovered, is a "soul vampire" who sucks creativity rather than blood from his victims. Although any homosexual elements are subjective, it is clear that Clarke's "evil influence" is at least allegorically homosexual, and muted homoerotic imagery is obvious throughout the story. The author later revealed the autobiographical basis of the novel.

VIERECK, GEORGE SYLVESTER, and ELDRIDGE, PAUL. The
Wandering Jew Trilogy. [F, M?]:

873 ▪ *My First Two Thousand Years; The Autobiography of the Wandering
Jew*. New York: Macaulay, 1928.

874 ▪ *Salome: The Wandering Jewess; My First Two Thousand Years of
Love*. New York: Liveright, 1930.

875 ▪ *The Invincible Adam*. New York: Liveright, 1932.

Viereck and Eldridge produced an important epic fantasy. The
first volume of the Wandering Jew trilogy concerns Cartaphilus, lover of
John the Apostle and Mary Magdalene. He makes love with a wide
variety of people, some of whom have both female and male genders,
but his primary love is the equally immortal and bisexual Salome.
Princess Salome is the subject of the best volume of the trilogy. Her life
is a revolt against the subjugation of women by both men and nature.
She declares war on the moon for its enslavement of women through
menstrual cycles, and she uses her power to advance strong women in
the church and on the throne. The third Viereck / Eldridge
collaboration deals with the life of Kotikokura, companion of
Cartaphilus and Salome. Kotikokura represents eternal Youth
struggling against his animal nature to bond with humanity. Throughout
his life, Kotikokura is confronted with male homosexuality – by the
decadence in Rome, the bisexual Michelangelo, and the Marquis de
Sade – but the youth's orientation remains heterosexual. Nonetheless,
Kotikokura's primary emotional relationship for over 2,000 years is with
Cartaphilus. There are secondary lesbian and gay characters scattered
throughout the trilogy.

Biographical Note

George Sylvester Viereck (1884-1962) began his writing career in 1904 when
his first volume of poetry was published, and his literary involvement in
poetry, prose, and criticism continued for decades. Viereck celebrated all
forms of sexual expression, both intellectually and personally, and his early
poetry was considered sexually radical and shocking. An amateur
sexologist, he later found a solid philosophical base for his liberated ideas in
the teachings of Sigmund Freud, and Freud's belief in the basic bisexuality
of humanity constitutes a major thread throughout Viereck's work. The other
Viereck/Eldridge fantasy collaboration, *Prince Pax* (London: Duckworth,
1933), contains none of Viereck's Freudian philosophy.

Despite his support of sexual emancipation and his strong, though dated,
feminist beliefs, he remained nationalistically loyal to his father's German
homeland, and his support of Germany during the two world wars brought
him into conflict with the United States authorities.

Autobiographical information can be found in *My Flesh and Blood: A Lyric Autobiography with Indiscreet Annotations* (New York: Liveright, 1931). Biographical information is in Elmer Gertz's *Odyssey of a Barbarian* (Buffalo, N.Y.: Prometheus, 1978) and in Phyllis Keller's "George Sylvester Viereck: The Psychology of a German-American Militant," in *Journal of Interdisciplinary History* 2, no. 1 (Summer 1971).

---

876 VINGE, VERNON. *Marooned in Real Time*. New York: Bluejay, 1986. [F]

An imaginative sequel to the author's acclaimed *The Peace War*. A worldwide war has destroyed the Earth. Clustered survivors from various times have "bobbled" into the future–awaiting safety in the timeless limbo of stasis. Under the guidance of Marta and Yelen Korolev, two lesbian lovers from a technologically advanced future, these few thousand individuals attempt to reestablish civilization. When one of the Korolevs is found murdered, Wil Brierson, a private detective from the twenty-first century, is drafted.

877 VIXEN, RICHARD M. [pseudonym]. *Deep Foot*. Eugene, Oreg.: Avant-Garde Creations, 1977. [f]

Science-fiction pornography containing female-female sexual imagery.

878 VIXEN, RICHARD M. [pseudonym]. *Deeper Foot*. Eugene, Oreg.: Avant-Garde Creations, 1977. [f]

Pornographic science fiction containing female-female sexual imagery.

879 VONNEGUT, KURT, Jr. *Breakfast of Champions*. Illustrated by the author. New York: Delacorte, 1973. [m]

Vonnegut writes novels that successfully bridge the gulf between science fiction and mainstream social satire. In *Breakfast of Champions*, the cataclysmic meeting between Vonnegut's philosopher / science-fiction writer Kilgore Trout and wealthy automobile dealer Dwayne Hoover becomes the focal point of a myriad of wacky characters and situations. Among these characters are three gay men: George "Bunny" Hoover, Wayne Hoobler, and Milo Maritimo. All are sympathetically presented.

880 VONNEGUT, KURT, Jr. *God Bless You, Mr. Rosewater*. New York: Delacorte, 1965. [f, m]

Eliot Rosewater is an exceedingly wealthy and eccentric humanitarian who refuses to adopt the lifestyle and social graces of the super-rich. Eliot's sanity is called into question by his relatives because he gives away all his wealth to the poor. They mandate that he will have to spend his life in a mental institution if he does not confine himself to respectable upper-class society far away from his beloved poor of Rosewater, Illinois. But Kilgore Trout, science-fiction writer extraordinaire, saves the day when he comes up with an acceptable explanation for Eliot's "odd" behavior. A lesbian and a gay man are minor characters. Entertaining.

881 WAGNER, KARL EDWARD. *Bloodstone*. New York: Warner, 1975. [f]

An enjoyable "Conan"-style Sword and Sorcery novel. The principal character, Kane, is a seemingly ageless barbarian who wanders through a world of myth and magic. Kane seeks power to dominate the world. His quest leads to his destruction. Central to the enjoyment of the novel is Teres, a major character throughout the book. Teres has been raised as a boy, and she first enters the story while fighting another soldier over a servant girl. She is strong and independent, though not exclusively lesbian.

882 WAGNER, KARL EDWARD. "Blue Lady, Come Back." In *Night Visions 2*, edited by Charles L. Grant. Niles, Ill.: Dark Harvest, 1985. [F, m?]

Alcoholic psychiatrist Russ Mandarin investigates a stolen manuscript, a possibly homosexual literary rival, two brutal murders, and a mysterious lesbian ghost in this suspenseful supernatural thriller.

883 WAGNER, KARL EDWARD. "More Sinned Against." In *Silver Scream*, edited by David J. Schow. Arlington, Ill.: Dark Harvest, 1988. [m]

An actress wreaks supernatural havoc on the bisexual man who brought her ruin.

884 WALLIS, DAVE. *Only Lovers Left Alive*. London: A. Blond, 1964. Reprint. New York: Dutton, 1964. [M?]

An intriguing science-fiction novel in which all the world's adults are mysteriously compelled to commit suicide. As a result, society disintegrates, and teenage mob rule develops. A small group of British adolescents survive the holocaust and attempt to reestablish civilization. The author briefly uses latent homosexuality as a motivation for a male character's action.

885 WALPOLE, HUGH. *The Killer and the Slain: A Strange Story*. Garden City, N.Y.: Doubleday, 1942. [M?]

Jim Tunstall is a loud, aggressive bully of a man worlds apart from the quiet, effeminate intellectual, John Talbot. Yet from early childhood the two have had an almost supernatural bond between them, unspoken but understood. The domination intrinsic in the bond proves unendurable for Talbot, and he is led to a desperate act: the murder of Tunstall. Unfortunately, Tunstall continues to dominate Talbot even after his death. In addition to the highly ambiguous love-hate relationship between the two central characters, a homosexual vicar is also mentioned. It is interesting to note that the book is dedicated "in loving memory and humble admiration" to the author of *The Turn of the Screw*, Henry James, with whom Walpole had a very close friendship.

Biographical Note
Hugh Walpole (1884-1941) was a British man of letters whose homosexuality was acknowledged after his death. He wrote several ghost stories, among them the marginally fantastic *Portrait of a Man with Red Hair* (London: Macmillan, 1925) and *All Souls' Night* (London: Macmillan, 1933). Information on Walpole can be located in *Twentieth Century Authors*, ed. Stanley J. Kunitz and Howard Haycraft (New York: Wilson, 1942) and in Rupert Hart-Davis's *Hugh Walpole: A Biography* (New York: Macmillan, 1952).

---

886 WALTON, SU. *Horace Sippog and the Siren's Song*. London: P. Davies, 1967. Reprint. New York: Morrow, 1968. [F, M]

Gay and bisexual characters roam freely throughout this strange mermaid fantasy tale. In one of the book's many subplots, all the girls in a young ladies' boarding school are enamored of the beautiful and androgynous-looking "K" (short for Katherine). K, however, only has eyes for Cynthia, a disguised mermaid, and their affair unfortunately leads to expulsion for Cynthia and suicide for K. Later, Cynthia visits her brother, Ian, at college where another lesbian, Vivian, falls madly in love with her. The two women commit a murder for which Cynthia's brother is blamed. He is forced to ride off on a white stallion to join a frequently mentioned, but possibly imaginary, group of Indians. He is accompanied by an effeminate gay man who is in love with him. Numerous other gay and lesbian characters appear within the rest of the novel. Surreal and amusing though tending toward a tragic style of humor.

887 WARNER, SYLVIA TOWNSEND. "The Blameless Triangle." *New Yorker*, no. 50 (20 May 1974). Reprinted in *Kingdoms of Elfin*. London: Chatto & Windus, 1976. Reprint. New York: Viking, 1977. [M]

When the Elfin queen Balzamine leaves with most of her court for a health resort, she discards five of her elfin lovers who promptly decide they must leave the Elfin Kingdom and seek serenity through meditation. They travel about the countryside until winter sets in and food becomes scarce. In desperation, four of the elves encourage the youngest and most handsome to prostitute himself to the notorious homosexual Mustafa Ibrahim Bey so that they will have a roof over their heads for the winter. When spring comes, four of the elves return to the queen's court, but the youngest, now in love with Mustafa, decides to stay and remain as his lover.

Biographical Note

Sylvia Townsend Warner (1893-1978), noted British novelist, often used witchcraft and the supernatural in her tales; note in particular her *Lolly Willowes* (London: Chatto & Windus, 1926), and the short-story collection *Kingdoms of Elfin* (London: Chatto & Windus, 1976).

Warner lived virtually her entire life with her woman companion, Valentine Ackland. Her novel *Mr. Fortune's Maggot* (London: Chatto & Windus, 1927) is of major importance to gay male literature though it is not fantasy, and her biography of the master fantasy author Terence Hanbury White, *T. H. White: A Biography* (London: Cape with Chatto & Windus, 1967), deals fairly and honestly with his homosexuality.

Biographical information on Warner can be found in Claire Harman's *Sylvia Townsend Warner: A Biography* (London: Chatto & Windus, 1989) and in Wendy Mulford's *This Narrow Place: Sylvia Townsend Warner and Valentine Ackland: Life, Letters, and Politics, 1930-51* (London: Pandora, 1988).

888 WATKINS, JEFF. "A Second Eden." *In Touch for Men* (Los Angeles), no. 39 (January-February 1979). [f, M]

Mission 21-sc is forced by radiation to make an emergency landing on an unsettled planet. The mission has little chance of reproduction (the crew is all male), until one of the crewmen genetically and surgically alters his male lover to a point where reproduction is possible. The resulting civilization is an open and free one, and it is supportive of all varieties of love. The plot is reminiscent of Marion Zimmer Bradley and Juanita Coulson's "Another Rib."

889 WATKINS, JEFF. "Sex in Space." *In Touch for Men* (Los Angeles), no. 26 (November-December 1976). [Nonfiction]

An overview of homosexuality in science fiction.

890 WATSON, IAN. *The Fireworm.* London: Gollancz, 1988. [m]

Psychiatrist John Cunningham becomes intrigued when one of his patients, Tony Smith, remembers a past life while under hypnosis. Tony recounts a bizarre tale involving two British schoolboys, a graphically depicted incident of sodomy, and a weird supernatural worm that lives in the cliffs near the village of Tynemouth. Cunningham is a closet author of horror novels and finds Smith's story to be inspiration for his fiction. But the deeper the doctor goes into Smith's psyche, the more Cunningham realizes that the horrible fireworm is real!

891 WATSON, IAN. *The Martian Inca*. New York: Scribner's, 1977. [f]
   An automatic Soviet spaceship bearing Martian soil samples crashes high in the Andes mountains near an isolated Bolivian village. The Indian village dwellers soon become seriously ill, and only two, Julio and Angelina, recover. They are aware that during their illness they have evolved into superior beings, and Julio interprets this metamorphosis as a divine message to lead the Indian people in revolt. Angelina has a lesbian past that is portrayed positively.

892 WAUGH, EVELYN. *Love among the Ruins: A Romance of the Near Future*. London: Chapman Hill, 1953. [m]
   This mainstream dystopian novel centers upon Miles Plastic and the joyless, omnipotent, and hopelessly bureaucratic British Welfare State in which he resides. Minor references to male homosexuality occur in the first chapter, which is set in a criminal rehabilitation center. Bleakly humorous.

893 WEATHERS, BRENDA. *The House at Pelham Falls*. Tallahassee, Fla.: Naiad, 1986. [F]
   In some respects, *The House at Pelham Falls* is comparable to Jane Chambers's *Burning*. Both novels are consciously feminist and involve contemporary lesbians caught up in the frightening affairs of their supernatural sapphic sisters. Dr. Karen Latham, Boston anthropology professor, flees her Ivy League existence and the emotional turmoil of her first lesbian affair. Seeking emotional tranquillity, she leases a charming century-old house on the desolate Maine coastline, but instead of peace Dr. Latham finds the ghost of a Yankee spinster who seeks to possess her. The author carefully delineates her coming-out story and effectively incorporates it into a spooky, but not particularly violent, horror novel.

894 WELLES, JESSE. "Succubus." In *The Dress / The Sharda Stories*. San Francisco: Library B Productions, 1986. [F]
   A sexually inhibited lesbian finds herself attacked by an erotic female demon, releasing some frightening incestuous sexual fantasies. A potent mix of horror and the erotic.

895 WELLES, PAUL O'M. *Project Lambda*. Port Washington, N.Y.: Ashley, 1979. [f, M]
   A fascist police state gains power in the near-future United States. A power-hungry senator begins an all-out, nationwide witch hunt

against male homosexuals, and concentration camps are secretly set up to facilitate "treatment" of sexual deviants. Throughout the country, gay men mysteriously vanish. The book contains a strong, positive statement regarding homosexuals and their rights, and it is horrifying in its vision, but one is left wondering why the author's fascists have entirely overlooked lesbians.

WELLS, JOHN J. [pseudonym of Juanita Coulson]. *See* BRADLEY, MARION ZIMMER (joint author)

896 WENTWORTH, ROBERT O. "World without Sex." *Marvel Tales*, May 1940. [F?]
There is no overt lesbianism in this man-hating far-future world where women completely dominate. Reproduction is done artificially and the last remaining men have been ordered exterminated. The men escape, kidnap and presumably rape some women, and rediscover heterosexuality.

897 WEST, WALLACE G. "The Last Man." *Amazing Stories*, February 1929. Reprinted in *The Pocket Book of Science-Fiction*, edited by Donald Wollheim. New York: Pocket Books, 1943. [F?]
Women have slowly taken over the world. They have discovered a chemical means of reproduction and dispensed with men. The few males left are museum specimens, retained to warn women of the horror they have escaped. "Women, no longer having need of sex, dropped it, like a worn-out cloak, and became sexless, tall, angular, narrow-hipped, flat-breasted and unbeautiful." Eve, one of these futuristic amazons, falls in love with the last remaining man, M-1, and frees him from captivity. Together they destroy the reproduction center, steal an aircraft, and head for the hills to birth a "new and finer race."

898 WESTON, SUSAN B. *Children of the Light*. St. Martin's, 1985. [f]
Jeremy Towers, a midwestern teenager, gets time-transferred into a postapocalypse future after eating some wild mushrooms. He stumbles into a small farming community on the shores of Lake Michigan comprised of several women and a few sterile men. Towers must adapt and settle into this struggling new world. Most of the women are at least situationally lesbian.

899 WHALEN, PATRICK. *Monastery*. New York: Pocket Books, 1988. [m]
The death of two elderly priests on a small island off the coast of Washington State unleashes a horde of ancient bloodthirsty vampires who slaughter most of the island's inhabitants. It remains for a hypermasculine paid mercenary, Braille, to single-handedly battle the

undead. Among the terrified humans hiding in Braille's shelter is a gay man, George Harden.

900 WHITE, TED. "Welcome to the Machine." *Amazing*, June 1976. [M]
A glimpse into the life of a male prostitute of the far future. Rael, seeking an escape from his oppressive pimp, sexually experiments with both men and women. A sordid and seedy portrait but not particularly homophobic.

901 WHITE, RICHARD A. "Deep Space Probe." *Honcho* 10, no. 5 (May 1987). [M]
Sexually explicit gay male science fiction.

902 WILDE, OSCAR. *The Picture of Dorian Gray. Lippincott's Monthly Magazine* (London and Philadelphia), 1890. Unauthorized reprint. Cleveland, Ohio: Arthur Westbrook Co., 1890. Reprint. London: Ward Lock, 1891. Reprint. New York: G. Munro's Sons, 1895. [M?]
This classic horror tale concerns a man whose outward appearance remains youthful and innocent; the inner corruption of his soul is mirrored only in his mysteriously changing portrait. The portrait reflects the "true" Dorian Gray, growing more and more hideous as the years go by, and it is because of this painting that Gray comes to his deserved end. Both the horror and the homosexual elements seem tame by today's standards, but at the time of its publication *The Picture of Dorian Gray* shocked the reading public with its sensuality and decadence. In addition to fleeting references to overtly homosexual characters (e.g., Pietro Riaria, the minion of Sixtus IV), the romantic friendship of the painter Basil Hallward for Gray is a major component of the novel, and there are homosexual allusions in Gray's own unspecified "sins."

Biographical Note

Oscar Wilde (1854-1900) was a noted Anglo-Irish dramatist, poet, and wit. His fantasy works also include two collections of fairy tales: *The Happy Prince and Other Tales* (London: David Nutt, 1888) and *A House of Pomegranates* (London: Osgood, McIlvaine & Co., 1891). His arrest, conviction, and subsequent imprisonment in 1895 on sodomy charges rocked the Western world, and his name has since become synonymous with homosexuality.

Biographical information is plentiful but beginning references are *Oscar Wilde*, by H. Montgomery Hyde (New York: Farrar, Straus & Giroux, 1975), and Richard Ellmann's *Oscar Wilde* (New York: Knopf, 1988).

---

903 WILHELM, KATE. *The Clewiston Test*. New York: Farrar, Straus & Giroux, 1976. [f]

Anne Clewiston is a brilliant scientist on the verge of a major medical discovery. Her career is in jeopardy because she is temporarily confined to a wheelchair and unable to get to the lab where the final stages of her experiment continue without her. While confined to her home, Anne becomes aware of the limitations that marriage imposes on her career and the extent to which her husband controls her sexuality. The determination Anne shows to continue her experiment and break her husband's subtle dominance is handled by the author with insight. Less satisfactory from a feminist perspective is the depiction of Deena Wells, Anne's colleague, who is portrayed as a "rabid" feminist and repressed lesbian.

904 WILHELM, KATE. "The Funeral." In *Again, Dangerous Visions*, edited by Harlan Ellison. Garden City, N.Y.: Doubleday, 1972. [F?]

Set in a repressive girls' school, this weird story concerns a young girl who flees the institution to save herself from becoming a lesbian sadist. Extremely odd and unpleasant but well-written.

905 WILHELM, KATE. *Let the Fire Fall*. Garden City, N.Y.: Doubleday, 1969. [m]

An alien spaceship lands in the middle of a quiet Ohio cornfield. Its crew quickly succumbs to an unknown disease leaving only one survivor, a small male infant. The alien child is secretly switched with a human newborn and is raised by a human family without his knowledge of his alien identity. The human child is raised as if it were the alien. An enormous, fascist religious movement arises to destroy the alien, and the world is edged toward a full-scale religious war. The author handles her tale with skill and makes this story of good versus evil entertaining and memorable. Two minor characters are derogatorily referred to as pansies, and the lesbians and gay men are specifically noted as being part of the evil evangelist's misguided followers.

906 WILHELM, KATE. *Where Late the Sweet Birds Sang*. New York: Harper & Row, 1976. [F, M]

A postholocaust story in which humans survive by cloning techniques. This method of reproduction is only intended to last for a few generations, but when the last human dies, the clones, all of whom are homosexual, decide never to reproduce sexually again. The clones come in single-gender groups of six to eight and utilize group sexuality to heighten their paranormal telepathic abilities. In the end, all of the clones are killed off and once again heterosexual humans make a comeback. Wilhelm won a Hugo Award for this homophobic novel.

907 WILLIAMS, MICHELLE D. "Moondancer." *Sinister Wisdom* (Berkeley, Calif.), no. 34 (1988). [F]

A lesbian starship captain picks up a mysterious and beautiful passenger and later keeps a rendezvous with an ex-lover in this excerpt from a novel-in-progress.

908 WILLIAMS, ROBERT MOORE. "World without Men." *Amazing Stories*, June 1950. [F?]

Four men are transported into the distant future where women are in control and men have become fugitives. Although homosexuality is not suggested, the women are definitely not heterosexual. Predictably, men win in the end and heterosexuality triumphs.

909 WILLIAMSON, CHET. ". . . To Feel Another's Woe." In *Blood Is Not Enough*, edited by Ellen Datlow. New York: Morrow, 1989. [m]

Williamson's sophisticated vampire tale is set amid the glittering Manhattan theatrical set. While auditioning for a part in *A Streetcar Named Desire*, a struggling actor meets a strangely compelling actress. A gay secondary character is described as "not at all flouncy."

910 WILSON, ANNA. "The Reach." In *The Reach and Other Stories*, edited by Lilian Mohin and Sheila Shulman. London: Onlywomen Press, 1984. [F]

A young lesbian feminist is recruited into an ancient feminist conspiracy.

WILSON, JOHN ANTHONY BURGESS. *See* BURGESS, ANTHONY (pseudonym)

911 WILSON, RICHARD. "The Hoaxters." *Galaxy*, June 1952. Reprinted in *Those Idiots from Earth*. New York: Ballantine, 1957. [M?]

Sam Black and Alex Hurd are stuck mining on an asteroid deep in space. Boredom sets in and they decide to stir up some excitement by playing a trick on the patrol ships that occasionally visit the area. Their relationship is very domestic, with Sam assuming the more dominant, "butch" role, but there is no overt sexuality expressed.

912 WITTIG, MONIQUE. *Across the Acheron*. Translated by David Le Vay. London: Peter Owen, 1987. Originally published as *Virgile, Non*. Paris: Éditions de Minuit, 1985. [F]

Retellings of classic myths and fantasy tales are not uncommon within contemporary science fiction. In *Across the Acheron*, Wittig offers a lesbian-identified rendition of Dante's famous visit to the inferno. Hell is somewhere near San Francisco; purgatory is the interior of a Valencia Street lesbian bar. The angels the author meets are leather-clad women on motorcycles. Dante's guide was Virgil, while Wittig is led by a wise woman named Manastabal. Poetic, hallucinatory, and radically feminist, Wittig's vision is wildly different than the Niven and Pournelle exploration of the same material.

913 WITTIG, MONIQUE. *Les Guérillères*. Translated by David Le Vay. New York: Viking, 1971. Originally published in Paris: Éditions de Minuit, 1969. [F]

Using a style that is more akin to poetry in its rhythmic quality than to a novel, Wittig writes angry and playful images of lesbians. Each paragraph forms a scene and conveys one complete aspect of the lesbians' culture. The paragraphs work as literary snapshots to form a colorful fantasy describing warrior women as they destroy the last vestiges of male domination. Because they are aware that language determines thinking patterns, the lesbians create a new language that relies on the symbol of the circle. The lesbians explore their environment, create their new culture, and express their physical and emotional love for each other. They are at war with men, but Wittig emphasizes the lesbians' creativity and love more than their responses to, and destruction of, patriarchal society. The author experiments with the French language, but her experimental usages do not translate easily into English. Nonetheless, her strong positive message is conveyed well.

914 WITTIG, MONIQUE. *The Lesbian Body*. Translated by David Le Vay. New York: Morrow, 1975. Originally published as *Le Corps Lesbian*. Paris: Éditions de Minuit, 1973. [F]

One need not know anatomy to enjoy *The Lesbian Body* even though anatomical terms are used extensively within the book to form lists of the female body's parts and to make more accurate the descriptions of the lesbians' bodies in movement. Unsanctioned by their lesbian community's collective expression of sexuality, two women on an island engage in many forms of physical sensation and expression that could loosely be called sex. The images created vacillate between tender and violent as the women possess and reject, dismember and rejoin each other's bodies. Men have no place in the love-hate relationship between these women and are not mentioned at all in the novel.

915 WITTIG, MONIQUE, and ZEIG, SANDE. *Lesbian Peoples; Material for a Dictionary*. New York: Avon, 1979. Originally published as *Brouillon pour un Dictionnaire des Amantes*. Paris: Grasset, 1976. [F]

Lesbian Peoples is a dictionary used in a far-future lesbian utopia. A wholly different history is used as a basis for this dictionary, making it void of patriarchal concepts that permeate our contemporary lexicon. For example, *woman* is defined as "obsolete ... once applied to beings fallen in an absolute state of servitude." This different perception is noticeable even in the definitions for words not traditionally associated with gender. Using a dictionary's format, the authors tell the glorious history of lesbian peoples from the Golden Age, through the Concrete Age (that of our own time), to the Glorious Age of the future. They also, by apparently assuming that men have never existed, illuminate how fully patriarchy is ingrained in our society and offer delightful woman-identified redefinitions for a myriad of concepts and myths.

Biographical Note

Monique Wittig (b. 1936) is a brilliant novelist whose first book, a nonfantasy, lesbian-relevant novel entitled *The Opoponax* (New York: Simon & Schuster, 1965), first published as *L'Opoponax* (Paris: Éditions de Minuit, 1964), won the 1964 Prix Medicis.

Wittig is openly lesbian. Biographical and critical information on her can be found in Pat Califia's article "Monique Wittig: Lover of Words and Women," in *Lesbian Tide* (Los Angeles), no. 7 (July-August 1977); in Margaret Crosland's *Women of Iron and Velvet* (New York: Taplinger, 1976); and in Helene Vivienne Wenzel's "The Text and Body / Politics: An Appreciation of Monique Wittig's Writings in Context," *Feminist Studies*, 7 (1981).

---

916 WOLFE, GENE. "Silhouette." In *The New Atlantis*, edited by Robert SILVERBERG, New York: Hawthorn Books, 1975. [f, m]

Johann, the protagonist of "Silhouette," finds life boring aboard a spaceship that searches year after year for a planet to colonize. That is, until he comes up against the unknown – in this case, an alien that takes the shape of Johann's shadow and pops into his life during a shipboard mutiny. Together Johann and his independently moving shadow take over the ship's command. References to the female captain's bisexuality and a male crew member's subtle sexual overtures toward Johann are diluted and almost lost in the plot. The novel does not probe into the intriguing alien's motivations but concentrates on the human's secret societies and other coping mechanisms that have developed during the long voyage.

WOLLHEIM, DONALD. *See* GRINNELL, DAVID (pseudonym)

WOODROW, TERRY. *See* BLUEJAY, JANA (pseudonym)

917 WOOLF, VIRGINIA. *Orlando: A Biography*. London: Hogarth Press, 1928. Reprint. New York: C. Geige, 1928. Reprint. New York: Harcourt, 1928. [X]

This charming fantasy is Virginia Woolf's gift and tribute to her lover, Vita Sackville-West. The title character represents Sackville-

West's literary heritage; Orlando's life during the four centuries from Elizabethan time to the present century parallels the progress of the English literary style. As a young man, Orlando is so beautiful that many women and a few men are quite attracted to him. During a seven-day sleep, he magically transforms into a woman. She then periodically masquerades as a man to enjoy better the freedoms and pleasures of the various ages she lives through. There are two other transvestites in the story, males, who attempt to capture Orlando's affections. These variant elements enhance the lighthearted and enchanting biography. Highly recommended.

918 WYAL, PG. "Border Town." *Amazing*, July 1971. [F]

A humorous story about three interstellar outlaws who are negotiating business on a small "border world." One of the outlaws, a rough and tough character named Queer Sal, is clearly labeled a lesbian.

919 WYAL, PG. "They've Got Some Hungry Women There. . . ." *Amazing*, March 1975. [F]

In another of the author's "Queer Sal" stories Sal is again defined as a lesbian. This time she is pitted against STRONZO, the interstellar crime syndicate.

920 WYATT, JACKSON. "Time Will Tell." *In Touch for Men* (Hollywood, Calif.), no. 149 (May 1989).

A young gay man tumbles into a time machine and emerges to have an erotic encounter with a Cro-Magnon male.

921 WYLIE, PHILIP. *The Disappearance*. New York: Rinehart, 1951. [f, m]

All over the world women suddenly see all the men vanish. The reverse happens to men: they watch all the women disappear. Life continues in two parallel worlds. In the men's world, looting erupts, war is started, martial law is declared, and a heavily role-identified form of homosexuality is adopted. In contrast, the women's world deals with the crisis rationally; although some of the women are petty and insecure, they find in themselves a competence they didn't know they possessed. Lesbianism is introduced when a neighbor's proposition is rejected by the female protagonist. Both worlds wish the opposite sex would reappear, but it is clear that they can live without each other. In fact, the male protagonist perceptively writes that the sexes have always lived separately, both psychologically and physically, and this new state of affairs is only an exaggeration of that separation. Although the author has an ambivalent message about homosexuality, his examination of sex roles is surprisingly detailed considering the date of publication.

922 WYNDHAM, JOHN [pseudonym of John Wyndham Parkes Lucas Beynon Harris]. "Consider Her Ways." In *Sometime, Never*. New York: Ballantine, 1956. [F]

This male-authored world-without-men story is different from the others of this type because it features a female protagonist and it ends with the woman-identified future society still intact. Jane Waterleigh, recently widowed and near suicidal, volunteers to try an experimental drug, chuinjuatin. She loses consciousness and awakens in a tidy, all-women's culture of the future. The future population is structured by a rigid class system that determines both body type and occupation. When it becomes clear that Jane cannot blend into the carefully controlled society, the women offer her a painless oblivion. Instead, Jane requests more chuinjuatin and wakes up in her own time again. She tries to change the course of events that she knows will lead to the all-female future, but her attempts are unsuccessful.

923 WYNDHAM, JOHN [pseudonym of John Wyndham Parkes Lucas Beynon Harris]. *The Midwich Cuckoos*. London: M. Joseph, 1957. Reprinted as *The Village of the Damned*. New York: Ballantine, 1961. [f]

Panic strikes a small English town as almost all the women mysteriously become pregnant. Some alien force has used the town as a kind of breeding ground. Among those afflicted by these unplanned pregnancies is one partner of a lesbian couple.

924 WYNNE, JOHN. *The Sighting*. New York: Tree Line, 1978. [M]

A short novelette combining 1950s nostalgia with flying saucers, vampires, and a delightful coming-out story. The gay male content is major and positive.

925 YARBRO, CHELSEA QUINN. *Blood Games*. New York: St. Martin's, 1979. [m]

Yarbro is skilled at writing vampire stories within a detailed, accurate historical context. Saint Germain, in contrast to most vampires, is not a villain. He is a gentle and gentlemanly vampire surrounded by far more despicable humans who thrive on others' suffering. Yarbro's vampire requires emotional and sexual intimacy, as well as blood, from his male and female victims. Since he prefers to share in as much of humanity as is possible, his vampiritic acts tend to occur within the context of ongoing relationships. Two of the relationships are with his slaves, a man and a woman. The third relationship, and the one that most pleases Saint Germain, is with a Roman lady, Atta Olivia Clemens. Olivia remains passive and resigned to the gross abuse inflicted upon her by her husband during most of the novel until finally she is rescued by the heroic vampire. Many of the Roman males in this novel are bisexual. This third volume about Saint Germain is filled with more carnage and violent sex than the previous two novels in this series.

926 YARBRO, CHELSEA QUINN. "Dead in Irons." In *Faster Than Light*, edited by Jack Dann and George Zebrowski. New York: Harper & Row, 1976. [m]
    Yarbro has a talent for creating spooky, evil, and macabre moods, and "Dead in Irons" displays this talent well. A young woman, Shiller, signs on as a steward aboard an intergalactic transport. Life within the starcraft is a human jungle dominated by one villainous man, Wranswell. Yarbro's story follows Shiller's confrontations with Wranswell through the course of the voyage. The author handles her female characters wonderfully but makes Wranswell a loathsome pederast.

927 YARBRO, CHELSEA QUINN. *Hotel Transylvania*. New York: St. Martin's, 1978. [m]
    This novel was the first written in a series that chronicles the adventures of Saint Germain the vampire. Set in French society in 1777, Madeline de Montalia, the beautiful daughter of a rich man, falls in love with Saint Germain, a noble and good-hearted vampire. Evil Parisian satanists, both homosexual and heterosexual, demand innocent virgins for their vile rituals. Madeline's father had once made a pact with the devil worshipers to give them his firstborn child and they come to claim her just as she is about to enter Parisian society. This is one of the few fantasy tales in which a vampire plays the heroic role. As is true of the entire series, it is a well-written and suspenseful novel, but the equation of satanism with sexual deviation is unnecessary.

928 YARBRO, CHELSEA QUINN. "Un Bel Di." In *Two Views of Wonder*, edited by Thomas Scortia and Chelsea Quinn Yarbro. New York: Ballantine, 1973. [m]
    A male government official sexually abuses a group of children. He then takes a lower government position on another planet until the scandal dies down and then he returns home, unchanged. Depressing.

929 YOLAN, JANE. *Sister Light, Sister Dark*. New York: TOR, 1988. [F]
    The first book in the author's Great Alta series offers readers much in the way of matriarchal myth. Combining legend, song, and storytelling, the prophecy unfolds of young Jenna who will bring about the end of matriarchy and the beginning of something new. Yolan's myth creation adds to the genre more than a new female hero (though this one is certainly a treat); it invokes the shadow sister, a dark sister called up from the eternal shadows to roam with her light sister, to

share her thoughts, her deeds, and her bed–but to appear only in moonlight or candlelight.

930 YOLAN, JANE. *White Jenna*. New York: TOR, 1989. [F]

In the second volume of the Great Alta series, Jenna gains mythic stature and continues to fulfill the prophecies surrounding the demise of the women's society. Most of the hames (villages of Alta's worshipers) have been destroyed. The War of the Genders has erupted, and Jenna joins with a young prince to overthrow an evil usurper to the throne. Again, the light sister / dark sister pairing is presented as a central part of the lives of Alta's women.

YOUD, CHRISTOPHER S. *See* CHRISTOPHER, JOHN (pseudonym)

931 YOUNG, DONNA J. *Retreat: As It Was!* Weatherby Lake, Mo.: Naiad Press, 1979. [F]

For the first time war comes to the lesbian planet, Retreat, located in a lesbian galaxy. The perpetrators of the violence are a species never before known by the women: men. Within this apocalyptic context a love story is told. Tolly, a messenger from another lesbian world, and Ria, a healer from Retreat, become lovers and exchange genes through cunnilingus. Ria becomes pregnant, but when her child is born its genitalia are exposed on the outside of its body. It is treated as a mutated female; the women do not understand that it is a boy child. This lesbian fantasy is poorly conceptualized, yet its descriptive episodes of lesbian sexual activity may make for enjoyable reading.

932 YULSMAN, JERRY. *Elleander Morning*. New York: St. Martin's, Marek, 1982. [m]

Mainstream novel about time travel and alternative realities. Minor gay male character.

933 ZANA. "Man Plague." *Sinister Wisdom* (Berkeley, Calif.), no. 34 (1988). [F]

A disabled lesbian separatist and her friends, just back from a two-month survivalist training camp, casually adjust to a plague that has destroyed every human male on the planet.

934 ZAROVITCH, Princess VERA [pseudonym of Mary E. Bradley Lane]. *Mizora: A Prophecy. Cincinnati Commercial*, serialized 1880-81. Reprint. New York: Dillingham, 1889. [F?]

One of the earliest-known female separatist fantasies to come out of the nineteenth-century American feminist movement. Princess Vera Zarovitch has been exiled to Siberia for condemning her government's treatment of a beloved woman friend. Courageously, she flees her imprisonment, and after living for a time with Eskimos she sets off alone and discovers a world located under the North Pole. Called Mizora, the world is populated entirely by beautiful blond women. The women have created a classless, scientifically advanced culture based upon universal higher education. Romantic love is scorned, and the only condoned emotion is that expressed between mother and daughter, yet nonsexual woman-woman friendships provide an important motivation for the plot. Despite a naive racism and Victorian attitude toward all forms of sexuality, *Mizora: A Prophecy* remains a landmark feminist utopia that is truly unique for its time.

ZEBROWSKI, GEORGE. *See* DANN, JACK (joint author)

ZEIG, SANDE. *See* WITTIG, MONIQUE (joint author)

935 ZELAZNY, ROGER. *Lord of Light*. Garden City, N.Y.: Doubleday, 1967. [f]
    This highly imaginative fantasy tells of an Earth-colonized world where a small group of individuals have seized control of the planet's entire technology. By using such things as radio communications, aviation, and immortality, members of this group have assumed godlike powers and attitudes. They have taken on the titles and attributes of the ancient Hindu pantheon and their domination of the world seems complete, until finally there arises an opponent equal in power to the "gods," Siddartha Mahasamatman. "Sam" believes that technological knowledge should be shared, and events culminate in a battle of epic proportions. Zelazny makes one of the gods a lesbian who constantly reincarnates in a man's body so as to seduce mortal women. The sexually disguised god is unhappy with herself, yet the hero calls her the envy of every lesbian in the world.

See also ELLISON, HARLAN (joint author)

Appendix 1
Selected Anthologies

Amazons! Edited by Jessica Amanda Salmonson. New York: DAW, 1979.
A World Fantasy Award-winning anthology of amazon fantasy stories. Includes Kaye's "Amazons," Lynn's "The Woman Who Loved the Moon," and others.

Amazons II. Edited by Jessica Amanda Salmonson. New York: DAW, 1982.
An anthology of amazon fantasy stories. Includes Busby's "For a Daughter," Clayton's "Nightwork," Lee's "Southern Lights," and others.

Aurora: Beyond Equality. Edited by Vonda N. McIntyre and Susan Janice Anderson. Greenwich, Conn.: Fawcett, 1977.
A pioneering anthology of explicitly feminist science fiction. Includes an excerpt from Piercy's *Woman on the Edge of Time*, Russ's "Corruption," Tiptree's "Houston, Houston, Do You Read?" Sheldon's "Your Faces, O My Sisters! Your Faces Filled with Light," and others.

Despatches from the Frontiers of the Female Mind. Edited by Jen Green and Sarah Lefanu. London: Women's Press, 1985.
An anthology of feminist science fiction. Includes Lee's "Love Alters," Russ's "Clichés from Outer Space," and others.

Eros in Orbit: A Collection of All-New Science Fiction Stories about Sex. Edited by Joseph Elder. New York: Trident Press, 1973.
An anthology of sex-themed science fiction. Includes Scortia's "Flowering Narcissus" and others.

Free Amazons of Darkover. Edited by Marion Zimmer Bradley. New York: DAW, 1985.

An anthology of amazon fantasy stories, all situated in Marion Zimmer Bradley's world of Darkover. Includes Bigelow's "Tactics," Bradley's "The Legend of Lady Bruna," Lackey's "A Different Kind of Courage," and others.

Kindred Spirits: An Anthology of Gay and Lesbian Science Fiction Stories. Edited by Jeffrey Elliot. Boston: Alyson, 1984.

An anthology of lesbian- and gay-themed science fiction and fantasy. Includes Conner's "Vamp," Gerrold's "How We Saved the Human Race," Lynn's "The Woman Who Loved the Moon," Malzberg's "Going Down," Novitski's "Nuclear Fission," Pangborn's "The Night Wind," Pollack's "Black Rose and White Rose," Russ's "When It Changed," Salmonson's "The Prodigal Daughter," Scortia's "Flowering Narcissus," Silverberg's "Passengers," and Thomas's "Broken Tool."

Memories and Vision: Women's Science Fiction and Fantasy. Edited by Susanna Sturgis. New Freedom, Calif.: Crossing Press, 1989.

An anthology of women's science fiction. Includes Casper's "Harmonic Conception," Champagne's "Womankind," Clark's "The Rational Ship," Hartwell's "Itu's Sixth Winter Festival," Katz's "The Amazing Disappearing Girl," Meluch's "Conversation with a Legend," and others.

Strange Bedfellows. Edited by Thomas Scortia. New York: Random House, 1972.

An anthology of sex-themed science fiction. Includes Carlson's "Dinner at Helen's," Leibscher's "Do Androids Dream of Electric Love?", Sturgeon's "World Well Lost," and others.

What Did Miss Darlington See? An Anthology of Feminist Supernatural Fiction. Edited by Jessica Amanda Salmonson. New York: Feminist Press, 1989.

An anthology of feminist-themed supernatural stories. Includes Brown's "There and Here," Phelps's "Since I Died," Trevanion's "A Ghost Story," and others.

When Women Rule. Edited by Sam Moskowitz. New York: Walker, 1972.

An anthology of "woman-dominant" science fiction. Includes Gardner's "The Last Woman," Keller's "The Feminine Metamorphosis," West's "The Last Man," and others.

Worlds Apart: An Anthology of Lesbian and Gay Science Fiction and Fantasy. Edited by Camilla Decarnin, Eric Garber, and Lyn Paleo. Boston: Alyson, 1986.

An anthology of lesbian- and gay-themed science-fiction and fantasy stories. Includes Bradley's "To Keep the Oath," Delany's "Time Considered as a Helix of Semi-Precious Stones," Fisk's "Find the Lady," Gomez's "No Day Too Long," Lee's "Full Fathom Five My Father Lies," Leibscher's "Do Androids Dream of Electric Love?", Lynn's "The Gods of Reorth," Pangborn's "Harper Conan and Singer David," Russ's "The Mystery of the Young Gentleman," Tiptree's "Houston, Houston, Do You Read?", and Varley's "Lollipop and the Tar Baby."

Appendix 2
Selected Films and Videos

Alien Prey. Dir. Norman J. Warren. Great Britain, 1983. [F]

A rather silly, and decidedly homophobic, mixture of science fiction and horror in which a pair of British lesbians, Jo (Sally Faulkner) and Jessica (Glory Annan) discover a strange man wandering around on their country estate who eventually turns out to be a bloodthirsty alien. Inadequate plot, horrendous makeup, and the lesbians get raped and eaten at the end of the film.

Aliens. Dir. James Cameron. United States, 1986. [f]

Cameron's sequel to the highly successful *Alien* is a big-budget thriller featuring Sigourney Weaver as Ripley, a strong female hero who battles insectlike aliens on a distant world. A secondary character is an obvious lesbian. Not as good as the original, but action-packed and adventure-filled.

All of Me. Dir. Carl Reiner. United States, 1984. [X]

In this wacky – but not entirely effective – comedy about sexual identity, the soul of cranky millionaire Lily Tomlin gets miraculously transported into the body of attorney Steve Martin, with many comic results.

Angel of H.E.A.T. Dir. Myrl A. Schreibman. United States, 1982. [f]

Silly spoof on espionage thrillers starring adult film star Marilyn Chambers as a secret agent and Mary Woronov as her lesbian assistant. The unusual duo battle a wacky mad scientist who has developed a metal-shattering device.

Barbarella. Dir. Roger Vadim. France, 1968.
[f, m]

Based on a popular comic strip by Jean-Claude, *Barbarella* features Jane Fonda as a sexy forty-first-century innocent who encounters handsome angels, man-eating dolls, and pleasure machines. Anita Pallenberg is notable as the evil lesbian space queen who has designs on the heroine, and John Philip Law plays a gay angel.

Barry McKenzie Holds His Own. Dir. Bruce Beresford. Australia, 1974. [M]

This is a crude, raunchy, but very funny Australian vampire comedy in which a young man (Barry Crocker) and his elderly aunt (played by noted drag queen Barry Humphries) are kidnapped by vampires and taken to Transylvania.

Because the Dawn. Dir. Amy Goldstein. United States, 1988. [F]

This short humorous vampire film has already become a cult favorite. Director Goldstein turns the traditions of the lesbian vampire genre on their heads. Her vampire (Edwige) is being pursued by an aggressive fashion photographer (Sandy Gray).

Bedazzled. Dir. Stanley Donen. United States, 1968. [m]

The acclaimed satirical revue "Beyond the Fringe" (featuring Dudley Moore) is featured in this humorous fantasy about a man who makes a pact with the Devil. His plans are undone by personifications of the Seven Deadly Sins; Vanity and Envy are portrayed as swishy gay stereotypes.

Blackula. Dir. William Crain. United States, 1972. [m]

An exploitative film about a black vampire (William Marshall) who begins terrorizing Los Angeles after a pair of gay antique dealers release him from his eternal sleep. The gay men are characterized as shallow, weak, effeminate caricatures who become, of course, victims of the vampire.

Blood and Roses. Dir. Roger Vadim. France, 1961. [F]

Roger Vadim's version of LeFanu's story "Carmilla" has a beautiful Italian woman (Annette Vadim) craving the blood of both women and men. The film was rendered nearly incoherent by American censors who removed over ten minutes of lesbian footage.

Blood of Dracula. Dir. Herbert L. Strock. United States, 1957. [F]

Set in an all-girls school, *Blood of Dracula* concerns a science teacher who turns a young student into a blood-sucking monster. There are numerous lesbian overtones throughout the film.

Blood-Splattered Bride. Dir. Vincente Aranda. Spain, 1972. [F]

A boring Spanish version of Lefanu's classic story "Carmilla" in which newlyweds meet the reincarnation of the long-dead *femme fatale*.

Born in Flames. Dir. Lizzie Borden. United States, 1982. [F]

An independently produced vision of the near future in which the United States government becomes entirely totalitarian and radical feminists begin a revolution. Includes strong secondary lesbian characters.

Celine and Julie Go Boating. Dir. Jacques Rivette. France, 1974. [F]

This magical movie has developed a devoted cult following. The beautiful magician Celine (Juliet Berto) and the librarian Julie (Dominique Labourier) fall in love and begin sharing an apartment. They tell each other stories, play games, and take on each others' identities, but when they stumble upon a haunted house, things really start getting bizarre. A fantastic, dreamlike atmosphere is maintained throughout the three-hour film.

Children Shouldn't Play with Dead Things. Dir. Bob Clark. United States, 1972. [m]

There are several secondary gay male characters in this off-beat zombie film. A second-rate theater company travels to a deserted island to stage an elaborate satanic ritual to awaken the dead. To their surprise, their ritual works and the dead begin to rise!

The Comeback. Dir. Peter Walker. Great Britain, 1977. [M?]

Jack Jones plays a popular singer planning his comeback when he is haunted by the ghost of his recently murdered wife. The film includes a minor transvestite scene with implied gay male content. Also known as *The Day the Screaming Stopped*.

Daughters of Darkness. Dir. Harry Kumel. Belgium, 1971. [F]

Daughters of Darkness is a fascinating lesbian vampire film which has developed a strong cult following. Countess Elizabeth Bathory (Delphine Seyrig) lives with her beautiful female lover (Andrea Rau) in a luxurious seaside resort hotel in Belgium. Together they seduce a moody young man and his battered wife. Compelling and erotic, the film's underlying feminist discourse has been noted by several critics.

The Day the Fish Came Out. Dir. Michael Cacoyannis. United States, 1967. [m]

A confused nuclear disaster film starring Candice Bergen. An atomic bomb, accidently jettisoned onto a tranquil Greek island, causes chaos. Several secondary gay male characters are featured.

Does Dracula Really Suck? Dir. unknown. United States, 1969. [M]
Sexually explicit gay male erotica utilizing a vampire theme.

Dr. Jekyll and Sister Hyde. Dir. Roy Ward Baker. Great Britain, 1971. [X]
An unusual variation on Robert Louis Stevenson's early science-fiction tale produced by Great Britain's Hammer Studios. Good Dr. Jekyll (Ralph Bates) performs an experiment in which he releases his evil self. In this version, his evil self is a female.

Dracula's Daughter. Dir. Lambert Hillyer. United States, 1936. [F]
Countess Marya Zaleska (Gloria Holden), the daughter of the infamous Count Dracula, seeks the help of a psychiatrist to escape her hunger for blood in this Universal Studios classic. One of Zaleska's victims is an attractive artists' model, and their interaction, though not specifically lesbian, is surprisingly erotic given the time.

Dune. Dir. David Lynch. United States, 1984. [m]
Director David Lynch creates a not-so-successful film version of Frank Herbert's best-selling novel. The desert planet of Arrakis is held hostage by the corrupt Baron Harkonnen. As in Herbert's original, Harkonnen is depicted as a sadistic homosexual.

Earth Girls Are Easy. Dir. Julien Temple. United States, 1989. [m]
Wacky comedy starring Geena Davis and Jeff Goldblum about aliens who crash in a Los Angeles swimming pool. Secondary characters include two gay police officers.

El Topo. Dir. Alexandro Jodorowsky. United States, 1970. [f]
A weird and surreal fantasy in which a black-clad gunslinger stalks the West, murdering, raping, and eventually achieving enlightenment. Laden with symbolism, this is a hopelessly confusing film. There is minor lesbian content.

Fear No Evil. Dir. Frank LaLoggia. United States, 1981. [m]
Three archangels arrive on Earth to battle the Anti-Christ, a young high school student. The action includes a homosexual hazing incident in the school shower room.

Fearless Vampire Killers. Dir. Roman Polanski. United States, 1967. [m]
Roman Polanski's spoof of vampire films follows a professor and his trusted assistant as they invade the dwelling of a vampire. The film features a nelly gay vampire as a minor character (played by Ian Quarrier). Not entirely successful, but it has its moments.

Flesh Gordon. Dir. Mike Light. United States, 1974. [f, M]

An amusing soft-core sex comedy based on the old Flash Gordon comic strip. Flesh Gordon and his girlfriend Dale Ardor battle the evil forces of Emperor Wang. Get the idea? There are several gay characterizations, including an amazon queen and a very gay Prince Precious (whom Gordon beds). Noted science-fiction author Tom Reamy is reputed to have helped with the screenplay.

Flesh 1995. Dir. Kennith Holloway. United States, 1985. [M]

Low-budget gay male erotica set in a postnuclear world in which sex is only allowed for procreation. A few of the most attractive men are licensed to perform gay sex acts on the state-approved television show "Sexarama."

Frankenstein Created Woman. Dir. Terence Fisher. Great Britain, 1967. [F?, X]

Mad scientist Baron Frankenstein (Peter Cushing) transplants a male spirit into the body of a buxom woman (*Playboy* centerfold Susan Denberg), with some obvious lesbian overtones.

Fright Night. Dir. Tom Holland. United States, 1985. [M?]

A spooky vampire thriller with Roddy McDowell as a horror movie video host. There is an implied relationship between the evil vampire Chris Sarandon and his assistant.

Le Frisson des Vampires. Dir. Jean Rollin. France, 1970. [F]

Soft-core fantasy of a "butch" lesbian vampire, complete with chains and black leather.

Gayracula. Dir. Roger Earl. United States, 1983. [M]

This surprisingly imaginative sexually explicit gay male film features Tim Kramer as the sexually active Count Gaylord who searches Los Angeles gay bars in search of his enemy, the Marquis de Suede.

God Told Me To. Dir. Larry Cohen. United States, 1976. [X]

Noted horror director Cohen produces an unusual thriller in which a religious New York cop investigates a series of senseless murders. In each case, the killer claims that "God told me to." "God" turns out to be a radiant, blond, androgynous being fathered by a flying saucer.

Goodbye Charlie. Dir. Vincente Minnelli. United States, 1964. [X]

In this film version of George Axelrod's play, a male scriptwriter is reincarnated in the body of a woman (Debbie Reynolds). Reynolds gets to act pretty butch, but otherwise this is not worth watching.

Gothic. Dir. Ken Russell. Great Britain, 1986. [M]

Moody horror film about the infamous meeting in 1816 of Lord Byron, John Polidori, Shelley, and Shelley's wife, Mary, that resulted in the writing of *The Vampyre* and *Frankenstein*. Polidori and Byron are portrayed as lovers (with Polidori being quite a swish) and there appears to be involvement between Shelley and Byron as well. As excessive as most Ken Russell films.

The Haunting. Dir. Robert Wise. Great Britain, 1963. [F]

A brilliant haunted house film based on Shirley Jackson's *The Haunting of Hill House*. A group of psychics investigate an old mansion that seems to have a will of its own. As in the original novel, there is a noticeable lesbian subtext throughout the story. Julie Harris and Claire Bloom are brought very close together by the house's sinister mystery. Wise's film is genuinely scary without any of the gore so common in horror films. Highly recommended.

Hellhole. Dir. Pierre De Moro. United States, 1985. [f]

A ridiculous "women in prison" story with a science-fiction twist. A mad scientist is using inmates of the Ashland Sanitarium for Women as guinea pigs in his brain surgery experiments. One of the best features of the film is Mary Woronov as a bisexual psychiatrist.

The Hunger. Dir. Tom Scott. United States, 1983. [F]

Chic lesbian vampires are featured in this stylish, beautifully photographed, high-budget thriller, which stars Susan Sarandon, David Bowie, and Catherine Deneuve. Based on the Whitley Strieber novel of the same name.

The Ice Pirates. Dir. Stewart Raffill. United States, 1984. [m]

Surprisingly funny spoof of space adventures like *Star Wars* in which adventurer Robert Urich and his companions battle the evil Templar Empire to locate the only planet in the galaxy with water. Includes a brief bit with a stereotypic gay barber.

The Last House near the Lake. Dir. Enzo G. Gastellari (Girolami). Italy, 1983. [f]

A young woman (Eleneora Fani), plagued by a witch's curse, collapses into a faint following orgasm and is unable to awaken until her lover dies. The curse is broken when the woman sleeps with another woman.

Liquid Sky. Dir. Slava Kerova. United States, 1983. [F, m, X]

Filmed on a very low budget, *Liquid Sky* is a visually exciting New Wave film set in New York's drug and rock underground. Young lesbian Margaret is visited by a flying saucer and suddenly finds her lovers disappearing after she has orgasm. Anne Carlisle plays a dual role as both the androgynous lesbian and a gay male model.

Logan's Run. Dir. Michael Anderson. United States, 1976. [m]
A totalitarian future world doesn't allow old people but accepts homosexuality. Michael York, Jenny Agutter, and Farrah Fawcett star.

Love Bites. Dir. Marvin Jones. United States, 1988. [M]
This independently produced feature-length video was designed specifically for the gay market. A handsome vampire hunter discovers a gay vampire living in the heart of West Hollywood and falls in love with him. The budget was low, but the humor is high and the video has a definite campy charm to it. Sexy, wholly gay-positive, yet not pornographic.

Lust for a Vampire. Dir. Jimmy Sangster. Great Britain, 1970. [F]
A lesbian vampire named Mircalla (an anagram of Carmilla), played by Yvette Stensggard, runs amok in a girls' finishing school in the second lesbian vampire film from Hammer Studios. Also known as *To Love a Vampire*.

The Man Who Fell to Earth. Dir. Nicolas Roeg. United States, 1976. [m]
Space alien David Bowie tries to return to his home planet, but he is eventually corrupted by society. Among his few friends is a gay attorney played by Buck Henry.

Mary, Mary, Bloody Mary. Dir. Juan Lopez Moctezuma. Mexico, 1973. [f]
Silly vampire film in which a beautiful vampire (Christina Ferrare) is cursed by the bloodlust that plagued her father (John Carradine). A very bad movie, with only an extended lesbian seduction scene to redeem it.

Miracle Mile. Dir. Steve DeJarnatt. United States, 1989. [m]
An unusual "what if . . ." science-fiction film about the reaction of a group of people in Los Angeles when they learn of an impending nuclear holocaust. A gay bodybuilder and his lover turn out to be heros.

Myra Breckinridge. Dir. Michael Sarne. United States, 1970. [X]
An awful film version of Gore Vidal's sex-change fantasy starring Raquel Welch, Rex Reed, and Mae West.

Nightmare on Elm Street; Part Two: Freddy's Revenge. Dir. Jack Sholder. United States, 1985. [M?]
The second in a series of highly successful films revolving around a psychotic killer named Freddie Krueger who invades the dreams of his victims. In *Freddy's Revenge*, Krueger enters the dreams of Mark Patton with some surprisingly gay nightmares. At one point Patton's sadistic gym

teacher is located in a leather bar and is stripped naked, whipped, and murdered by occult forces.

Once Bitten. Dir. Howard Storm. United States, 1985. [m]
Sophomoric vampire film featuring Lauren Hutton as an ageless vampire. Cleavon Little plays a prissy, mincing homosexual.

Picture of Dorian Gray. Dir. Albert Lewin. United States, 1945. [M]
The first film version of Oscar Wilde's classic fantasy tale. Hurd Hatfield portrays the youthful Dorian Gray, who is lured into debauchery by the decadent aristocrat played by George Sanders.

A Polish Vampire in Burbank. Dir. Mark Pirro. United States, 1983. [m]
Low-budget vampire comedy cheapened by sophomoric and sometimes offensive humor. The plot revolves around an adolescent vampire trying to lose his virginity by making his first kill. Among the characters is "Queerwolf," a young man who becomes homosexual during the full moon.

Requiem pour un Vampire. Dir. Jean Rollin. France, 1971. [F]
A lesbian vampire film.

Road Warrior. Dir. George Miller. Australia, 1981. [m]
A sequel to the trend-setting action film *Mad Max*, this film is notably violent and homophobic. In a brutal, postholocaust future world, policeman Mel Gibson battles a band of barbarian, punk, homosexual motorcycle thugs who threaten the stability and decency of the struggling new world.

Rocky Horror Picture Show. Dir. Jim Sharman. United States, 1975. [M, X]
Originally a London stage musical, this film has become a true cult classic that satirizes nearly all of the science-fiction and horror film conventions. Newlyweds Barry Bostwick and Susan Sarandon stumble into the castle of mad scientist (and transvestite) Dr. Frank N. Furter (Tim Curry) who is creating, with his friends from the planet Transsexual, the perfect male sex partner. Everyone ends up sleeping with everyone. Great fun.

Secret of Dorian Gray. Dir. Harry Alan Towers. Italy and Germany, 1971. [M]
A low-budget updating of Oscar Wilde's classic horror tale. Helmut Berger plays the slowly corrupting Dorian. Unlike the 1945 film, this version contains overt homosexual implications.

The Sentinel. Dir. Michael Winner. United States, 1977. [f]
Based on Jeffrey Konvitz's novel of the same name, this occult thriller revolves around a portal to hell located in an old New York brownstone.

Homosexuals are part of Satan's minions; Sylvia Miles and Beverly D'Angelo play repellent lesbian lovers.

Sex Drive, 2020. Dir. unknown. United States, 1988. [M]
Gay male pornographic science-fiction film.

Shadey. Dir. Phillip Saville. Great Britain, 1985. [X]
An inventive British fantasy about a mechanic with psychic powers who wants to use his talents to get a sex change.

The Shining. Dir. Stanley Kubrick. United States, 1980. [m]
Stanley Kubrick's adaptation of Stephen King's best-selling novel about the haunted Colorado resort hotel, the Overview. Jack Nicholson and Shelley Duvall star as the hotel's winter caretakers. King's original had several minor gay male characterizations, and the film leaves in a fleeting gay male sequence late in the film.

Sleeper. Dir. Woody Allen. United States, 1973. [m]
A hilarious future fantasy in which Woody Allen is frozen alive in 1973 and awakens 200 years later. Among the characters he meets are a swishy gay couple and their equally swishy robot.

Streets of Fire. Dir. Arthur Hill. United States, 1984. [F]
Hill's *Streets of Fire* oddly mixes elements of an action-packed adventure film with the sound and excitement of a rock video. In an unnamed city in the unspecified future, attractive rock star (Diane Lane) is kidnapped by a violent street gang named the Bombers and boyfriend Michael Pare must rescue her. One of the film's best features is Pare's sidekick, a tough-talking, hard-boiled lesbian portrayed by Amy Madigan.

Theatre of Blood. Dir. Douglas Hickox. United States, 1973. [m]
Vincent Price thriller about a failed Shakespearean actor who begins to murder, one by one, the drama critics who destroyed his career. There are certainly fun elements to the film: Price is deliciously campy and Diana Rigg looks great in man-drag. But unfortunately the only overt gay character is an outrageously stereotypic Oscar Wilde-type dilettante, played by Robert Morley, who is forced to eat his beloved poodles.

They Came from Within. Dir. David Cronenberg. Canada, 1976. [f, m]
The first feature film of Canadian director David Cronenberg is a strangely symbolic horror film with graphic violence and overt sexual overtones. A large Toronto housing complex is invaded by a human-eating, phallus-appearing parasite that causes its host to become sexually pathological. The residents of the complex begin an orgy of violence and sex, including lesbian and gay sex.

The Toxic Avenger. Dir. Michael Herz and Samuel Weil. United States, 1985. [m]

The wimpy janitor in a fitness gym falls into a vat of industrial waste and emerges as the "Toxic Avenger," a deformed monster who only attacks criminals. The film's humor is broad, with countless sight gags and horrible puns. The film's two gay characters are comic stereotypes – effeminate hairdressers who fight over the monster – but they at least are not among the monster's victims. Vulgar and exceedingly graphic, but not without some appeal.

Turnabout. Dir. Hal Roach. United States, 1940. [X]

A classic Hal Roach comedy based on Thorne Smith's wonderful novel of sex change. Carole Landis and John Hubbard exchange bodies, with predictable results. Family entertainment by today's standards, this film was risqué in its day.

Twins of Evil. Dir. John Hough. Great Britain, 1971. [F]

Peter Cushing portrays a nineteenth-century witch-hunter who battles two beautiful lesbian vampires (Mary and Madelein Collinson) in the third lesbian vampire film produced by Great Britain's Hammer Studios.

The Vampire Lovers. Dir. Roy Ward Baker. Great Britain, 1970. [F]

Ingrid Pitt stars as Mircalla, a vampire who seduces numerous women until stopped by Peter Cushing. The first in a series of intentionally titillating lesbian vampire films produced by Hammer Studios.

Vampyres. Dir. Joseph Larras. Great Britain, 1974. [F]

A pair of lesbian vampires (Marianne Moore and Anulka) lure unsuspecting men to a remote castle and gruesomely murder them until two tourists interfere. A soft-core feature with lots of nudity and heavy breathing.

The Velvet Vampire. Dir. Stephanie Rothman. United States, 1971. [F]

The Velvet Vampire is an unusual entry into the lesbian vampire film genre because of its female director and its feminist twist. A female descendant of Sheridan Lefanu (the author of *Carmilla*), living in the desert outside of Los Angeles, picks up a young hippie couple at an art gallery. She turns out to be a bisexual vampire who proceeds to seduce both husband and wife. Although Rothman never allows full expression of lesbianism, the director is clearly sympathetic to same-sex love. Extremely dated and "hippie" in style.

Venus in Furs. Dir. Jesus Franco. United States, 1970. [f, m]

A strange and kinky film about two spirits, James Darren and Barbara McNair, who don't know they are ghosts. Both are drawn to the sadomasochistic underworld of Europe where they meet lesbians and gay men.

Le Viol du Vampire. Dir. Jean Rollin. France, 1967. [F]
   A lesbian vampire film.

Virgin Witch. Dir. Roy Austin. Great Britain, 1970. [F]
   Two young women arrive in London to work as models but soon find themselves involved in a coven of sinister lesbian witches.

Voodoo Island. Dir. Reginald Le Borg. United States, 1957. [f]
   Boris Karloff investigates a tropical island that seems to be cursed by voodoo. Jean Engstrom plays a lesbian who lusts after Boris Karloff's secretary and then gets eaten by a giant Venus's-flytrap. Pretty silly.

Appendix 3
Selected Fan Organizations

FRIENDS OF DARKOVER
(A national organization for
readers of Marion Zimmer
Bradley)
P.O. Box 472
Berkeley, CA 94701

QUEEN'S OWN
(A national organization for
readers of Mercedes Lackey)
P.O. Box 43143
Upper Montclair, NJ 07043

ANNE RICE'S VAMPIRE
LESTAT FAN CLUB
(A national organization for
readers of Anne Rice)
P.O. Box 58277
New Orleans, LA 70158-8277

APA-Lambda
(A gay and Lesbian Amateur Press
Association)
P.O. Box 1006
Elgin, IL 60121

GAYLACTIC NETWORK
(A national network of Gaylaxian
fan organizations)
P.O. Box 1051
Boston, MA 02117-1051

THE GAYLAXIANS (Gaylaxian
Science Fiction Society, Inc.)
(Boston fan organization for
lesbians, gay men, and their
friends)
P.O. Box 1059
Boston, MA 02103

CAPITOL DISTRICT
GAYLAXIANS
(New York fan organization for
lesbians, gay men, and their
friends)
P.O. Box 66054–Fort Orange
Albany, NY 12206

TRI-STATE GAYLAXIANS
(Tri-State fan organization for
lesbians, gay men, and their
friends)
c/o 55 Mercer St. #1
Jersey City, NJ 07302

GREAT LAKE GAYLAXIANS
(Great Lake fan organization for
lesbians, gay men, and their
friends)
c/o 51 Spokane Villa #13
Pontiac, MI 48053

PHILADELPHIA AREA
GAYLAXIANS
(Philadelphia fan organization for
lesbians, gay men, and their
friends)
c/o 219 Talbot Dr.
Broomall, PA 19008-3728

NORTH COUNTRY
GAYLAXIANS
(Minnesota fan organization for
lesbians, gay men, and their
friends)
P.O. Box 25026
Minneapolis, MN 55458

LAMBDA SCI-FI: D.C. AREA
GAYLAXIANS
Washington, D.C. fan organization
for lesbians, gay men, and their
friends)
P.O. Box 10087
Silver Spring, MD 20914

Chronological Index

Note: References are to entry numbers, not pages.

Nonfiction works are not listed in this index.

Alphabetical Index to Titles

Note: References are to entry numbers, not pages.

Index to Biographical Notes

Note: References are to page numbers.